Business and Finance

Needham & Dransfield

BUSINESS AND FINANCE

for working in organisations

Dave Needham and Rob Dransfield

HEINEMANN
EDUCATIONAL

Heinemann Educational,
a division of Heinemann Educational Books Ltd,
Halley Court, Jordan Hill, Oxford OX2 8EJ

OXFORD   LONDON   EDINBURGH
MADRID   ATHENS   BOLOGNA   PARIS
MELBOURNE   SYDNEY   AUCKLAND   SINGAPORE   TOKYO
IBADAN   NAIROBI   HARARE   GABORONE
PORTSMOUTH NH (USA)

First published 1992

A catalogue record for this book is available from the British Library on request

ISBN 0 435 45523 0

Designed by Bob Prescott
Typeset by Taurus Graphics, Abingdon, Oxon
Printed by Bath Press Ltd, Bath

CONTENTS

Acknowledgements

The authors would like to thank the following individuals for their support, encouragement and contributions:

Margaret Berriman, Alex Clark, Roger Parker, Mary Hamley, Tony Newbould, Ian Millard, John Merchant, Sue Friery, Alastair Clelland, Stephanie Swain, Bryan Oakes, Julie Ashton, Steve Wain, Aubrey Nokes, Kate Johnson, Michael Bushby, John McGrath, Marilyn Elliott, Robert Young, Roger Newman, Liz Robertson, Brian Yeomans, Phil Guy, Sue Woollat, Don Clarke, Justine Lindley, Colin Bunn and Martin Turner.

In particular, we would like to express our gratitude and appreciation to both the teaching and library staff at Darlington College of Technology and Nottingham Polytechnic, the editorial, production, marketing and sales teams at Heinemann Educational and finally our families for their patience and understanding.

The authors and publishers would also like to thank the following for permission to reproduce photographs and other material, and for providing advice and information:

Amalgamated Engineering Union; Apricot Computers Ltd; B & Q PLC; BT; British Airways; British Bakeries; British Nuclear Fuels PLC; The Burton Group PLC, Business and Technician Education Council; East Midlands Electricity PLC; The Economist Newspaper Ltd; Eden Vale Ltd; Ford Motor Company Ltd; Hanson PLC; IBM United Kingdom Ltd; The Independent; Japan Information and Cultural Centre; Jus-rol Ltd; Kettle Foods; Marks & Spencer PLC; Midland Bank PLC; Mintel International Group Ltd; Money Management Review; National Westminster Bank PLC; Nissan Motor Manufacturing (UK) Ltd; Procter & Gamble Ltd; Shell Education Service; Tesco PLC; Thorn EMI PLC; Northern Electric PLC; Understanding Industry; Whitbread PLC; Yorkshire Bank PLC.

We would also like to thank the following for permission to reproduce photographs on the pages noted:

Dick Barnatt p51; J Allen Cash p115; Hulton-Deutsch Collection p97; Philip Parkhouse p125; Press Association Ltd p370; Universal Pictorial Press and Agency Ltd pp56, 60.

This book has been written specifically to reflect the recent revisions which have taken place to the BTEC National Qualification in Business & Finance and Public Administration. In particular, it focuses upon the core unit Working in Organisations which has replaced the Organisation in its Environment, People in Organisations and Finance.

In writing this book we have been profoundly aware of the need to provide a *particular* classroom resource designed to help teachers and lecturers to deliver the revised BTEC National core unit. The crucial element in the design of the book has been to provide a text which is capable, in terms of size, structure, presentation and content, of being used *actively* in a classroom. In order to provide such a resource, extensive research and consultation has taken place to discover the sort of text which teachers of BTEC courses feel they require. As a result this book appears as an active-learning text in which each area is supported by a variety of tasks and frequent case analyses. The book is particularly suitable for resource-based learning. Regular case analysis has been deliberately used to avoid the necessity for detailed listings, and is intended to create a work-centred approach to learning.

We have also attempted to adopt a broad approach to areas covered by the text. Case analysis not only allows current events to be analysed but also allows areas such as business ethics, environmentalism, equal opportunities and Europeanisation to be viewed as influential upon the way in which people work, think and operate in a modern working environment.

The book is divided into six themes, and three chapters appear within each theme. Though it is designed to cover all areas in the core, themes will vary from institution to institution depending upon how each BTEC team approaches the course. We hope that our particular approach serves to provide a useful reference and a source of ideas for BTEC teams. It is important, however, that the text is supported by:

(a) experienced teachers and lecturers who develop, expand and support work within the text.

(b) access to library facilities, not only for books but also for magazines, periodicals and reference materials.

(c) the use of IT facilities and resources.

Key features of the book

- Each chapter is preceded by a short introduction.

- Case studies are integrated into the text and serve as a vehicle for developing learning and understanding.

- Tasks appear frequently throughout the text. Many are designed to be completed individually, others are designed to provide a basis for ground work or just for discussion.

- Each chapter aims to integrate common skills, and provides a framework which allows options to be integrated with core blocks.

- The book seeks to provide and enhance an understanding of working in organisations.

At the heart of the text is our belief in BTEC values, styles and ideas, and our hope is that we have provided a framework within which these can be delivered in the classroom in a way which emphasises good teaching practices.

1

The Organisation

In this opening chapter we set out to show that an organisation is a unit that makes decisions which affect people. These decisions need to be taken because societies use scarce resources to produce goods that people want and need.

Organisations operate as systems which are critically influenced by the environment in which they operate. This chapter explores these environmental influences, in particular the economy and different types of economic systems. It examines some of the main goals and objectives of organisations and considers different types of structures, and the way in which they are changing in the modern world.

In this book we set out to explore some of the many ways in which business organisations operate today.

Businesses exist because they meet **needs** and **wants**. The person or people who run these organisations have identified a need. This applies equally to:

- the ice-cream van selling cones and choc-ices outside a park or a school gate
- the large multinational clothes manufacturer selling its brands throughout the world
- the public service organisation, such as the meals-on-wheels service
- the charity organisation such as Oxfam working to provide famine relief.

What are needs and wants? At a basic level we all need a minimum standard of food, shelter and clothing (although a walk through Central London makes it apparent that not everybody achieves this).

Our wants go beyond our basic needs, and it would appear that many of them are insatiable. The tennis enthusiast who buys a tennis racket, balls, trainers, wristband and clothes soon moves on to a better racket, more sophisticated trainers and a more extensive wardrobe of 'designer' tennis clothes. Consumers aspire to bigger, better and more up-to-date goods. Producers seek to provide the goods and services that will meet these wants and needs by chanelling resources into producing them.

Production resources are relatively scarce. If we use a particular piece of wood to make a table, we cannot use the same piece to make a chair. Decision-making over the use of resources involves:

- making a *choice* (we can do either this or that)
- making a *sacrifice* (if we choose to do this with a resource we cannot also do that).

Opportunity cost

The concept of **opportunity cost** is an important one in all decision-making and particularly in the business world. Opportunity cost means the next

Figure 1.1 The market-place brings together consumers and producers

best alternative that is sacrificed when we carry out a particular action. Individuals, groups, communities and nations are continually making decisions. When you make a decision to buy one thing you sacrifice *options*; for example, when you decide to buy a compact disc the real cost to you is the thing that you have to go without. When the government decides to build a new hospital, the real cost may be a new school that might otherwise have been built. When a business decides to invest in new computers the alternative sacrificed might be a wage increase to staff.

Task

Explain how an understanding of opportunity cost would affect the business decision-making of each of the following groups or individuals.

1. Jill works for herself illustrating children's books. She works from home and frequently takes commissions over the phone from clients. Jill has been asked to give a talk at a school 100 miles from home. She will be paid a fee of £150 but no expenses. Jill has worked out that it will cost her £15 for petrol and about £10 for wear and tear on the car. She therefore anticipates making a profit of

£125 for the day. She thinks that this will be worthwhile.

2. Southampton Boat Builders and Repair Yard is a business that normally does a lot of small repair jobs, and makes small fishing boats. They have recently received an order for three larger fishing boats from a big company. They have decided to refuse all other new work to meet these orders. The job will take them six months and may lead to a larger order. They have calculated that they will make twice as much profit from concentrating on the large order.

3. John normally works a 30-hour week for £5 an hour. He has been offered a rate of £6 an hour if he will agree to work a 35-hour week. John has calculated that he will be better off by £60 a week.

Business works

In examining the way that businesses operate, we need to be constantly aware of these very basic ideas of **scarcity** and **choice**, and understand the implications of the concept of opportunity cost.

A *good idea* will normally be the starting point for a new business. However, many good ideas have fallen at the first hurdle. Any good idea needs support and organisation for it to develop. Examine the following 'good idea'.

Case Study – Chip vending

The world's first chip vending machines, the dream of the fast food business for many years, have been trialled at 15 selected test sites in California. The first man to deliver such a product was a 60-year-old inventor from Leeds, William Bartfield, who had spent ten years researching production of the machine. His Prize Frize company, backed by investors, spent £5 million on research and development.

Mr Bartfield first found a company which produced reconstituted potato for the armed forces and then began to develop a machine which would turn out hot, fresh chips within seconds of coins being deposited.

The machines cut the potato concentrate into 33 chips, then a conveyor moves them to a fryer for a 15-second fry in vegetable oil. They drop into a second cooking basket for 30 seconds and finally fall into a paper carton.

The consumer deposits the equivalent of about 30 pence, waits for 45 seconds, and then receives a cardboard carton containing a portion of chips complete with ketchup and salt.

By late 1991 Mr Bartfield already had orders for more than 1000 machines. The cost of the machines was high, and he recognised that an important task would be to reduce his costs.

At the same time a rival company backed by Heinz was seeking to produce a chip vending machine which would deliver chips cooked from the frozen potato.

1. *Why is a chip vending machine a good idea?*
2. *Explain how the following might be helpful in turning the idea into an effective business proposition:*
   - *a planning*
   - *b finance*
   - *c organisation*
   - *d research and development*
   - *e teamwork*
   - *f record-keeping*
3. *What else is needed to turn the idea into a business?*

Potato concentrate mixed with hot water

Potato partly cut into oblongs

Conveyor moves chips to fryer

Cooked for 15 seconds

Cooked another 30 seconds

Ketchup and salt at base of cup

Figure 1.2 The chip vending machine

What is a 'good business'?

A good business has a number of distinguishing characteristics:

- It makes a profit by supplying products or services that people want to buy.
- It contributes to its own and the community's long-term prosperity by making the best use of resources.
- It minimises waste of every kind.
- It respects the environment, locally, nationally and globally.
- It sets performance standards for its suppliers, and helps in their achievement.
- It offers its employees good career prospects, professional training and job satisfaction.
- It expects the best from its employees and rewards them accordingly.

If a business is to remain a 'good business' it needs to fulfil all these criteria. For example, no business can continue to make a profit if it fails significantly to make the best possible use of available resources. It would simply be overtaken by competitors who do.

In making the best possible use of resources – whether raw materials or human potential – it automatically contributes to the general prosperity.

Of course, 'best possible use' implies more than simply 'best possible use in the short term'. Any company short-sighted enough to exploit resources simply for immediate gain, at the expense of the environment or the customer's best long-term interests, would risk failure. For example public hostility and a customer boycott. A good business should always be a good citizen.

Given that the most important resource available to any company is its people, they must be looked after, trained and generally enabled to fulfil their potential.

Converting inputs into outputs

One of the prime concerns of any business is to convert **inputs** (what goes in at one end) into **outputs** (finished goods) in order to satisfy the wants and needs of its consumers.

Case study – Making dog biscuits

A company that makes dog biscuits carries out a number of processes within its factory. Look at the diagram below to see how the dog biscuits are made.

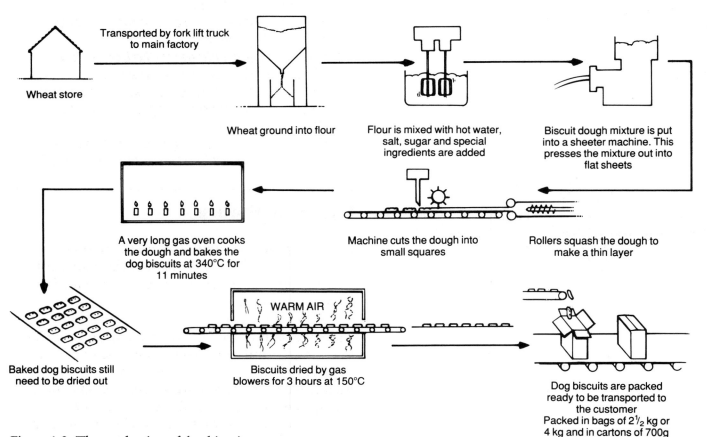

Figure 1.3 The production of dog biscuits

1 *What processes (grinding, transporting etc.) can you identify in the production of dog biscuits?*

2 *What inputs can you identify in the production of dog biscuits?*

3 *Try to illustrate the inputs, processes and outputs involved in dog biscuit production in a simple diagram.*

The company knows that to stay in business it must produce a good quality product. It needs to keep the costs of making the biscuits as low as possible, and it must sell them to its customers at a price they can afford. The money it receives for the biscuits is used to pay its costs, including wages. Any money left over is profit.

The company needs certain things to make the dog biscuits. They are shown in Figure 1.4.

The company produces 11 500 tonnes of dog biscuits every year. The annual costs of the inputs needed to make this quantity are shown in the table.

Ingredients	£1 466 250
Energy	£ 126 500
Labour	£ 28 750
Maintaining buildings and machinery, heating and lighting	£ 11 500
Administration	£ 74 750
Haulage and distribution	£ 202 975
Packaging	£ 718 750

Total cost of producing 11 500 tonnes is £ _____

1 *Which input costs the most?*

2 *Which input costs the least?*

3 *How much does energy cost the company each year?*

4 *How could the company cut costs?*

5 *How much does the company spend on packaging?*

6 *How much does it cost the company to make one tonne of dog biscuits? (We can call this the average cost per unit.)*

7 *How many 4kg boxes of dog biscuits could be produced by the company?*

8 *If the company sold each 4kg box of dog biscuits for £1 would it make a profit?*

9 *Calculate the profit the company would make if it sold the 4kg boxes of dog biscuits for £1.10, £1.25 and £1.40.*

10 *Design a packet for dog biscuits. What would, or should, the customer want to know about?*

Systems theory

A system **processes** inputs to produce outputs. For example, in the dog biscuit factory the ingredients and other inputs are processed by the production system to produce outputs.

The production process takes place within defined **boundaries,** which are usually fairly obvious. The inputs flow into this system. Some of the resources used will be **current resources** – for example, salt, sugar, wheat and energy. What actually goes into the production process will be '**filtered**' to ensure that only desirable inputs are accepted. For example,

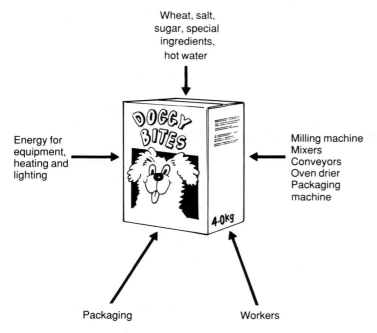

Wheat, salt, sugar, special ingredients, hot water

Energy for equipment, heating and lighting

Milling machine
Mixers
Conveyors
Oven drier
Packaging machine

Packaging

Workers

Figure 1.4 Inputs needed to make dog biscuits

quality control ensures that no fragments of glass enter the production system. Current resources then 'combine' with elements (or fixed assets) such as machinery and buildings, and flow from one element to another element across **links** between the elements. For example, the dough for dog biscuits flows from the dough mixing element, through the rollers, and into the gas ovens.

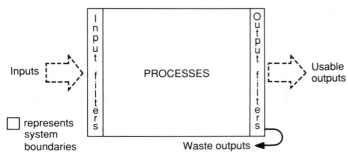

Figure 1.5 The input/processes/output model for an open system

The system is **controlled** by a user, who puts in the **primary** inputs and the **secondary** inputs. The primary inputs are the settings (control parameters) which control the operation of the system (e.g. the speed of the line, the temperature, the quality standards, the hours worked and so on). The secondary inputs are the current resources.

Closed and open systems

The systems model described above illustrates an **open system**. In an open system the outputs *do not affect the inputs.*

In a **closed system** the outputs do affect the inputs. A comparator compares the outputs with a pre-established value, and if the outputs do not meet this value the inputs are adjusted. For example, a thermostat in a room regulates a heating system to produce a chosen temperature; when the temperature reaches a given higher level the heating is turned off, and when it then reaches a certain lower level the heating is turned on. In the same way, if a particular product does not meet its specifications, then the comparator instructs the system to alter the inputs appropriately. If the dog biscuits proved to be too

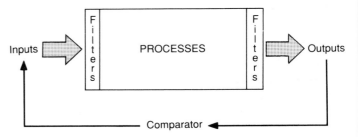

Figure 1.6 A closed system

brittle the comparator might decide that more water must be added to the mix, or that the baking temperature needs to be reduced.

In setting up a production system it is important to establish definite goals. These should be expressed in terms of **performance indicators**. For example, target quantities of output can be established, or standards can be set for minimising waste or breakdowns to machinery.

Tasks

1 The text has mentioned a number of terms related to systems theory. Try to familiarise yourself with them. In your notebook or folder define the following:

Open system	Closed system	Inputs
Outputs	Process	Boundaries
Filter	Current resources	Elements
Links	Controller	Primary inputs
Secondary inputs		

2 Look at a production system in a local business, and try to identify each of the elements outlined above.
   a *What are the goals of this system?*
   b *What performance indicators are used to check whether these goals are being achieved?*
   c *What happens when the system falls short of its goals.*

Sub-systems

In all but the smallest organisations there are usually a number of **sub-systems** operating at the same time, and these interact with each other. There may be an accounting system, a production system and a marketing system, for example, but it would be unrealistic to assume that the boundaries between these sub-systems can be drawn rigidly.

The wider environment in which businesses operate

The operation of a system is critically influenced by its **total environment**. This is best studied under several headings:
- the *natural* environment
- the *social* environment
- the *legal and political* environment
- the *technological* environment
- the *industrial relations* environment
- other environments.

The natural environment

Nature has always had a great influence on the way in which businesses operate. At a basic level, for the manufacturer of dog biscuits a good wheat harvest means lower raw material costs.

The **natural environment** provides opportunities and exerts constraints on human activities. Rain and sunshine both make crops grow, but a lack of rain may lead to famine and starvation.

In recent years we have become increasingly aware that certain human activities can have dreadful consequences. Some chemicals deposited in the atmosphere from power stations and factory chimneys return to earth in the form of acid rain, whilst certain gases rise to deplete the ozone layer.

The social environment

A **social system** is the fabric of ideas, attitudes and behaviour patterns that are involved in human relationships. Within a society, ideas and attitudes arise, for example, as to how long people should work, what is 'men's work' and what is 'women's work', and how new technology ought to be used. The dog biscuit manufacturer might find that he or she cannot recruit sufficient labour on a Sunday to run a particular shift efficiently.

The legal and political environment

Every society has its foundations in a set of **laws** and ethical **codes**, and business systems operate with similar opportunities and constraints. For example, food production is governed by laws relating to the handling of foodstuffs, the types of allowable ingredients, and the labelling of packets.

In the wider field the way in which businesses operate is influenced by **political considerations**. In 1991 British Aerospace was unable to accept an order from Iran for passenger aircraft, because the American producers of essential components were prevented from supplying those parts by a US government restriction on trading with Iran.

The technological environment

We live in an age of technological developments, and businesses that make use of the newest **technologies** are frequently at a considerable **advantage**. In the 1990s many Eastern European countries are disadvantaged because they still use older technologies.

We can relate the changing technological environment to our dog biscuits example. *A gas oven* has for a number of years been used to bake the biscuits. This works in just the same way as a domestic gas oven, so a gas flame warms the inside of the oven and heat energy is transferred to the biscuits to cook them. The biscuits travel through a long oven on a conveyor belt, and they are in the oven for about 11 minutes at a temperature of 340°C. The heat energy travels to the inside of a biscuit, and a crust forms on the outside before the inside has completely dried out. The crust traps moisture inside the biscuit.

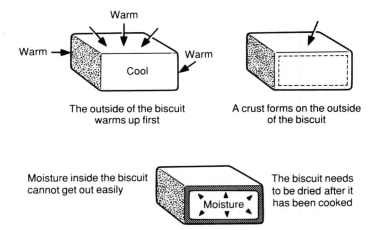

Figure 1.7 What happens when a biscuit is cooked in a gas oven

When the biscuits come out of the oven they have to be dried for three hours. A gas burner warms the air for this purpose. After drying, the biscuits must be left for a further 24 hours to settle before they can be packed.

Today, a different form of energy can be used to cook the biscuits. *Radio-frequency energy* is similar to the energy used in domestic microwave cookers, and these energies very quickly reach the inside of the foodstuffs being cooked. Cooking times are shorter, and the biscuits dry out before a crust forms on them. There is no need to dry the biscuits or let them settle, so they can be packed shortly after cooking. Because cooking times are faster, radio-frequency ovens are shorter and so take up less room.

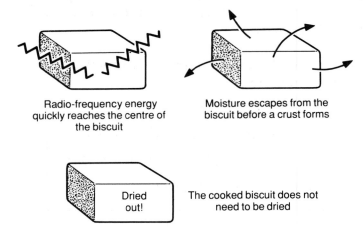

Figure 1.8 What happens when a biscuit is cooked in a radio-frequency oven

The industrial relations environment

The most important resource of a company is the **workforce** – the people who work for it. **Industrial relations** is concerned with communication between representatives of the employer and representatives of the employees. Business performance is always keenly influenced by the quality of this communication process. An organisation is most likely to be successful when employees feel a sense of responsibility for what they are doing and are concerned to produce a quality product.

Businesses may also be affected by the wider industrial relations environment. When a particular type of labour is in short supply and wages are rising nationally, employees are influenced to seek pay rises for themselves.

Other environments

We shall be exploring the economic background against which firms operate both in this chapter and throughout the book. Here we can mention that businesses are continually influenced by many other outside factors – such as population changes and changes in taste.

Conflict or consensus?

Do businesses operate in a society in which people share values, or is there a fundamental **conflict** of interests? There are different schools of thought on this issue.

Figure 1.9 Demonstrating a point of view

Figure 1.10 **Demonstrating another point of view**

When we examine a global issue such as the use of nuclear power, there are clear differences of opinion between various groups. The same can be said about acid rain, and the greenhouse effect. However, while it is obvious that conflict exists over specific issues, is conflict an *inherent* part of society? Marxist thinkers (people whose ideas have been influenced by Karl Marx) believe that, while certain values serve to keep society together, these values represent the interests of the 'ruling classes'. Education and other systems encourage conformity. Marx believed that beneath the surface societies are fundamentally based on conflict between those who own the means of production (e.g. the shareholders in a capitalist society) and those who do not. Marx felt that the 'working class' is misled into being loyal and hard working and into accepting the ideology (ideas, values and justifications) of a society in which it is exploited. Realisation of this position then inevitably leads to conflict.

In contrast, many other people believe that society is based more on **consensus** – that is, on shared ideas. For most, the national and local communities are units on which they can focus these shared values, which may include patriotism, loyalty, community spirit and obedience to the law. The American writer Talcott Parsons argued that 'fundamental values underpin the social system and without them it could not function'.

A synthesis (coming together) of these two contrasting theories is represented by the idea of **pluralism**. A plural society is made up of many different groups – ethnic groups, religious groups, age groups, style and fashion groups, interest groups etc. Members of these share many of the same and similar values, but some of their values are so fundamentally different that consensus is disturbed by periods of conflict.

Large-scale or small-scale studies of societies

When studying a society we can take an **holistic** view (looking at things as a whole), or alternatively study small-scale interactions. An holistic study might, for example, be concerned with looking at the relationship between unemployment and inflation in the whole economy. A small-scale study might be concerned with looking at how individuals in a small business interact with each other. Both perspectives are valuable in their own way.

The economy and business

Resources are said to be scarce relative to our wants and needs. This assertion is, however, being increasingly challenged today, and questions are raised as to how we **manage** our resources. For example, the continent of Africa is by no stretch of the imagination overpopulated, yet year after year people living in vast tracts of it suffer famine. These areas tend to coincide with military conflicts supported (financed) by richer countries. Yet in the early 1990s the world has *record supplies of grain and meat reserve*s – indeed a major 'problem' is lack of storage space.

These issues bring to light the fundamental economic questions:

> WHAT SHOULD BE PRODUCED?
>
> HOW SHOULD IT BE PRODUCED?
>
> WHO SHOULD GET IT?

The function of an economic system is to resolve these three questions.

A simple circular flow model illustrates the way in which resources are used by firms to produce goods which are purchased by households. The four main factors of production are:

- **Land** – including all the gifts of nature
- **Labour** – all mental and physical effort
- **Capital** – including all goods that are used to create further outputs (e.g. machinery)
- **Enterprise** – the skill of taking risks to bring together all these factors.

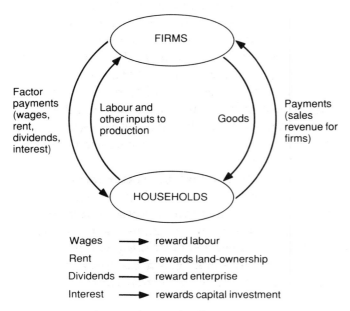

Wages   ⟶ reward labour
Rent   ⟶ rewards land-ownership
Dividends ⟶ reward enterprise
Interest ⟶ rewards capital investment

Figure 1.11 The simple circular flow system

Different types of national economy

Not all countries operate identical economic systems. One way of classifying economies is by the amount of government involvement in decision-making. At one extreme a **free market** system has no governmental interference. At the other extreme, in a totally **planned** system, the government plays a considerable part in making business decisions.

Free market systems

A **free market** exists where the government plays no part in controlling markets. Decisions are made freely (without interference) by buyers and sellers. Buyers continue to buy items provided they feel that they are getting value for money. If consumers consider that they would get better value for money from buying an alternative brand, they will buy it. Producers adjust their output of goods in response to **consumer demand**.

Free market systems do not exist in perfect form in the real world because governments of all countries today insist on at least a small role in controlling economic activity.

Advantages of the free market system

1 Consumers are able to 'vote with their money' for the goods they want to be produced. Popular items are likely to be produced in large quantities and at relatively low prices.
2 Because demand represents consumer needs and wants, resources are channelled mainly into these lines. There is a disincentive to channel resources (wastefully) into unpopular lines.
3 Because the government does not interfere in the economy, consumers can spend their own money in ways they see fit. The argument is that individuals know what purchases will give them most satisfaction. A government official spending money on your behalf is less in tune with your needs and wants.
4 A free market system can respond to changes. In other words it is *dynamic*. In the 1960s and 70s teenagers bought records, but as cassettes and CDs became available so teenagers showed their preference for these by buying them. The music industry helped by bringing about the changes, and today music shops supply what the consumer wants.
5 Scarce resources do not have to be wasted on administering the system.

Disadvantages of the free market system

1 There are no checks against monopolist practices by large producers.
2 Large and powerful interests (such as big companies) have far more influence than smaller ones.

3 Although consumers can vote with their money, some will have far more money than others.

4 The market system does not *guarantee* that a minimum standard of needs will be achieved by everyone. Market economies tend to be characterised by great inequalities in wealth and income.

5 Some goods are 'non-excludable' – supplying these goods to one person means that other people also benefit. For example, if we improve pavements in the town centre then everyone who goes there will benefit; it would be impossible to make just the users of the pavements pay more for this service.

6 A free market only works effectively if we assume that all consumers have perfect knowledge of the features of all goods available in the market. This is clearly unrealistic. Buying decisions are frequently made on the basis of imperfect knowledge. I may buy 10 litres of petrol from a particular service station, not realising that there is another outlet 200 metres up the road selling cheaper petrol.

7 In the real market-place consumers are fed a lot of misinformation, particularly through advertising.

The planned system

In some economies all major decision are made by a **central planning** body. The planning authority collects information about the quantities of resources (e.g. coal, steel, bricks) that are expected to be available in a given time period (e.g. five years).

The central planners ask local planning bodies to say what they will need and how much they will produce, before deciding on how to allocate (give out) the available resources. They have to give careful thought to this in order to ensure the best value to society in a given period of time. In theory, plans can be adjusted from time to time to deal with any problems that arise.

In the 1990s the number of planned economies in the world is falling as many countries (particularly those in the Commonwealth of Independent States) switch to market systems. Planning is still, however, important in China and Cuba.

Advantages of the planned system

1 The system allows targets and plans to be established for the whole economy. The central planning body is able to issue instructions to all the enterprises in the economy informing them of their own individual targets. In effect the central plan is the solution of an enormous set of simultaneous equations because all the enterprises in the economy will be interdependent – the output of the coal industry will form the input of energy and steel industries. It follows that the ability of the steel industry to meet its targets will depend, to a large extent, on the performance of the coal industry.

2 Revisions can be made by the central authority which has access to a great deal of information, especially on how the total economy is operating.

3 Plans can be made to ensure that basic needs are met for all of the people. For example, until recently unemployment was unheard of in the Russian economy, and bread was heavily subsidised.

4 Long-term planning is possible for all resources, and all industries.

5 Wasteful duplication of products and services can be cut out.

6 Goods and services can be distributed more evenly.

Disadvantages of the planned system

1 There is no competitive spur. Competition tends to increase the quality of products. If the state produces everything then it does not operate in a competitive environment.

2 A major danger is that local planners can deliberately overestimate the resources they need in order to get projects finished more quickly, so boosting their local output and prestige. Resources can be wasted in this way.

3 The costs of running a planned system are high. Bureaucrats are needed to make the plans, and run enterprises from their offices.

4 Bureaucrats may slow down progress in order to keep their jobs. For example, an official working for a declining industry may have a vested interest in making that industry seem vitally important to the national economy.

5 The absence of the profit motive removes the spur to individual effort and enterprise.

6 Black markets may develop when the official economy fails to deliver the goods that consumers want.

Case Study – Weaknesses of a planned economy

The following letter appeared in *Pravda* (a Soviet newspaper) in late 1989:

'To obtain your coal coupon is one thing: you are only half way there. Now as for actually getting your coal . . .The night before, you take your place in the square at the gates of the coal depot. You queue all night long only to discover that there isn't enough coal for everyone. The reasons vary: sometimes lorries don't arrive, sometimes people are off sick.

How can it be that in a centralised system, with fixed prices, providing people with adequate supplies of heating fuel is such a complicated procedure? It's been a whole year since our local paper raised the issue and still no results.

Another problem: the allocated maximum amount of coal per family – 1.5 tons – is not enough, particularly during severe winters like last year. What's more, all we get is low-grade coal. Only half of it is any good – the rest is dust. As a result, towards the end of the winter, people are compelled to buy coal illegally on the black market and to pay the earth for it.

Something should be done about the whole system: people should be able to buy coal at official coal depots without coupons. Not, of course, for 15 to 18 roubles per ton, but twice or even three times as much. And the coal would have to be better quality.

V. Karieko

1 Does this letter indicate that the planning system provided for the needs of all the people?
2 What weaknesses does the article expose in the planning system?
3 How were consumers able to combat weaknesses of this system?
4 What alternatives to the planning system was the letter writer suggesting?
5 What suggestions would you have made for improving the distribution of coal in the Soviet Union?
6 What problems have been encountered in changing this system?

The mixed economy

Mixed economies involve a blend of private enterprise and government involvement in economic activity. In economies such as those of the European Community and Japan, decisions are made by three groups – producers, consumers and the government.

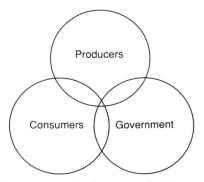

Figure 1.12 **Interconnection between decision-makers in a mixed economy**

In these countries a large proportion of business capital is privately owned. Private owners are free to decide how their resources ought to be employed, their own production targets, the quantity and quality and the amounts of factor inputs they feel are necessary.

Governments in such countries make contributions to the economy in two senses:

● They are owners of resources in their own right because they are responsible for running certain services for the nation – such as defence, public health and welfare.

- They have the power to change and influence private decisions made by producers and consumers when they feel that these decisions may not otherwise serve the best interests of the community. For example, the government sets high rates of taxes to discourage cigarette smoking and excessive drinking of alcohol.

Views as to how the mixed economy should operate change over time. In the United Kingdom, the government sector of the economy has grown substantially in the twentieth century (up until 1979). Successive governments gradually built up the Welfare State and nationalised industries increasingly took over the 'commanding heights of the economy', including rail, coal, steel, airways, postal services and telecommunications. Since 1979, the government sector has been reduced. The 'Thatcher years' were characterised by **privatisation**. Government-run industries such as gas, steel and telecommunications were returned to private ownership. The ideology behind this was based on industries moving upwards and away from dependence on the government. After 1990 the Conservative government continued with the policy of privatisation, but moved toward recognising that government industries still have an important part to play in a mixed economy. It stressed that government industries need to be increasingly accountable to their consumers.

Advantages and disadvantages of the mixed economy

The main advantage of a mixed economy is that it combines the best elements of planned economies and free markets. The government is able to coordinate major areas of industrial policy, to provide a safety network for weaker members of society, to make sure that markets run smoothly, and to enable effective competition. The main disadvantage is that it combines the worst elements of the two systems. Government interference stifles initiative and enterprise whilst competition favours the strong at the expense of the weak.

Tasks

1 Look at the purchasing situations below. In a mixed economy would a decision be made by a planning official or a private citizen?

- **a** Buying new school books.
- **b** Employing more doctors at a local hospital.
- **c** Buying a word processor.
- **d** Maintaining the local leisure centre.
- **e** Maintaining public parks.
- **f** Expanding the services of a local bank.
- **g** Buying medical syringes.
- **h** Reducing the mileage travelled by police vehicles.
- **i** Increasing holiday expenditures.
- **j** Having a haircut.

2 Look at the decisions about production which need to be made below. Do you think they would be made by a planning official or a private entrepreneur in a mixed economy?

- **a** Building a new airport.
- **b** Building a new road.
- **c** Building a new daycare centre for the elderly.
- **d** Building a new town hall.
- **e** Cutting back on military services.
- **f** Cutting down further on opening times at the local library.
- **g** Making a new aircraft engine.

3 Look at the situations below and decide whether you think decisions should be made by private individuals or government officials.

- **a** Building of new roads.
- **b** Provision of parking facilities.
- **c** Creating a law that requires drivers to wear seatbelts.
- **d** Programming and scheduling television.

Dislocation of new market economies

One of the key issues in international business education today revolves around how Eastern bloc countries can be supported in reforming their central planning systems to include free market principles. Free market principles include:

- competition
- extensive privatisation
- the use of prices to decide what goods will be produced.

However, a centrally planned system cannot be dismantled overnight to be replaced by a market economy. We have seen the enormous problems that can occur whilst countries are trying to reform their economic systems from recent events in the Commonwealth of Independent States. The desire to reform is often not unanimous and may be opposed by those who still adhere to the principles of the previous system.

Within a system, organisations and attitudes develop over a long period of time. Once they are established they are very difficult to change. For example, people in Eastern European countries have become used to full employment and subsidised food, and are apprehensive of changes that they believe will involve huge job losses and soaring prices. The move to market forces leads to an initial collapse of distribution systems. The governments of some Eastern European countries have been reluctant to allow market forces to prevail in one step and have chosen instead a diluted form of **partial markets**. Being neither one thing or the other these partial markets have been ineffective.

Opponents of change have tried to sabotage new reforms and have brought about destabilisation. Foreign multinationals such as Western car giants have invested in large-scale industry at the expense of the small and medium-sized companies. They have also sought monopoly status (where they are the only firm in the market), which goes against the whole ethos of competition. Inevitably Eastern bloc countries will experience a great deal of dislocation and hardship before things start to get better. They must also overcome traditional mistrust between the West and the Eastern bloc.

In many situations, aid given to developing economies can be of mutual benefit. For example, European Community countries offered to provide technical support to the Commonwealth of Independent States so that it could develop its substantial oil and gas industries. These were seen as alternative sources of supply to some of the unstable Middle Eastern countries.

Organisational goals and objectives

Etzioni (*Modern Organisations*, Prentice Hall) defines organisations as:

> 'social units that pursue specific goals which they are structured to serve under some social circumstances.'

The goals can be defined as a future state of affairs which the organisation strives to achieve. Most organisations will set down guidelines for activity which serve as standards by which the success (i.e. the effectiveness and efficiency) of the organisation can be judged.

Task

Choose three organisations with which you are familiar and find out what their prime goals are. What guidelines have the organisations used to measure their success?

Some thinkers argue that the behaviour of members of an organisation is mainly governed by the goals which its decision-makers have set for it.

Task

Think back to your three organisations. Who would you say has the power to determine the goals of these organisations? To what extent are they able to influence the behaviour of members of these organisations? Why does this influence vary between the organisations that you have examined?

Once those with power in an organisation have established its goals, they can then establish its objectives for getting there.

The goal of an organisation might be:

- to gain promotion at the end of the season (football club)
- to become a market leader (confectionery company)
- to be re-elected to government (political party).

What else can you think of for other organisations?

Perceptions of an organisation

There is likely to be a considerable difference between the organisation that people think they are operating, the organisation that actually exists, and the organisation that is best suited to the needs of the market at that time. I may think that I am running a first-rate, modern and interesting business studies course, my students might think that it is boring, and the reality may be that I am twenty years behind the times (of course this is not true!). As times change, organisations move on.

We might have clearly set out our goals and objectives when we set up a company initially. An outsider examining our business at a later date might find that we have moved away radically from our stated aims and objectives. The company that set out to be the market leader may in fact have modified its goals simply in order to survive.

The business plan

Most businesses today set out their aims and objectives in some form of business plan. We can regard this as representing the formal goals of the organisation. However, within an organisation's day-to-day running there will be many informal elements. The partners who agree on paper to work from Monday to Friday may in fact work a seven-day week. On paper all grievances may have to be presented to a senior manager, but informally they may be taken to someone else.

Organisations operate in an ever-changing environment. It is therefore important for the organisation to be flexible. Etzioni talked of an **effectiveness systems model** whereby the organisation explores changes which have occurred and how they affected the ability of the organisation to serve its goals. Organisational change (whether it is modest or fundamental) requires adaptation of existing processes and patterns of behaviour, and in some cases major changes in attitudes. Earlier in the chapter we saw that if Eastern European countries are going to assimilate change then they need to use an effectiveness model. The same is true of large companies in a recession, when old and new practices need to be re-evaluated so that changes can be made to improve effectiveness. You can soon see that this model is helpful in many circumstances.

Developing goals

Professor Kotter (*A Force for Change*, Macmillan) argues that:

> 'The development of good business direction is not an act of magic. It is mostly a tough, sometimes exhausting, information-gathering and analytical process. People who help develop such visions and strategies are not magicians. They tend to be broad-based strategic thinkers who are willing to take risks.'

When Robert Horton became Chairman of BP in 1989 his first task was to spend months on research and discussions with people throughout the company. This resulted in Project 1990, a vision for BP's future. Horton's vision was that BP could become 'the world's most successful oil company in the 1990s and beyond'. In the case of General Electric in America, Jack Welch set out to be best or second best in every field of GE's business. Everything else was ruthlessly cut out.

Today managers and employees sit down to work out **mission statements**. A mission statement is an expression of what an organisation stands for, and members of that organisation are involved in agreeing its terms and details. This mission must then be communicated throughout the organisation. With clearly established goals everyone involved can work with shared values towards a common point which they have helped agree on.

Establishing goals

We have seen that every organisation needs to establish its goals, perhaps encapsulating its philosophy in a mission statement. The major route to achieving these goals will depend on strategy. It is important to be clear what is meant by the terms **strategy** and **tactics**. These terms originate from military use, where strategy before and during a battle was the general policy overview of how to defeat the enemy.

Strategy involves defining the major aims and objectives and developing means for achieving them.

Figure 1.13 Goals, strategy and tactics

Having established its general strategy an organisation can work out the necessary day-to-day tools and tactics to meet the strategic goal. Such tactics may change at short notice to satisfy changing circumstances.

Tactical decisions need greater flexibility. A tennis player's strategy might involve playing with great power to force opponents into errors. The player may practise his or her game to perfect the skills and power to implement this strategy (by, for example, practising forceful serving). During particular games he or she may alter tactics by serving long or short, or playing to different sides of the court.

Task

Describe three situations in which you apply strategies to seek to attain particular goals. What sort of tactics do you apply to back up your strategy? How often do you have to alter your tactics? In what ways? How frequently do you have to modify your underlying strategy? How does this affect your actions?

Business aims

Businesses are set up for many different reasons. Profit is usually an important motive but is certainly not the only one. Many people are prepared to take a cut in salary because of the satisfaction and freedom of working for themselves. Businesses generally have a wide range of possible aims, including:
● to make as much profit as possible
● to have the number-one product in a given market
● to maximise sales
● to grow quickly
● to operate in a wide range of markets
● to provide owners with a steady income
● to provide the freedom for the owner/s in the work they enjoy.

Profit maximisation

Profit maximisation occurs when there is the greatest possible difference between the total cost of production and the revenue gained from selling the goods. If we assume that all goods can be sold at a given market price, revenue can be shown on a diagram by a line which rises from left to right (see Figure 1.14). We shall see later on that in fact most businesses have considerable freedom in setting prices so that in the real world the line would be more complicated.

Costs rise as a firm increases its output. Initially as this happens, the total cost of production rises, but the rate of increase falls. Place a ruler on the total cost curve in Figure 1.14 and you will see that as you move it up the curve the ruler begins to tilt downwards to the right. This is because as you increase output you are able to spread fixed costs (such as rent and rates) over a wider area. Then the total curve begins to rise again more steeply – check this out with the ruler. Profit maximisation will occur at the point of greatest difference between total cost and total revenue.

For businesses to operate in this way in the real world we need to assume that:

- they want to maximise profits
- they have the necessary market information to calculate the point of profit maximisation
- their markets do not change.

A firm may be reluctant to act as a pure profit maximiser because this might involve losing public goodwill, and could in some circumstances encourage the government to investigate its practices. However, all organisations do need to consider carefully the question of profitability; a firm that goes out of business can help no-one.

Market leadership

Many firms seek to be **market leaders**. They may want to sell more products than all rival brands combined, or simply to sell more than the next best selling brand.

The most reliable indicator of market share is relative – that is, the ratio of a company's market share to that of its largest competitor.

$$\text{Relative market share} = \frac{\text{Market share of the company}}{\text{Market share of nearest competitor}}$$

A well-known study argued on the basis of statistical evidence that a ratio of two (i.e. twice the market share of the nearest competitor) would give a firm a 20% cost advantage. The implication is that if you dominate a market you are able to produce on a larger scale than your rivals. You can therefore spread your costs over a larger output and produce more cheaply than your rivals. You can then plough back your higher profits into research, advertising and expansion in order to sustain your market leadership.

Task

Find out who the market leader is in specific markets such as disposable nappies, washing powder and lawn mowers. What advantages do they have over competitors? How do they seek to protect their market leadership?

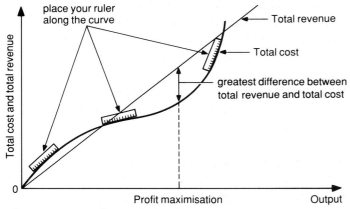

Figure 1.14 **Profit maximisation**

Sales maximisation

Some business organisations seek to maximise sales. **Turnover** is a term that means the value of sales in a given period of time. Clearly, if you are making sales then you may well be taking revenue away from competitors. The larger the volume of sales, the more your fixed costs can be spread.

Business managers have an interest in the sales of their branch or department being high. For one thing, this helps to boost the size of their department and hence also their salary.

Task

Take a firm that has fixed costs of £100 000 and additional costs of 50 pence for each unit produced. What will be the average cost per unit to produce:

a 5000 units?
b 20000 units?
c 500000 units?

Growth

Firms can benefit from **growth**. A firm that grows quickly will find it easier to attract investors and will be able to produce on a larger scale. However, one of the biggest mistakes that entrepreneurs make in their early days is that of over-trading. Running a large business is quite different from running a smaller one. Large businesses are quite different to manage and all sorts of problems arise from over-trading; for example there might not be enough cash to pay bills in the short term, managing staff can be difficult, and so on.

Wide range of markets

Operating across a number of markets makes it possible to spread the risk. If one market fails another may support the loss. However, breaking into new markets also exposes a business to fresh risks. It may be better to operate in a small number of well-known markets rather than exposing yourself to new risks.

Steady income

Satisficing is an alternative to maximising. A firm may set itself the task of attaining clearly realistic goals rather than stretching itself to the limit. This makes considerable sense when an organisation does not want to take unnecessary risks. It may feel that it is better to be able to meet its orders with a margin to spare, to meet financial targets comfortably and to build up a reputation for meeting delivery dates and quality standards.

This does not indicate complacency. It may indeed be seen as sound business sense as successful small businesses have traded and operated over many generations. Indeed, in the longer term a satisficer may make larger profits than a short-term high-flying profit maximiser. Throughout the 1980s the Polly Peck company was heralded as the high-flying company of the decade, but in the early 90s the company collapsed – it had over-traded and failed to keep proper account of its activities.

Task

Look at the financial pages in some newspapers. Which firms can you identify as being:
● sales maximisers?
● growth firms?
● satisficers?
From the information that is available, which of these companies would you think to have the best long-term prospects?

Freedom of expression

Many people set up a small business simply because it provides them with an opportunity to be creative and to work for themselves. Why work for someone else, when you can be your own boss, make your own decisions, and take the profit?

Types of business organisation

Businesses are in either the private sector or the public sector of the national economy.

- Private sector businesses are owned by private individuals and groups.
- Public sector businesses are owned by the state.

Type of enterprise	Who owns the business?	Who controls the business?	Usual sources of finance
Sole trader	One person	One person	Owner's savings, bank loans or overdraft, profits
Partnership	Two or more partners	The partners	Partners' savings, bank loans or overdraft, profits
Company	Two or more shareholders	The directors	Share issues, bank loans or overdraft, venture capital, profits
Co-operative	Two or more members	Managers and other co-operators jointly	Share issues, bank loans or overdraft, profits

Figure 1.15 Main types of business organisation in the private sector

Shareholders in companies and co-operatives have the legal protection of **limited liability**. Sole traders and ordinary partners cannot have limited liability.

Limited liability means that, if the business goes bankrupt because it is unable to meet its debts, the shareholders/owners will not be liable (responsible by law) to lose their possessions to pay the money that is owed. The maximum amount that they could lose is the amount that they have put into acquiring their shares.

The sole trader

The **sole trader** is the most common form of business ownership and is found in a wide range of activities (e.g. window cleaning, plumbing, electrical work, busking).

No complicated paperwork is required to set the business up, decisions can be made quickly, and close contact can be kept with customers and suppliers. All profits go to the sole trader, who also has the satisfaction of building up his or her own business.

There are disadvantages. As a sole trader you have to make all the decisions yourself, and you may have to work long hours to achieve your earnings target (what do you do if you fall ill or want a holiday?). You do not have limited liability, and you have to provide all the finance yourself at your own risk. As a sole trader you may need to be a jack-of-all-trades, and just because you are a good hairdresser does not necessarily mean you have a head for business!

Task

Write a short case history of a sole trader in your neighbourhood. When did he or she set up? What is the business? What are the advantages and disadvantages to this person of being a sole trader?

The partnership

An ordinary partnership can have between two and 20 **partners**. People in business partnerships can share skills and the workload, and it may be easier to raise needed capital.

A group of vets is able to pool knowledge of different diseases and groups of animals, and two or three vets working together may be able to operate a 24-hour service. When one of the vets is ill or goes on holiday, the business can cope.

Partnerships are particularly common in professional services (think also of doctors, solicitors, accountants). A small business such as a corner shop may take the form of a husband and wife partnership.

There are disadvantages in partnerships. People can fall out (he doesn't work as hard as me!). Ordinary partnerships do not have limited liability, and partners can rarely borrow or raise large amounts of capital. Business decisions may be more difficult to make (and slower) because of the need to consult the partners. There may be disagreements about how things should be done. A further disadvantage is that profits will be shared (but so are losses).

Partnerships are usually set up by writing out a 'deed of partnership' which is witnessed by a solicitor. This deed sets out important details, such as how much each partner should put into the business, how the profits and losses will be shared, and the responsibilities of each partner. There is also a special form called a 'limited partnership'. Limited partners – sometimes called 'sleeping partners' – can put money into the business and have the protection of limited liability, but they play no part in the running of the business. It must be run by at least one non-limited partner.

Task

Find one business in your locality that runs as a partnership. Who owns it? What is the relationship like between the partners? What are the advantages and disadvantages of this form of organisation to the partners? Compare your results with other students' work.

Companies

A company is set up to run a business. It has to be registered before it can start to operate, but once all the paperwork is completed and approved the company becomes recognised as a legal body.

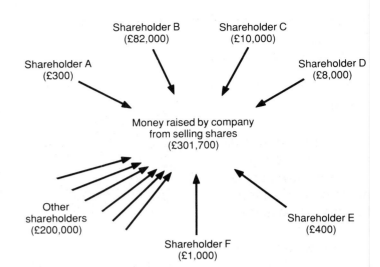

Figure 1.16 **A company raises money from its shareholders**

The owners of a company are its **shareholders.** However, other individuals and businesses do not deal with the shareholders – they deal with 'the company' in the shape of the directors and other employees.

Shareholders put funds into the company by buying **shares.** New shares are often sold with a face value of £1 per share, but this is not always the case. Some shareholders will only have a few hundred pounds worth of shares, whereas others may have millions of pounds worth.

The capital of the company

The directors of the company can apply to the Registrar of Companies for permission to issue new shares. The amount that the Registrar agrees to is called the **'authorised capital'** (or sometimes 'approved capital').

The **issued capital** is the value of the shares which are actually sold. The directors may decide not to issue shares to the full value of the authorised capital straight away, but may instead hold back a certain amount for sale at a future date.

Alternatively, all the shares can be issued at once, with payment required in stages over a period of time. Each stage is then termed a 'call' and there may be three or four such calls before the full price is finally paid. The **paid-up capital** is the money that has been received for these partly paid shares.

Task

Obtain the prospectus of a new company. This will show details of the offer of shares for sale. What is the value of the authorised capital? How much capital is actually being sought? What arrangements are being made for payment for the shares?

Private companies

Private companies tend to be smaller than public ones (discussed below) and are often family businesses. There must be at least two shareholders but there is no maximum number. Shares in private companies cannot be bought on the Stock Exchange, and it is quite usual for the permission of the **board of directors** to be required before shares can be transferred to new ownership outside the existing shareholders.

The board of directors is a committee set up to protect the interests of the shareholders. The members of the board choose the managing director, who is responsible for the day-to-day running of the business. The rules of the business set out when shareholders' meetings will take place and the rights of shareholders.

Private companies may find it possible to raise more cash (by selling shares) than unlimited-liability

Figure 1.17 Choosing the management in a public company

businesses. The shareholders can also have the protection of limited liability.

There may be disadvantages. In a private company the profits must be shared among the shareholders. It may not be possible to make decisions quickly. Finally, private companies cost more to set up and this involves a deal of paperwork.

Task

Study a local private company. Who owns it and who controls it? How much share capital does it have? What are the advantages and disadvantages of this organisational form for this particular company?

Public companies

A **public company** has its shares bought and sold on the Stock Exchange. Companies can go to the expense of having a 'full quotation' so that their share prices appear on the dealers' VDUs. Alternatively they might choose to enter the 'unlisted securities market', or what is known as the 'third market' – whereby they only trade a small proportion of their shares and prices are not quoted in the financial press.

The main advantage of selling shares through the Stock Exchange is that large amounts of capital can be raised very quickly. One disadvantage is that control of a business can be lost by the original shareholders if large quantities of shares are purchased as part of a 'takeover bid'. It is also costly to have shares quoted on the Stock Exchange.

In order to create a public company the directors must apply to the Stock Exchange Council, which will carefully check the accounts. A business wanting to 'go public' will then arrange for one of the merchant banks to handle the paperwork. Selling new shares is quite a risky business. The Stock Exchange has 'good days' (when a lot of people want to buy shares) and 'bad days' (when a lot of people want to sell). If the issue of new shares coincides with a bad day a company can find itself in difficulties. For example, if it hopes to sell a million new shares at £1 each and all goes well, it will raise £1 million; but on a bad day it might only be able to sell half its shares at this price.

One way around this problem is to arrange a 'placing' with a merchant bank. The merchant bank recommends the company's shares to some of the share-buying institutions with which it deals (pension funds and insurance companies, for example) who may then agree to buy, say, one-tenth of the new shares. In this way the merchant bank makes sure that the shares are placed with large investors before the actual date of issue comes round. Then, even if it is a bad day on the Stock Exchange when the shares are issued, the company's money is secure.

Another common method by which public companies raise share capital is by offering new shares for sale to the general public. The company's shares are advertised in leading newspapers and the public invited to apply.

When a company is up and running, a cheaper way of selling is to write to existing shareholders inviting them to buy new shares. This is a **rights issue.**

Co-operatives

Co-operatives are increasingly popular as a means of business organisation. At one time they were only to be found in agriculture and retailing, but in recent years the biggest growth areas have been in service occupations and in small-scale manufacturing.

The basic idea behind a co-operative is that people join together to make decisions, work and share profits. There are many different types of co-operative; we consider here the three most commonly found in business.

Retail co-operatives

The first successful co-operative in this country was set up in the northern town of Rochdale in the last century. Twenty-eight weavers clubbed together to start their own retail shop, selling a few basic grocery items. The profits were to be shared according to the amount spent, and everyone would have an equal say in how the shop was run.

The basic ideas started in Rochdale continue in today's Co-op. On buying a £1 share in the Co-op you are entitled to go along to the annual general meeting to discuss policy.

Consumer co-operatives are usually registered as limited liability companies.

Producer co-operatives

Producer co-operatives are usually registered as companies 'limited by guarantee', which means that each member undertakes to fund any losses up to a certain amount. There are many types. A workers' co-operative, for example, is one that employs all or most of its members. In a workers' co-operative members:

- share responsibility for the success or failure of the business
- work together
- take decisions together
- share the profits.

Other examples of producer co-operatives are groups to grow tomatoes, to make furniture or to organise child-minding.

The main problems that such co-operatives face are finance and organisation. Co-operators sometimes find it difficult to raise capital from banks and other bodies because they are not groups that seek to make profits primarily. A number of co-operatives in recent years have, however, been able to raise finance by selling shares. Some larger co-operatives have also found that it is necessary to set up a management structure in order to get decisions made.

Marketing co-operatives

Marketing co-operatives are most frequently found in farming areas. The farmers set up a marketing board to be responsible for, among other things, grading, packaging, distributing, advertising and selling their produce.

Franchising

In America over one-third of all retail sales are made through firms operating under the **franchise** system. It is a form of business organisation that is becoming increasingly popular in the United Kingdom.

Franchising is really the 'hiring out' or licensing of the use of 'good ideas' to other companies. A franchise grants permission to sell a product and trade under a certain name in a particular area. If I have a good idea, I can sell you a license to trade and carry out a business using my idea in your area. The person taking out the franchise puts down a sum of money as capital and is issued with equipment by the franchising company. The firm selling the franchise is called the *franchisor* and a person paying for the franchise is called the *franchisee*. The franchisee usually has the sole right of operating in a particular area.

This type of trading is common in the fast-food industry, examples being Spud-U-Like and Pizza Hut.

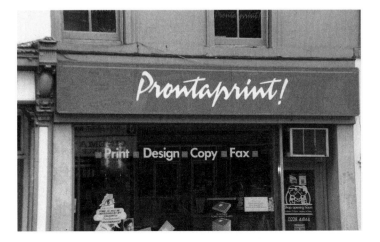

Further examples are Dyno-Rod (in the plumbing business), Tumbletots, Body Shop.and Prontaprint.

Where materials are an important part of the business (e.g. hamburgers, confectionery, hair conditioners) the franchisee must buy an agreed percentage of supplies from the franchisor, who thus makes a profit on these supplies. The franchisor also takes a percentage of the profits of the business, without having to risk capital or become involved in the day-to-day management.

The franchisee benefits from trading under a well-known name and enjoys a local monopoly. Training is usually arranged by the franchisor. The franchisee is his or her own boss and takes most of the profits.

Task

Write down two lists to summarise the advantages of franchising to:

a the franchisor
b the franchisee.

Can you think of any more examples of firms operating under this system?

Small and large firms

Under the Companies Act, a small firm was defined as one having fewer than 50 employees. The Bolton Committee defined a small company as being one with fewer than 200 employees.

A small firm is likely to be a sole trader, a partnership or a private company. It is also likely to operate on one site and to have a limited amount of specialisation of departments.

Small firms often serve a niche in the market. Communications between members are almost invariably good, and the company is able to respond to changing circumstances.

Task

Study two small firms. What are the advantages and disadvantages of this form of organisation? Compare your findings with those of other students. Can you make any general comments?

Large firms are most likely to be public limited companies, although some private companies and even partnerships are large. They may operate from several locations in more than one country. They may employ many people, have extensive specialisation, and use considerable quantities of capital. All this means that large firms can produce larger outputs with lower unit costs.

Task

Study one large company (the company report will give you ample information). Where does it operate? How many people does it employ? What is its turnover? How much profit does it make? What evidence is given in the report that it benefits from being large?

Businesses in the public sector

The government has a shareholding in some businesses and direct ownership of a number of major enterprises. Local government also has a stake in some business activities.

Local government enterprises

Local councils often run business activities. For example, in municipal car parks attendants may be employed to collect parking charges and to check that no-one is using the car park without paying. Swimming pools, day nurseries, bus services, parks and leisure centres may all be run by the council, although services are increasingly being offered to tender by private firms.

Finance to run municipal enterprises usually comes from **local taxes** and from charges for using the services.

The local council may also sponsor **job creation schemes**. For example, it might set up **enterprise workshops** where people can start up a business in premises with a very low rental charge.

Central government enterprises

In the United Kingdom certain business activities are run by one of the following:

- a government department
- a company in which the government has a shareholding.
- a public corporation.

Activities run by a government department

When an activity is run by a government department a Minister is in overall charge, and the department is staffed and run by **civil servants**. An example of this is the Department of Inland Revenue which deals with the collection of some taxes.

CENTRAL GOVERNMENT ENTERPRISES

Run by a government department

Example: Inland Revenue

Run by a company in which the government has a shareholding

Example: UK Nirex Ltd

Run by a public corporation

Example: British Rail

Figure 1.18 Central government's involvement in business

From a business point of view there are a number of criticisms of such an organisation:

1 Decisions are made slowly because there are many links in the chain of command.
2 The organisation is not forced to be efficient because of competition.
3 It is difficult to protect the public's interest by checking on how the department is run.

Companies in which the government has a shareholding

Over the years the British government has had shareholdings in a number of public companies, including BP and Rolls-Royce. The shareholding has often been a form of **subsidy** to the company to help it carry out research, compete with overseas companies, or avoid **unemployment** of the workforce.

In recent years the government has been selling off these shareholdings in the belief that companies should stand on their own feet. Can you insert an example on Figure 1.18?

Activities controlled by public corporations

Public corporations, the main form of direct government involvement is business, are owned by the state on behalf of the people. They are felt to be a suitable form of **public ownership** because, although the state owns the corporations, their controllers are given a lot of freedom to make their own decisions.

Public corporations are set up by Act of Parliament, an example being the Coal Industry Nationalisation Act 1946. They are also called **nationalised industries**.

Although a public corporation provides a marketable good or service, it is different from a normal company in that the managers are not accountable to shareholders – instead they are accountable to the government. Also, although today public corporations are expected to be profitable, in the past they were given wider **social responsibilities**.

Public corporation	Public company
Set up by Act of Parliament	Set up by issuing prospectus and offer to buy shares
Owned by government	Owned by shareholders
Run by chairperson and managers appointed by government	Run by management team chosen by directors representing shareholders
Aims to provide a public service as well as having commercial goals	Commercial goals

Figure 1.19 Constrasting public corporations and public companies

Once a public corporation has been set up by Act of Parliament a government Minister is made responsible for the industry concerned. For example, the Minister of Transport is responsible for British Rail. However, the Minister chooses a chairperson (not a civil servant) to run the industry on a day-to-day basis.

The government sets yearly **targets** for the particular industry to meet, and the chairperson and managers must then decide on the best way to meet these. The government might, for example, set the British Broadcasting Corporation a target of making a 15% return on capital employed in 1995. The corporation must then decide on how to meet this target in conjunction with its commitment to provide a high quality of programmes. In other words, it must decide on how much to spend on programmes, how much to pay in wages and so on. The corporation is supposed to have the freedom to make these day-to-day decisions and there is a lot of heated debate in the press and Parliament if the government tries to interfere.

Up to 1979 many public corporations were given large financial **subsidies** by the government. There were two main reasons for this:

- to try to maintain jobs in declining industries (e.g. coal and steel) because they were major employers
- to encourage the corporations to continue to run services which, although not profitable (and so of no interest to private firms), were of great social benefit to certain individuals, groups or communities.

Today public corporations are encouraged to concentrate more on meeting financial targets, and to be more profit and client conscious. Members of the public do have some control over the running of public corporations. They can make a complaint to their local MP who can then raise the matter when the corporation is being discussed in Parliament. In addition, a committee of MPs has the job of keeping an eye on each of the corporations, and each has a **consumer council** to which complaints can be made.

Privatisation

One of the major policies of the Conservative governments of the 1980s was **privatisation** – that is, putting public sector businesses into private hands. Examples of privatisations are British Airways, British Telecom and British Gas.

The usual build-up to privatisation is to remove inefficient parts of an industry, cutting back on employment and redundant equipment. Shares are then offered to the public.

A number of reasons have been given for privatisation. Firstly, it creates wider share ownership – the idea is that, by owning shares in public services like the telephones, electricity, water or gas, people will feel more involved. Secondly, privatisation is supposed to make these industries more competitive. It is felt that if some of these industries are encouraged to compete more they will produce a better service. In the past losses were made up by taxes; losses today could lead to bankruptcy. Thirdly, money from the sale of the industries should enable the government to lower taxes. And finally, the industries themselves can raise money more easily for investment.

Task

Study an example of a privatisation (either in the UK or another country). Why was the industry privatised?
How is the ownership of the industry changed?

What problems were involved in the privatisation? How can you measure the success of the privatisation? Is the privatisation likely to be a success?

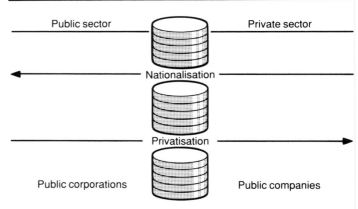

Figure 1.20 **Privatisation and nationalisation**

There are many opponents of the principle of privatisation. They say that the public already owns these industries, so why should they be asked to pay for shares in order to continue to participate in ownership? Some opponents also say that in competing to make profits these industries tend to cut services which are a real benefit to certain individuals, groups and communities, and that the money raised from the sale really helps to cut the taxes of the better off.

Task

Presentation of the case for privatisation or nationalisation of a particular firm or industry
Each member of the group should prepare a 20-minute presentation to the whole group using three overheads. The presentation should demonstrate your ideas in favour of or against a particular case.

Use the following checklist to prepare your presentation

To plan and organise the presentation
Plan to:
- [ ] Set out your objective.
- [ ] Set out a main idea and a clear conclusion.
- [ ] Set out your introduction clearly.
- [ ] Think about your audience, their interests and their level.
- [ ] Brainstorm some main ideas.
- [ ] Plan handouts and overheads.
- [ ] Keep a clear thread linking main points.

To prepare for the presentation
Make sure you:
- [ ] Practise.
- [ ] Check the equipment.
- [ ] Order your notes and handouts.

To develop the visual aids
Make sure you:
- [ ] Make them clear and easy to look at.
- [ ] Choose the correct type of chart.
- [ ] Have clear titles.
- [ ] Talk to the audience, not to the visual.
- [ ] Place yourself in the centre of the stage.
- [ ] Use a pointer, but not too often.

To stop being nervous
Plan to:
- [ ] Take deep breaths.
- [ ] Move during the presentation.
- [ ] Establish eye contact.

Delivering your presentation
Plan to:
- [ ] Be aware of what you say and how you say it.
- [ ] Speak with a strong clear voice, and don't speak too quickly.
- [ ] Be animated, clear and enthusiastic.
- [ ] Use eye contact to make the presentation conversational and personal.

Questions and answers
Plan to:
- [ ] Prepare for questions and practise the answers.
- [ ] Ask for questions by stepping forward with hand raised.
- [ ] Watch the questioner and listen carefully.
- [ ] Repeat the question to make sure everyone has heard it.
- [ ] Keep the same bearing as in your presentation.
- [ ] Use eye contact and look at the whole audience.

Case Study – Making railways more competitive

In July 1991, John Major introduced his Citizen's Charter which set out consumer rights as the 'central theme of public life' for the 1990s. The proposed consumer rights would extend throughout the National Health Service, education and transport to the privatised gas, water, electricity and telecommunications utilities.

The White Paper (a document setting out the government's intentions for new laws) indicated that the officials with responsibility for supervising public utilities (the utility regulators) would have new powers, including the option to award compensation for reasonable complaints by consumers. This would mean clearer commitments to quality of service, fixed appointment times and new means of seeing complaints through. There would be a charter standard for public service quality which would entitle those who can prove they meet the high standards to use a new 'chartermark'.

In the rail service, passengers whose trains are 'unreasonably' late or cancelled will be able to call on tough new compensation rules. Proposals are to be spelt out for privatising British Rail.

Passengers who cannot take their normal train because of cancellation should get a refund. Annual season ticket holders should be entitled to a renewal of their tickets to compensate them for poor service in the previous year.

It is proposed that British Rail privatisation should include ending BR's monopoly over running trains, and the appointment of an independent regulator to ensure fair access to the rail network for private train companies, and fair charging for track use. The charter states that: 'Exposing the railways to the discipline of the private sector will be by far the most effective way of making sure the passenger gets a fair deal.'

1 What do you understand by the following terms: regulation, privatisation, competition, monopoly, and the 'discipline of the private sector'?
2 What benefits might result from the new suggestions for competition?
3 What do you think are the likely costs of the suggestions?
4 How will it be possible to determine whether benefits will exceed costs?
5 Why is it likely that different groups and individuals will have different views about the changes?
6 Do you think that 'the discipline of the private sector' is likely to make British Rail more effective. Explain your reasons.
7 What are the main arguments for the government running the railways?

Case study collection

Try some of the case studies *below*. They cover some of the important topics that you have learnt about from reading this chapter. Each case will give you the opportunity to use knowledge and skills that you have built up, and will help you to tackle the later activities in the book.

Case Study 1 – The political environment in which businesses operate

The table below illustrates the difference in emphasis between the policies of major political parties in 1992. In groups of two or three students choose a particular area of policy (for example, competition and utilities). Show how a change in government would affect the

environment in which businesses would operate. What, for example, would be the effect of a change in government from Conservative to Labour? Groups of students should present their findings back to other groups, to lead to a discussion on what general conclusions can be drawn about changes in the political environment.

HEALTH
CONSERVATIVE: Maximum waiting times for operations; fixed appointments for hospital outpatients.
LABOUR: Patients to have right to access to the GP or hospital of their choice; no-fault compensation in the event of injury.
LIBERAL DEMOCRAT: Operations within a specific time limit, choice of doctor and hospital; no-fault compensation; local ombudsman for complaints.

TRANSPORT
CONSERVATIVE: Compensation for poor service for holders of British Rail season tickets; revision of BR's 'conditions of carriage'; independent regulator of BR after ending of monopoly. London buses to be privatised.
LABOUR: Consumer protection commission to investigate complaints against BR; penalties for failing to meet higher standards; repeal of BR's carriage condition exempting it from liability for delays.
LIBERAL DEMOCRAT: A private-sector input on the rail network; ombudsman to resolve complaints; financial compensation where trains are late.

UTILITIES
CONSERVATIVES: New powers for the watchdog bodies regulating water, electricity, gas and telephones to enforce compensation payments.
LABOUR: Customer service contracts setting out time limits for repairs; compensation if promises broken.
LIBERAL DEMOCRAT: Greater competition in telephones and restructuring of the privatised gas and electricity industries; tougher regulation of water.

Source: *The Independent on Sunday*

Case Study 2 – Marks and Spencer knickers

One of Marks and Spencer's most successful lines over the years has been women's knickers. It got into the business in the late 1920s, when womenswear was becoming simpler, less restrictive and capable of being manufactured on a big scale. M&S had 34 per cent of the market in 1991. Wherever you are in this country – at whatever function – you can say with a conviction bordering on certainty that one in three of the women present is wearing M&S knickers.

The company takes about £500 million a year from selling women's underwear. The gross margin or mark-up is probably about 40 per cent. The economies of scale are extensive: M&S can sell knickers for a fiver and women think they are getting a bargain in places as far afield as Madrid and Brussels. If smaller firms wanted to compete they would have to go for much larger margins to compensate for smaller production runs. Marks and Spencer underwear is thus one of the best protected business lines in the country.

1   Explain three factors that have made Marks and Spencer knickers so successful.
2   As a market leader, how is the company able to benefit from a cost advantage in knickers.
3   Why are economies of scale so important?
4   How could other firms compete in the knicker market?
5   What factors in Marks and Spencer's business environment offer fresh opportunities for knicker sales?
6   What factors in their business environment offer threats to knicker sales?
7   How can we measure the company's success in knickers?

Case Study 3 – St Paul's aims to balance books with entry fee

In June 1991, St Paul's Cathedral in London started to charge for admission in an attempt to solve its financial problems.

The Dean of St Paul's, Eric Evans, said: 'Excellence is expensive. When people enter St Paul's for the first time it is something most of them never forget. The worship itself, the music, the organ, the choir are all in a way unique.'

An entrance fee of £2 for adults and £1 for pensioners and children was set, although there would be no charge on Sundays. In the past visitors on average put 15p in the collection box.

Many people have commented that the fees are not excessive. Indeed the fees are a fraction of those for tourist attractions like Madame Tussauds and the Tower of London.

The move is intended to ease the cathedral's deficit, which in 1991 would have been nearly half a million pounds. The introduction of charges will undoubtedly lead to a fall in the 2.5 million annual visitors to St Paul's. Calculations have been made that if the cathedral lost 40 per cent of all tourists it would still make £1.7 million pounds and be almost able to balance its books.

The move by St Paul's is expected to be followed by a similar announcement from other great churches.

1   Do you think that the public should pay to go into churches? Give reasons for your answer.
2   How could St Paul's be made into a commercial proposition?
3   What criteria should be used to set an entry fee to St Paul's?
4   Explain the importance of the calculations described in the extract above?
5   What risk is the cathedral taking in setting a £2 charge?
6   What would be the implications of charging more? Or less?
7   How could you evaluate in future years whether St Paul's had made a sound decision?
8   Outline three different views that individuals might have about charging to enter St Paul's.

Case Study 4 – Changes in the coal industry

British Coal exists in a difficult environment. It is high on the government's list of targets for privatisation, the intention being to start selling the organisation in the mid-1990s.

The biggest threat to British Coal comes not from its own privatisation but from the privatisation of the electricity supply industry. The new competitive environment in which the generators, National Power and PowerGen, have to survive has meant radical changes in how they view the purchasing of fuel. The electricity industry, once the customer on which British Coal relied to take almost all of its output, is looking for new sources of fuel.
British Coal is protected until mid 1993 by contracts with the generators – they have to buy an agreed quantity at set prices. However, it is likely that after 1993 the generators will have other suppliers.
British Coal has two big problems: its coal is expensive compared with prices in the international market, and its suphur content is high. Sulphur emissions from power stations are regarded as a major cause of acid rain and are under attack by the European Commission rules.

For a company that has undergone massive restructuring and achieved great increases in efficiency over the past few years, taking further action to make its product more attractive will be hard. Since the miners' strike of 1984–85, the workforce has been cut back from 170 000 to 60 000 at the beginning of 1991. The number of pits has fallen from 169 to 68. In 1991–92 another seven pits are due to be closed.

1 What does the information tell you about the environment in which British Coal has been working in recent years?
2 How will the slimming down of British Coal help its own privatisation?
3 Is the reduction of the UK coal industry a good or bad thing?
4 What benefits will the UK coal industry gain from privatisation?
5 What do you think that a privatised coal industry will look like?
6 How are the policies of coal producers likely to alter as a result of privatisation?

Database Activity

Carry out research to find details of four public corporations, five recently privatised companies, and four long-term public companies.

Find out the date when each organisation was set up, nationalised, or privatised. Who is the chairperson and/or managing director of each organisation? What lines of business is it involved in? How many people are employed? What is the annual turnover? What is the latest profit figure?

1 Load a database package and set up a file to contain the information you have collected. Use the following headings: company name, date, chairperson or MD, activities, employees, turnover, profit.
2 Sort the file into alphabetical order, and print it.
3 Sort the file using various measures of size/success, and reprint it.
4 As you progress with the course, you may want to update information. Perhaps you can also add new organisations to your file.

2
Working for an Organisation

As organisations grow, develop and employ more people they have to define roles for each of their employees through a framework known as an organisational structure. Such a structure will serve to divide work within the organisation and enable managers to coordinate, monitor and control the activities of the relevant parts of the workforce.

This chapter looks at why organisations need to structure their activities and how they divide them up. It examines the need for different levels of authority, responsibility and accountability. Frequent references are made to the ways in which many large organisations structure their activities, and the relationships created by such structures.

Nearly everyone at some time or other thinks about starting a business of their own. You often hear people say 'Someone could make a fortune out of that' or 'I wish I had thought of that idea first'. So imagine that you decide, having left college and having worked for a large organisation for a few years, to 'go it alone' and set up your own business buying and selling jewellery by mail-order.

Consider your role in this new organisation. If you did not employ anyone else at the start, you would soon find that you needed to become a jack-of-all-trades, able to turn your hand to every aspect of the business. For example, you would be involved in buying the jewellery, designing a catalogue and having it printed, finding out the sort of people who would like to buy the jewellery, putting together a mailing list and sending the catalogues out, taking order by phone and mail, dealing with all correspondence, sending the orders out, keeping the accounts, getting the money in and banking it, as well as all the other issues needing daily attention.

We can show diagramatically how this business is organised. Your role would be at the centre of a

range of functions for which you would be personally responsible (see Figure 2.1).

Operating on your own is rarely easy. There are times when, as owner, you require the help or advice of others with special skills, such as an accountant, a bank manager or a solicitor.

As the business expanded you would find it necessary to employ some form of help, possibly part-time at first and then full-time. As you began to employ other people you would relinquish some of the work you had been doing, and this would require a reappraisal of your role as well as the creation of roles for others within an **organisational structure.**

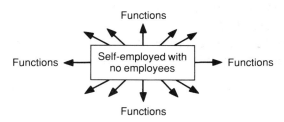

Figure 2.1 Organisation in a one-person business

Task

Assume that you start up and run a jewellery mail-order business. In the business's first year you decide you can afford to employ four other people. What roles would you expect for each of these staff? Draw a simple diagram of the organisational structure.

This simple example shows that, as an organisation develops, it has to consider the roles of everybody within it. It has to be **organised** in the best possible way to meet its objectives efficiently. This involves defining the relationships between departments, as well as between managers and other employees, so that all employees know what they should be doing, where they fit into the organisation, and to whom they are responsible.

Organisations in history

If we look back in time we can see that there has always been a need to organise people. Probably the first large-scale organisations were Egyptian state monopolies used for building the pyramids. At the head of the organisation was the Pharaoh whose authority was invested by divine right and who delegated authority to a **vizier** who acted as prime minister, chief justice and treasurer over an elaborate bureaucracy, at the bottom of which were the slaves.

Over the medieval period serfs replaced slaves at the bottom of the economic and social order and, for a long time, businesses were viewed as a necessary evil. By about 1750 the ideological and cultural stage was set for the advent of the **industrial revolution**. Industrialisation resulted in the birth, growth and development of a massive number of organisations. At the same time there was a growing awareness of the need for **division of labour** and **specialisation**.

Specialisation

Division of labour involves the breaking down of a production process into a number of clearly defined specialist tasks. It is based upon the fact that the total output of a group can be increased if, instead of each person trying to do everything, each specialises in a particular skill or activity. The most famous early observation of division of labour was that by Adam Smith in a pin factory and quoted in *The Wealth of Nations*. He noted that where operations were divided and where workers specialised, output was far greater than it would otherwise have been.

Task

Consider the organisation you either work in or attend. To what extent do employees in this organisation specialise? Make a list of the advantages and disadvantages of this division of labour.

Specialisation is fundamental to modern societies and, as well as division of labour, includes:

- specialisation of equipment
- specialisation by plant
- specialisation by firms
- specialisation by industry
- specialisation by region or nation.

If we consider the massive number of goods or services consumed weekly by an average household, we can begin to appreciate how so much depends on people and organisations specialising in order to satisfy our needs and wants.

Specialisation is often explained in terms of the theory of **comparative advantage**. This states that resources are used in the most cost-effective way when they are used in areas where they are most **efficient**. For example, a golf professional might be good not only at her sport but also as a solicitor. However, she concentrates on her golf because golf is her best line. By specialising she is concentrating on an area where she is more talented.

Task

Make a list of ten large organisations (e.g. BP, Glaxo, Marks and Spencer, your local hospital). In what ways do these organisations specialise? How does such specialism contribute to the quality of the goods or services the consumer receives in each instance?

The advantages of specialisation

1 Resources can be concentrated where they are most productive.
2 Factors of production become more efficient if they are directed towards a set task. For example, labour becomes more efficient the more skilled the worker becomes at a particular task.
3 Specialisation allows a larger output to be produced at a lower unit cost.
4 Concentrations of specialists can lead to sharing of skills and experience.
5 Specialisation makes it possible for us to have a higher standard of living. By specialising, people and nations can develop their talents and then trade their goods and services.
6 Specialisation means that one job can be done well rather than a number of jobs done badly.

The disadvantages of specialisation

1 Specialisation can lead to a boring lack of variety. If workers repeat the same task over and over again they may become disillusioned and this will affect their morale.
2 Specialisation can present a problem where one stage of production is dependent upon another stage.
3 Specialisation may lead to workers becoming little more than machine operators and this could lead to a loss of skills.
4 Narrow specialism may make it difficult for factors of production to respond to change.
5 Generalism is often more useful than specialism. A generalist is often in a better position to look at the various parts of an organisation to devise an overall strategy.

Case Study – Anglia motorbikes

Anglia motorbikes have captured the attention of nostalgia lovers throughout the world over many generations. The stylish, slow-revving, large-capacity machines built using traditional skills and techniques were products caught up in a time-warp.

Until recently, each of the six available models was custom-built by craftsmen to customer specifications. However, dwindling profits and increasing costs per unit led to the management of Anglia realising that the organisation had come to a crossroads. If the business was to continue to exist, it had to modernise. Out went all of the traditional practices and in came massive investment in technology, the installation of production line working and greater specialisation. The table at the top of page 34 shows some relevant figures.

Year	Number of models	Output	Profits £(000)	Sales £(000)	Days lost in industrial disputes	Days lost by sickness
1991	6	534	85	1602	18	1245
1992	2	1658	541	4974	1420	3460

1 Study the figures and comment upon how production line working, greater division of labour and specialisation appear to have affected Anglia's:

a employees　*c shareholders*
b management　*d customers.*

2 Suggest an alternative business strategy to the one adopted by Anglia.

Modern theories

Great lessons were learnt from the industrial revolution. As entrepreneurs (people with 'good ideas') directed their efforts to increasing their share of resources and the sizes of their businesses, they realised that it was just not possible for one person to control all aspects of a business's activities and that human inputs were more than just tools of business. Such ideas about business, administration and bureaucracy have been further developed by theorists.

Henri Fayol was one of the first people to try to work out what managers should do and how they should do it. In 1916, after many years thinking about his job as a manager, he published a small book called *General and Industrial Management*. In this book Fayol identifies five functions of management:

- **Planning** – looking ahead and making provision for the future
- **Organising** – making sure a business has everything it needs and managing its resources
- **Command** – directing and managing people
- **Coordination** – harmonising activities to achieve successful results
- **Control** – making sure things happen the way they were planned.

Task

Look at Fayol's five functions of management. Consider whether it would be possible to do without any of these functions. Give reasons for your answer.

Having outlined five functions of management, Fayol then identified the following fourteen principles or guidelines for management:

1 *Division of work* – the need to specialise
2 *Authority and responsibility* – the right to command others
3 *Discipline* – firm but fair
4 *Unity of command* – an employee receives orders from one superior only
5 *Unity of direction* – everyone pulls the same way
6 *Subordination of individual interest to general interest* – the group's needs come first
7 *Remuneration* – the pay must be fair
8 *Centralisation* – the extent to which authority is delegated through departments

9 *Chain of authority* – ranging from ultimate authority to lower levels

10 *Order* – there must be a place for every employee

11 *Equity* – treating employees well fosters loyalty

12 *Stability of tenure of staff* – 'job security'

13 *Initiative* – thinking out a plan and executing actions

14 *Esprit de corps* – teamwork and harmony build up the strength of the organisation.

Case Study – Finding a job for the Prime Minister

If we want to consider seriously what the Prime Minister is for and what the role of PM entails, there is no easy answer because there is no job description. Asquith's famous one-liner was that the office of Prime Minister is 'what the holder chooses and is able to make of it'. The roles of other Ministers are not a problem because their duties are laid down by law.

Professor Anthony King of the University of Essex has examined the job of the Prime Minister and has concluded that 'outlines of the job remain roughly the same and change only slowly through time, but the way in which the job is done varies enormously'. He does, however, point to seven tasks regarded as mandatory for Prime Ministers:

- the appointment and dismissal of Ministers
- the appointment of certain civil servants
- chairing the Cabinet and its committees
- appearing twice a week for PM's question-time
- representing the government at Summit meetings
- acting as Minister for the secret services
- choosing the moment to dissolve Parliament.

1 Comment on the role of the Prime Minister. For example, is the role as limited as that indicated by Professor King?

2 Think about how you would feel in a Prime Minister's role. Look at Fayol's fourteen principles and guidelines for management and consider how you would apply them to the office of PM. For each principle, state how you think it is applicable and how you would apply it.

F. W. Taylor also contributed to organisation theory by pointing out that there is **inefficiency** in nearly all of our daily acts. He showed that the remedy for inefficiency is not solely the appointment of an unusually talented administrator, but rests with scientific (that is, methodical) management. His idea was that management is a true science.

Task

Analyse carefully (and truthfully!) how efficient you are at a few specific chores. Could you improve your efficiency? Discuss your answers with others.

PRIME MINISTER

JOB DESCRIPTION

1 ...
2 ...
3 ...
4 ...
5 ...
6 ...
7 ...

Figure 2.2

Max Weber considered the growth of large organisations and predicted that this growth would require a formal set of procedures for administrators. He felt that bureaucracy could be used with large and complex organisations and described bureaucracy as having:

- a well-defined *hierarchy* of authority
- a clear *division of work*
- a system of *rules*
- a system of *procedures*.

Each of the theories from the early days of Adam Smith has been designed to improve our understanding of the working of organisations. From such theories we can see that every organisation needs division of work supervised by a hierarchy which has some form of structure.

Organisational structure and design

As we saw earlier in this chapter, an organisational structure is designed to coordinate and monitor people, activities and resources. A formal structure ensures that everybody can see their role within the organisation.

Consider again the small organisation we mentioned at the start of the chapter. If you as owner of the jewellery mail-order business employed four people you might have given them the roles of buyer, office junior, mail room clerk and accounts clerk. One possible organisation chart is shown in Figure 2.3.

Notice that the business has been organised to reflect the **activities** of each of the members of staff. We can also see that each of these staff is responsible

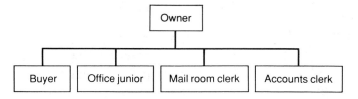

Figure 2.3 Organisation chart of small mail-order jewellery business

to one manager only, the owner. The chart therefore has a **pyramid structure**, in which the authority for management decisions starts from the top and extends downwards in a hierarchical pattern.

Task

Obtain an organisation chart either from your place of work or from the institution you attend. You will be asked to study this later.

What would need to happen if the jewellery business expanded? Perhaps a second warehouse is purchased, professional managers are taken on and more staff are employed. The business might also move into other product lines such as watches and clocks. As the organisation grew the organisational structure would have to change to reflect such developments. At this stage the crucial decision would be *how to divide up the business* so that the various parts could be managed efficiently.

Dividing up an organisation

Dividing up an organisation is often referred to as **departmentation**. For example, because customers are all over the country it might be sensible to divide the business by regions. Or would it be easier to divide by functions, processes etc.? The **design** of the new organisational structure would be crucial to the success of the business. It would have to:

- bring together every part of the organisation
- relate each part of the organisation to every other part
- show where the authority of individuals and departments lies
- enable those within the organisation to assess their roles and status.

Departmentation is the process by which certain activities or sections of an organisation are grouped logically and then assigned to managers. The way in which this is done depends on the aims of the organisation. The five main methods of grouping employees are by:

- function
- product
- process
- geographical area
- type of customer.

As we shall see later, a **matrix structure** can be used to combine grouping methods.

Task

Look at the organisation chart you have obtained. Is the organisation divided up by one of the five methods we have mentioned?

Division by function

This is probably the most common way of grouping employees. **Functional organisation** means that the business is divided into broad sectors, each with its own specialism or function. Examples are 'Production' and 'Sales'. Though every organisation will have its own method of structuring its functions, we shall look at some typical divisions within a large organisation.

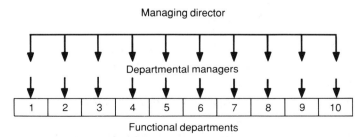

Managing director

Departmental managers

| 1 | 2 | 3 | 4 | 5 | 6 | 7 | 8 | 9 | 10 |

Functional departments

Figure 2.4 Division by function

The company secretary

The law requires that every company has a **company secretary**, who is responsible for all legal matters, and often advises other departments. Duties include filling in the Memorandum and Articles of Association when the company is started. He or she also acts as a link between shareholders and directors and handles correspondence to and from shareholders, informing them of company meetings and other important matters. Often a company secretary will have some other responsibilities, such as that of **office manager**.

The administration department

Many large organisations have a central **administration** office which is responsible for controlling paperwork and supporting other departments with facilities such as filing, mail, word processing and data handling. Modern offices use computers and information technology extensively.

It is common practice for an administration department to appoint an office manager with the responsibility for coordinating **office services** and offering expert advice to departmental managers. The work of an office manager might include organising clerical training, advising departments on layout, equipment and practices, coordinating the supply of equipment and stationery, standardising office practices and setting up an effective communications system within the organisation – such as mailing or phone systems.

Case Study – Centralisation of office services

Many organisations prefer to centralise their office services within an administration department. This means that all paperwork is filed together centrally, that a typing pool deals with all word processing

37

requirements and that mail is dealt with by a mail room. It is thought that greater efficiency can be obtained if these and other services are carried out by a specialist department.

Viewpoint 1 – Rob Butcher had been working at Smartco for 20 years in the accounts office. He enjoyed his job and felt that all the amenities and services he required were always at his fingertips. When office services were centralised the departmental secretary was moved to a typing pool, the photocopier was taken away so that all requirements were met by a print room, and all of the correspondence files were now filed centrally. If he required a service he found that he had to fill in a form to request it.

Viewpoint 2 – Jan Smith was responsible for the reorganisation at Smartco. Despite resistance to the changes from some staff, it was her opinion that centralisation of office services led to easier covering for staff absences, a fairer distribution of work amongst clerical staff, and greater uniformity of procedures. She also felt that many of the savings could be spent upon better systems and equipment.

1 Examine the two viewpoints and explain whether your sympathies lie with Rob or with Jan.
2 Why might it be necessary to take into account the special requirements of some departments when centralising services?

The accounts department

The **chief accountant** supervises the work of the accounts department. The managers of an organisation need to be constantly aware of relevant financial matters. Computers and calculators help to speed up accounting procedures.

The accounts department may be further sub-divided into two sections. Then the *financial accounting section* will be responsible for keeping

records of events as they occur. Records need to be kept of both cash and credit transactions. As well as keeping day-to-day records the section will be responsible for producing periodic records such as the annual accounts. The *management accounting section* will influence the direction of the organisation based upon its analysis of figures for the present and predictions for the future. Costings, budgets and targets for achievement are all vital.

The marketing department

The **marketing** function is responsible for identifying, anticipating and satisfying consumer requirements profitably. Although sometimes marketing and sales departments are combined, there is an important distinction between the two. Whereas marketing is concerned with ensuring that the organisation produces what the customers want, sales is about selling what the organisation has.

The marketing department will therefore be primarily concerned with investigating consumers' needs and wants. This will involve **market research** to find out who comprises a particular market, what they want, where they want it, how much they will pay for it and the most effective way of promoting it. So that the wishes of consumers can be tied in with new product development, there will be close co–operation between the marketing department and the production planning/research and development departments.

The sales department

The main responsibility of the sales department is to create **orders** for goods and services. The size of the department and the ways of operation vary considerably. For example, some organisations employ a large sales force working on a regional basis. Other organisations depend upon advertising to stimulate sales and employ only a small sales team.

Task

Look at the distinction between marketing and selling. Comment on how the roles differ, and consider which of the two areas you would prefer to work in. Give reasons for your answers.

The information technology department

In a modern organisation, staff may work either directly with or have access to **information technology**. Information technology (IT) refers to the large and developing body of technologies and techniques which are used to obtain, process and disseminate information to employees.

The responsibilities of this department would include computing, telecommunications and office developments. Though these three areas used to be viewed as distinct, they are progressively merging together and playing a greater role in business activity.

The IT manager is there to exploit IT in the organisation and provide the guidance, support and expertise necessary to accomplish this.

The production department

Production involves the performance of activities necessary to produce a good service that satisfies the customer. It is often argued that this part of the business is the most difficult to carry out. It involves getting the quality of the good or service just right, and it usually employs the largest amount of capital, assets, labour and other factors in the organisation.

The personnel department

The **personnel** function has three principal areas of responsibility:

- It is responsible for the recruitment and training of staff within the organisation.
- It is responsible for ensuring that their terms and conditions of employment are appropriate, competitive and properly administered.
- It is responsible for employee relations policy.

Task

In 1991 the economy of the United Kingdom moved towards recession. Jobs were lost across a range of industries. Those in work, more often than not, saved for a jobless day despite the continuing slide in interest rates. Industrial pay awards fell sharply. Working in groups, explain how such events might affect the operation of a *personnel department*.

The community projects department

Larger organisations in the UK are aware that they are more likely to thrive in a successful and receptive community. A **community projects manager** might be appointed with the responsibility of overseeing a range of projects – such as help to local small businesses, an educational service and environmental concern units.

Case Study – The Bank of England

The Bank of England was founded in 1694 because William III was short of money to finance the war against France. Today, if anybody is asked what the Bank does they probably say 'prints money'.

However, issuing new money is only a small part of its work.

The Bank now occupies a privileged position at the centre of our financial system. It is administered by a Court of Directors which in many ways is similar to the board of a company. The Court consists of the Governor, Deputy Governor, four executive directors and twelve non-executive directors, all appointed by the Crown on the advice of the Prime Minister.

Though the Bank's main business is carried out at Threadneedle Street in London, it also occupies other offices in the City and has branches in major cities throughout England. For operational purposes the Bank is divided by function as shown in the table.

The Governor and Deputy Governor The Court of Directors	
Banking department	carries out the banking business – providing services to City institutions, government, overseas banks and other customers
Registrar's department	maintains a register of government and other stocks (much of the work is heavily influenced by the mood of the financial markets)
Corporate services	provides support services for the Bank – such as personnel, administration, finance, business systems etc.
Policy and markets division	responsible for activities in the financial markets
Finance and industry divisions	monitor industry and commerce throughout the UK
Banking supervision	responsible for protecting bank depositors and ensuring the health of the banking system
Printing works	designs, prints and destroys banknotes.

Figure 2. 5 How the Bank of England is organised

1 *Explain why the Bank of England divides its activities by function.*
2 *What are the benefits it gains by doing so?*
3 *How important is it for employees in the Bank of England to understand clearly how their organisation is divided?*

Division by product

As an organisation grows, so too may the range of products it offers. At the beginning it may be straightforward to handle all the products with common facilities. As the range of products increases it may become more practicable to handle each type of product in a separate division of the company, so structuring the organisation upon **product lines**. For example, some publishers have a newspapers division, a magazine and periodicals division and a book publishing division.

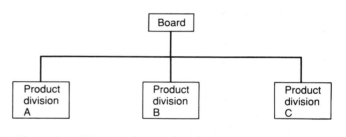

Figure 2.6 Division by product lines

Case Study – Hanson PLC

Hanson

As a multinational organisation with several types of business interests, Hanson PLC structures its activities in the UK by product. It has the following divisions:

a The *consumer group* includes Imperial Tobacco with names such as Embassy, John Player Special, Lambert & Butler, St Bruno, Henri Wintermans and Castella; Ever Ready with Silver Seal and Gold Seal; and Seven Seas, the world's largest supplier of vitamin and mineral supplements in capsule form.

b *Building products* includes ARC, Greenways, London Brick, Butterley Brick, Crabtree and Marbourn.

c *Industrial products* includes Robinson Willey, Smith Meters. Switchmaster, Berry Magicoal, SLD Pumps and Rollalong.

1 Comment briefly upon how Hanson PLC structures its UK activities.

2 Why might an organisation like Hanson PLC, which is a vast conglomerate, be more likely to structure by product?

The great advantage of dividing by product is that all divisions can concentrate on their own market areas. It also becomes possible to assess the profitability and effectiveness of each sector. For example, some organisations sell off or merge unprofitable divisions if the particular industry or area shows little promise; this allows the company to concentrate on more profitable areas. Division by product can also allow parts of organisations to engage in joint ventures with other companies. CocaCola and Nestlé both have interests in drinks and beverages, and they recently entered into a joint venture to manufacture a fresh range of ready-made beverages under the Nescafé and Nestea brand names. Deals like this are expected to become more common and are viewed as preferable to takeovers.

Division by process

Many manufacturing or service operations consist of a series of sequences or processes. Each of these requires division of labour with separate skills, different types of machinery, and often in a different working environment (e.g. a paint shop, an upholstery workshop, a production line). Where this happens it could be appropriate to set up a department to monitor and manage each **process**. For example, a manufacturer of chicken nuggets could be divided by process as shown in Figure 2.7.

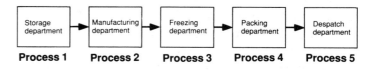

Figure 2.7 **Division by process in a manufacturer of chicken nuggets**

Task

Make up an example of a situation in which an organisation could divide its activities by process. Indicate how you would divide its activities.

Division by process allows an organisation to set up teams of specialists involved with each stage. It also allows points in the production process to be identified if things go either well or badly. Division by process will, however, only work effectively if there is a steady flow from one process to another. If one process department produces too much or too little, problems can occur as stocks build up or run out. This might occur if workers in one process department go on strike or if one department has particularly high absenteeism. Another problem might arise if the departments fail to communicate with each other.

Division by geographical area

A large organisation may have branches and divisions not only throughout the country but also across the world. For example, ICI boasts of its operations in more than 70 overseas countries. Such organisations, rather than attempting to control all their activities directly from a head office, may decide to divide up their operations according to regions or countries. A large retailer such as Marks & Spencer, which has shops on every major high street in the UK as well as in cities across the world, will have groups of shops organised into regional and international divisions.

Figure 2.8 illustrates a company with five domestic divisions and three overseas divisions.

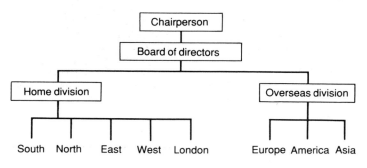

Figure 2.8 Grouping by geographical area

Case Study – Yorkshire Water

Yorkshire Water is the guardian of a water environment which stretches from the industrial conurbations of south and west Yorkshire to the rural and recreational areas of the Yorkshire Dales, Moors and North Sea coast. Every day, around the clock, Yorkshire Water collects, treats and puts into the supply system on average some 302 million gallons of water serving around four and a half million customers and some 160 000 commercial premises. The scale and spread of activities across a large geographical area necessitate dividing the region into distinct areas (see figure 2.9).

1 *Yorkshire Water is 'one of the ten water and sewage businesses of England and Wales'. Why do you think water companies are split according*

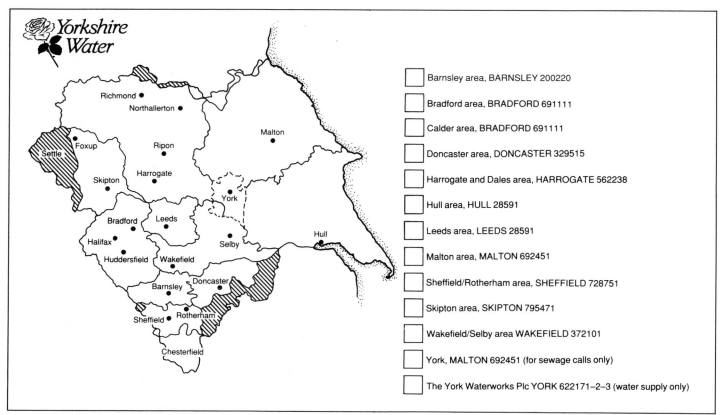

Figure 2.9 The region served by Yorkshire Water

to regions and have then further divided
themselves geographically?
2 Make lists of the advantages and disadvantages
of organisations being divided geographically.

Being organised geographically makes it easier for a large enterprise to respond quickly to local issues and problems and to tailor its strategies to local conditions (language, laws, customs etc.). At the same time it might be possible to cut through a lot of 'red tape' if regional divisions are allowed to make their own decisions. In addition, governments often look more kindly on divisions of foreign multinationals if there is a local head office and manufacturing facility.

However, having too many regional divisions can lead to duplication of facilities, lack of coordination and communication breakdowns. An extensive regional structure requires a series of management positions, and this might lead to a division taking on a life of its own, pulling against the parent organisation and ending up at loggerheads with the head office.

Division by type of customer

This type of division is particularly common where it is felt that different categories of customers require different treatment. For example, an organisation may treat its industrial customers differently from its retail customers.

Banks, in particular, are divided in order to cater for various customer requirements. They have a foreign currency desk, a mortgage advisor, a separate desk for enquiries, and departments dealing with account services for private and business account holders.

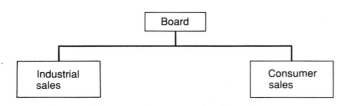

Figure 2.10 Division by type of customer

The main advantage of this approach is that each department can concentrate on the special needs of its customers. However, the departments may be costly to set up and run, particularly in terms of staffing, and may only be cost-effective when there is sufficient demand from all types of customers.

Task

Find an organisation that is divided by customer type. Comment on how this has been done and then indicate whether you feel the strategy has been successful.

The matrix structure

A **matrix structure** can be used to combine the grouping methods we have identified. In such a matrix it is probable that each member of the organisation belongs to two or more groups. A matrix is thus a combination of structures which enables employees to contribute to a mix of activities.

For example, in Figure 2.11 employees are organised both by function (personnel, marketing) and by product (product division). In this example some workers from each product division will be accountable to a personnel manager and a marketing manager, as well as to their divisional manager.

The matrix enables the organisation to focus upon a number of aims at the same time, and gives it the flexibility to respond to new markets where there is an increase in demand for its goods and services – for example, servicing different types of customers with different products in different regions. Another great benefit is the cross-fertilisation of ideas between departments.

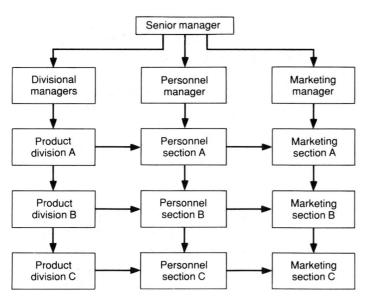

Figure 2.11 Part of a matrix structure

On the other hand, a matrix may be difficult to understand, so that employees lose sight of operational aims. The system might also involve more than one chain of command, leading to power struggles, contradictory orders and general confusion.

Span of control

Span of control refers to the number of employees who are directly supervised by one person. The manager who tries to supervise too many people may be overworked so that his or her staff are unable to perform their duties effectively. On the other hand, if a manager has too few people to supervise, their time might be wasted.

Task

How many people come under your supervisor's or lecturer's span of control? Does this number appear to be too few or too many? What do you believe to be the optimum span of control in their situation?

The question of how many immediate subordinates one manager can cope with has been debated for a long time. A principle followed in many large organisations is that no manager can deal effectively with more than five or six. In 1921, General Sir Ian Hamilton wrote that between three and six is the ideal number, depending on the level in the organisation. Various surveys show, however, that managing directors deal with anything between one and 24 managers directly. Clearly a lot depends on the level – it is probably considerably easier for a manager to supervise 20 shop-floor employees undertaking menial tasks than for a managing director to supervise the work of four directors.

Unity of command

Just as one person cannot be expected to supervise too many people, each person should themselves have only one superior to whom they have to report. This is known as **unity of command**. If an employee is accountable to more than one supervisor it can be difficult for him or her to know which of their assignments to do first, or there could be conflicting instructions on the same assignment. This can affect both morale and the way the task is done.

Task

Are you subject to unity of command either at work or at college? How does this affect the way you perform your tasks?

Responsibility, authority and accountability

The number of hierarchical levels and the span of control are two important dimensions in an organisation's structure. The board of directors is **responsible** to the shareholders for the performance of the organisation. In return for this the shareholders give the directors **authority** to make decisions on their behalf. When the directors use their authority they are then **accountable** to the shareholders for what they have done and from time-to-time might have to justify their actions.

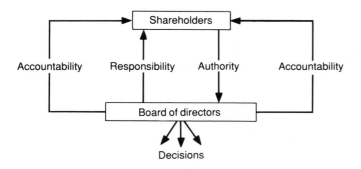

Figure 2.12 **Responsibility, authority and accountability**

We have looked at two levels of control, but in each part of the organisation there will be different levels of responsibility, authority and accountability. The more senior managers will be concerned with making **strategic decisions** affecting the overall policy of the organisation. As we look down the hierarchy, decision-making will become more **tactical** and designed to meet the short-term, constantly changing circumstances of the organisation.

Delegation and decentralisation

These are terms associated with authority. **Delegation** is simply the passing down of authority from a superior to a subordinate. **Decentralisation** goes much further – it is a philosophy of management which determines what authority to pass down. It then develops policies to guide the staff who have this authority delegated to them, and implements controls for monitoring their performance.

Case Study – Delegation and decentralisation

Phil works for a small company as a buyer. Though he normally works under close supervision, the Managing Director has asked him to cover while the Purchasing Manager is on holiday.

Sally works for a large company as a buyer. She is given an annual budget and a series of guidelines which determine what she can do and what she cannot do. The particular aspect of her job she likes is the freedom to make decisions. Her activities are constantly monitored in regular meetings with her supervisor, and each year she has an appraisal interview.

1 Explain how the two examples help to emphasise the principles of delegation and decentralisation. Which situation would you prefer to work in?

2 What are the dangers of too much delegation and decentralisation?

Organisation charts

A large enterprise – one with many employees – may have a **flat** or a **tall** organisational structure (see Figures 2.13 and 2.14), depending on the nature of its business.

Task

Consider to what extent the management structure in the organisation you attend or in which you work is either flat or tall. Which type of structure would you feel to be the best for morale? Which type would be best for efficiency?

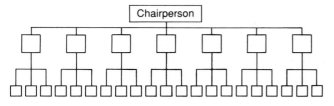

Figure 2.13 A flat organisational structure

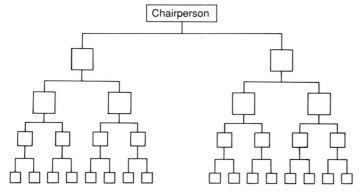

Figure 2.14 A tall organisational structure

An organisation chart is a *visual device* which shows the structure of the enterprise and the relationships between workers and divisions of work. Thus the chart:

- shows how the organisation is structured
- indicates each employee's level of responsibility and to whom each reports
- shows lines of communication
- indicates possible lines of promotion.

Many organisations make their charts public, and they may issue a copy as part of their promotional materials, sometimes in a house magazine and often in an annual report. It is not uncommon for names and/or photographs to be put on the chart in order to emphasise the personal aspect of management. This is also a common practice in education to familiarise pupils with names and faces when they start secondary school.

An organisation chart thus provides a clear, simple picture of an organisation's structure. This is also helpful when the roles and performances of individual elements have to be assessed. The chart can also help a manager to decide whether to delegate and decentralise.

Task

Outline the advantages and disadvantages of putting both names and pictures on an organisation chart.

Relationships

Organisation charts depict a series of **formal** relationships and patterns of authority. There is an important distinction between line, functional, staff and lateral relationships.

A **line relationship** is a traditional relationship in a hierarchical body. There are direct communication links between *superiors* and *subordinates*. Each member of the organisation has a clear understanding of the chain of command, to whom they should report and for whom they are responsible.

A **staff relationship** exists where a member of staff has an assistant who supports him or her in day-to-day activities. This assistant will have an advisory role and have no direct line relationship (see Figure 2.17).

A **functional relationship** occurs when a department exists to provide specialist advice and services to

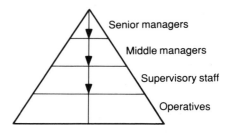

Figure 2.15 The downward flow in a line relationship

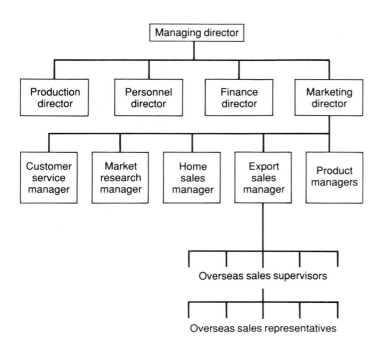

Figure 2.16 Line relationships in one part of a large marketing department

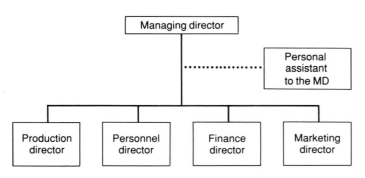

Figure 2.17 An example of a staff relationship

other departments across the organisation. Purchasing, personnel, information technology and office administration are all departments which cut across an organisation to provide a series of specialist services.

Medium and large organisations often *combine* elements of line and functional relationships. Whereas a line department (such as marketing) tends to concentrate on achieving the organisation's business objectives, functional relationships complement such activities to improve the way they

are carried out. This also means that line departments only need to familiarise themselves with their core activities and can rely on help through their functional relationships.

___

Task

Is there ever likely to be a situation where a functional relationship might hinder or conflict with a line relationship? Explain your answer.

___

A **lateral relationship** occurs where managers and other employees at or around the same level of responsibility and from different departments co-operate on projects – particularly in a matrix. For example, a project might involve assistant managers from marketing, production, purchasing, sales and research and development.

Informal relationships

In the real world no organisation can function solely on the basis of a **formal structure** of relationships as depicted in its organisation chart. There are also **informal relationships** in the workplace between employees at all levels and from all backgrounds which help to ensure that things get done. For example, an accountant from the finance department may regularly check details with a particular clerk in the purchasing department before making decisions, because he or she knows that this particular person is 'on the ball' and close to the core activities of the organisation. Other informal relationships arise through social groups, organised outings or sports and recreational activities. Wherever people meet there is some form of social system, and the relationships established from these meetings may become useful in the workplace.

Case Study – Yorkshire Bank PLC

Over the last 70 years Yorkshire Bank has undergone a phenomenal growth in its activities and is today recognised as one of the foremost banking organisations in the UK, with branches across the country providing a comprehensive range of services. Study the bank's organisation chart (Figure 2.18).

1 Comment on how Yorkshire Bank is divided up.
2 Taking into account the nature of the organisation, does the chart seem to indicate a flat structure or a tall structure?
3 Show examples from the chart of lateral, functional and line relationships.
4 How might such a chart help employees at the bank?
5 Why are organisation charts often shown in landscape form?

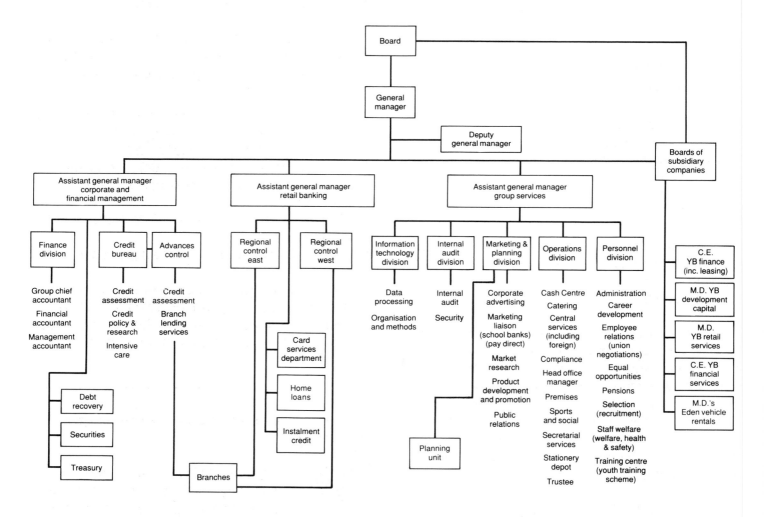

Figure 2.18 Yorkshire Bank's organisational chart

Case Study – Splitting up the railways

British Rail is a public corporation with a turnover of nearly £3 billion. It employs well over 100 000 staff, with a passenger volume of over 20 billion passenger-miles in addition to freight activities. The organisation is currently split up into five manageable units (see Figure 2.19).

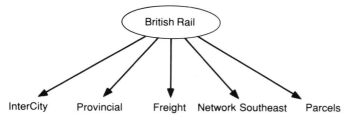

Figure 2.19 The units of British Rail

For several years British Rail has been directed by the government to prepare itself for privatisation. Many people, however, feel that the organisation is too unwieldy to privatise, and there have been rumours that the privatisation might be dropped altogether.

The crucial question seems to be, if the enterprise is privatised should it be sold as a lump or as discrete packages? If it is sold as packages, how should these be structured?

The Secretary of State for Transport, against the advice of BT senior managers, has decided not to sell BR in a single lump. He fears that this would merely create a private-sector monopoly and would not improve the service. He is also opposed to a scheme of dividing the organisation into seven regional packages, as a romantic way of returning to the situation that existed before the railways were nationalised.

Current thinking is to sell the *freight* division first. This division is profitable, and should boom as road congestion increases and can be helped by the opening of the Channel Tunnel and new technology. Many feel that if this division is privatised it will be able to respond more quickly to business developments and overcome the image of unreliability. *InterCity*, too, will probably be easy to privatise as it is another money-maker. Other areas, however, are supported by large subsidies and will be tougher to sell off.

Another idea is to put each part of the organisation out to tender, perhaps line by line, in the same way that bus services have been deregulated. Bidders would get a subsidy but would have to compete on price and quality. The problem with this is that breaking the organisation up into small units would result in inefficient use of resources.

Whatever ideas are put forward over the next few years, the future of the railways as we know them, and the structure of the organisation, hinge upon many external factors.

1 *Comment on the present structure of British Rail. Can you make a guess at the type of organisation chart it has (flat or tall)?*
2 *How would the conversion of British Rail into small units affect line, functional and lateral relationships?*
3 *What might the break-up of BR do to the morale of the workforce?*
4 *Why would the break-up of the organisation into small units be inefficient?*
5 *Working in groups, suggest how you would (assuming you are given the powers to do so) divide the railways business? Report your ideas back and then compare them with those from other groups.*

Case Study – Eight-freight Ltd

Eight-freight is a small private company providing courier delivery of envelopes and parcels to guaranteed time schedules. The following staff are employed by Eight-freight:

Managing Director: Sarah Williams
Personal Assistant: Sue Jones
Marketing Director: Ron Atkinson
Marketing Managers: David Platt and Mark Walters
(each with two assistants)
Personnel Director: Joe Jordan
Personnel Officer (Staffing): Jane Whitehouse
Personnel Officer (Training): Robin Fitzwarren
Finance Director: Shelia Williams
Finance Manager: Adrian Mole (who has four
assistants)
Operations Director: Jimmy Saville
Operations Managers: James Schultz and
Jimmy Edwards (both of whom have responsibility
for 20 couriers) – James takes responsibility for all
northern work and Jimmy for all southern work
Company Secretary/Administrator: Peter Williams
Administrative Officer: Jane Redmond (who has
responsibility for two typists, a reprographics
operator and a receptionist).

1 *Draw an organisation chart for Eight-freight Ltd.
Give one example each of a line, staff, functional
and lateral relationship.*
2 *Comment on how Eight-freight Ltd is divided.*
3 *Jimmy Saville has suggested that Eight-freight
Ltd form a mixed hockey team to play regularly
on Sunday mornings. How might this affect
relationships in the organisation?*

3

The Needs of the Employee

A good organisation seeks to make the best use of the people employed. In order to do this the leaders of the organisation must try to understand how the employees behave, and then provide the sort of environment for them which caters for their individual needs and encourages them to perform well.

In this chapter we look at the culture of an organisation and at how this might affect the ways in which people operate. We also look at how managers and leaders use human-relations skills to satisfy the needs of employees. Finally we analyse the importance of motivation, as well as monetary and non-monetary rewards.

Upon what does the success of a business in a competitive environment largely depend? If you were asked to put your ideas down on paper you might mention:

- quality products or services
- competitive prices
- an efficient system of production
- a good reputation
- a broad customer base.

All of these factors are, of course, very important, but how do they come about? When you consider how each is achieved, you realise that all are very dependent on the *people* who work for the organisation and that its destiny rests firmly on their shoulders.

Human beings have reasons for the things they do. External influences in the environment, as well as intelligence, personality and interests, all help to determine the shape and pattern of their needs. The leaders of an organisation concerned about its performance must understand why the employees react in a certain way.

What happens when an employee becomes dissatisfied with their job or enters into dispute with their supervisor? For a short time there may be no noticeable problems, but over a longer period the quality of their work is bound to suffer. This might directly affect the quality of the product or service, leading to customer complaints. Absenteeism might increase, and the employee will look for another job.

Failure to pay attention to the reasonable needs of employees will have a negative effect on any organisation. The management of an American telephone company suffering from high labour turnover once stated: 'Something is wrong, and we are going to have to look closely at our work, our measurements and our style of supervision.'

Task

A recent ICI report said: 'People are the Group's most valuable resource; our competitive edge depends upon their talents.'

1 Consider the organisation you work for or attend. How important are its employees as an influence on its success?
2 Make up a table with two columns. In the first column list the positive ways in which employees can be treated (such as training), and in the second column put negative points (poor pay, bad conditions etc.).

The culture of an organisation

Organisations are as individual as nations and societies. They have vastly different **cultures**, reflected by their own values, ideals and beliefs. The culture influences the way an organisation operates, so that it is necessary to understand the culture before deciding how people might contribute to the organisation's success or failure.

Organisational cultures, therefore, determine the way in which things get done. This might involve:

- the ways in which people interact
- the way they dress for work
- the image of the organisation
- the way in which employees are treated
- the general environment of the organisation
- organisational rules
- goals and objectives
- the use of technology.

Case Study – Comparing two organisations

In Organisation A, ideas are considered from individual employees. The staff are responsible, motivated and capable of governing themselves, and decisions arise through consultation. Members of the organisation see themselves as a family who take care of each other.

In Organisation B, ideas are considered from older and high-status individuals. There is loyalty and discipline, and relationships are well defined, so everyone has a niche. The organisation takes care of its members.

In Organisation A there is a general air of informality, whereas in B formality permeates everything. Neither of these organisations is wrong in its approach to employees – they are just different.

1 Make lists of the advantages and disadvantages of working for each of the two organisations.
2 Which of the organisations would you prefer to work for, and why?
3 Why do organisations differ so widely?

Types of organisational culture

Cultures are founded and built over years by the dominant groups in an organisation. We shall consider the four main types of culture.

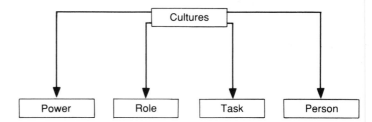

Figure 3.1 Types of culture

The power culture

Centralisation of **power** is the key feature of this type of culture. It is frequently found in small entrepreneurial organisations where control rests with a single individual or a small group of individuals.

Its structure is best pictured as a web (see Figure 3.2). There is a central power source and rays of influence spread out from that central figure. In this

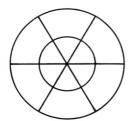

Figure 3.2 **A simple way to visualise the power culture**

type of organisation the emphasis is on individuals rather than group decision-making, enabling it to move quickly to make decisions and react well to threat or danger.

However, the danger of this sort of culture is that, because it is autocratic, there can be a feeling of suppression and lack of challenge in the workforce. Size is also a problem for power cultures, and the web can break if it tries to support too many activities. Power cultures tend to suffer from low morale and high staff turnover in the middle management layers.

Case Study – Apricot Computers

apricot

One of the organisations to receive the attentions of Sir John Harvey-Jones's expertise in his television series 'Troubleshooter' was Apricot Computers, which was run by Roger Foster, its flamboyant founder. In his investigation Sir John found that Roger Foster wanted to get involved in almost every aspect of the business – often with quite trivial decisions – a technique which was appropriate when the company was small but no longer appropriate as the company grew.

1 Speculate on how important a power culture was for Apricot Computers in its earlier years.

2 Why does a power culture tend to become less important as an organisation grows?
3 Outline the advantages and disadvantages of working within a power culture.

The role culture

The **role culture** is typical of bureaucracies. An organisation is arranged according to a set of functions which are determined by formal rules and procedures concerning the way in which the work is to be conducted. The culture works by logic and rationality, and the simple diagram depicting this type of culture bears a resemblance to the temple of Apollo, the Greek god of reason.

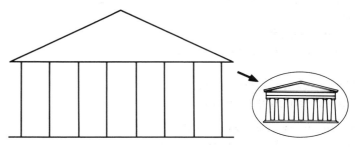

Figure 3.3 **The role culture**

In a role culture, power is hierarchical and derived from the employee's position in the organisation. Its strength lies in its pillars or functions – such as the finance department or the purchasing department. The interaction of these pillars is determined by job descriptions and defined communication procedures. Indeed, in this culture the job description is often more important than the person who fills it, and performance over and above the role is not required. 'Position' is the main source of power, and 'rules and procedures' are the main source of influence.

Role cultures tend to offer security and predictability, a good example being the civil service. Their efficiency depends on the allocation of work rather than individual personalities. They can encourage a more-than-my-job's-worth approach and be slow to respond to change.

Task

Explain how an employee benefits from working in a role culture.

The task culture

A **task culture** is job- or project-orientated and places emphasis on completing a specific task. It is a team culture. The task determines the way in which the work is organised, rather than either the individuals or the formal rules of operation.

A task culture is best represented as a net, with some strands thicker and stronger than others. Much of the power and influence lies at the interstices of the net at the knots.

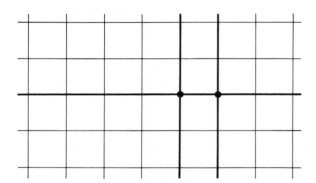

Figure 3.4 The task culture

The **matrix** is a form of task culture. It brings together people and resources and is based on expertise rather than position or personal power. The matrix relies on the unifying power of the group to complete a specific task. Teams are formed for specific purposes and then abandoned, allowing the system to be flexible to short-term needs.

In a task culture workers have considerable freedom, and the opportunity to be flexible makes them rewarding environments to work in. However, lack of formal authority and a considerable number of strands can make management and control of the task culture difficult.

Case Study – Introducing the matrix into colleges

Over recent years many colleges of further education and colleges of technology have introduced the task culture through some form of matrix. As a result many heads of departments who formerly engaged in traditional role cultures have become assistant principals with college-wide functions. At the same time new levels of management have been created with cross-college responsibilities for areas such as information technology, school liaison, resources, client support and research and development.

1 Explain the advantages of working in an organisation which operates some form of task-orientated matrix. Relate your answer to the college situation.
2 For a large organisation operating a matrix, such as a college, explain how this could make the organisation more difficult to manage.

The person culture

In a **person culture**, individuals are central. The organisation only exists to serve the interests of those within it. Not surprisingly, person cultures are more likely to be found in communities such as kibbutzim rather than in profit-motivated enterprises. Other examples may be co-operatives, barristers' chambers and architects' partnerships, where there is a cluster of individuals or a galaxy of stars all operating at the same level.

In a person culture, hierarchies are impossible except by mutual consent. An individual may leave the group but the organisation does not have the power to evict the individual. In this sort of culture the

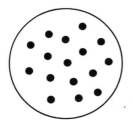

Figure 3.5 The person culture

individual has almost complete freedom to adopt any direction and to do as he or she pleases. Given the opportunity many people would have a preference for this sort of culture.

Cultural changes

Most organisations start with power cultures. Then, as they mature and become less dependent upon the founder, they tend to become role cultures. When the role culture needs greater flexibility, there might be a further change towards a task culture to fit the requirements and needs of each part of the organisation.

Culture and commitment

There is a strong relationship between culture and the level of **commitment**, job satisfaction and stress felt by individuals at work. Many employees prefer to know where they stand by working within a rigid framework, rather than in an organisation that gives them too much responsibility for decisions (see Figure 3.6).

Task

Find out what sort of culture prevails in the organisation you work in or attend. Try to discover why the organisation has this sort of culture and comment on how effective it is in terms of commitment and job satisfaction.

Leadership

Individual workers have their own goals and needs. The closer the work of the organisation meets the needs of the employees, the greater their satisfaction will be. Managers are people who decide what should be done and then get others to do it. They must satisfy the needs of each employee while also meeting the goals of the business. Being able to do so involves **leadership**.

The activities of managers cover many areas, but perhaps a manager's most important function as a leader is to encourage employees to produce their best work in order to improve the performance of the organisation. Leadership therefore involves more than just policy-making, planning, organising, control and coordination – it also involves achieving results by working with other people using **human relations skills**.

Task

Explain why a good manager must also be a leader. List five powerful and influential figures alive today whom you would describe as leaders. What special qualities do these people have?

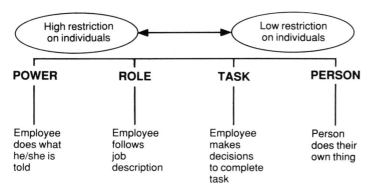

Figure 3.6 Effect of culture on employees

Categories of leadership

A leader, as we have seen, is someone who exercises influence over other people in order to achieve organisational goals. Being able to exercise leadership depends entirely on the *opportunity* to be able to do so. Many people have 'leadership qualities' but never have the opportunity to use them, while others become leaders by virtue of inheritance or an accident of birth.

A **charismatic leader** is someone with exceptional personal qualities who influences others by sheer strength of personality. Examples from history include Napoleon, Churchill and Hitler.

Case Study – Margaret Thatcher's leadership

Whatever one's political beliefs, there is no doubt that one has to describe Margaret Thatcher as a charismatic leader. During her years in office as Prime Minister she articulated her vision and gave strong expression to her beliefs in such a way that others in her party accepted her ideas and pursued the common objective of 'Thatcherism'.

Margaret Thatcher has also been described as a **transformational leader** – one who seeks and

Margaret Thatcher

brings about radical change. Such leaders are capable of being ruthless in pursuit of what they believe to be right and can be willing to take huge risks. Margaret Thatcher's strong sense of direction ('This lady's not for turning') and her ruthless determination earned her the label Iron Lady. Huge risks – such as those taken in the Falklands war – as well as her personal charisma generated strong feelings amongst colleagues and the electorate.

Some of the Thatcher qualities were her high energy level (long hours and little sleep), her mental power (ability to absorb, digest, retain and recall information, to keep in touch with details and to focus on major issues), her courage (the Brighton bombing) and the conviction that she was right. This conviction has, however, been described as her Achilles' heel. If you are completely convinced of the correctness of your own views this often stirs up challenges.

Another of her weaknesses, it has been said, was her inability to build a cohesive and stable team. Theorists tend to believe that transformational leaders should transform and then move on to look for fresh challenges – and that Margaret Thatcher's mistake was to stay too long. It is often argued that 'nothing is so dangerous as yesterday's success'.

1 How important is it for a head of government to be a charismatic leader?
2 Why should transformational leaders move on?
3 Make up your own lists of other charismatic and/or transformational leaders. Give a short explanation of why you believe them to be so.

A **traditional leader** is someone whose leadership is determined by their birth and inheritance. Members of the royal family adopt a role of traditional leadership.

Situational leaders provide leadership of a temporary kind by being in the right place at the right time. We hear of the courage and valour of people who make crucial decisions in times of disaster or natural crises.

At work, leadership is often exercised by an **appointed leader** whose influence arises from ambitions and promotion. The person's power stems from his or her position within a hierarchy.

Another type of leadership at work is **functional.** This leadership is determined by the particular skill or expertise of an employee – for example, a building surveyor, an accountant or a solicitor. The person's behaviour will adapt to the needs of each situation he or she advises on.

Theories of leadership

Most people have some leadership qualities, but such qualities vary considerably from person to person. **Personality** is an important influence, as is position at work and the opportunities arising to demonstrate leadership. To be an effective leader you have to have a **positive self-image** and the ability to face many obstacles.

Task

Assess your own leadership qualities by answering the following questions:

a Do you tend to lead or to follow others?
b How frequently do people look to you for guidance?
c Are you an 'ideas' person?
d Do you often put ideas into action?
e Do you try to build upon your strengths?
f Are you aware of your weaknesses?
g Do you have objectives?

h Do you learn from your mistakes?
i Do you try to help others with your leadership qualities?
j Are you a confident person?
k Do you ever speak to large groups of people?
l Are you a good communicator?
m Are you respected by others for what you do?

n Are you a dependabel person?
o Could you deal with people effectively?
p Could you delegate?

q Are you a good organiser?
r Can you use your initiative?

Leadership must be seen against a background of one or other of the organisational cultures, and this will have important implications for the level of power exercised by the leader as well as the style of leadership. There are three main categories into which theories of leadership can be placed (see Figure 3.7).

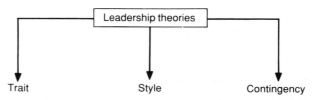

Figure 3.7 Categories of leadership

Trait theories

Trait theories assume that to get others to perform well requires certain personal characteristics in the leader. Some examples are physical stature, social background, intelligence and energy. One American study identified the following 15 attributes for leadership:

- judgement
- integrity
- energy
- human relations skills
- dependability
- fairness
- dedication
- co–operation
- initiative
- foresight
- drive
- decisiveness
- emotional stability
- ambition
- objectivity

Having these traits (or most of them) will not always ensure that a person becomes a good leader, because leaders also must understand the work that needs to be done, and work for an organisation that is efficiently run. Each leadership situation differs and requires more or less of a certain trait.

Leadership traits are an important aspect of the working world. Managers are often employed and periodically appraised on the basis of such traits. With extensive training people can develop traits and improve the quality of their decision-making.

Style theories

Style theories focus on *what the leader does* and the way in which he or she treats and directs employees, handles problems and makes decisions, rather than on individual traits. Leadership style can be influenced by numerous factors, and all managers are different.

Since the 1960s many style theories have been put forward. Often they have been expressed in terms of autocratic versus democratic, or people-orientated versus task-orientated. One such theory is that of **D. McGregor** who looked at leadership and motivation at work. He came up with two contrasting approaches to management which he labelled 'Theory X' and 'Theory Y'. A Theory X manager is tough and autocratic, supporting tight controls with punishment/reward systems – this person is authoritarian. A Theory Y manager is benevolent and participative, with a belief in self controls – the democrat.

Task

What experiences have you had – either in education or at work – of autocratic and democratic leadership styles? What sort of leader would you prefer to work for?

Case Study – Two contrasting styles

When Sir Kit McMahon resigned from Midland Bank in 1991 after unveiling poor results for the previous year, his place was taken by *Sir Peter Walters*, the former chairman of British Petroleum. Sir Peter revels in his 'hardman' image and does not deal in half-measures. He compares business to military situations and does not believe in waiting for the enemy to appear. He has often rid himself of managers because he has lost faith in their ability. He also believes in absolute power and is prepared to 'lead but not to drive'.

Paul Judge was the chairman of Premier Brands – the Smash, Marvel and Typhoo Tea company – which was forced to sell the business to Hillsdown Holdings, a food conglomerate. Paul was described by his colleagues as 'professional, analytical and nice'. His tutor at university thought of him as pleasant, sensible and quiet, and likely to be a conformist. When Paul sits down at meetings he suggests measured and practical solutions. He resigned after the sale to Hillsdown because he felt that staff commitment would be damaged by the sale.

1 To what extent do the two leadership styles of Paul and Sir Peter indicate contrasting approaches?

2 Explain why each type of approach represents an effective style of leadership.

Rensis Likert devised another model of leadership style. This highlights four types:

- *System 1 – the exploitive, authoritative system.* This epitomises the authoritarian style. Threats and punishments are employed and communication and teamwork are poor.
- *System 2 – the benevolent authoritative system.* This is paternalistic and allows some opportunities for consultation and delegation.
- *System 3 – the consultative system.* This moves forward to greater democracy and teamwork. Rewards are used instead of threats.
- *System 4 – the participative group system.* This is the ultimate democratic style, leading to commitment to organisational goals.

Task

If you were given a leadership role, where would you fit into Likert's four management systems? Give a supporting reason for your answer.

Tannenbaum and Schmidt came up with a continuum of leadership styles which fall between the authoritarian and the democratic. This is easier to understand when looked at in diagrammatic form (see Figure 3.8).

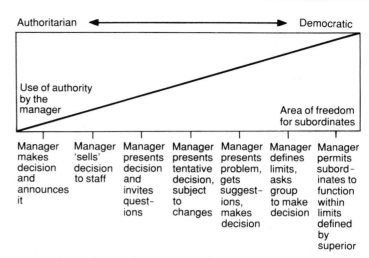

Authoritarian						Democratic
Manager makes decision and announces it	Manager 'sells' decision to staff	Manager presents decision and invites questions	Manager presents tentative decision, subject to changes	Manager presents problem, gets suggestions, makes decision	Manager defines limits, asks group to make decision	Manager permits subordinates to function within limits defined by superior

Use of authority by the manager — Area of freedom for subordinates

Figure 3.8 The continuum of leadership styles

Task

How does Tannenbaum and Schmidt's continuum relate to your own personal experiences?

The **managerial grid** is a matrix model of management which, instead of concentrating on autocratic versus democratic styles, looks at 'concern for people' and 'concern for production'. Again, this is easiest to understand in a diagram (see Figure 3.9).

Of the five styles of management shown in the grid, only 'Team' is the ideal style because it combines concern for people with concern for production, gets things done and keeps everybody happy. Looking at the others:

- 'Country Club' is too concerned with people and gets very little done.
- 'Task' is too concerned with production and creates an atmosphere of low morale.
- 'Impoverished' has no concern for people or output.
- 'Middle-of-the-road' shows some concern for people and some concern for production.

A manager can study the grid, assess where his or her leadership style lies, and consider where improvements are possible.

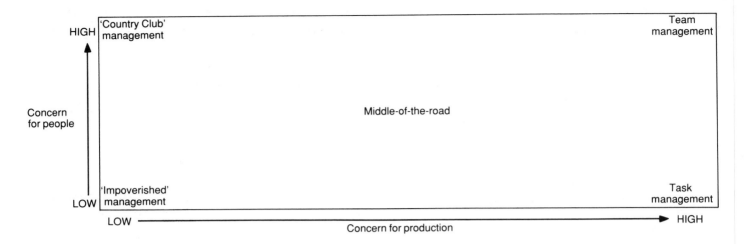

Figure 3.9 The managerial grid

Task

Place the following leading figures in the managerial grid:

Paddy Ashdown
Ron Atkinson
Richard Branson
Brian Clough

Edwina Currie
Princess Diana
Graham Gooch
Neil Kinnock

John Major
Anita Roddick
Clare Short
Margaret Thatcher

Contingency theories

Contingency theories argue that the most appropriate style of leadership depends largely on the nature of the situation into which a leader is put.

One modern theory along these lines is due to **Fielder**. He pointed to three variables which appear in any situation to determine the leader's approach. These are:

- leader–member relations
- the degree and structure of the task
- the power and authority of the leader's position.

Another contingency theory is represented by **Adair's functional model** of leadership. Adair sees

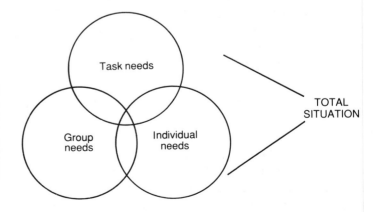

Figure 3.10 Functional model of leadership

three main variables at work which determine how a person behaves in a leadership situation – task needs, group needs and individual needs. Effective leadership involves creating the right balance between the three sets of needs in the light of the total situation. The circumstances of each situation (urgency, danger etc.) affect the priority due to each area of need.

Case Study – A British cure for a German company

As many British firms wallowed in the trough of recession, fork-lift truck manufacturer Lancer Boss of Leighton Buzzard was buying into Europe. In the process it revived a German manufacturer with a dose of management discipline.

Lancer Boss had itself suffered from a crisis in its recent past and had trimmed back at a time other UK companies had kept their ample layers of blubber. This meant that when times of high interest rates and an exchange rate crunch came they were well prepared. At that time they were looking for a European partner, and Steinbock – a Bavarian lift-truck maker – became available because of poor trading results.

The Germans were surprised by a British takeover, and even more so at the recovery plan which was brutal and swift. A factory was shut down, a production line was cut to half capacity and the workforce was reduced. Sir Neville Bowman-Shaw, the Lancer Boss chairman, found that the Germans were amenable to strong management disciplines 'because they were well educated and well trained'. As the British company used leadership skills to turn the company round, confidence was restored. From the seventh month after the takeover Steinbock was back in profit, and Lancer Boss had the European partner it wanted. Since then investment in the German plant had contributed to a doubled market share in Germany.

1 Explain why the situation of the takeover in this case required a particular type of contingency leadership.
2 Were there any alternatives to a strong dose of management discipline?

Summary of leadership effects

Trait, style and contingency theories of leadership all have considerable merit when trying to understand how a leader should operate. No organisation chart or job description will ever be able to specify every action that a leader has to perform. Effective leadership goes above and beyond a job description – it provides direction for the organisation as it works towards goals and, at the same time, helps to build relationships, affects morale and improves the motivation of employees.

Motivation

Motivation is what causes people to act or do something in a particular way. By understanding why people behave in the ways they do, managers can improve the design of jobs, rewards and the working environment to match more closely the economic, social and personal needs of their employees.

We all have different motives for the things that we do. For example, some people strive for achievement, status and power while others strive for money. Our personality, our expectations and our social background strongly influence the way we act. Managers must understand the needs of employees.

Task

Identify your personal goals. To what extent are these goals influencing the things that you do now?

Case Study – Understanding managerial commitment

A recent survey supplied evidence of a critical lack of motivation affecting the leadership and management of many major British companies.

The survey found that modern organisations tend to allow managers greater freedom to work within a smaller, separately budgeted unit, but that many found it difficult to work in such an environment and would prefer a more tightly controlled hierarchy. They were often experiencing stress and were finding it difficult to adapt to the new demands of their managerial roles. Stress was reducing their commitment to their organisations. Their views were reinforced by a feeling that they were under-paid and that there were limited opportunities for promotion. As a result many managers were developing their personal sources of motivation and satisfaction outside rather than inside work.

The survey concluded that management potential was being wasted because of a lack of attention to motivation, and this was affecting the quality of leadership in British companies.

1 Why did many of the managers in the survey lack motivation?
2 How could the commitment of managers be improved?

Satisfying needs

There has been extensive research into motivation and the behaviour of people at work. One of the leading theories is that of **Maslow** which provided an insight into people's needs. Maslow's study of human behaviour led him to devise a **hierarchy of needs** with basic needs at the bottom and higher needs at the top (see Figure 3.11).

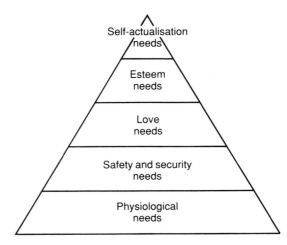

Figure 3.11 Maslow's hierarchy of human needs

Maslow claimed that people want to satisfy a lower level of need before moving on to a higher need.

- *Physiological needs* are basic. Food, shelter and clothing are required to meet the needs of the body and for physical survival. This basic level of need will be typically met at work by the exchange of labour for a wage packet or salary and by the physical conditions of the working environment.
- *Safety and security needs* involve protection from danger and the provision of a predictable and orderly work space. Security of employment, and pension and sick-pay schemes, are also relevant here.
- *Love needs* are concerned with the individual's need for love and affection. This involves relationships and a feeling of 'belonging'. At the place of work these needs can be satisfied by the companionship of fellow workers, working in a group or team, and company social activities.
- *Esteem needs* are based on an individual's desire for self-respect and the respect of others. Employees have a need to be recognised as individuals, to have a job title or some form of status or prestige, and to have their efforts noticed.
- *Self-actualisation needs* are concerned with personal development and individual creativity to achieve one's full potential. In order to meet these needs at work individuals need to be provided with the opportunity to use their creative talents and abilities fully.

Maslow felt that as an employee moves up the hierarchy he or she becomes more 'complete', someone who enjoys work and feels a direct involvement in it. However, the theory has its critics who question the realism of a hierarchy where needs are structured in such an ordered way. Maslow has also been criticised for producing a theory which only reflects middle-class values in American society.

Task

Can you recognise the needs in Maslow's theory in your own behaviour? If so, at what point in the hierarchy are you currently concentrating? How does society influence the way you satisfy these needs?

Job satisfaction

Another famous theory of motivation is that of **Herzberg**, and this in many ways complements Maslow's findings. Hertzberg investigated how **satisfied** people were at work. Following a series of interviews he came to the conclusion that certain factors tended to lead to job satisfaction while others frequently led to job dissatisfaction.

Factors which give rise to satisfaction Hertzberg called **motivators** or **satisfiers**; those tending to give rise to dissatisfaction he called **hygiene factors** or **dissatisfiers**.

The most important motivators or satisfiers are:

- a sense of achievement
- recognition of effort and performance
- the nature of the work itself
- responsibility
- the opportunity for promotion and advancement.

Hygiene factors or dissatisfiers include:

- company policy and administration
- supervision and relationship with supervisor

- working conditions
- salary
- relationships at the same level in the hierarchy
- personal life
- relationships with subordinates
- status
- security.

The main difference between motivators and hygiene factors is that motivators *bring satisfaction* whereas hygiene factors can at best only serve to *prevent dissatisfaction*. The theory thus makes a distinction between factors causing positive satisfaction and those causing dissatisfaction.

Task

Look at Hertzberg's motivators and hygiene factors. If you were a manager or employer, how useful would a knowledge of these be if you wanted to improve the morale and commitment of your workforce?

Enrichment and enlargement

The work of Hertzberg has led to considerable research on **job enrichment** and **job enlargement**. Job enrichment involves loading a job *vertically* to maximise responsibility, achievement and recognition. This may mean increasing the variety of individual tasks an employee undertakes at different levels of responsibility. It could also mean increasing his or her area of supervision so that the person's contribution is perceived as more highly valued. Other possibilities are to upgrade the job, give more control over the job, provide more challenging tasks, provide feedback etc. Hertzberg did, however, recognise that not every job can be enriched with other levels of responsibility, and that some employees feel happier in conditions of predictability.

Job enlargement, on the other hand, involves loading a job *horizontally* with more tasks of a similar nature.

The idea behind this is to increase the challenge and variety of the work and provide employees with a broader range of skills to cover work at that level. Increasing the variety of an individual's tasks can satisfy more work needs and allow him or her to see their contribution to the whole.

Task

Interview someone who has employment. To what extent is the job horizontally loaded or vertically loaded? Explain how the job could be enriched or enlarged.

Quality circles

An organisation can attempt to motivate employees by developing special groups or teams (see Chapter 9). For example, **quality circles** have been a particularly important motivator in recent years. Quality circles are typically small groups of seven or eight people who voluntarily meet on a regular basis to identify, investigate, analyse and resolve quality-related matters or other work-related arrangements using problem-solving techniques. Members tend to be from the same work area or do similar work.

Quality circles are about participation, teamwork, job satisfaction, self-esteem and organisational commitment as well as resolving work and quality-related problems. They have been particularly effective in Japanese industry where they have been responsible, it is claimed, for loyalty coupled with high productivity.

Case Study – Nissan Motor Manufacturing (UK) Ltd

On 1 February 1984, Nissan and the UK government signed an agreement to build a car plant near Sunderland in the North East of

Final assembly area – Nissan Sunderland

England. Within months the company had appointed its first British employee, the personnel director. Since then their short British tenure has been a success story, with forecast production of 270 000 cars by 1993, 70 per cent of which will be exported to continental Europe and the Far East.

Nissan's philosophy is to build profitably the highest-quality car sold in Europe. The company also wants to achieve the maximum possible customer satisfaction and ensure the prosperity of the enterprise and its staff. To assist in this, Nissan aims to achieve *mutual trust and co-operation* between all people in the company and to make Nissan a place where long-term *job satisfaction* can be achieved.

Nowadays, '**kaizen**' is a word much used in Sunderland. It is Japanese, the literal translation being simply '*continuous improvement*'. The improvement is gained by slow and steady change, and once achieved it is maintained at that level until such time as the next step of improvement takes place.

During the 1950s, Japanese industry made great efforts to improve the image of its product quality. These efforts were assisted by two prominent American specialists who visited Japan. Their influence caused Japanese industry to take a fresh look at its strategy, and in 1962 the first *quality circles* were formed and registered. By the mid-1960s most of the larger Japanese companies were supporting a great many quality circles, and currently Nissan in Japan has over 3900 active circles. Throughout the whole of Japan there are over 10 million members of some 1.2 million quality circles covering manufacturing industries, service industries and commerce. Such circles have been viewed as a powerful force for promoting a company-wide quality awareness and for encouraging contributions from an organisation's greatest resource – the workforce.

At Nissan's UK plant the 'kaizen' programme has been developed as a replacement for periodic quality circle activity. It encourages constant quality awareness and is better suited to the needs and aspirations of the British workforce. 'Kaizen' assumes the total involvement of all employees but recognises that participation depends on individuals genuinely feeling part of the Nissan team. The company policy is that:

- all staff have a valuable contribution to make as individuals, and this contribution can be most effective within a team environment
- 'kaizen' team activity helps develop leadership and presentation skills as well as enabling people to understand, acknowledge and learn from others
- 'kaizen' is one way in which employees may participate in issues that affect their workplace.

The 'kaizen' philosophy may be applied anywhere at any time. Everyone is encouraged to participate in the activity and, as members of a team, learn how to analyse situations logically and factually and discuss issues meaningfully and efficiently. People who contribute to the activity include:

- leaders who receive special training in the 'kaizen' process and then apply these skills to team activities
- members who participate in the activities, often from the same work unit or area
- specialists who assist a team with a particular project.

A steering committee develops the policies and guidelines under which the activity operates.

The 'kaizen' process is designed to enable a team to move on from the stage of dealing with current problems or areas in need of improvement to a stage where sources of concern are dealt with in advance of their actual occurrence.

1 *Explain how and why 'kaizen' activity or the process of participation through quality circles might motivate employees.*
2 *Refer to a group or team activity with which you have been involved (e.g. sports, hobbies, clubs). Explain how membership of the group or team affected your approach to the activity.*

Monetary and other rewards

Monetary and non-monetary **rewards** should be designed to attract, maintain and motivate employees. They should also be designed to meet the objectives of the organisation. The reward system is one of the key ingredients in motivation. Careful thought needs to be applied to structuring a payment system in a way that encourages motivation and performance.

In establishing a system of rewards an organisation will agree a **policy** for salaries and benefits. It will then **evaluate jobs** and place them into levels and scales. Assessment of the effectiveness of this policy of rewards will take place through some form of **staff appraisal**.

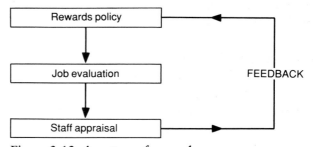

Figure 3.12 A system of rewards

The policy of rewards

The **policy** of rewards should:

- ensure that the organisation can recruit both the quality and the quantity of staff it requires
- foster staff loyalty
- provide rewards for good performance as well as incentives

- create differentials between jobs
- reflect market rates for different skills
- be easy to understand
- be cost-effective.

Task

Interview someone who is in employment. To what extent do they feel that their reward system matches the aims listed in the text? Do you feel that any other factors ought to be added to this list?

Job evaluation

Job evaluation aims to:

- establish the rank order of jobs within the organisation
- evaluate the differences in value of jobs and place them into an appropriate pay structure
- ensure that judgements about jobs are made on objective grounds.

Ranking is the process of analysing all jobs and determining their relative positions in terms of importance by comparing one job with another. For this purpose an office manager would be ranked above a typing pool supervisor but below a director. The purpose of ranking is to collect jobs of comparable responsibility into broad **bands** before pricing the structure by attaching rewards and salary brackets to the bands.

Task

Name 10 jobs or positions which appear in the organisation you either work for or attend. Rank them by dividing the jobs into bands or grades of

comparable responsibility. Indicate what you think each grade is worth in terms of monetary and non-monetary rewards. If possible, compare your answers with others in a group.

Graded salary structure

A **graded salary structure** consists of a sequence of salary bands, each with a maximum and a minimum amount of reward. The structure gives an indication of the different levels of importance of jobs in the organisation. It also establishes differentials and helps to create some form of career path.

Organisations vary in the number of grades, the widths of grades and the overlaps between them. Some examples are shown in Figure 3.13.

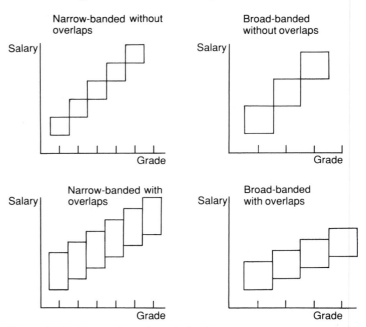

Figure 3.13 Examples of graded salary strucutres

Task

Find out details of two different graded salary structures. Into which category does each fall? Comment on any other differences between the two structures. In particular, refer to the effect each grade structure might have on staff motivation.

___

Incidental (or occasional) rewards

Incidental rewards are often linked with certain grades of job. They may also be given to encourage commitment to the organisation or to reward any special efforts made. They might include:

- a bonus scheme in the form of a lump sum related in some way to either individual or group performance
- the availability of overtime for extra monetary reward
- a profit-sharing scheme in the form of shares or special payments.

Other 'perks' that can be mentioned are pension schemes, insurances, sick pay, private health care, redundancy cover, extra holiday entitlement, bridging loans, relocation assistance, credit cards, fees to professional bodies, subsidised product purchase, a company car, payment for courses, and luncheon vouchers. The list is literally endless and stretches the imagination of the employer.

___

Case Study – Why industry thrives on the carrot

Industry in the UK spends at least £1 billion a year on staff motivation. Though some of the money is spent on involving the workforce in improving productivity, quality and level of customer service, most is spent on more obvious rewards such as holidays, gifts and bonuses for meeting performance targets.

As companies are reluctant to divulge information about incentives it is difficult to estimate the exact value of the incentive market. There are, however,

four main areas – cash, travel, merchandise and bonus shares (vouchers or bonds). All incentives have their own limitations. For example, cash is subject to taxes and it soon gets forgotten as a reward, and there are limitations with merchandise – how many video recorders will a high-flying salesman need?

Not every company thinks it is necessary to offer a vast array of material rewards. TGI Friday, the Whitbread-owned restaurant chain, operates on the principle that the greatest benefit is *recognition*. Staff are awarded merit pins for technical ability, sales acumen and leadership qualities.

A project was recently completed on behalf of Ireland's state-owned electricity board. As prices were frozen from 1989 to 1992, even though the organisation expected to have increased fuel bills, a cost-saving programme called Bright Ideas was designed to motivate staff. Nine out of ten staff responded to the scheme when they were offered one-third of the saving in its first year. Massive savings were made and staff felt they had made gains in teamwork, staff communications and achieving their sense of 'belonging'.

The indications are that, for the 1990s, motivation programmes in industry will move away from short-term incentives towards more long-term methods of investing in people.

1 What are the advantages of providing employees with short-term rewards for the efforts they make?
2 Of the four main reward types mentioned, what in your opinion would provide the greatest incentive?
3 How important is recognition as a motivator? If you were running a small chain-store, explain how you would try to recognise the efforts of your staff.
4 Comment on the Bright Ideas scheme, and outline any ideas you have for providing a more permanent long-term method of motivating employees.

___

Staff appraisal

Staff appraisal, while designed primarily to assess an employee's performance, also provides an opportunity to judge the effectiveness of a policy of rewards. Such appraisals concentrate not on jobs but on *individuals*. A manager can discuss an employee's needs on a one-to-one basis.

Task

If you, as a manager, wanted to find out more about the needs of your staff, what questions would you ask them on an appraisal form?

Case Study – Finding the vital motivation

A senior director of a large company was surprised by the poor performance of an employee who had been with his company for only a short time. This man had all the right qualities for the job, including the relevant technical skills, but was not doing as well as expected.

He was running a technical department with 30 highly qualified specialists, and his role was to lead and motivate the team in order to pursue the company's objectives. Despite a generous salary, help with relocation costs, free health insurance, a company car and a pension scheme, the employee's heart did not seem to be in the job and, instead of taking a real pride in running his department, he busied himself in technical work where he could see the fruits of his labours.

When the man was asked to comment on this observation, it was discovered that he felt the role was no longer challenging. Though he had been recruited on the basis of his technical competence and management potential, the company had not realised that he needed to be constantly involved in challenging projects that used his technical skills. As a result he had started to lack motivation in the management role.

A theory of human behaviour relevant to this case is the one devised by **Professor McClelland**, who sought to produce a theory of practical use to companies and individuals in search of job satisfaction and fulfilment. He identified three primary social motives which govern our behaviour:

- *Group energy* – the need to establish and maintain good relationships, often as part of a team
- *Influence energy* – the need to have an impact, be perceived as influential and accomplish tasks through the efforts of others
- *Task energy* – the need to improve one's performance and accomplish tasks through one's own efforts, often in innovative and entrepreneurial ways. People high in task energy are motivated by challenging goals.

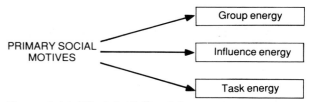

Figure 3.14 The McClelland theory

The man discussed above was found to be particularly high in group and task energy. Whereas his new job had initially satisfied both 'energies', his task energy has become unfulfilled. Subsequently, therefore, he was put in charge of a smaller team of project design experts where he could see the direct results of his efforts.

1 *Apart from monetary and incidental rewards, what do people look for at work?*
2 *How high are you in each of the three energy types?*
3 *Interview two or three people in different types of employment. How closely do their 'energies' seem to match their involvement at work? Do you think this is a good theory?*

4

Assessing Customer Needs

In this chapter we set out to show that no modern organisation, whether it be in the private or the public sector, can afford to disregard the preferences or views of its customers. In order to achieve objectives, the organisation has to discover what existing and potential customers really want. This requires a thorough understanding of human behaviour patterns and trends, coupled with a logical approach to market research activities.

Little more than forty years ago – immediately following the Second World War – there was rationing of food and many other goods. There was not much choice, and incomes were generally low. Since then there has been a massive expansion of product ranges, and the average income has risen faster than prices of the basic necessities of life. We have entered the 'age of the consumer'.

The importance of the customer

All organisations, whether in the public sector or in the private sector, have **customers** (sometimes called users or clients). A customer may be either a person or another organisation. In most cases the recipient of the good or service being provided has to pay for what is on offer, but in other cases there is no charge. For example, whereas a customer in a newsagent's shop is clearly a person buying the goods on offer, in the public sector it might be an organisation asking for *advice* from the Department of Trade and Industry. You yourself – in your capacity as a student – may be a customer of a school, college or other training institution.

Organisations never operate in an unchanging environment, because outside **influences** and **customer preferences** are constantly changing. If an organisation ever hopes to succeed it has to take these changes into account. It has to find out what goods or services its market requires now and in the future, and become **customer orientated.** Assessing customer needs is therefore a process of **discovery**, so that an organisation can **direct its activities** towards supplying customers with the good-quality, reliable products and services they want.

A classic example in the United Kingdom of the failure to monitor customer needs comes from the motor-cycle industry. Twenty-five years ago British roads seldom saw a foreign motorbike. Great names such as BSA, Triumph, Ariel and Norton graced the roads with heavy, slow-revving, large-capacity machines. Imports from Italy in the form of lightweight, high-revving machines were hardly given a second glance by British manufacturers – they did not make them so customers could not have them! Someone *had* noticed these machines, however, and thousands of miles away research and development programmes were under way – Japan was about to enter the market-place. Today the transformation is complete; motorbikes on British roads are nearly all Japanese and there are very few British manufacturers left. If the British had researched their market and found out what their customers really wanted, the position might be very different today.

Definition of marketing

The process of discovering and assessing customer needs is called **marketing**. The Chartered Institute of Marketing has a definition for this:

> MARKETING is the anticipation, identification and fulfilment of a consumer need – at a profit.

The implication is that for an organisation to pursue its objectives *and* continue to make a profit, it has to discover in good time what its customers want to buy and then set out to meet their needs.

Case Study – What do customers really want?

Corky Ra is an entrepreneur who likes a challenge and feels that he knows what his customers really require. In the 1970s he bet his father that he could open a vineyard in Utah, the American state where the mainly Mormon population consider drink and the devil to be cousins. He won his wager by building a 12-metre-high pyramid in Salt Lake City, making sacramental wine in it, and selling the produce to religious groups!

Seeking to diversify, Mr Ra moved into an industry ripe for some innovative marketing – the funeral business. Until his company arrived, burial and cremation were the two choices, but his research indicated that some potential 'clients' wanted something different – they wanted a way of preserving their remains so that they could be remembered.

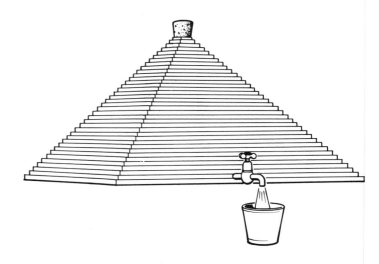

Mr Ra's answer was a type of mummification. For around $7700 clients can be pickled for eternity. Another $26 000 buys a bronze sarcophagus filled with an inert gas which does not allow body-eating bacteria to survive. One client has even specified a bejewelled interment costing $150 000. To help offset the expense to customers, Mr Ra has managed to persuade the US tax authorities that, unlike conventional funerals, mummification funerals should be tax-deductible.

There is, however, a snag – none of his clients has yet died. So far only his dog and cat have succumbed and sit mummified in his headquarters!

1 *To what extent did Corky Ra find out what his customers really wanted?*
2 *What does it mean, he 'moved into an industry ripe for some innovative marketing'?*
3 *Working in groups if possible, try to identify a good or service that does not appear to be offered by any organisation. Discuss your findings with other groups.*

Understanding customer behaviour

The process of buying a good or service is not as simple as it might at first appear. A customer does not usually make a purchase without thinking carefully about his or her requirements. Wherever there is choice, **decisions** are involved and these are influenced by complex motives. An organisation that understands *why* customers make particular decisions, *who* buys, *what* they buy, and *how* they buy, can design products to attract the attention of consumers, cater more closely for their needs – and thereby become more profitable.

Task

Think of the last item or service you purchased. Describe *what* you bought, *why* you bought it and *how* you bought it. Why might the knowledge of this be useful for the supplier?

As we suggested at the beginning of this chapter, customers can be divided into two distinct types:

- consumers, and
- organisations.

Consumer markets are made up of individuals who purchase items for personal or domestic consumption, typically from **retailers**. The purchases can, for example, be goods with a short 'shelf life', manufactured for immediate consumption (such as food and confectionery) or durable goods with a longer life and which are bought less frequently (such as cars and video recorders).

Organisational markets consist of buyers who purchase goods and services to use towards the production of other goods or services. In this category we can mention goods with a pattern of frequent purchase but limited life (such as chemicals, stationery and lubricants) and durable goods with a longer life (such as machinery and equipment). These are, of course, just examples.

Some organisations provide goods or services for both consumer and organisational markets. A motor retailer may sell cars to private customers as well as commercial vehicles (vans and trucks) to businesses.

Consumers

If an organisation is to match appropriate products with a group of consumers, it must have fairly detailed knowledge of **economic, social and cultural differences** in consumer behaviour. For example:

- Different consumers are able to afford different types of products.
- Some consumers might be offended if offered particular products.
- Products vary considerably between the regions.

Case Study – Party, party, party

At a time when airlines are struggling to win passengers, an older rival is building up steam. Sea cruising, once the province of the leisured rich, is booming.

The typical passenger booking a cruise today is successful, in his or her mid-thirties and looking for a good time. In response to this trend, ships have been transformed into floating fun palaces. Discos with laser lights and lavish floor shows have replaced a game of whist on the sun-deck. Gambling is an additional attraction. Customers also want shorter breaks – three to five days is the fastest growing segment of this holiday market.

1 *If you were a cruise operator, given the nature of the market indicated, how and where would you reach this particular type of consumer?*
2 *Where else is there a market for cruises? Are there other groups of consumers for whom you could gear particular types of cruises? How would you do this?*

Economic factors

A group of factors which clearly affect consumer behaviour are the **economic determinants of consumer demand.**

At the top of the list of determinants is probably the **real disposable incomes** available to consumers to spend on goods and services. An increase in real incomes (that is, after inflation has been taken into account) generally increases the demand for goods and services.

A second economic determinant is the relative price of a **substitute product** whose purchase might be preferred or seen as better value for money.

Thirdly, the **size of a population,** or its composition, can affect the demand for products. For example, how many elderly people are there in the market-place, and how many infants?

Tastes, fashions and habits, too, constantly influence the pattern of demand for goods and services. Think of how the markets vary for beverages such as instant tea and chocolate drinks, 'green' products, satellite televisions, CDs, frozen confectionery products, and so on.

Finally, **government measures** in areas such as credit controls and safety requirements influence the demand for a host of commodities.

Task

Think of a number of products that are currently in fashion. Comment briefly on the intended market for each, and how they are promoted.

Social factors

A provider of products or services must be interested in what inspires a customer's **individual motivation** to purchase a particular type of commodity. In Chapter 3 we looked at the work of Abraham Maslow who developed a hierarchical picture of human needs. As well as relating such needs to motivation and behaviour at work, it is also possible to relate them to purchasing behaviour. Let us look again at the five broad categories of need:

- *Physiological needs* are concerned with acquiring food, shelter and clothing.
- *Safety and security needs* are concerned with physical well-being and the need for protection. If these needs are threatened by events such as increased car-thefts and burglaries, then manufacturers can develop appropriate products.
- *Love needs* centre on the desire for acceptance. Purchases are linked to wanting to belong to a community, and examples are a barbecue apparatus or a football strip.
- *Esteem needs* stem from a desire for status, for a sense of achievement and for respect for one's accomplishments. This might lead to a lavish life-style and the possession of prestigious items such as an expensive car, a sauna, a swimming pool, a box in a stand at a football ground etc.
- *Self-actualisation needs* are concerned with full personal development and individual creativity. To achieve this level individuals try to use all their creative skills and capacities.

The implications of Maslow's system are easy to perceive as different products and services are related to different needs. It is noticeable that in Western societies there are far more products and services related to higher needs than in poorer countries. Such a theory also helps to bear the consumer more closely in mind when undertaking advertising and marketing activities.

Task

Identify two products which you feel would appeal to each of the needs in Maslow's hierarchy.

Another theory which seeks to explain the behaviour of consumers is the **self-image theory**. The 'self-image' is an individual's thoughts about himself or herself as a person of a certain type. There are various ways to maintain and enhance this image, and in particular the individual makes choices of car, music, clothing and places to shop which fit into his or her perception of 'self'. By discovering how consumers wish themselves to be perceived, organisations can design, promote and retail goods that are consistent with the image sought. For example, the Rover Group recently altered the nature of its advertising to try to match its products (that is, the way they are perceived) more closely with the 'self-image' of the prospective purchasers.

Task

Identify a number of products that you have recently purchased which match your own self-image.

Closely related to self-image is the **personality** of the consumer. Considering customers with similar personalities, it may be possible to divide up the market on the basis of such stereotypes. For example, various models of cars, records and fashion products all reflect the personality traits of customers.

Task

Which newspaper you read regularly tends to reflect your personality. Make a list of national papers and indicate the sort of personality to which you feel each paper is likely to appeal.

Cultural factors

Culture encompasses standard patterns of behaviour and plays an important role in shaping our purchasing patterns. It stems from the traditions, beliefs and values of the community in which we live. For example, our religious beliefs, our attitudes towards alcohol, the food we eat and the importance of the family are all part of our culture. Though a nation may be characterised by one dominant culture, there may be a series of sub-cultures existing within it. Sub-cultures are important for organisations that wish to target their output to those who share the values of that particular sub-culture – for example, youth markets, ethnic groups and senior citizens.

Socio-economic factors

One way of meeting customer choices is to divide the customers into **socio-economic groupings** based on the types of jobs they do. Dividing people into classes is called **social stratification** and is a controversial issue. The underlying assumption is that, as particular jobs tend to have certain life-styles attached, if the market can be divided, more appropriate products and services can be targeted towards particular groups.

One of the best-known classifications used to divide the UK is shown in Figure 4.1. In this scheme, an exclusive product would be advertised to groups A and B because they would be more likely to be able to afford it.

Whatever one may think of the fairness or correctness of socio-economic grouping, it does provide a reliable picture of the relationship between occupation and income for the purposes of marketing. Members of each group have similar priorities which influence their wants and needs. For example, we could expect those in groups A, B and C1 to spend some of their income on private education, private health care, a new car, antiques etc., whereas those in groups C2, D and E spend a significantly higher proportion of their income on necessities.

Socio-economic group	Social 'class'	Most likely types of occupation	Examples
A	'Upper' or 'upper-middle'	High managerial Administrative Professional	Surgeon Director of large company
B	'Middle'	Intermediate managerial Professional Administrative	Bank manager Headteacher Surveyor
C1	'Lower-middle'	Supervisory Junior managerial Junior administrative Clerical	Bank clerk Nurse Teacher
C2	'Skilled working'	Skilled manual workers	Joiner Welder Foreman
D	'Working'	Semi-skilled Unskilled	Driver Postman Porter
E	Lowest subsistence level	Low-paid Unemployed	Casual worker State pensioner

Figure 4.1 An example of a socio-economic classification

Over recent years organisations have paid increasing attention to the **life-styles** of their consumers. A life-style is a behaviour pattern adopted by a particular community or a sub-section of it. Products can be developed and targeted to support such a life-style. For example, someone upwardly mobile and ambitious would be seeking an affluent life-style and a higher material standard of living. The UK 'yuppy' is reputed to be young (24–35), well-educated, professional and upwardly mobile.

Case Study – Launching new products

A feature of all markets is the development and launch of new products. Here are a few examples.

Cadbury introduced 'Strollers' as an 'adult, functional' product in the bagged chocolate 'selfline' sector of the chocolate market.

Whitbread launched Boddington's Draughtflow, a

draught ale in cans, and is planning a similar product for Murphy's Irish Stout. A successful launch opens up other possibilities for Whitbread's wide range of cask-conditioned ales.

Pepsi-Cola is selling 1.5 litre plastic bottles in six-bottle crates for the first time, to match the industry trend to package colas in larger units.

Wander, makers of Ovaltine, is offering Cafetino, a complete coffee drink available in mint chocolate and orange blends with milk and sugar. It only needs hot water.

Alfa Romeo launched its fastest ever car – the 164 Cloverleaf. This completed their range and was designed to become the flagship of Alfa Romeo's saloon range.

1 *Comment on the consumer needs intended to be met by each of the products outlined above. In each case mention the economic determinants of consumer demand, appeal to motivation, self-image, the personality of the consumer, culture, social stratification and life-style.*
2 *Briefly explain why consideration of each of these factors is important before launching a new product.*

Organisational behaviour

In an organisational market, organisations buy products and services which are used directly or indirectly in the production of other goods or services or which are stocked in order to be resold.

Think of a complex manufactured product such as a motor car. It is made up of numerous parts obtained from several suppliers. We tend to think of a product as a single item when, in fact, it really represents the culmination of a process that has brought together a vast number of items. A car typically has about 12 000 parts in it, and probably only half of these are produced by the car manufacturer, who buys the other 6000 from other companies. The organisations supplying these parts will also have suppliers from whom they buy raw materials and components.

Whereas a consumer market might have a potential 56 million users, the total number of organisations in the UK is fewer than three million and the likelihood is that the product on offer will appeal to only a very small number of organisations. However, items to be used in a production line may be ordered in large quantities.

The demand for organisational products and services is called **derived demand** because the amounts purchased are determined by the demand for related goods and services. For example, the amount of flex required by a manufacturer of electric lawnmowers depends on the demand for new lawnmowers, which must therefore be estimated by the flex manufacturer. The organisational supplier is aware that he is supplying goods to help produce someone else's product so that the demands of the final consumer can be met.

Being dependent on derived demand can have serious consequences for a business. Organisational markets are subject to **business cycles**, and the demand for industrial products and services may fluctuate violently when the pace of business activity changes. The recessionary business conditions in 1991, for example, saw severe cutbacks in the derived demand for inputs, and this led to a record number of business failures, with rising unemployment as a result.

Companies supplying goods in organisational markets face constantly changing circumstances which are often called **contingency factors**. Organisations need to be constantly aware of these factors. Here are a few examples:

- The supplier is usually expected to provide credit facilities for the customer.
- There is a risk of a takeover by the customer.
- Buyers deliberately exercise their buying power to influence the conditions of supply – such as discounts.
- Large companies often use small companies as suppliers simply in order to exercise their buying power.
- Buyers in any size of company may deliberately pursue a policy of delaying payment for goods and services received.
- There is a risk of a supplier becoming dependent on one customer.

Task

Working in groups, discuss the dangers associated with each of the *contingency factors* mentioned in the text.

Vertical and horizontal markets

Organisational markets are described as either vertical or horizontal. Where a product or service is used by only a small number of buyers, it has a

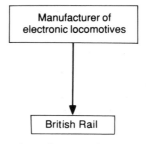

Figure 4. 2 **A vertical market**

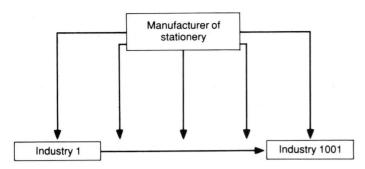

Figure 4.3 A horizontal market

vertical market. For example, there are very few buyers or passenger aircraft or electric locomotives. A product has a **horizontal market** if it is purchased by many kinds of organisations in different industries – examples are stationery and lubricants.

Market research

As we have seen, an organisation must be aware of changes in its external environment as well as changes in the needs of its customers. It requires **information**. The gathering of such information helps it to plan its activities and reduce uncertainty.\

The American Marketing Association uses a simple working definition of market research:

> MARKET RESEARCH is the systematic gathering, recording and analysis of data about problems related to the marketing of goods and services.

We can break this definition down into its important ingredients:

- *systematic* – in other words, using an organised and clear method or system
- *gathering* – knowing what you are looking for, and collecting appropriate information
- *recording* – keeping clear and organised records of what you find out
- *analysing* – ordering and making sense of your information in order to draw out relevant trends and conclusions

- *problems related to marketing* – finding out the answers to questions that will help you to understand your customers and other details about the market-place.

It is the responsibility of the market research function within an organisation to find out as much as it possibly can about customers, markets and products. This is essential for all organisations if they are to meet the needs of their customers and remain competitive and profitable. It is an organised way of finding answers to questions or solutions to problems and *should be an on-going activity*.

In order to sell to people *what* they want to buy, *when* they want to buy it, it is essential to build up a profile of customers – what they do, when and why they do it, and what would encourage them to use your products and services. In other words, you have to study their habits and motivations.

Market research also needs to find out what might make customers choose a rival product in preference to your own. For example, might falling sales be as a result of changes in demand, the existence of an aggressive competitor or poor service on your part?

Case Study – Researching consumer needs

For Procter & Gamble (a major international manufacturer of detergent, personal care, cosmetic and food products), market research surveys are a way of life. In fact, they never stop. Over 200 thousand consumers respond to their questions each year, resulting in a research report virtually every day. The changing patterns they reveal are fundamental to the firm's core business activities.

For example, in the immediate post-war years only 3 per cent of households had any form of washing machine, and these were not automatic. Today 80 per cent have one, and automatic machines account for more than four out of every five machines bought. Sales of low-suds powders and liquids necessary for automatic washing machines grew for several years at a rate of around 20 per cent a year.

Over the last 25 years the cotton content of fabrics has halved, and today man-made fibres account for over half of fabrics sold and around 80 per cent of articles washed are coloured. In response, washing products have had to be developed which don't eventually bleach out colour and which wash as well or better at lower temperatures.

There has also been rapid change in the social patterns which affect the clothes-washing task. Today's variations across family sizes, occupations, leisure pursuits and so on are considerable. Sophisticated research techniques are required to build up an accurate picture of washing habits.

All of these different consumer needs have to be met by products which, though highly sophisticated and chemically complex, are easy and quick to use and relatively inexpensive. Only 20p of every £100 of household expenditure goes on washing products.

1 Describe briefly what has happened to the market for washing materials over the last 25 years.
2 Explain how market research helps P & G to meet consumer needs.
3 What might have happened to their core business activities if P & G had not sufficiently researched the market?

Internal information

Much of the information that an organisation requires about the market-place is already held within its various departments. A lot of this **internal information** might be in filing cabinets, and at least

some of it will be out-of-date. The secret is to know what you need, to discover where to find it, and then to retrieve it.

Nowadays, a lot of internal information is held on **computer files**. Computers have revolutionised the way information is stored, analysed and retrieved, and this has made the task of dealing with internal information much easier.

For example, in the past it was often difficult to get regular and reliable feedback from **sales representatives**, because their 'paperwork' was kept in their vehicles, was disorganised and bulky, and was rarely filed. This information was potentially enormously valuable as it represented **feedback** from first-hand experiences with customers – it is often said that a sales force is an organisation's 'eyes and ears'.

Computers have provided the means whereby information of this nature can be recorded in a simple manner, and contacts with each customer can be 'processed' so that information can be retrieved very quickly and then displayed in a way that is easy to understand, perhaps with the aid of a graphics software package. Techniques like this improve the quality of the market research process and enable organisations to direct goods and services to those customers who are most likely to make a purchase.

Task

What sort of information are sales representatives likely to be able to supply from customers?

In organisations using computerised records, files of information are stored on a **database**. This is a large amount of information which is stored in such a way that it can easily be found, processed and updated. The database may be central so that it can be accessed by users from all parts of the organisation.

Case Study – The electricity distribution company

We can show how one type of database works by looking at the activities of an electricity distribution company. Customers are given a *customer reference number* (CRN). To the CRN the electricity company can then attach a vast array of information which tells it about the consumer. For example:

Tariff type – The price a customer pays for electricity can vary according to whether they are a home or business, a large or small customer.

Consumption – The company can track the *amount* of electricity a customer uses, and *when* it is used.

Method of payment – Some customers prefer prepayment rather than credit, others prefer to pay monthly rather than quarterly.

Change of tenancy – The company knows when customers move out of and into a property.

New buildings – The company knows when and where new buildings that use electricity are being erected, because an electricity supply is applied for.

From such information it is possible to obtain answers to an almost endless list of questions, such as:

- What is the size of the market?
- What type of user uses the most/least electricity?
- How do customers prefer to pay?
- What is the average credit period?
- What type of customers are bad payers?
- How many new users are coming on-stream?
- How many users is the company losing?
- What is the average consumption per user?
- What is the profitability for each type of customer?
- How does the use of electricity vary during the day?
- Where is the market expanding/contracting?

1 How will the answers to the sort of questions indicated here improve the way the electricity company manages its business?
2 What other questions might be answered from this type of database?

External information

The internal information that has been collated needs to be put into context, since on its own it simply provides a snapshot of the organisation and its customers. In particular it tells the organisation nothing about how effective its performance is relative to that of its competitors, nor how the business could be threatened by those competitors.

External information is more commonly called **secondary data** because it is often in the form of published materials, collected by somebody else. It can provide a broader dimension to data previously collected and can be used in two main ways.

Firstly, external information can **enhance** the company's existing knowledge. For example, postcodes help the computer to group customers geographically. By identifying and labelling certain characteristics of its customers, a company can make assumptions about their needs. Two examples of useful external sources are:

- *Domestic socio-economic data* – Customers are classified by their house type, the assumption being that a certain lifestyle is associated with that type of house.
- *Industrial classification* – Organisational customers can be classified according to the nature of their activities. Certain types of organisations can then be expected to have predictable demands for services.

Secondly, external sources can complement an organisation's own information by providing direct comparison with competitors, by putting performance within the context of the economy as a whole, and by identifying markets offering potential.

Task

Imagine that you are the owner or manager of a small shop selling sports equipment in your local neighbourhood. What sort of information might give you a better understanding of the decisions you have to make?

Government statistics

The government's statistical service is coordinated by the Central Statistical Office (CSO). Government departments prepare statistics and the CSO publishes both a monthly and an annual analysis. In addition, Business Monitors are published quarterly to provide a range of information about various markets. Information on particular groups of industries is identified by a code which relates to their Standard Industrial Classification (SIC) – for example, 'agriculture, forestry and fishing' and 'energy and water supply industries'. As the SIC is the government's official way of classifying organisations and markets, it is frequently used in market research.

Another useful source of information, particularly for industries selling in consumer markets, is **census data** published by the Office of Population, Censuses and Surveys. A full census is carried out every ten years, the last one being in 1991. This office also carries out two continuous surveys on Family Expenditure and General Households, which might also be useful for organisations to analyse for market research purposes.

Other sources of information

Mintel is a **commercial research organisation** which, in return for a fee, provides a monthly journal containing reports on a variety of consumer markets

– for example, bread, alcoholic drinks, insurance. The **Mintel reports** are up to about 20 pages long, with information such as market size, main competitors, projected growth, market share of main producers, advertising spend of main brands, trends etc. Mintel also produces in-depth reports on certain markets.

Task

How might the information published in a Mintel Report be useful?

Another research outfit which operates in a similar way to Mintel is **Euromonitor.** Key Note Reports cover a range of businesses and, at around 75 pages long, provide a good introduction to markets.

Some research establishments work exclusively in one particular sector. For the food industry, for example, there is the Leatherhead Food Research Association and the Food Policy Research Unit. **Business-to-business reports** are available for many sectors.

A. C. Nielson and **Retail Audits** are research outfits which collect data of retail sales through supermarkets and large chains, and sell the figures to organisations wishing to buy them. These figures enable manufacturers to work out their share of the market, the sales of different products, and the effects of any recent strategy such as a price change or a promotion campaign. These audits therefore offer a window directly onto the market-place.

Another way of finding out what is happening in the market-place is to set up **panels**. These are groups of consumers who record their purchases and/or media habits in a diary. The purpose of the diary is not just to record purchases but also to provide research information which relates purchasing habits with social status, occupation, income, demographic details, neighbourhood etc.

There are many sources providing **information about the media** which might be of use to organisations wishing to look at how to get their promotional messages across to customers. **Benn's Media Directory** gives details of TV and radio companies, newspapers and magazines. **British Rate and Data** (BRAD) provides comprehensive coverage of virtually all the media selling advertising space, together with rates. **The Advertisers Annual** makes detailed comparisons of advertising agencies.

Information about companies is available from several sources. **Kompass** publishes two volumes of products and services listed by the SIC codes mentioned earlier. **Extel** provides details extracted from the published accounts of all the public companies and from many of the larger private companies. The annual publication **Who Owns Whom** gives details of the ownership of subsidiary companies.

Task

Visit both the reference section and the periodicals section of your college library or your local library. Identify which sources of information may be of use for market research purposes. Ask the librarian for help if necessary.

Primary sources of information

Internal and external data may not answer all the questions an organisation wants to ask. It may be out-of-date or it may not cover exactly the right market sector. Then, to meet an organisation's specific needs, **primary research** has to take place.

Primary data is first-hand knowledge, 'straight from the horse's mouth'. Information a company compiles from its own research efforts is called primary.

Surveys are the most common method used to collect primary data; they involve contacting **respondents** to find out how they react to a range of issues contained in a **questionnaire**. There are two types of survey, a census and a sample. A **census** involves questioning everybody in a particular market – but, unless the market is very small, this is unlikely to be practicable. Taking a **sample** involves questioning a *selection* of respondents from the target market. In order to ensure that the results of a sample survey are accurate, the market research process must identify a representative group of consumers. If the selection of the sample is fair and accurate, then information should be **statistically reliable**. If the sample is incomplete and does not accurately represent a group of consumers, misleading data are obtained – the sample is said to be **biased**.

Choosing a sample

One way to ensure that a selection is free of bias is to use **random sampling**. Individuals and organisations are selected from a 'sampling frame', which is simply a list (usually numbered) of all the members of the market or population due to be surveyed. We shall consider several popular forms of sampling.

Simple random sampling

With this method the researcher chooses the size of the sample required and then picks the sample on a random basis. The sample must be selected in such a way that every item in the sampling frame has an equal chance of being selected. One way of doing this is to use a computer to draw names or numbers from the list at random.

Another way is to use **systematic sampling**, which involves selecting items from the list at regular intervals after choosing a random starting point. For example, if it is decided to select a sample of 20 names from 1000, then every 50th name (1000 divided by 20) should be selected, after a random start in the first 50. If 18 is chosen as the starting point (possibly by using a table of random numbers), then the sample series would start: 18 . . .68 . . .118 . . .168 . . . etc.

Stratified random sampling

If some customers are more important than others, then simple random sampling can distort the results. **Stratified random sampling** therefore weights the sample on the basis of the importance of each group of customers in the market.

For example, if an organisation has 5000 small users of products accounting for sales of £1 million, 4000 medium users accounting for £1 million, and 1000 big users accounting for £2 million, a random sample of 200 would not be representative of the whole market. To make the sample more representative would involve allocating the big users 1/2 the sample because they make up 1/2 the sales, with 1/4 of the sample to medium users and 1/4 to small users. The stratified random sample would then include 100 big users, 50 medium users and 50 small users, all randomly chosen from their respective categories.

Cluster sampling

With **cluster sampling** the population/customers are divided up into small areas, but instead of sampling from a random selection of these areas, sampling is carried out in a few areas which are considered to be typical of the market in question. For example, you might divide the city of Newcastle into 200 segments and then, because of the nature of your survey, decide that you will only sample from a segment which contains at least one school, one church and one shopping centre, and any segments without these facilities are avoided.

Quota sampling

Although random sampling, if properly conducted, produces the best results, it can be expensive and

time consuming, and in some situations it is not possible to identify a random sample. **Quota sampling** is more commonly used.

Interviewers are given instructions as to the number of people to interview with certain characteristics – such as sex, age, socio-economic group or other demographic detail. For example, if the interviewers are asked to investigate housewives aged 36–50, they will quiz every housewife 'fitting the bill' (possibly in interviews in the high street) up to their maximum quota. The problem is that there is no assurance that the housewives interviewed are typical of housewives in that band, and the statistical accuracy of such sampling is questionable.

Convenience and judgement sampling

Convenience sampling involves gathering information from anybody available for the interviewer to survey, no matter what their background. **Judgement sampling** involves selection of the respondents by the interviewer based on his or her judgement that they seemed to be and looked representative of the group of customers in the market being researched.

Task

Study each of the sampling methods described and then comment on which methods you feel would provide:

a *the greatest accuracy, and*
b *the greatest cost-efficiency.*

Preparing a questionnaire

When the sampling problems have been settled, the researcher must design a questionnaire. This is a systematic list of questions designed to obtain information from people about:

- specific events
- their attitudes
- their values
- their beliefs.

Questionnaire design is probably the most crucial part of a survey. Though it is easy to design questions, it is difficult to produce a good questionnaire – and a badly designed questionnaire may lead to biased results. For instance, if the people completing the questionnaire are unaware of its purpose, they may place the wrong emphasis on the questions. Another problem may arise if very few completed forms are returned, or if those returned are only partially completed. In addition, if the questionnaire is being administered by an interviewer, there is always a danger that the interviewer may misinterpret the questions and introduce his or her own personal bias in a way which prompts certain answers from respondents.

Task

Think back to any questionnaire or form which you have recently had to answer. (If necessary, use your course enrolment form as an example.) What was the purpose of the questionnaire? Was it simple and easy to understand? Do you feel that it was well designed? If not, why not?

A good questionnaire will:

- ask questions which relate directly to information needs
- not ask too many questions
- not ask personal questions
- fit its questions into a logical sequence
- have unambiguous questions.

It will also have been extensively tested, possibly with trial interviews, before being administered.

The questions in a questionnaire may be 'open' or 'closed'. **Open questions** allow the person answering to give an opinion and may encourage him or her to talk at length. **Closed questions** usually require an answer picked from a range of options (which may be simply yes/no). Most questionnaires used closed questions, so that they can be answered quickly and more efficiently, and the answers are easier to analyse (see Figure 4.5).

The purpose of a closed question is to get people to commit themselves to a concrete opinion. If you ask an open question, the likelihood is that your survey will prompt a wide range of answers which are very difficult to analyse. Closed questions tie respondents down so that they have to make a decision within a range of choices.

To help interviewers operate a questionnaire, sometimes a **prompt card** is used. This means that, if several or all of the questions in the questionnaire have the same range of set answers, these can be numbered and then the respondents' answers can be recorded as numbers (see Figure 4.6).

Some questionnaires are designed so that respondents can concentrate on the questions that are relevant, and then skip over questions which do not relate to them (see Figure 4.7).

Case Study – Jus-rol Ltd

As a manufacturer of frozen food, Jus-rol Ltd is conscious of the need to take into account the views of its customers. The company is also aware of the valuable information that its customers might hold. The questionnaire in Figure 4.7 was recently sent to a sample of known consumers of frozen fillo pastry. Read through the questionnaire and then answer the questions that follow.

JUS-ROL LIMITED 21ST MARCH 1991

1 HAD YOU EVERY PURCHASED FROZEN FILLO PASTRY PRIOR TO BUYING THE JUS-ROL BRAND OF FROZEN FILLO? (PLEASE TICK THE APPROPRIATE BOX)

YES	
NO	

2 HOW OFTEN DO YOU BUY JUS-ROL FILLO PASTRY? (PLEASE TICK THE BOX WHICH IS NEAREST TO YOUR PURCHASE)

FORTNIGHTLY	
MONTHLY	
EVERY 3 MONTHS	
ONCE A YEAR	

3 HAVE YOU PURCHASED JUS-ROL FILLO PASTRY ONLY THIS ONCE? IF SO, WHY IS THIS? (PLEASE EXPLAIN BRIEFLY)

4 IS JUS-ROL FILLO OBTAINABLE IN THE STORES YOU NORMALLY SHOP AT? (PLEASE TICK THE APPROPRIATE BOX)

YES	
NO	

5 WHERE DO YOU NORMALLY SHOP? (IT IS LIKELY YOU SHOP AT SEVERAL STORES. PLEASE PUT A TICK AGAINST THE STORE YOU NORMALLY VISIT AND THE RELEVANT FREQUENCY)

STORE	WEEKLY	MONTHLY	FORT-NIGHTLY
SAINSBURY			
TESCO			
SAFEWAY			
ASDA			
ICELAND			
CO-OPS			
GATEWAY			
OTHERS			

6 WHICH PRODUCTS DO YOU NORMALLY PREPARE USING FILLO PASTRY? (PLEASE TICK RELEVANT BOXES AND PROVIDE ANY ADDITIONAL INFORMATION IN THE SPACE BELOW)

SAMOSAS	
STRUDELS	
SAVOURY SNACKS	
SAVOURY MEALS	
DESSERTS	
OTHER	

7 FOR WHAT MEAL OCCASION DO YOU NORMALLY USE PRODUCTS MADE WITH FILLO PASTRY? (PLEASE TICK APPROPRIATE BOXES)

BREAKFAST	
MAIN MEALS – lunch	
MAIN MEALS – dinner	
SNACK OCCASIONS – day	
SNACK OCCASIONS – evening	

8 WHICH OF THE FOLLOWING CATEGORY ARE YOU? (PLEASE TICK THE APPROPRIATE BOX)

FULL TIME EMPLOYED	
PART TIME EMPLOYED	
HOUSEWIFE/ HOUSEHUSBAND	

9 IF EMPLOYED, WHAT IS YOUR OCCUPATION? PLEASE SPECIFY

10 IS THE TEXTURE AND TASTE OF JUS-ROL FILLO TO YOUR SATISFACTION? (PLEASE TICK THE APPROPRIATE BOX)

YES	
NO	

11 DO YOU FIND JUS-ROL EASY TO USE (PLEASE TICK APPROPRIATE BOX) IF NOT, WHAT IS THE PROBLEM?

YES	
NO	

12 WHAT IS YOUR VIEW ON THE PACK SIZE OF JUS-ROL FILLO I.E. 300G (PLEASE TICK THE APPROPRIATE BOX)

ABOUT RIGHT	
TOO LARGE	
TOO SMALL	

13 AT PRESENT THE SIZE OF EACH JUS-ROL FILLO SHEET IS 12″ × 6″. WHAT IS YOUR VIEW ON THIS SIZE? (PLEASE TICK THE APPROPRIATE BOX)

ABOUT RIGHT	
TOO LARGE	
TOO SMALL	

14 IF YOU FELT AN AMENDMENT TO THE PACK AND SIZE OF SHEETS IS DESIRABLE, WHAT WOULD YOU RECOMMEND? (PLEASE TICK PREFERRED WEIGHT AND SIZE)

WEIGHT: 400G	
WEIGHT: 250G	
WEIGHT: 200G	
SIZE: 20″ × 10″	
SIZE: 12″ × 12″	
SIZE: 15″ × 12″	

15 DO YOU HAVE A COPY OF JUS-ROL'S FILLO RECIPE BOOKLET (PLEASE TICK THE APPROPRIATE BOX)

YES	
NO	

16 IF YOU HAVE A JUS-ROL FILLO RECIPE BOOKLET, DO YOU USE IT . . . (PLEASE TICK THE APPROPRIATE BOX)

OCCASIONALLY	
OFTEN	
NEVER	

17 PLEASE WRITE YOUR NAME AND ADDRESS IN THE BOX PROVIDED.

Figure 4.4 Questionnaire

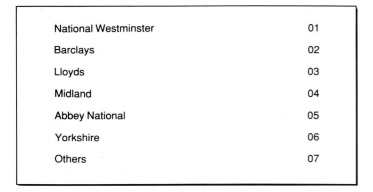

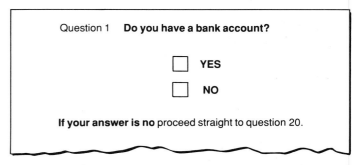

Figure 4.5 Three examples of closed questions

Figure 4.6 An interviewer's prompt card for the third example in Figure 4.4

Figure 4.7 An example of a 'skip' question

1 Stating specific examples, explain how the answers provided to questions in the questionnaire will help Jus-rol to market its products.

2 Comment on the nature of the questions (open/closed, easy to understand etc.).

3 How easy (or difficult) would it be to analyse information from the questionnaire?

4 How would you suggest that this information be recorded?

5 Why do you think the questionnaire asks for the names and addresses of respondents?

Task

Set out a questionnaire (with at least ten questions) to find out whether members of your group have ever thought of setting up their own business and, if they have, what lines of business they would like to follow. Apply the questionnaire and keep the results, which will be used in a later task.

Administering the questionnaire

There are three different ways of using the questionnaire:

- with a face-to-face interview
- by telephone
- through the post.

Face-to-face tends to be the best form of contact. It allows two-way communication between the researcher and the respondent. It is flexible and also allows gestures, facial expressions, signs of impatience and boredom all to be noted.

A questionnaire put to a person in the street is likely to be less friendly and detailed than a group discussion in the home. A street interview is brief, impersonal and uses a broadly defined sample group, whereas a home discussion can be exactly the opposite – detailed, personal and with a tightly defined sample group. Different results can be expected.

Telephone interviewing is usually more appropriate for business surveys as the respondents are often busy people and unavailable for group discussion. However, this method is often regarded as intrusive since it catches people unawares, especially in the home. This means that the respondent can start the interview with a negative view, which questioning will not necessarily help to overcome. However, it is a cost-effective means of reaching people, and the replies received are likely to be truthful. The rate of response will probably be higher than with the third method, the **postal technique**.

The level of response to a questionnaire sent through the post will vary enormously, depending on its relevance to the reader and his or her interest. Response rates are often as low as 10 per cent, so that answers are not particularly representative – they might just be representative of those who like filling in forms! The way to avoid this outcome is to ensure that the questionnaire is brief, succinct and sent only to those for whom it is directly relevant. A good postal questionnaire can achieve a response rate as high as 70 per cent.

Other primary sources

Another simple primary source is **observation** – for example, looking at how consumers behave when shopping. Information obtained like this can help to decide on packaging, or suggest offers which seem to attract the attention of consumers.

Discussion groups are an inexpensive method of obtaining useful qualitative information from consumers. For example, under the guidance of a chairperson, a group of users of the same product may be invited to give opinions upon its use.

Opinion polls are often used to find out about consumer awareness, opinions and attitudes. Perhaps the most famous organisation in this field is **Gallup**, but there are others. Questions are short and are designed to find out how consumers respond to issues such as image, product lines etc.

Electronic interviewing is a market research technique based on an interactive system with a telecommunications network. A respondent need only be a television and telephone subscriber and can respond instantly with a range of answers while a television campaign is actually being carried out.

Task

Make sure you know the difference between *qualitative* information and *quantitative* information.

Organising the data

When an organisation has completed the important task of gathering information, it has to decide what to do with it. There are three stages involved:

- sorting and storing the information
- presenting the information
- making sense of the information.

Each of these three stages has been transformed by the use of information technology.

Today, compilation, storage and analysis of market research may be undertaken using **specialist software,** of which examples are the Statistical Package for Social Sciences (SPSS) and Minitab. Use can also be made of information received from **bar code analysis** derived from electronic checkout and scanning systems located at the point of sale.

Electronic data processing (EDP) is frequently used for compiling and then categorising and summarising the results of market research. Questionnaire answers can be numerically coded for data entry. EDP makes it easy to deal efficiently and quickly with the results of lengthy questionnaires.

Task

Use the information obtained from your questionnaire in the task on page 84 to create a *database.* Interrogate your database by asking your own questions, and then comment on the conclusions you draw from the results.

Presentation of data

Once statistical data has been obtained from all sources, it needs to be broken down and presented in such a way that its significance can be appreciated easily. Information can be displayed as text, tables, charts, or graphs.

A **table** is just a matrix of rows and columns defining the relationships between variables; it summarises information into a form that is clear and easy to read. With suitable computer software, a table can be shown on a screen in the form of a **spreadsheet** – a grid of columns across the screen and rows going

down the screen (see Figure 4.8). It can also be manipulated through a series of calculations to show what would happen if alterations were made to any of the figures. As a result, one of the great benefits of spreadsheets is that they allow '**what if?**' questions to be asked and answered quickly.

OUTPUT	FIXED COSTS	VARIABLE COSTS	TOTAL COSTS	AVERAGE COSTS
10	300	20	320	32
20	300	120	420	21
30	300	200	500	16.6666667
40	300	260	560	14
50	300	300	600	12
60	300	320	620	10.3333333
70	300	390	690	9.85714286
80	300	460	760	9.5
90	300	620	920	10.2222222

Figure 4.8 A spreadsheet

Pictorial **charts** are eye-catching and enable information to be presented in a form that can be readily understood. For example, in a **pie chart** each slice of the pie represents a component's contribution to the total amount. A circle is divided up in proportion to the figures obtained and, in order to draw the segments accurately, a protractor is necessary to mark off the pieces. The following formula can be used to find the angles (in degrees) for each segment:

$$\text{Angle for segment A} = \frac{\text{Amount of A}}{\text{Total}} \times 360 \text{ degrees.}$$

Task

A company's sales are made up as follows:

	Sales (£million)
Home	15
USA	4
Australia	3
EC	8
Middle East	10
Total	40

Draw an accurate pie chart to present these sales figures. Label the chart.

In **bar charts** the areas for comparison are represented by bars – which can be drawn either vertically or horizontally. The lengths of the bars indicate the relative importance of the data.

Task

Look at the bar chart in Figure 4.9, which shows the proportions of men and women in each job category in the marketing industry. Comment on:

a the nature of the information, and
b the form of presentation.

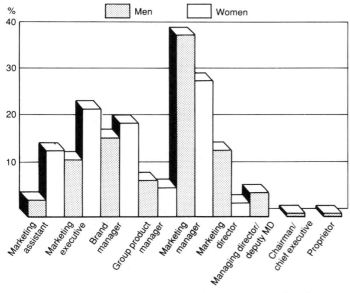

Figure 4.9 **Proportion of men and women in each job category**

Graphs are another visual way of displaying data. They show the relationship between two variables either in the form of a straight line or in the form of a curve. In particular, a graph shows how the value of one variable changes given a shift in the value of another. A graph may, for example, be constructed to show:

- sales over a time period
- the way the total cost of production varies according to the units of output produced.

If a computer is being used it can be applied as a powerful tool to present information using **graphics packages** (programs) – drawings or pictures stored in a computer are known as graphics. A graphics package might be able to show a 'three-dimensional' shape as well as reduce and enlarge an image. Some programs allow bar charts, pie charts, graphs and other characters to be built up. Figure 4.10 shows a

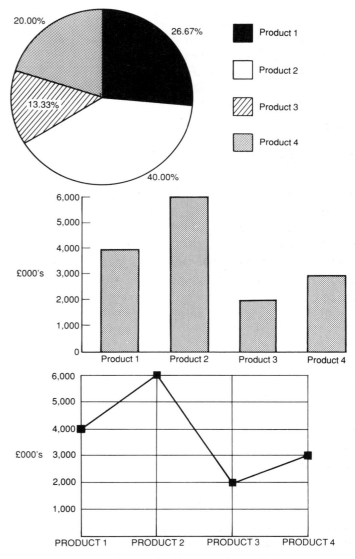

Figure 4.10 **Sales figures for four products shown as a pie chart, a bar chart and a graph, using a computer graphics package**

simple set of information displayed in three different ways, for comparison.

Making sense of the data

Statistical analysis of the hard-won information enables forecasting to take place. Decision-making techniques applied to the data allow decisions to be taken with greater precision and probability of success. Statistics are, therefore, a **tool of management** which tell managers what has happened in the past and what is happening now, thus providing a more secure direction for the future.

Case Study – Mintel on personal savings

Tessa – the tax-exempt special savings account – has prompted feverish promotional activity by many banks and building societies. Judging by Mintel's findings (summarised in the pie chart) their efforts appear to have paid off; but whether anyone is saving more of their income than before is less than certain as many of those opening Tessa accounts have simply transferred funds from an existing savings vehicle.

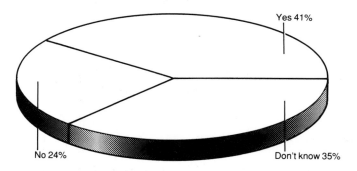

Figure 4.11 Mintel's findings on the percentage of AB consumers intending to open a Tessa account

1 What is meant by AB consumers?
2 Why would Mintel produce a report on Tessas?
3 Comment briefly on the way the results have been presented?

Case Study – Market research reports

Tourists desert Mediterranean – British tourists are deserting the Mediterranean beaches and many are turning their attention to locations such as the Caribbean and the Far East.
SOURCE: *UK Tourism and Holiday Travel*, Key Note Publications, £295.

Sober reading – Consumption of low-alcohol and alcohol-free beers were set to triple by 1991: sales were to grow from 0.5 to 1.6 million barrels.
SOURCE: *Leisure Futures Report* (Quarterly), Henley Centre, £875 per annum.

Increases in home shopping – Home shopping in the UK is set to grow.
SOURCE: *Homeshopping UK* (Databrief), MSI, £110.

PR agencies need a PR job – Advertising agencies are thought to make the most genuine contribution to clients' marketing strategies and PR consultancies the least.
SOURCE: Mintel Report, £650.

1 To whom might each of the reports mentioned be of interest?
2 How might these reports be useful to them?
3 Comment on the price tags attached to each of these reports.

5
The Market-place

In this chapter we set out some of the key principles underlying the running of any market. The market-place is any situation in which buyers and sellers come into contact to make an exchange. The market-place communicates the wishes of buyers and sellers most effectively when these two groups are well-informed and there is no interference from outside forces.

When buyers and sellers are restricted in some way, 'black markets' can arise with a consequent waste of resources, coupled with racketeering. This was graphically illustrated in the Second World War by the restriction on cosmetics manufacture. Racketeers bought up liquid paraffin and other materials intended for the war effort and made colossal profits – a lipstick bought on the black market for 6s 6d (32p) cost only 7d (3p) to manufacture.

We look at the major forces shaping demand and supply in the market-place, including power relations between buyers and sellers.

A **market** exists when buyers and sellers come into contact. In some markets the buyer and seller may meet face to face every day. In some markets they may rarely meet – they may simply contact each other by letter, phone, fax or messenger.

Task

1 *List three markets where buyers and sellers meet regularly.*
2 *List three markets where buyers and sellers rarely meet.*
3 *List three markets where buyers and sellers may never meet.*

Why is it that in some markets buyers and sellers frequently meet, whilst in others they rarely meet?

The market-place has a number of ingredients. The key players are the **buyers** and the **sellers,** and these two groups **interact**. The interactions involve:

- **communication**
- an **offer for sale**
- an **exchange** (usually goods or services for money or credit).

Figure 5.1 The market-place

Power relations in the market-place

The distinguishing feature of a **market economy** is that **consumers** are free to spend their money in the ways they think fit. Consumers are free to choose one pair of jeans rather than another, Coke or Pepsi, margarine or butter, and so on. This freedom of choice is supposed by many people to support the argument that 'the consumer is king' in a market economy. The consumer effectively 'votes' (with his or her income) for resources to be channelled into certain goods rather than others. The clothes shop that fails to keep up with fashion trends will rapidly find out that sales fall off. But how much **power** does the consumer really have? Inevitably, there are a number of important restrictions to consumer power.

Firstly, individual consumers only have limited **incomes**. With the development of new market-based economies in Eastern Europe in the early 1990s, it did not take consumers long to find out that without incomes they had very little power in the market-place. This is true of any market economy – the possession of a sizeable income gives an individual far greater power to claim scarce resources for his or her own use.

Secondly, the power of consumers depends in part on the intensity of **competition** in the market-place. If there are three petrol stations at the end of your street they are far more likely to respond to your wishes than if there is only one petrol station within twenty miles.

Thirdly, consumers have more power **the greater the proportion of a commodity** they purchase. For example, a wholesaler who buys half the output of a potato farm may be able to influence the size, type and quality of potatoes grown on the farm. The wholesaler may also be able to negotiate a bulk discount. A person who turns up at the farm gate to buy one bag of potatoes will have far less influence.

Fourthly, consumers have greater influence if they can organise themselves into **buying groups**. For example, departments within a college may buy stationery in bulk on special terms.

Fifthly, consumers have greater influence the more they know about a product. The greater the

knowledge the better the opportunity to make an informed purchase from a position of strength. An experienced computer operator is unlikely to be taken in, for example, by 'woolly' sales talk.

Finally, consumers are in a stronger position if they are supported by **consumer rights organisations** and government **legislation**. Consumer and government bodies can help to spread information, and to insist on minimum standards in production and selling.

Task

1. *Describe five situations in which consumers have considerable influence in the market-place. Explain why in each case consumers have such influence.*
2. *Describe five situations in which consumers have little influence in the market place. Explain why in each case the consumer's influence is limited.*
3. *To what extent do you think the consumer is king in the market place?*

To summarise these points, we can say that consumers have more power in markets in which:

- they have considerable buying power
- competition exists
- individual consumers are responsible for significant proportions of all purchases
- they are organised into buying groups
- they are informed
- they are protected.

It follows, then, that *producers* have more power when all or some of these considerations do *not* apply. For example, producers have considerable powers when consumers have little information about what is available, there are few suppliers, or there are many consumers.

At the end of the day, one of the key factors determining power relations is the **urgency** with which a purchase or a sale needs to be made.

Task

1 Can you remember times when you were asked to pay what you considered to be 'extortionate' prices and still made a purchase? Why did you buy the goods?
2 Can you think of situations when a seller is likely to have to make a sale at a price well below what he would have wished? Why might he be forced to make the sale?

Demand and supply

Relations between buyers and sellers in markets can be better understood when we have explored **price theory**. This involves bringing together two elements – demand and supply.

> DEMAND is the quantity of a good that a consumer will be prepared to buy at a given price.

If the price of a printer for a computer if £500, John will be prepared to buy one printer. If it is more than £500 he will not be able to afford one. If the price fell to £300 he might be prepared to buy two – one for home and one for his office. We can set out John's demand for computer printers in a little table:

Price	Quantity
More than £500	0
£500	1
£250	2

Quite clearly, as the price of printers falls they will become more affordable, and consumers will be prepared to purchase them instead of spending their money on alternatives. One printer will be very useful to John, as will two. However, if the price continues to fall there will come a point at which John has enough printers, and then further price falls will not entice fresh purchases at the same rate.

Market demand

In the example above we concentrated on *individual* demand for a product. Some markets may be made up of just a few consumers, some will be made up of a few hundred, whilst others will be made up of thousands or even millions of consumers. We talk of **global markets** where demand for a product is worldwide.

Task

1 Identify four products for which total demand is limited to under ten customers.
2 Identify four products that have a few hundred customers.
3 Identify four products that have a nationwide demand.
4 Identify four products that have a global demand.

Demand schedules can be set out by adding together the individual demand schedules of all consumers in a particular market. For example, the demand schedule below shows the likely national market for a particular type of printer in a six-month period – the figures have been collected from the market research carried out by the manufacturers:

Price of printer (£)	Quantity demanded
1000	500
800	1000
600	10 000
400	12 000
200	14 000

Task

Study the demand schedule given in the text for printers.

1 What do you think would be the best price to charge for printers? Explain your answer.
2 Why would other prices be unsuitable?
3 What further information would you require to be able to select the most appropriate price to charge? (You may want to select a price which is not indicated in the table.)

The information in the demand schedule table can be illustrated in the form of a demand 'curve' (see Figure 5.2). It is convenient for us to think of demand as fitting a nicely drawn demand curve, but of course in the real world demand patterns are not so simple. The demand for products varies considerably with fresh price changes. Some price rises will have little effect on quantities bought, whilst other quite small price rises may be critical.

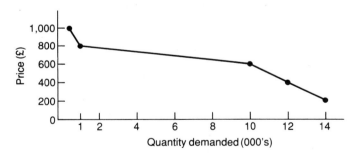

Figure 5.2 Demand for a company's printer at various prices

Elasticity of demand

Elasticity of demand is a measure of how much the quantity demanded of a good responds to a price change.

● Demand is said to be **elastic** if the proportional change in quantity is greater than the proportional change in price – for example, if the price increases by 5 per cent and the quantity demanded falls by 6 per cent.
● There is **unitary elasticity** of demand when the proportional change in quantity is equal to the proportional change in price – for example, if the price falls by 5 per cent and demand rises by 5 per cent.
● Demand is said to be **inelastic** if the proportional change in quantity is less than the proportional change in price – for example, if the price falls by 5 per cent and demand increases by only 4 per cent.

For all normal goods a rise in price will lead to a fall in demand and a fall in price will lead to a rise in demand.

The responsiveness of consumers to price changes is critical when considering price changes. We can safely conclude that sellers may consider price reductions if demand is *elastic*, and they may consider price rises if demand in *inelastic*.

However, as we have seen, elasticity varies considerably as we alter the price. We can use Figure 5.3 to describe the implications for a soft drinks manufacturer of increasing his price. If he does this, at first sales will not fall off by much, because consumers will remain loyal to his cheaper brand which is better than slightly higher priced (but inferior) substitutes. At first, then, demand will be inelastic as the price rises. However, as his price rises into the bracket of prices charged by comparable and superior products, then demand for his brand

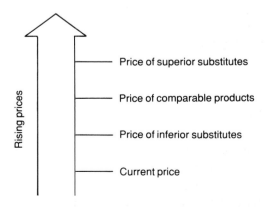

Figure 5.3 Prices of soft drinks in the market-place

will become increasingly elastic. Sellers need to carry out extensive market research to find out what will be the likely effects of raising prices.

Measuring elasticity of demand

Elasticity of demand can be calculated in the following way:

$$\text{Elasticity of demand} = \frac{\text{Change in quantity demanded (\%)}}{\text{Change in price (\%)}}$$

Demand is said to be elastic when the value of such a calculation is greater than 1, and inelastic if less than 1. Unitary elasticity is when the result is equal to 1 (unity).

Task

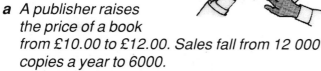

Calculate the elasticity of demand in the following instances.

a A publisher raises the price of a book from £10.00 to £12.00. Sales fall from 12 000 copies a year to 6000.

b An ice-cream seller raises the price of cones from 50p to 60p and sales drop from 600 a week to 500.

c A clothes shop reduces the average price of garments from £50 to £40 and weekly sales rise from 100 garments to 120 garments.

d Fares on the London underground are reduced by 10 per cent and the number of passengers increases by 25 per cent.

The slope of the demand curve

We can make a useful simplification by showing that when demand is elastic the slope of the demand curve is relatively flat; when demand is inelastic the slope is relatively steep; and when demand is unitary the shape will be what is called a 'rectangular

hyperbola' (see Figure 5.4). For unitary elasticity movements along a curve are proportional to movements down it.

It is important to stress that in setting out these general guides we are, in fact, simplifying mathematical reasoning.

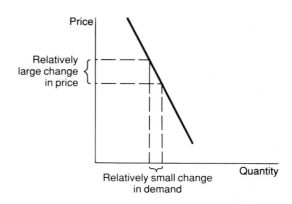

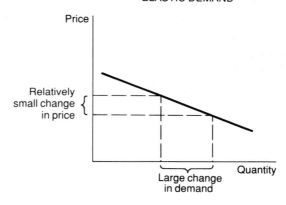

Figure 5.4 Simplified demand curves

Factors influencing elasticity of demand

Correct pricing is critical. If prices are judged by consumers to be too high then the lack of sales may ruin a business. If prices are too low it may not be possible to recover costs. We shall consider the important factors influencing demand elasticity.

The price of competitive products. In competitive markets sellers have little choice over what prices they charge. When competitors alter prices firms may have to alter their prices too, particularly when prices fall.

The proportion of income that households spend on a particular commodity. Most households spend a lot on housing, clothes, fuel and food. When the prices of items in these categories rise, households may be forced to cut back spending. However, there are items that are bought rarely and cost relatively little – for example, salt, food seasoning, shoe laces, and so on. When these items rise in price, quantities bought will not be greatly affected.

The price of a good or service. We have already seen that the current price is critical (Figure 5.3). If it is already considered to be high, then a price rise may lead to a greater fall in demand than if the initial price is considered low.

The necessity of making a fresh purchase. When my watch is old I can still use it provided it works well – I do not have to purchase a new one. This is not the case with soup – when I have finished one tin I will want to buy another fairly soon because I like soup. The demand for **consumer durables** may therefore be more elastic as a result of a price increase than the demand for **consumer disposables** such as foodstuffs.

Whether a good is a basic necessity or not. Goods which are 'essentials' will have inelastic demands. We cannot easily do without items such as bread and milk, but we can do without many exotic and fancy foods that we only buy on special occasions. The same applies to many other commodities such as clothes and luxury models of cars.

Perhaps the most important factor influencing elasticity of demand is the **time period** in question. In the short term, consumers may feel it is necessary to buy a particular good or service. Given more time, however, they may better appreciate the benefits of looking around and switching to alternatives. A product which at one time seemed indispensable may lose its sales base as time moves on and new substitutes replace it.

Task

1 Identify a product which you think has an inelastic demand at its current price level. Carry out some research to find out if other consumers agree with your perception.
2 What factors may lead the elasticity of demand for the product you have chosen to become more elastic in the course of time?
3 Identify another product which appears to have an elastic demand at its current market price. What strategies can the seller adopt to try to decrease the elasticity of demand for his product (perhaps so that he can raise its price).

Group Task

In this activity you will need to work together with two or three others. The object is to find out how a *local firm* makes a pricing decision for a particular product or small range of products. Obviously some product pricing decisions are sensitive areas for some companies. However, for many products this is not the case and local business owners will be pleased to discuss the matter with you.

The aim of the assignment is to find out:

a how the firm arrives at a pricing decision
b the likely effects on sales of charging higher or lower prices.

Choose a group leader who will be responsible for coordinating the work. The duties of the group leader will be to ensure that the group works as a team, to manage the working environment, and to make sure that records are kept. A record sheet (see Figure 5.5) should be set out on a word processor and a suitable number of copies run off.

1 At the beginning of each session the group leader should collect earlier record sheets and take note of any memos from the lecturer or supervisor. It is a good idea to keep a record of attendance.
2 The first few minutes of each session should be spent on group discussion, and checking progress on the assignment.
3 Ten minutes before the end of each session the group will need to discuss progress, update record sheets and prepare a memo for the lecturer or supervisor.

To start off the assignment the group will need to think about the sort of questions to ask a local business manager about pricing decisions. **Hints**: Who at the company has this sort of information? When and how are they most likely to be able to supply you with the information? Will it be best to work through contacts that a group member has? Is there someone at the place where you work part-time who may be prepared to talk to your group? Will it be best to look at a range of contacts, bearing in mind that some companies will not be able to talk to you? Will you need to do some background research so that you know a bit about the company and its products before you start the assignment?

You should then draw up a checklist of key questions about pricing. Set these out in a logical order.

In your group, draft a letter to make the necessary arrangements to visit the company or have someone come to talk to you. Discuss the draft with

---

LOCAL PRICING ASSIGNMENT:
Group record sheet

The group leader should hand this form to the supervisor or lecturer before the end of each session.

Group name......................................

Date..

Absentees..

Checklist (tick when completed)

All group members' record sheets completed and returned

Textbooks returned/signed out

Discs returned

Computers switched off or left on main menu

Area tidy

Group task completed

Memo for supervisor or lecturer

Signed

....

Supervisor or lecturer's reply:

....

Figure 5.5 Group record sheet

your lecturer or supervisor, who should countersign the letter before it is sent.

If you decide to make the initial contact by telephone, you will need to follow this up with a letter confirming the arrangements.

Organise the work
When you start to gather information try to organise it in a way that is easy to understand. Put your ideas in the form of a report which you can present to other members of your group – and perhaps to members of the company that you have been working with.

Movements along the demand curve

For convenience we will now draw the demand curve as a straight line in order to simplify the text (see Figure 5.6).

- If the price of a good rises we can refer to 'a move up the demand curve'. What happens to demand as the price rises to P_1 in Figure 5.6?
- If the price of a good falls we can refer to 'a move down the demand curve'. What happens to demand as the price falls to P_2 in Figure 5.6?

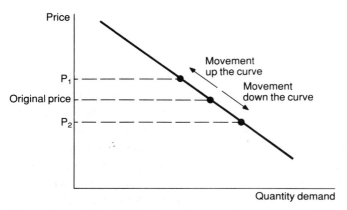

Figure 5.6 A simplified demand curve drawn as a straight line

Shifts in the demand curve

Price is not the only factor that alters demand. Other factors include:

- the price of complementary products
- the price of substitute products
- changes in tastes
- changes in incomes
- changes in population.

However, at the time we draw a demand curve we assume that these other influences do not come into play *at that particular time*. As time moves on, however, one or more of these other factors may exert an influence and cause the original demand curve to shift to the left or right. Indeed, in the real world these factors are constantly changing. Some may work in the same direction, or at other times against each other. It will be clearer if we first look at

them in isolation before looking at a combination of their influences.

Complementary products

Complementary products are those you use together. For example, my computer keyboard complements my screen and printer; my business studies textbook is complemented by a workbook; and my car radio is complemented by my car. When the price of a desktop computer falls I may be more inclined to buy a printer as well. If the price of ham rises I may be inclined to buy fewer eggs.

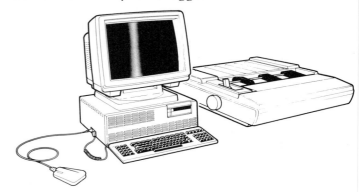

Figure 5.7 Complementary products

Substitute products

Many goods **compete** with one another. When one brand of soap powder becomes more expensive I may switch to a cheaper rival. The same is true for canned drinks such as Coca-Cola and Pepsi-Cola, for brands of petrol such as Shell and BP, and for newspapers such as the *Sun* and the *Daily Mirror*. In Figure 5.8 we can see the effect of a rise in price of Coke on the demand for Pepsi, whose price remains unaltered.

Tastes

Tastes obviously affect demand. Clothing fashions change not only with the seasons but from year to year. Many of this year's garments will end up as cast-offs. This year's car registration will drop in

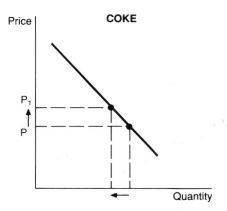

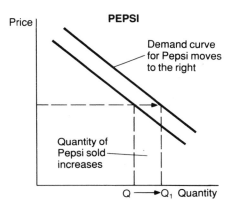

Figure 5.8 **What happens to the demand for Pepsi when the price of Coke increases**

Income

Income is an important determinant of expenditure. In a period of recession, high street sales will slump and expenditure on most goods will fall. This is particularly true of luxury items and incidental extras. In the boom years of the late 1980s, **niche marketing** developed. We saw the growth of firms such as Tie Rack, Knicker-box and Sock Shop. In the early 1990s, with a period of recession, the profits of these concerns slumped as consumers had to hold back their expenditure for more essential items.

Population

When the population increases generally, so too will the demand for goods – in a particular country as well as on a global scale. However, population tends not to rise uniformly, and marketeers are more interested in the **distribution of population**. For example, they will be interested to note the current trend towards an ageing population. As we move towards the twenty-first century we have a far higher percentage of people past official retirement age – so that products can be developed for this group, with promotion geared towards the channels that reach them.

popularity once next year's appears. The life-cycle of a product depends very much on whether it is in a fashionable sector of the market or in a sector that lasts for a long period of time. When tastes move in favour of a good its sales will boom, and when tastes move against a good its sales will fall. If it is quite difficult to think of products and brand names that are in decline, this is because many of them slip gradually from memory.

Task

Explain what movements are likely to occur in the demand for products in each of the following examples:

1 *Reading becomes less popular in a time of recession. What will be the effects on the demand curve for fiction books?*
2 *The number of young children increases at a time when it is fashionable for children to have 'designer' clothes. What will be the effects on the demand curve for designer clothes for children?*

3 The prices of cameras rise at a time when average incomes are increasing. What will be the effect on the demand for camera films?

4 The prices of newspapers rise at a time when people are reading fewer magazines, and people are using teletext as a common substitute for receiving news items. How might this affect the demand for newspapers?

5 The price of ice-cream falls owing to improvements in production methods during a long hot summer. How might these changes affect the demand for ice-cream cornets?

6 Firework parties at home become more popular at a time when incomes are falling and people have fewer children. How might this affect the demand for fireworks?

Need for market research

We can see from the foregoing examples that there are many factors influencing demand and that these frequently work against each other. Demand in the market-place will be in a constant state of change. Market research is therefore essential to predict future changes and to raise awareness of current changes.

Case Study – The changing demand for white bread

In the 1980s, white bread acquired something of a social stigma. As a result, sales fell in volume by 7 per cent while sales of other types of bread jumped by nearly 20 per cent. Since about 1960, consumption of white bread has fallen from close to 40oz per person per week to just 15oz. Britain remains bottom of Europe's bread eating league, consuming about 56 loaves per person per year against 100 in Italy and Germany.

But white bread looks to be back in favour. While wholemeal brands account for 22 per cent of the market, brown bread 9 per cent and wheatgerm and ethnic bread 1 per cent, white bread sales can still claim a massive 67 per cent of a market worth £2 billion.

That share seems certain to grow, according to market research. The average white loaf today now costs about 12p less than the equivalent wholemeal loaf (because of cheaper flour, economies of scale and lower profit margins for distributors and retailers).

A recent survey by advertising agency Coley Porter Bell found that more than two in five consumers had not changed their shopping habits in the interests of health. Around 44 per cent said that they had not stopped buying anything because they thought it was unhealthy, and 43 per cent had not added anything to their weekly grocery basket on health grounds. Half of those asked were unable to name a manufacturer they associated with either healthy or unhealthy products.

The report concluded that nutritional value remains at the bottom of the list of reasons consumers give for buying food. Only 17 per cent thought it was the most important factor, against 60 per cent who cited taste and 23 per cent who put cost first.

1 Identify different segments of the bread market highlighted above.

2 Explain how demand has altered in two of these segments in recent years. What factors might have affected these shifts in demand.

3 How would you go about finding out about possible future shifts in demand patterns? What sort of questions might you need to ask to elicit information?

4 What is your opinion of the interpretation of the figures for changes in demand?

5 Carry out your own research into what factors influence the demand for different types of bread. What factors cause changes in demand?

Task

Movements along the demand curve and shifts in demand

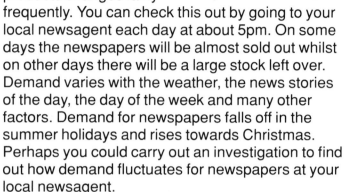

Demand for most products changes fairly frequently. You can check this out by going to your local newsagent each day at about 5pm. On some days the newspapers will be almost sold out whilst on other days there will be a large stock left over. Demand varies with the weather, the news stories of the day, the day of the week and many other factors. Demand for newspapers falls off in the summer holidays and rises towards Christmas. Perhaps you could carry out an investigation to find out how demand fluctuates for newspapers at your local newsagent.

In the section on demand we have seen that the slope of the demand curve changes. Sometimes it is steep (relatively inelastic) whilst at other times it is flatter (relatively elastic). When the conditions of demand change, the demand curve will shift to the left or right.

In each of the situations below explain what the likely effect on the demand curve will be for a particular newspaper, *The Daily News*.

1 *A rival newspaper,* The Daily Planet, *goes out of business.*
2 *More people switch to newspaper reading and away from journals and magazines. This is because newspapers such as* The Daily News *begin to publish their own magazines and supplements.*
3 *In a period of recession people cut back on general household expenditures.*
4 *A new paper with a similar format to* The Daily News *enters the market.*
5 *The prices of all newspapers increase.*
6 *The average length of commuter journeys by train decreases.*
7 *The government bans the use of newspapers for wrapping up fish and chips.*

Market supply

As we saw in Chapter 1, organisations have many different reasons for existing. Some may want to maximise profits or sales, while others will be content to break even or make a modest profit. To simplify our supply analysis we will assume that companies seek to make profits.

The profit from selling a good is the difference between the price at which it is sold and the cost of producing it. The quantities of the good that the company offers will therefore depend on the price it receives for each unit sold relative to the cost of producing each unit.

As price rises (other things remaining the same), the company will at first make a larger profit on each item it sells. This will encourage it to make and sell more. However, the company may face rising costs as it expands production beyond the limit that it had originally planned (for example, the cost of paying employees at overtime rates will increase). For these reasons we should expect that companies will offer more for sale at higher prices, and as they increase their output they will ask for higher prices.

We can either draw a supply curve for an individual company, or a market supply curve from adding together all the individual supply curves. A typical supply curve will slope upwards from left to right (Figure 5.9).

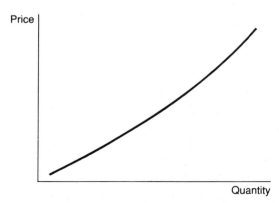

Figure 5.9 A simple supply curve

Task

Study the supply curve in Figure 5.10.

1 *How much of the commodity would be supplied at:*

a 15p	**c** 13p	**e** 11p	**g** 9p
b 14p	**d** 12p	**f** 10p	**h** 7p

2 *Draw in the supply curve and explain its shape.*

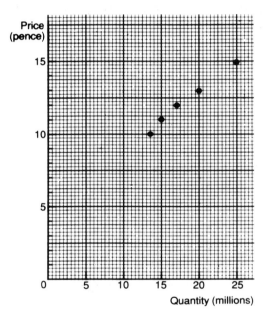

Figure 5.10 Supply curve

Elasticity of supply

Elasticity of supply measures the responsiveness of supply to changes in price. It can be measured by:

$$\text{Elasticity of supply} = \frac{\text{Change in quantity supplied (\%)}}{\text{Change in price (\%)}}$$

Supply is said to be elastic when the quantity changes by a greater proportion than the price change. Inelastic supply is when the quantity changes by a smaller proportion than the price change.

The time factor

Time has a great influence on elasticity of supply. We can identify three time periods.

The momentary period. At a moment in time it is impossible to alter supply. In a shoe shop at 3.30pm on a Saturday afternoon there may be only three pairs of size 7 trainers. In business we define the momentary period as that in which it is impossible to alter both our fixed factors of production (such as the machinery or buildings in a processing plant) and our variable factors (such as labour and energy).

The short period. Between 3.30pm and 4.00pm on a Saturday afternoon it may be possible to rush extra training shoes to the shop from a local warehouse. In business we define the short period as the period in which fixed factors remain fixed, but variable factors can vary.

The long period. Because of a general increase in the demand for trainers, a factory producing trainers may expand its plant and equipment. In business we define the long period as the period in which all factors of production can become variable.

We can illustrate elasticity of supply in different time periods as in Figure 5.11. Momentary supply is represented by a vertical line, short-period supply by a relatively inelastic supply line, and long-period supply by a relatively elastic supply line.

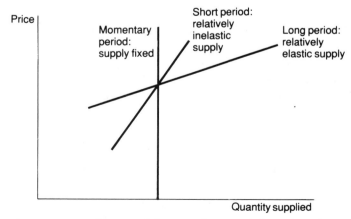

Figure 5.11 Influence of the time factor on elasticity of supply

What constitutes a short or long period varies from company to company and from industry to industry. For example, it takes a lot longer to increase fresh flower production than it does to expand artificial flower production. Some products have an extended long term (e.g. coffee and rubber production), while others have a shorter long term. If you have ever grown cress on your window sill you will know that it can be grown within days.

Task

Try to think of ten products with extended long periods and ten with very short (long) periods. What factors cause these differences?

The effect of spare capacity

Elasticity of supply also varies according to how close to **capacity** a company or industry is running. For example, if a factory is using only half its machines, it would be relatively easy to expand production. However, if the factory is already working at full capacity, then the company would have to invest in new plant in order to expand its supply.

The availability of components and raw materials

In order to expand production it is necessary to increase **inputs**. If inputs are readily available, then supply will be far more elastic than if inputs are scarce.

The cost of producing additional outputs

If the **extra cost** of producing additional units is rising sharply, then producers will be reluctant to expand output in response to higher prices.

Shifts in the supply curve

The cost of production of an item is made up of the prices of the various inputs, including raw materials and the machinery used to make it. Rises in the prices of some of these factors will increase production costs, and this results in a reduction in supply at each and every price (see Figure 5.12). The supply curve shifts to the left – at any given price less will be produced and offered for sale than before. For example, 1990 saw a rise in interest rates (i.e. the cost of borrowing money), and this increased the cost of production of many goods. Of course, a fall in production costs has the opposite effect.

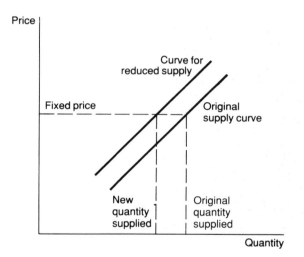

Figure 5.12 **Shift in the supply curve**

Taxation imposed on output or sales has the same effect – producers and sellers are effectively taking less money at each price. On the other hand, improvements in **technique**, which make it possible for any given quantity of a product to be made or sold at a lower cost than before, will have the opposite effect.

The **conditions of supply** may be altered by such things as changes in the weather, fires, floods, duststorms or earthquakes, although such changes are often only temporary. Weather conditions can lead to large or small harvests, and hence increases or shortages in the supply of wheat and other crops.

Task

State what will be the likely effect on supply in each of the following instances:

a *improvements in technology in the car industry*
b *very high demand for tickets on cup final day*
c *the development of more effective pesticides for use on cereal crops*
d *an increase in the cost of the raw materials required for housebuilding*
e *an increase in demand for small-engined cars.*

The interaction of demand and supply

Figure 5.13 shows the outline demand and supply curves for jars of strawberry jam in a particular week. We can combine these two curves on a single drawing to illustrate how prices are determined in the market-place. The point at which the two curves cut is the point at which the wishes of both consumers and producers are met (Figure 5.14).

We can now see that at a price of 60p for a 350g jar, 100 thousand tonnes of jam would be bought in the market-place each week. At this price consumers are happy to buy 100 thousand tonnes and sellers are

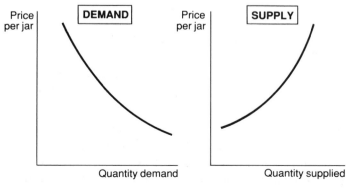

Figure 5.13 **Demand and supply curves for strawberry jam**

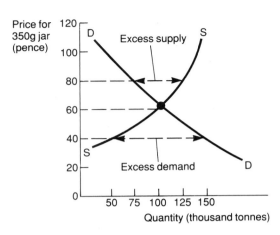

Figure 5.14 **Market equilibrium for strawberry jam**

happy to supply this quantity. This is called the **equilibrium point** because there is nothing forcing a change from it.

We can see why this point is an equilibrium one by considering non-equilibrium points. For example, at 80p a jar consumers would be prepared to purchase only 75 thousand tonnes while suppliers would be prepared to make 125 thousand tonnes available to the market. At this price sellers would be left with unsold stocks and would quickly contract supply to the equilibrium point. If the price was below the equilibrium – at say 40p – demand would be for 150 thousand tonnes with producers only willing to supply 50 thousand tonnes; in this situation, strawberry jam would be snapped up as soon as it was put on the shelves, and stocks would run out. Prices would soon be raised towards the equilibrium point.

Markets in motion

The simple explanation of demand and supply of strawberry jam provided above gives us an important insight into how markets operate. Producers and consumers respond to **price signals**, and in this way their wishes and plans are coordinated by the **market mechanism**. These wishes and plans change regularly since the factors influencing supply and demand are in a constant state of change.

For example, improvement in standards of living in a country will increase demand generally, but it will also affect costs – the money paid to an employee as wages for his or her work is *income* from the employee's point of view, but to the employer it is a *cost*. Furthermore, improvements in manufacturing techniques often increase the supply of particular goods without increasing costs. It is obvious that *any* change has knock-on effects throughout the market-place. These changes are not isolated, and they are happening all the time. Consider the case of up-market cook-chill meals sold by outlets such as Marks and Spencer and Sainsbury's.

If an increase in supply is coupled with a decrease in demand, the price of the good will fall. If a decrease in supply is coupled with an increase in demand, the price of the good will rise. However, if an increase in supply is coupled with an increase in demand, or a decrease in supply by a decrease in demand, we know that output is likely to increase in the first case and contract in the second – *but we cannot be sure what will happen to price* in these circumstances.

Changes in the market-place lead to adjustments by consumers and producers. Demand and supply curves change shape and position, and very quickly a new equilibrium position is established. However, this will only be a temporary equilibrium point because markets are characterised by **change**. Indeed, one beauty of the market-place is that it can quickly accommodate changes. However, Eastern European countries that are converting their economies away from central planning (see Chapter 1) are finding that adjustments cannot be made quickly when the price mechanism has been suppressed for a long time.

Consumer and industrial markets

Organisations can be classified according to the goods or services they produce. As we saw in Chapter 4, one simple division is into consumer

markets and organisational markets. Another name for the latter is industrial markets.

Consumer markets are made up largely of individuals who buy things for personal and home use. Consumers typically buy from retailers and purchases tend to involve fairly low money values. Examples are:

- goods with a short shelf-life, made for immediate use (e.g. foodstuffs)
- durable goods with a longer life and which are bought less often (e.g. cars and televisions).

Industrial or organisational markets are made up of buyers who purchase goods and services to use in making or providing other goods and services. They include:

- industrial consumption goods which have a frequent purchase pattern but a limited life (e.g. chemicals and fuels)
- industrial durable goods which have a longer life (e.g. machinery and equipment).

Some organisations sell products in both consumer and industrial markets. A motor manufacturer like Volkswagen produces private motor cars as well as lorries.

Identifying markets

Manufacturers and sellers need to have a great deal of information about potential customers. Chapter 4 deals extensively with how to obtain this information.

Interdependent markets

The links between industrial and consumer markets are just one aspect of the **interdependent market process**.

A large multinational motor vehicle manufacturer, for example, makes a range of moulded metal parts in a factory, usually called a foundry. In the foundry, iron is melted and poured into moulds, which are made of sand. Metal products that are made by pouring molten metal into moulds are known as 'castings'.

The moulded parts produced in the foundry include brake discs, brake drums and engine manifolds. Look at Figure 5.15 to see where they are located in the finished motor car.

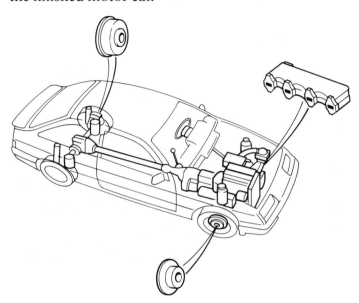

Figure 5.15 **Brake and engine castings**

If the demand for motor vehicles increases, there will be an increase in demand for brake discs, brake drums, manifolds and many other components. In turn this creates a demand for **intermediate products** such as iron and sand. In addition it creates further demand for more moulds, more capacity at the foundry, and so on. More employees are required, and more managers. As more employment is created incomes begin to rise – people can therefore spend more on cars and many other items. The market economy is thus an interdependent one.

Prices provide **signals** to all sectors of the market economy. Decisions can then be made in response to these signals. No army of people sitting in offices could possibly work as effectively as the price system in signalling changes to the millions of components that make up an economy.

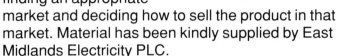

Task

Here is a task that is best tackled by a group. It involves looking closely at a particular product, finding an appropriate market and deciding how to sell the product in that market. Material has been kindly supplied by East Midlands Electricity PLC.

Introduction

Everyone knows that East Midlands Electricity sells electricity to firms and households, but do you realise that it also sells appliances which use electricity?
Can you list ten products which are likely to be sold from East Midlands Electricity shops?

In this activity you are asked to help East Midlands Electricity to promote **one** of its popular products – either cordless kettles or satellite dishes.

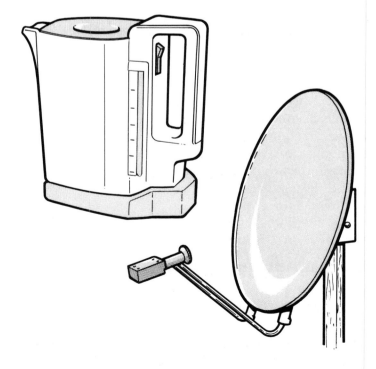

First you must do a SWOT analysis of one of the products. Then you must decide who you are going to sell the product to and how you will reach them. Lastly, you may like to produce a creative advertisement for the product.

What is a SWOT?

SWOT stands for:

- strengths
- weaknesses
- opportunities
- threats

When you are marketing a product you should work out what are its **strengths** and **weaknesses** – then try to work out what are the **opportunities** that will help you to promote the product and the **threats** likely to be faced by your product in the near future.

For example, if Rowntree wanted to do a SWOT analysis of its product Smarties, it might say that:

- *its strengths include* – the fact that everyone knows what a Smartie is; that children love the different colours; that they are not expensive; the packets look attractive in the shop, and so on
- *its weaknesses might include* – they are primarily a children's sweet, rather than for adults; they have been around a long time (perhaps people are getting bored with them)
- *its opportunities are* – new European markets for Smarties are opening up, not just in the European Community, but also in Poland, Hungary and so on; blue Smarties are new and exciting
- *its threats might include* – the wide range of new sweets that are being sold; the arrival of M&M's and competition from European chocolate manufacturers, and so on.

What Rowntree needs to do then is promote and improve strengths, play down and cut out weaknesses, make the most of opportunities, and be aware of and respond to threats.

Do your SWOT analysis

Do your SWOT analysis for EME cordless kettles **or** satellite dishes. Can you list **three** strengths, **three**

weaknesses, **three** opportunities and **three** threats? Decide how you will:

- maximise the strengths
- minimise the weaknesses
- make the most of the opportunities
- reduce the threats.

Use the SWOT analysis sheet on the next page.

Who are you selling to?

You need to be able to identify your **target** market. This is the group of people you think will be interested in your product or service and who have the money to spend on it.

- Try to identify the target audience for your chosen product. You will probably target two or three groups to concentrate on. An example of a target group might be single women in the 18–24 year age-group on high income.
- What type of media will be most suitable for reaching the target audience you have chosen?

Guidelines for promotions

To help you choose the most effective media for your promotions, consider the following guidelines. You will have detailed costs of these media outlets, and you should make a sensible selection to suit your chosen product. This will be your **media plan**.

Television. In order to have a meaningful TV campaign you need at least 10 on-peak and 20 off-peak spots in any one month. Some months are cheaper than others. Do you feel that spots during particular programmes are more desirable (e.g. Coronation Street)?

Local Radio. For maximum effectiveness you need 50 spots per month. This medium is particularly effective with the 16–25 years age-group and has high listening ratings during 'drive time'.

Press. Which newspapers would you use? Which magazines?

Electricity account inserts. Each quarter of the year, 1.8 million customers receive an electricity bill, which gives an excellent opportunity to include promotional literature (the cost of postage is already paid by the accounts department).

Direct Mailing. This is an excellent means of communicating with small customer groups (e.g. recent purchasers of cars, videos, microwave cookers) whose addresses can be readily obtained from existing sources. Hand delivery of direct mail can be employed. These will not be personally addressed, but posted through letter-boxes of everyone in a selected area. This is therefore suitable for products that have a wider appeal.

Telephone sales. A member of staff is employed to phone direct to the customer.

Shop displays. This is a facility in all 76 shops to display products.

Exhibitions. The company may take part in local or national exhibitions, building its own stands, staffed by trained advisers who can promote the various appliances featured.

Leaflets. These are a very useful promotional aid which a potential customer can take home, to help their decision whether to buy after visiting a shop or an exhibition.

Producing a creative advertisement

Can you, as a group, produce an advertisement for a newspaper or magazine?

Preparing a media plan

Now that you have a clear idea about who your customers are, you should now prepare a Media Plan for the next 12 months.

You can either do this on the 'MEDIA PLAN' sheet provided or set out your media plan on a spreadsheet.

Here are your media guidelines:

You have a budget of £750 000 to spend over 12 months. If the campaign is going to be a success you will need to use several different types of promotion. You would almost certainly use the power of television as part of your campaign. Show on your chart or spreadsheets:

● During which months you will spend your money.
● How much you will spend.
● Remember to put in your sub-totals.
● Your total spending should not be greater than £750 000.

Finally you need to produce a creative advertisement

How will you present your ideas? To finish off this activity you will do a presentation to the rest of your class. This presentation should be rounded off by a Creative Advertisement – a poster, a video, a talk, or some other creative advert.

The presentation time will be divided as follows:

2 minutes To set up.
2 minutes To explain your SWOT analysis and to discuss your media plan, explaining how it will effectively communicate with your target customers.
4 minutes To present your creative execution in any way, shape or form, using chosen media.
2 minutes To pack away.

You should explain during your 4 minute presentation how you expect to maximise the strengths and overcome the weaknesses of the product which you have identified in the SWOT analysis.

You should also indicate how your presentation may relate to the target audience you have previously identified.

Points to consider:

● Do I need a personality? If so who?
● Do I need music? If so, what type?
● Do I need any promotional offers, e.g. interest-free credit, buy now pay later, etc?
● How do I make it interesting, amusing, memorable, credible and original?

SWOT ANALYSIS

PRODUCT_____

STRENGTHS	WEAKNESSES
OPPORTUNITIES	THREATS

TARGET CUSTOMERS

PRODUCT_____

STATUS	AGE	INCOME H –HIGH L – LOW	TARGET AUDIENCE	SUITABLE MEDIA
MALE (MARRIED) NO CHILDREN	18 – 24	H		
		L		
	25 – 45	H		
		L		
	OVER 45	H		
		L		
FEMALE (MARRIED) NO CHILDREN	18 – 24	H		
		L		
	25 – 45	H		
		L		
	OVER 45	H		
		L		
MALE (MARRIED) + CHILDREN	18 – 24	H		
		L		
	25 – 45	H		
		L		
	OVER 45	H		
		L		
FEMALE (MARRIED) + CHILDREN	18 – 24	H		
		L		
	25 – 45	H		
		L		
	OVER 45	H		
		L		
MALE (SINGLE)	18 – 24	H		
		L		
	25 – 45	H		
		L		
	OVER 45	H		
		L		
FEMALE (SINGLE)	18 – 24	H		
		L		
	25 – 45	H		
		L		
	OVER 45	H		
		L		

MEDIA PLAN

PRODUCT _____

MEDIA			£ COST	JAN	FEB	MAR	APR	MAY	JUN	JUL	AUG	SEP	OCT	NOV	DEC	SUB-TOTAL COSTS	COMMENTS
TELEVISION (CENTRAL AREA)	30 SECOND COMMERCIAL OCT, NOV, DEC, MAR, APR, MAY	OFF PEAK	600														
		ON PEAK	4,000														
	30 SECOND COMMERCIAL JAN, FEB, JUN, JUL, AUG, SEP	OFF PEAK	400														
		ON PEAK	3,000														
LOCAL RADIO	30 SECOND SPOT		100														
NATIONAL PRESS	ONE INSERTION PER NEWSPAPER		5,000														
LOCAL PRESS	ONE INSERTION PER NEWSPAPER		500														
FREE TRADE PRESS	ONE INSERTION PER NEWSPAPER		200														
ELECTRICITY ACCOUNT INSERTS	ONE FOR EACH DOMESTIC CUSTOMER PER QUARTER		30,000														
DIRECT MAILING	1000 PACKAGES DELIVERED BY THE POST OFFICE (SELECTED ADDRESSES)		450														
	1000 PACKAGES HAND-DELIVERED (SELECTED AREAS)		300														
TELEPHONE SALES	PER HUNDRED CALLS		10														
EXHIBITIONS	SMALL		250														
	MEDIUM		1,500														
	LARGE		4,000														
LEAFLETS	PER THOUSAND		250														
SHOP DISPLAYS	76 SHOPS		10,000														

109

6
Marketing Products and Services

This chapter looks at the practical aspects of marketing activities. Marketing is the essential point of contact between every organisation and its clients. It is the key strand of the business fabric – it runs though everything an organisation does. Using information from the market-place, organisations segment the market into different groups of customers and then use the ingredients of the marketing mix to suit the precise requirements of each market segment. As markets are dynamic, the marketing mix requires constant adjustment and management to suit the changing requirements of each group of customers. Throughout this chapter tasks and case analysis encourage you to relate the marketing activities highlighted to your own experience of the market-place.

The nature of competition

An organisation must at all times be aware of its competitors and the nature of what they are doing. There is **competition** when two or more organisations act independently to sell their products to the same group of consumers. In some markets there may be a lot of competition, signified by an abundance of products and services so that consumers have a massive choice. These markets are characterised by promotional activities and **price competition**. In other markets, competition is limited and consumers are able to choose from a limited range of products and services on offer – perhaps only one. In these circumstances consumers may feel that prices are too high – they are not getting **value** for their money.

Task

Look at the market for one particular type of product (e.g. cars,

electricity, insurance, beer, confectionery). Comment briefly on how the organisations supplying this market behave. In particular, is there a link between the numbers of competitors in this market and prices, promotional activities and choices being offered?

Direct competition exists where organisations produce similar products and appeal to the same group of consumers. *The Daily Star* is direct competition for *The Sun*; and if you want to have a wall built, all the builders in your area looking for this type of work are in direct competition.

Even when an organisation provides a unique end-product with no direct competition, it still has to consider **indirect competition**. Potential customers might examine slightly different ways of meeting the same need. Instead of buying a car they might buy a moped; instead of buying a bag of sweets they could buy a box of chocolates from a different supplier.

It is frequently argued that competition is good for consumers and organisations alike. It forces organisations to act reasonably, stimulates the market-place, increases **choice** and boosts sales. Organisations have to become **more efficient** and offer **better products** at prices acceptable to the market. As a result customers have a wider selection of goods and services and better value for money. Without competition customers would have to accept a limited range of goods and services at higher prices.

Case Study – Computers in schools

Acorn Computers recently commissioned a survey of the computer market in schools from market research company Taylor Nelson. The survey revealed that the best selling computer was the Acorn A3000 with about 30 per cent of the market of 106 000 classroom computers sold in 1990. Second was the Nimbus 186 selling about 20 per cent. The BBC Master was third at around 15 per cent. Nimbus came fourth again with its PC-clone 286 range capturing about 10 per cent, and fifth was Acorn with the Archimedes 400 series with around 8 per cent.

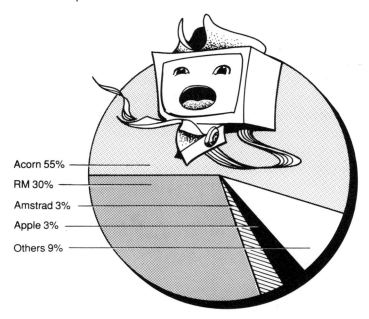

Acorn 55%
RM 30%
Amstrad 3%
Apple 3%
Others 9%

Figure 6.1 Schools market share based on research by Acorn

The survey was based on a telephone sample of 600 schools throughout the UK covering primary, secondary, independent and special schools banded by size, and the results are consistent with a Department of Education and Science survey recently undertaken.

Acorn's survey showed that its market share in the last three quarters of 1990 was 55 per cent. In other words, 55 out of every 100 computers sold into schools in the UK between 1 April and 31 December 1990 were Acorn machines (see Figure 6.1). In the 'others' category, no company had more than 1 per cent of the market.

Acorn estimated that at the time of the survey there were 430 000 computers in the UK's 34 000 schools, and that 106 000 were bought in 1990.

1 *Working in groups if possible, comment on the nature of the market for school computers. Analyse:*
   a *the features of Acorn machines*
   b *reasons for their success*
   c *possible reasons for the absence of major competitors other than RM*
   d *the benefits of such a large market size for Acorn*
   e *the direct and indirect competition for Acorn.*
2 *How might Acorn use the results of this survey?*
3 *Estimate the annual market value of the school computer market.*

Market share will constantly change as new competitors and products come into the market-place. Spain used to be the most popular destination for UK tourists overseas, but in recent years its popularity has been affected by, for example, Miami, EuroDisney and Legoland. The Spanish tourist industry has had to respond to change by providing better packages to entice customers. Competition thrives upon such changes and provides consumers with greater benefits through better products.

Competition and market share can also be affected by changes in an organisation's **external environment** which may be completely beyond its control. Some changes may be cosmetic and almost imperceptible, while others – such as the takeover of a competitor, technological discoveries, high interest rates or the creation of a single European market – can have a dramatic affect on the behaviour of organisations. Every organisation should be aware not only of its own market, the actions of its competitors and new ideas and products, but also of changing business conditions within a wider environment. It should be prepared to respond with appropriate measures.

If the competitive forces within a market lead to a **trade war** between rivals, they sometimes call for a 'ceasefire' if the competition is so fierce as to make their activities virtually unprofitable. To cite a famous example, the cigarette card war was ended by mutual consent of the tobacco companies in the late 1930s. Competition may also be overcome by taking over (that is, buying) a rival – Iceland took over Bejam, Nestlé took over Rowntree Mackintosh. Competition may be reduced by engaging in **joint-ventures** with rivals – Courage, the Australian brewing company, recently signed a host of lager brewing and distribution agreements with the brand leaders Carlsberg.

Task

In your local library, scan the newspapers for an example illustrating competition deliberately reduced by agreement, takeover or a joint-venture in a

market. Why do you think this has taken place? Indicate to what extent consumers might be affected.

Market segmentation

Customers exhibit different needs, wants, likes and dislikes. Not every person likes the same make of motor car or has the same taste in clothes. If cost and production time were of no importance, manufacturers would make products to the exact specifications of each buyer. Unfortunately, this is not at all practicable – an organisation cannot provide a different product for each customer. On the other hand, neither can it serve its customers successfully if it groups all of their needs and wants together.

Instead of trying to serve all consumers equally, an organisation may focus its efforts on different parts of the total market-place. Within the total market-place it is possible to group customers with similar characteristics into **market segments**. Market segmentation is therefore a process of separating a total market into parts so that different strategies can be used for different sets of customers.

If you attempt to market a single product to the whole population, this is sometimes said to be like using a blunderbuss, firing shots to pepper the whole market-place. When it is not possible to satisfy all its customers' needs with a uniform product, an organisation will use market segmentation to divide consumers into smaller segments consisting of buyers with similar needs or characteristics, so that marketing becomes like firing a rifle instead of a blunderbuss. A rifle with an accurate sight will hit the target more efficiently, without wasting ammunition.

Figure 6.2 Marketing by blunderbuss

Figure 6.3 Marketing by rifle–hitting the target segment

Figure 6.4 A range of credit cards is available

Case Study – Credit card services

National Westminster Bank has widened its range of credit cards, as have many other financial institutions. By dividing the market up into segments the bank is now able to provide a credit card specifically geared to the needs of identified groups of customers and, at the same time, give customers a choice. A few years ago the only credit card this bank offered was an Access Card.

National Westminster now offers four different cards:

- the regular credit card (Access or Visa) with a credit limit to suit the customer's circumstances, and an annual fee
- a Visa Primary card, with a lower annual fee and a fixed credit limit of £500
- a Mastercard, which is similar to Access and Visa but offering the facility of converting an outstanding credit balance into a fixed-term loan at any time
- a Visa Gold card, with a *minimum* credit limit of £2500.

So National Westminster has created a range of products, each providing different benefits to cater for each group of customers. Having created such a portfolio of products, the bank now has to monitor and develop each one to ensure the success of each in the market-place. It needs a **range strategy**.

1 *What are the benefits of dividing a market into segments for:*
    a the National Westminster Bank?
    b the bank's customers?
2 *Explain the difference between a blunderbuss strategy and one that carefully targets a specific group of customers.*
3 *Chapter 3 dealt with 'assessing customer needs'. Using examples, explain how knowledge of consumer behaviour helps an organisation to segment its product range.*
4 *Why must an organisation monitor the success of its range strategy? What might happen if it failed to do so?*

Positioning

Segmentation enables an organisation to follow **marketing objectives**. It also provides a means whereby an organisation can position its brands and product varieties in the market-place. The marketing department can, by suitable promotion, establish a particular position in the market for each brand (e.g. up-market, mid-market or down-market) and then tailor selling strategies for each position.

The marketing mix

By splitting the market-place and developing strategies to position products, an organisation can choose an appropriate **marketing mix** for each target segment.

The marketing mix comprises a complex set of variables which an organisation combines in order to ensure that objectives are achieved. It includes strategic, tactical and operational elements and techniques.

The concept is usually analysed on the basis of the four P's. To meet customer needs an organisation must develop **products** to satisfy them, charge them the right **price**, get the goods to the right **place** and make the existence of the product known through its **promotion**.

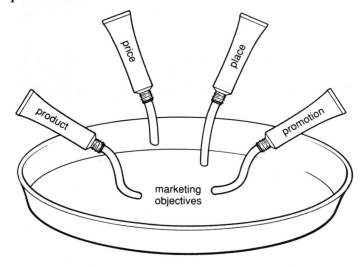

Figure 6.5 The marketing mix

'Mix' is an appropriate word to describe the marketing process. A mix is a composition of ingredients blended together to fulfil a common purpose. Every ingredient is vitally important and each depends on the others for their contributions. Just as with a cake, each ingredient is not sufficient on its own – but blended together it is possible to produce something very special. In the same way that there are a variety of cakes to suit various tastes, a marketing mix can be designed to suit the precise requirements of the market.

The marketing mix must have a **time scale**. An organisation must have a plan that indicates when it expects to achieve its objectives. Some objectives will be set to be attained in the near future. Others might be medium-term (one to five years), and yet others might be visionary objectives for attainment in the longer term.

The mix must have **strategic elements**. These will involve the overall strategy or the organisation. They require considerable use of judgement and expertise and are only made by senior managers. Such decisions might involve the development of a new product or a new market strategy.

The mix must also have **tactical or medium-term elements**. The business environment has to be constantly monitored and decisions have to be taken according to whatever changes take place. External events might affect pricing strategies, product modifications or amendments to marketing plans.

There must also be **short-term operational elements**. These involve predictable everyday decisions such as contacts with customers, analysis of advertising copy and minor decisions about packaging.

The commitment and support of a programme of planning with sufficient resources will underlie the manipulation of the marketing mix and will ultimately determine how capable an organisation is of achieving its objectives.

Task

Choose a product you use regularly and comment briefly on:

a the nature of the **product**
b its **price**
c its availability (**place**)
d how it is **promoted**.

If you were given overall responsibility for this brand, how would you use the marketing mix to develop its core strength?

The product

The **product** is the central point on which all marketing energies must converge. Organisations have to analyse what their products mean to their customers. People and organisations buy goods and services for a variety of reasons, and a wide range of characteristics influence the decision to buy. For example, on the surface there are often clear and **tangible benefits** such as:

- shape
- colour
- size
- design
- packaging
- appearance.

The **intangible features** are not so obvious. They may include the reputation of the producer on certain issues, such as:

- after sales service
- availability of spare parts
- customer care policy
- guarantees.

Task

Choose a product. List both its tangible and its intangible benefits.

At a basic level, people buy woolly jumpers to keep warm. They buy umbrellas to keep dry in the rain, and watches to tell them the time. However, human behaviour is a complex process. It is not uncommon to hear someone say 'I wouldn't be seen dead wearing one of those'. In other words, for many of us it cannot be any old jumper, umbrella or watch – it needs to be an item that fits in with a particular perception or self-image. Products are not usually purchased to meet a single need; the ownership and use of a product involves a whole range of factors that make up the **product concept**.

For example, it may appear that a person chooses to holiday in the West Indies because he or she is attracted by the sand, sun and surf. However, it may come to light that the person is more concerned with 'image' – friends and associates will become aware that he or she is able to afford to holiday in the West Indies. Holidaying in the West Indies is therefore associated with a particular life-style. In the public imagination it may represent being rich and able to afford exotic things.

Turtle Beach, Jamaica

Product benefits can be broken down into a number of important dimensions, of which we shall consider three:

- **Generic dimensions** are the key benefits of a particular item. Shoe polish cleans shoes. Freezers store frozen food. Deckchairs provide a comfortable seat on a sunny day. Hairdressers cut and style hair.

- **The sensual dimensions** of a product are those that provide sensual benefits. These include design, colour, taste, smell and texture. A ring doughnut has a shape, appearance, texture, taste and smell all of its own. The sensual benefits of products are frequently highlighted by advertisers.
- **Extended dimensions** of a product include a wide range of additional benefits. Examples are servicing arrangements, credit facilities, guarantees, maintenance contracts and so on.

Research and development

Many people associate the **research and development** function of an organisation with the invention of new products. Whilst this is very important, the development of existing products is also significant. The task of product research and development is to combine with marketing activities to cater for the changing preferences of consumers and come up with the goods and services that will meet the needs of tomorrow's customers. Product research and development therefore goes hand in hand with market research, and considerable liaison is required between these two areas. For example, they will attempt to investigate all of the questions in Figure 6.6 before a final decision is made to go into production.

Task

Imagine that you have come up with the idea of a mailbox which opens at the top, for the delivery of newspaper and post to households. The idea is that the box will be attached to the outside of front doors. Highlight areas of market and product research that will need to be covered before going into final production of the boxes at a factory unit. What are the key questions that you will need to consider? What are the key tasks that will need to be carried out?

Product researchers use marketing information to help them develop well-designed products. **Design** involves developing goods and services in a form which both attracts customers and serves the intended purpose. The layout of a department store, for example, must be designed so that a customer is able to find the item he or she wants quickly – the right use of space is vital to ensure profitability. Product researchers must also consider production costs, ease of manufacture and selling price.

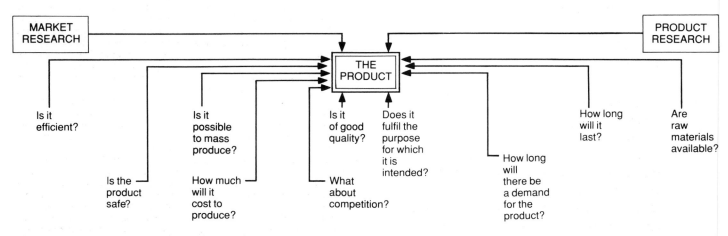

Figure 6.6 Key questions about the product

A company might be reluctant to change an existing design, particularly if it provides status (e.g. the radiator grill on a BMW car). Conversely, small changes may be made to products to give them a more up-to-date feel. A company logo may be updated to give it a 'modern look'.

Built-in obsolescence

Built-in (or planned) **obsolescence** can be, and frequently is, a feature of many products. Fashion clothes are designed to last for a season, and cars are built to last for only a few years. A manufacturer is able to sustain long-term market demand by limiting the life-span of a product. Some commentators argue that this leads to a huge waste of resources, while others see it as boosting demand, employment and output in the economy.

Task

Draw up a list of arguments an environmentalist might put forward against built-in obsolescence. How might a major manufacturer respond to such arguments?

The product mix

Many organisations produce more than one product. One advantage of **diversification** is that it enables the company the spread its risks. The **product mix** is the complete range of items produced by an organisation. These products have to be managed and positioned in appropriately targeted market segments. The mix comprises all the brands, line extensions, sizes, and types of packaging on offer.

Task

Design three charts to show the product mixes of three well-known companies.

The key to a good product mix is having an effective balance of products in line with the organisation's strategy. Effective management involves creating this balance. If a product is losing pulling power, it may need to be revamped, relaunched or replaced.

Case Study – New product development in Japan

WESTERN companies are supposed to be the masters of innovation, marketing and incisive management. Japanese firms have a reputation for borrowing ideas from abroad, making painstaking improvements and then, when everything is ready, churning out better-quality products in huge volumes at low prices. This reputation may still be partly true for Japanese companies abroad. At home almost the opposite is the case, as many American and European companies trying to compete in Japan have been shocked to discover.

Foreign firms entering the Japanese market with a four-year technical lead have seen their products quickly matched – not copied, mind, matched – and then left behind. Once Japanese manufacturers relied on slick production techniques to make them into awesome competitors. Today their most effective weapon is rapid innovation.

Take Sony's best-selling CCD-TR55, a miniaturised video camera and recorder ('camcorder') that weighs a mere 790 grams (1.5lb). To make the product palm-sized, Sony had to shrink 2,200 components into a space one-quarter the size they occupy in a conventional camcorder. Yet only six months after introducing the CCD-TR55 in June 1989, Sony had competition. Matsushita, followed by its stablemate, JVC launched even lighter look-a-likes. Within a year, Sanyo, Canon, Ricoh and Hitachi were selling palm-sized camcorders as well.

The process of rushing out instant imitations is known in Japan as **product covering**. Rival manufacturers rush to produce their own versions just in case the pioneer's should prove to be a best-seller. With a target to aim at, the coverers know that the innovation is at least technically feasible. Reverse engineering – taking the product apart to see how it works – provides short-cuts. The top priority of companies is to prevent distributors and retailers from deserting their own camp.

Product covering is really just a part of an even more formidable Japanese process known as **product churning**. When developing a new product, western firms use a 'rifle' approach, testing the market constantly and revising the product each time until it exactly meets the customer's needs before launching it. Japanese manufacturers, by contrast, tend to use a 'shotgun' approach. For instance, around 1,000 new soft drinks appear annually in Japan, though 99% of them vanish within a year. New-product ideas are not tested through market research, but by selling the first production batch.

Kevin Jones, a consultant in McKinsey's Tokyo office, points out that nobody could imagine why people would want a hi-fi with not one, but two, compact-disc players. The doubters included Sharp, the firm that launched the machine. Nevertheless teenagers bought the machines to mix tracks from separate CDs onto tape. Within months both Sanyo and JVC followed with their own twin-CD machines.

Firms also engage in **parallel development** – developing second-and-third-generation products along with the initial version. As soon as the pack catches up, the original innovator has a replacement for its own hit product ready to go. Only weeks after Matsushita launched a rival to Sony's palm-sized camcorder, Sony hitback with two new models – oneeven lighter, the other with yet more technical features. Companies that fail to ride each successive waveof innovation risk being washed away.

This looks wasteful. But according to a study by McKinsey, Japanese companies develop new products in a third to half the time spent by their western counterparts, at a quarter to a tenth of the cost. Three factors help Japanese companies pull off this feat:

● **Japan's army of engineers.** Japanese companies are reaping the benefits of the country's enormous investment in education, especially in engineering schools. Technical literacy is now more widely diffused throughout Japanese business than anywhere else in the industrial world. Japan has 5000 technical workers for 1 million people. The comparable figure for America is 3500, for western Germany 2500; no other country comes close.

● **Catalogue design.** Instead of designing every component of a new product from scratch, Japanese engineers reach instinctively for the parts catalogue. By using off-the-shelf components wherever possible, they devote their most creative engineering skills to fashioning a product that is 90% as good as a product designed from scratch might be – but only half the price of a completely original version.

● **Free flow of information.** Unlike western firms, which tend to hand their suppliers the skimpiest of

Figure 6.7 His master's CD

specifications when seeking a price quotation for a new component, Japanese manufacturers share their most secret plans, send their top staff to help out and hand over any proprietary know-how needed. They then leave the supplier to get on with the job of developing the part needed for the new product. With so much trust and exchange of staff, product-development information can flow between a company and its suppliers while a new product is still only a gleam in an engineer's eye. The lack of job-hopping among Japanese engineers limits the leakage of information to competitors.

Even Japanese firms have not been able to transfer all these practices abroad. Flooding the market with new products, even imitations, is important in Japan because firms are determined not to lose access to scarce, and often rigid, dealer and distribution networks. Abroad, this matters less. Tarnishing their reputation with a poor product is also less of a concern because many new versions are aimed at a small core of sophisticated consumers who will try anything new. The extraordinary appetite of all Japanese consumers for new gizmos can also make an aging product-line fatal to a firm's prospects, as many failed camera manufacturers discovered in the 1980's.

Abroad, new products still have to be chosen and developed more carefully. A single dud can damage a carefully nurtured image. And falling a small step behind is not so threatening once brand loyalty has been established. Nevertheless, the new-product treadmill Japanese companies face at home has already given them an eviable prowess in foreign markets. Moreover, any western firm hoping to grab a chunk of the huge Japanese market will have little choice but to step on to the new-product treadmill too.

Source: The Economist Newspapers Ltd

1 Explain why it is difficult for many American and European companies to compete in Japan.
2 What are the dangers of rushing out instant imitations too quickly?
3 Explain what is meant by:
   a product covering
   b product churning
   c parallel development.
4 How do the Japanese benefit by using off-the-shelf components?
5 Identify the areas of new product development in Japan which, in your opinion, use:
   a good marketing practices
   b poor marketing practices.
6 How is the Japanese consumer affected by such activities?

The price

Of all the aspects of the marketing mix, price is the one which creates sales **revenue** – all the others are costs. The Oxford English Dictionary has the following definition:

> THE PRICE is the sum or consideration or sacrifice for which a thing may be bought or attained.

However, to produce a watertight definition of pricing which gives a clear indication of its importance in the marketing mix is like trying to define the length of a piece of string. In some contexts a particular definition will be appropriate, in others it will not. The problem stems from the fact that 'price' has different meanings for different groups of people:

● For **buyers**, price may be regarded as an unwelcome cost. Price involves sacrificing the next-best alternative that could be bought (as we saw in Chapter 1, this is sometimes referred to as the **opportunity cost**). Price can also be used as a measure of the **value** of an item.

● For **sellers**, price is a key element in the marketing

mix. It is an important selling point. 'Getting the price right' is an important tactical decision and as such it is a key factor influencing revenue and profit. We all know of a business that sold wonderful products which were just a little too expensive – it went bust. We also know of businesses that sold themselves too cheaply – not enough revenue was generated to cover costs adequately.

- For the **government**, the price of individual products is an influence on the general price level – and hence votes!

The importance of price within the marketing mix varies from one market to another and between different segments in the same market. In low-cost, non-fashion markets, price can be critical (for example in the sale of white emulsion and gloss paint for decorating). In fashion markets, such as fashion clothing, it can be one of the least relevant factors. Certain products are designed to suit a particular price segment (e.g. economy family cars) whilst others perform a specific function regardless of cost. For consumers with limited budgets, price is a key purchasing criterion, whilst for others for whom 'money is no object', price is less important.

Task

Identify a range of similar products or services. Comment briefly on the differences and similarities in their prices.

Pricing objectives

There are many possible objectives in establishing prices. A key assumption of many business theories is that **profit maximisation** is the most important pricing target. Studies of actual business behaviour,

however, reveal a wide range of objectives other than short-term profit maximisation.

A **competitive price** is one that gives a competitive edge in the market-place. It is not necessarily lower than that of a rival because other elements of the marketing mix add to the competitive edge. For example, it is possible to argue that Gillette razor blades are better quality than those of rivals, giving scope to charge a higher yet more competitive price than those applying to other blades.

A further aim of competitive pricing is to set a price that deters new entrants in a particular market. Large organisations with some degree of monopoly power may be inclined to keep prices relatively low in order to secure their long-term market dominance. From time to time you might hear the owner of a small organisation say: 'Of course we would like to diversify into producing X but we simply cannot compete with the prices being offered by the big boys.'

H.A. Simon put forward the view that a business may want to **satisfice** – that is, achieve given targets for market share and profits from sales which may not maximise profits but which instead inflate boardroom egos. This can arise when the managers of an organisation are clearly different from the owners. If the managers can provide sufficient profits to keep the shareholders satisfied, then a proportion of the profits can be diverted to provide more perks for managers and large departments.

There are many other possible objectives in establishing prices. For example, a company might feel that it is important to **maximise sales** to create **brand leadership,** or it might want to establish a high price to create a **reputation for quality.**

Pricing strategies

Once a pricing objective has been established, it is necessary to establish an appropriate strategy. Three broad strategies can be considered: low-price, market-price and high-price.

A **low-price strategy** should be considered when consumers respond positively to small downward changes in price. In technical terms we can measure this response by calculating the **elasticity of demand** (see pages 92 and 93 in Chapter 5). Elasticity of demand can be used to express the changes in quantities purchased as a response to price changes. In Chapter 5 we saw that demand is said to be *elastic* if the change in quantity demanded is of a greater proportion than the change in price that initiated it. If the price of a brand of washing powder were to fall by 10 per cent and there was an increase in sales of 20 per cent, then the demand for the product would be said to be elastic – the change in price leads to a more than proportionate response in quantity demanded. In this example:

$$\text{Elasticity of demand} = \frac{20\%}{10\%} = 2.$$

Products with a value greater than 1 are said to have an elastic demand. However, it needs to be remembered that elastic demand does not always mean that a producer will benefit from price reductions. If a company in a **price-sensitive** market lowers its price, there is a strong chance that other producers will follow suit. Another consideration is cost – if a company lowers its price, and sells more, it will have to pay out more in expenses and other variable costs.

A low-price strategy is important wherever it is easy for consumers to compare competitive products. When brands of similar washing powders sit side by side on the shelves of a supermarket there is a strong incentive to set a lower price.

In many situations organisations will tend to set prices at the **market-price level**. This will happen where:

● products are bought frequently
● competitive products have very similar characteristics
● a few large organisations dominate the supply in a specific industry.

In any of these situations, an organisation could quickly lose all its business if it set its price above those of the competition. Conversely, if it lowers its price the competitors may be forced to follow. Organisations tend to set prices at market-price level so that the role of the price is neutral.

A **high-price strategy** can be a long-term or a short-term policy. A long-term policy implies that the firm seeks to sell a high-quality product to a small, select market, high prices being an essential feature of up-market products. A short-term policy is based upon the advantages gained by selling a patented product (when there is also heavy investment in new equipment) or when there is some form of barrier to others entering the market.

Task

Give two examples of situations where it would be appropriate to use:

a low-price strategy
b a market-price strategy
c a high-price strategy.

Pricing techniques

How are prices set in practice? Important influences upon pricing techniques include:

● cost
● demand
● competitors' prices.

Practical pricing involves elements of all three. Below we explore some commonly used pricing techniques.

Any study of how organisations price products or services inevitably reveals a very high proportion using no other basis than a mark-up. This is known as **cost-plus pricing**. Information about costs is usually easier to piece together than information about other variables such as likely revenue. The unit cost is the average cost of each item produced; if a company produces 800 units at a total cost of £24 000 the unit cost is £30. The price is then arrived at by adding on a certain percentage of the unit price.

Contribution pricing involves separating out the different products that make up a company's portfolio, in order to charge individual prices appropriate to each product's share in total costs. Two broad categories of costs can be identified:

- **Direct cost**s vary directly with the quantity of output produced – for example, costs of materials and wages.
- **Indirect costs** are amounts that have to be paid irrespective of the level of output – for example, the salaries of permanent staff and the cost of maintaining a plant.

When an organisation produces a range of individual items or products it is easy to determine the direct costs of each, but not the indirect costs. For example, in a food processing plant producing 100 different recipe dishes it is easy to work out how much goes on each line in terms of raw materials, labour input, and other direct costs. However, the same cannot be said of indirect costs, and the organisation has to decide on a policy of allocating reasonable amounts of the total indirect costs to each product line in order to calculate prices.

Contribution is the sum remaining after the direct costs of producing individual products have been subtracted from revenues. Figure 6.8 makes clear how this works.

Demand-orientated pricing involves reacting to the demand for a product, so that high demand leads to high prices and weak demand leads to low prices even though unit costs are similar.

When an organisation can split up the market in which it operates into different sections, it can carry out a policy of **price discrimination**. This involves selling at high prices in sections of the market where demand is intense and at relatively low prices where demand is elastic. Price discrimination may be carried out in the following circumstances:

- **In a customer-orientated situation**. Some customers may have a high demand for a product while others may have only a weak demand. Discrimination would involve selling the same type of product to the first type of customer at a high price and to the second type at a lower price.
- **In a product-orientated situation**. Slight modifications can be made to a product to allow high-price and low-price strategies.
- **According to time**. Sellers are able to discriminate between customers at different times of the day or according to seasons or the time of year.
- **According to situation**. Prices can vary according to the situation associated with the product. For example, house prices vary according to the area of a town or city in which they are located.

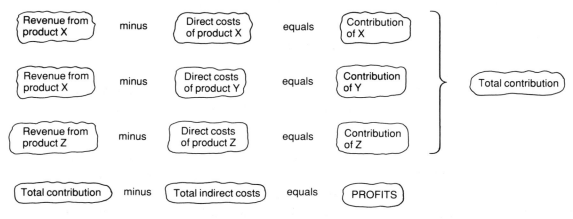

Figure 6.8 Calculating profits using contribution pricing

Task

BT uses discriminatory pricing according to time. Find out in detail how BT currently applies this policy. List and explain examples of other forms of price discrimination according to customer, product and situation.

Competition-orientated pricing is frequently adopted in extremely competitive situations. If a product is faced with direct competition from highly similar products in the market-place, this may constrain pricing decisions so as to keep them in line with the actions of rivals. In contrast, when there is only indirect competition in other sectors of the market, there will be more scope to vary price.

Markets are sometimes classified according to the level of competition. One extreme is called **perfect competition** (it exists in theory rather than in practice). In perfect competition there would be no limitations to new firms entering the market-place, and buyers would know what was on offer and have to accept the ruling market price. The other extreme is **monopoly**, where a single company dominates a market-place, giving it considerable powers to set high prices – to be a **price maker**. In the real world, most markets lie between these extremes and involve some level of imperfection.

Figure 6.9 Decreasing levels of competition

Task

Identify one market in which there is little competition, and one in which there is a lot of competition. Comment on prices in these two markets.

Short-term pricing policies

Pricing can be used as an incisive to pursue short-term marketing and selling targets for an organisation. Typical attack-based policies include:

- skimming pricing
- penetration pricing
- destroyer pricing
- promotional pricing.

Skimming pricing is used when there is little competition in the market. It involves setting a relatively high initial price in order to yield a high initial return from those customers willing to buy the new product. Once the first group of customers has been satisfied, the seller can then lower prices in order to make sales to new groups of customers, and this process continues until a large section of the total market-place is catered for. This sort of pricing often takes place when new electrical products are launched.

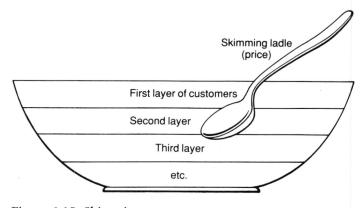

Figure 6.10 Skimming

Penetration pricing is appropriate when the seller knows that demand is likely to be elastic. A low price is therefore required to attract customers to the product. Penetration pricing is normally associated with the launch of a new product for which the market needs to be penetrated. Because price starts low, the product may initially make a loss until consumer awareness is increased. As the product rapidly penetrates the market, sales and profitability increase and prices can creep upwards.

Task

Identify examples of penetration pricing – products or services that have been launched at low prices to establish themselves in markets.

A policy of **destroyer pricing** can be used to undermine the sales of rivals or to warn potential new rivals not to enter a particular market. Destroyer pricing involves reducing the price of an existing product or selling a new product at an artificially low price in order to destroy competitors' sales. This type of policy will almost certainly lead to short-term losses.

Prices can be lowered from time to time to promote a product or service to new customers. **Promotional pricing** can be used to inject fresh life into an existing product or to create interest in a new product. Supermarkets frequently use a **loss-leader** to boost sales of other items.

Case Study – Car wars

The plunge in car sales in 1991 cost the motor trade more than £2.5 billion in the first half of the year and sparked a savage price war. Nissan fired the first volley with the announcement

of price cuts across its entire range. Ford, the market leader, followed with a dramatic move which led to it slashing list prices on many of its models by up to £2000. Vauxhall, down from number two in the car market to third place behind Rover, came in with a cash-back offer to pay a refund of up to £1500 to customers taking delivery of a new car within a three-month period. Fiat cut showroom prices by between £500 and £2000 across its range.

The reason for the price battle became clear when the latest monthly sales figures were released by the Society of Motor Manufacturers and Traders. New car sales for June were the lowest for 21 years and served to confirm the dismal trend. Car sales were running 24.8 per cent down, with registrations barely scraping past 800 000, compared with well over a million in the previous year. The deep depression throughout the motor industry is also having a serious knock-on effect upon component manufacturers.

The action of four major car manufacturers in slashing prices inevitably set the scene for a dramatic price war. Soon after the price cuts there was evidence that business warmed as a result. One motor retailer said: 'There seem to be people around in a buying mood who have been holding back, not quite confident enough to take the plunge, and the price reductions might just tip the balance.' He also pointed out that customers coming into showrooms were much more aggressive – they knew there were discounts to be had and were determined to push for them.

Few car manufacturers have escaped the icy draught blowing through the car market. For manufacturers in 1991, every customer counts.

1 Comment generally on the nature of the car market in 1991.
2 Look at the pricing techniques outlined in this chapter. Which of the pricing techniques contributed to the actions of motor manufacturers in 1991? Explain why they used these techniques.
3 Make a list of those who benefit from a price war in the car market.

4 What techniques other than price could motor manufacturers use to sell more new cars?

5 What knock-on effect might the recession and a price war for new cars have on the market for second-hand cars?

The place

Though figures vary widely from product to product, roughly a fifth of the production cost of an item goes on getting it to the customer. The issue of **place** deals with various methods of transporting and storing goods, and then making them available to the customer. Getting the right product to the right place at the right time involves the **distribution** system. Distribution is the process of moving goods and services to the places where they are wanted. It may involve a single step or any number of steps. The local baker might supply bread directly to customers. In contrast, the furniture store might supply chairs and tables produced in Scandinavia which have passed through a number of hands and have been stored two or three times before arriving at their final destination.

Transport

Transport can be a key cost component in many products. Choosing the 'best' possible transport system involves weighing up and 'trading off' a number of key elements. What forms of transport should be used – road, rail, air, sea? Can these forms of transport be integrated? What are the best possible routes? Do you use your own fleet or outside carriers? How do you maximise safety? How do you minimise costs? How do you make sure that products arrive on time and in the best possible condition?

Task

Imagine you are the transport manager for an organisation that manufactures and delivers fresh cream cakes from Shildon, in County Durham, around the North East of England – particularly to Darlington, Sunderland, Durham, Newcastle and Consett. Work in groups to research and then discuss each of the transport issues mentioned in the text.

Different forms of transport have their own distinctive advantages and disadvantages. Pipelines are expensive to construct, cheap to run and expensive to repair. Roads give door-to-door delivery, are fast over short and some long distances, and make it possible to use your own fleet relatively cheaply. However, road travel is also subject to traffic delays and breakdowns, and drivers may only drive their vehicles for a certain number of hours in a day. Rail transport is relatively cheap and quick over long distances, particularly between major cities. However, it is not always appropriate for reaching out-of-the-way destinations and is costly for guaranteed speedy deliveries. Air is very fast between countries, provided the ultimate destination is not off the beaten track. Air is generally used for carrying important, urgent, relatively light and expensive loads. Sea transport is a cheap way of carrying high-volume bulky loads when speed is not of the essence.

Containerisation of loads has made possible the integration of these different forms of transport. Routes and services have been simplified to cut out wasteful duplication. Special types of vehicles have been developed to carry certain loads. Direct motorway connections between major cities have proved to be of major importance in determining factory location decisions, as have fast intercity rail services and air links. Different methods of transport may prove to be more or less cost effective in different situations depending on the cost of transport relative to the type of good being transported, the price of the good, or the speed with which it is needed.

Channels of distribution

Distribution is not just concerned with moving goods physically from manufacturers to consumers.

It is also concerned with choosing the appropriate **channel** of distribution – for example, whether to sell direct to the consumer or to sell primarily to wholesalers or retailers (see Figure 6.11).

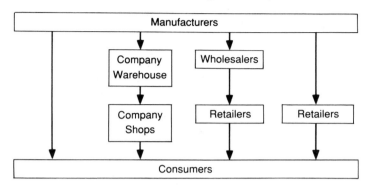

Figure 6.11 **Some of the many channels of distribution**

Choosing appropriate channels for distribution involves highly significant policy decisions which can have an important effect on other areas of the marketing mix. For example, if you choose to distribute through a chain of readily accessible cut-price stores this will have obvious implications for the public perception of your products.

Modern commerce uses thousands of channels and methods of distribution. The traditional way of distributing goods from a manufacturer to a market is through a small number of **wholesalers** who then sell the goods to a large number of retailers. In this way a wholesaler is a go-between who buys in bulk from manufacturers and breaks the bulk down into small units for retailers. Wholesalers often provide a variety of services which benefit both manufacturers and retailers, such as warehousing, credit arrangements transport and packaging. However, the involvement of a wholesaler adds to the selling price.

If a manufacturing company sells to a retailer directly, it can exert firmer control over its sales, and the manufacturer and retailer can work together on sales promotion schemes. Selling direct to retailers involves a larger sales force and increased transport charges when sending smaller consignments. If circumstances allow, it can be possible for manufacturers to sell directly to consumers,

particularly if the product is a high-cost one and has a good reputation within the market.

Case Study – Developing a fast answer to fashion fads

Britain's chain stores are working to eliminate their risk from the notoriously high-risk clothing industry. Alarmed by almost unprecedented volumes of unsold stock caused by recession, high street fashion chains are trying to solve this costly problem by working more closely with the manufacturers. In order to reduce losses from marking down clothes, they have developed a solution: a **quick response** to changes in fashion.

'Quick response' means developing a system of working which produces a much closer relationship between demand and supply. Methods of achieving QR vary at each stage of the clothing supply chain. The aim is to provide the right product in the right quantity in the right place in the quickest possible time, with minimum inventory and costs.

QR has profound implications right down the supply chain. It helps to eliminate some of the complacency in the modern fashion market which developed in the late eighties when the consumer boom kept factory order books full. Today fashion has become much more unpredictable and retailers and manufacturers can no longer anticipate what their customers will want to buy a year in advance. They recognise the need to respond quickly to the uncertain twists of fashion. They no longer want to have to guess customer requirements months in advance of the season.

Marks and Spencer, the UK's biggest clothing retailer, is expected to step up its QR programme in coming months. By 1993 the company wants its suppliers to replenish clothing lines twice weekly instead of once a week. Woolworths is introducing QR throughout its children's wear divisions and plans to reduce **lead times** to under 10 days on some lines that currently stand at 5–10 weeks.

Domestic clothing manufacturers believe QR is an essential tool for fighting competition from the Far East. Suppliers to the Burton Group say buyers want greater flexibility and want merchandise fast. Research suggests that QR can develop a 7.5 per cent increase in sales for retailers and improve margins through reduced mark-downs. The development of QR seems to be transforming the industry.

1 *Explain what is meant by quick response (QR).*
2 *How will QR benefit the 'place' ingredient in the marketing mix?*
3 *Make a list of the groups who benefit from QR.*
4 *Investigate how retail technology might help an organisation to implement QR.*
5 *What other 'unpredictable' markets might benefit from QR?*
6 *Imagine you are responsible for clothing sales in a large chain. How would you attempt to introduce QR?*

Promotion

Since early days individuals have used hand signals, vocal patterns, symbolic drawings and facial expressions for the purpose of communicating. Today, the exchange of information takes place through sophisticated media in order to accomplish the same goal. An efficient network of communications is essential for successful promotional activity.

The **promotional mix** comprises all the marketing and promotional communication methods used to achieve the promotional objectives of the marketing mix. These methods can be broken down into two distinct areas: non-controllable and controllable.

Non-controllable methods are marketing messages which take place on the basis of word-of-mouth, personal recommendations and a consumer's overall perception of a particular product or service. For example, consumer opinions are influenced by a number of factors, such as whether their family has regularly used the product. A brand heritage, character, colour and image will also have helped to create brand loyalty and influenced regular purchasing patterns. On the other hand, public displeasure with a particular organisation, country or range of products might influence purchases; examples are CFCs in aerosols and 'dolphin-unfriendly' tuna.

Controllable methods are marketing messages which are carefully directed to achieve the objectives of an organisation's promotional campaign. We shall consider four main areas.

Advertisements

Advertisements are messages intended to inform or influence the people who receive them. A message is paid for by an advertiser in order to sell a product or service or to seek support or participation. This category includes adverts on TV, radio and in magazines, but does not include promotional materials supplied with a product, promotional events, branding or company brochures.

To plan a campaign, an advertiser usually consults an **advertising agency**. Such an agency is a vital link between the advertiser and the consumer. The role of an advertising agency is to create, develop, plan and implement an advertising campaign for a client. The extent to which an agency does so will vary according to its type. Some agencies offer all kinds of services while others specialise, for example, in creative work.

The interaction of ideas with creativity forms a major factor in the success of an advertising campaign. The message might be a combination of works, symbols, characters, colours, sounds and gimmicks. It must be conveyed to the right people in the right place at the right time, as 'good' advertising will not work if it is misdirected.

At the heart of advertising is identification of where the interests of the consumers lie, and knowing how they will respond to different messages. Good copywriting is important. Buzz words such as 'new' and 'free' try to encourage the consumer to do something. Straplines are associated with a brand name and can help to develop an image – for example, 'Once driven, forever smitten' or 'Ralgex has the muscle'. Sometimes a character is used to identify the qualities of the brand – for example, Mr Sheen and Mr Kipling. A brand's heritage is often an area that advertisers like to build upon. Artwork, sex appeal, humour and repetition all help to communicate the identity of the brand as well as provide a foundation for the other areas of the promotional mix.

Case Study – Using sex to promote ice-cream

Combatants in Europe's $7 billion a year ice-cream war are using sex to turn on the public. The use of naked flesh to market new products is nothing new, but fierce competition in the 'adult' market is inspiring advertisers to new heights. In Britain, campaigns by two manufacturers in the gourmet market have raised eyebrows as well as brand awareness. The UK's television watchdog, the Independent Television Commission, recently banned from national TV a series of erotic advertisements for ice-cream, saying they were 'too hot' for British viewers. The Advertising Standards Authority has also received complaints about ice-cream adverts, all expressing surprise that sex should be used in such a blatant way to sell ice-cream.

Unilever's best-known adverts featured the pan-European Cornetto gondola. It, too, has recently turned to sex appeal with the girl-licks-lolly

formula to help it to double the sales of Magnum, the chocolate covered ice-cream on a stick. With predicted sales of 200 million in Europe this year, it shows that the proof of the pudding is in the eating!

1 Why might using sex-appeal to sell ice-cream sometimes be considered to be against the public interest?
2 Outline the benefits of using such a strategy for:
   a advertisers
   b consumers.
3 What other methods of promoting ice-cream might also be successful? Working in groups, consider what themes you would emphasise if you had to promote a new ice-cream product in the luxury 'after-dinner' segment of the adult market.

A key element in advertising is media selection. Media selection will depend on the target audience – that is, the number of **potential customers** the advertiser will wish to reach (**coverage**) – as well as the number of times the advertiser wishes the message to be transmitted to customers (**frequency**).

Task

List as many types of media as you can think of. Comment on the advantages and disadvantages of using each to reach a *carefully selected target audience.*

Advertising is an essential part of the promotional mix and requires particularly large levels of expenditure. It is therefore crucial that organisations try to analyse the effectiveness of their investment. The success of a campaign will depend upon the way it appeals to the attitudes of its target audience.

Sales promotion

Sales promotion describes a set of techniques designed to encourage customers to make a purchase. It usually complements advertising, personal selling and publicity, and might include point-of-sale materials, competitions, demonstrations and exhibitions. The essential feature of a sales promotion effort is that it is a short-term inducement to encourage customers to react quickly, whereas advertising is a much more long-term communication process involving the building of a brand image.

Promotions into the pipeline are techniques used to sell more stocks into the distribution system. Examples are 'dealer loaders' such as thirteen for the price of twelve (the baker's dozen), point-of-sale materials, dealer competitions, extended credit to dealers, sale-or-return and promotional gifts.

Promotions out of the pipeline assist in promoting and selling products to the end-user. These might include free samples, trial packs, coupon offers, price reductions, competitions, premium offers, demonstrations, charity promotions and point-of-sale displays.

Task

Do some fieldwork. Interview a retailer to find out more about sales promotions into the pipeline. Also look at those offered out of the pipeline. Which are the most common? How effective do they seem to be?

The effects of individual sales promotions vary widely. Though most promotions using free samples lead to an immediate (if temporary) increase in sales, sales promotions are a short-term measure on the whole and have little effect on brand loyalty over a longer period.

Personal selling

Personal selling involves persuasive communication between a seller and a buyer which is designed to convince the consumer to purchase the products or services on offer. The objective of personal selling is therefore to obtain a sale and is the culmination of all the earlier marketing activities. It involves matching a consumer's needs with the goods and services on offer – the better the match the more lasting the relationship between the seller and the buyer.

Personal selling is important in both customer and organisational markets. In consumer goods markets, advertising is often the driving force which has **pulled** a product through the distribution network so that most consumers know what they want to purchase. In organisational markets, the purpose of a sales force is to **push** the product through the market.

The sequence of events used in personal selling is often described as the **five P's** (do not confuse with the four P's of the marketing mix!). They are:

- *Preparation* – Sales staff should be adequately trained and familiar with the product, customers, competition and the market.
- *Prospecting* – Prospective customers (prospects) are identified before the selling can take place.
- *Pre-approach* – Learning about the projected customer.
- *Presentation* – Use of active selling skills.
- *Post-sale support* – Following up the sale to create repeat business.

Task

In what ways is personal selling likely to be easy? In what ways is it likely to be difficult?

Those involved in personal selling operate as an information link between the suppliers and their customers. As a result, personal selling involves a boundary role – being at the boundary of a supplying organisation as well as in direct and close contact with its customers. The role is often one not only of selling but also of interpreting the activities and policies of supplier and customer. The role of personal selling has changed considerably in recent years. However, despite database management and changing patterns of distribution, personal selling continues to play an essential role in the promotional mix.

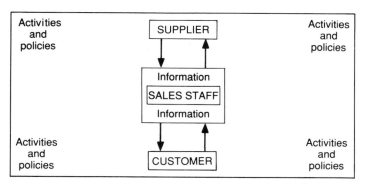

Figure 6.12 The information link between customer and supplier

Public relations

Public relations (PR) encompasses all of the actions of and communications from an organisation. The forces in an organisation's **external environment** are capable of affecting them in a variety of ways. The forces might be social, economic, political, local or environmental and could be represented by a variety of groups such as customers, shareholders, employees, special interest groups and by public opinion. Reacting to such elements in a way that will build a positive image is very important.

The purpose of public relations is therefore to provide an external environment for an organisation in which it is popular and can prosper. Building **goodwill** in such a way will require sound organisational performance and behaviour and the communication of such actions and attitudes to its many publics.

The direct selling of products or services is *not* an objective of public relations. Whereas advertising is about relatively short-term objectives, public relations is long-term; it works by sending free messages to various groups through the activities of the organisation in order to improve its reputation and maintain its positive image.

PR can be used as a strategic device to develop a more positive public perception and image of an organisation. Activities might include charitable donations and community relations, hospitality, press releases, visits, event sponsorship, free literature etc. Public relations can provide an organisation's many publics with information about what it does and how it responds to different circumstances. It can help to build confidence in its activities, develop goodwill in the community and provide benefits for its publics.

Case Study – Ski uses rock 'n' roll for cerebral palsy

Yoghurt brand Ski recently pledged £200 000 in its biggest programme for the cerebral palsy charity the Stars Organisation for Spastics (SOS). To mark SOS's tenth anniversary, Eden Vale, the parent, will sponsor a single title 'The Spoken Word of Rock 'n' Roll', featuring seventeen SOS celebrities. The proceeds will go to the Dame Vera Lynn Children's Project. Each record contains an SOS information leaflet and a coupon for 20p off a pack of four Ski yoghurts. At the same time an on-pack promotion will ask consumers to take part in a competition with cash prizes by calling a Ski hotline and identifying some of the voices on the record. Ski will donate 10p for every call.

The £65 million Ski brand has backed the charity – whose supporters include founder Dame Vera Lynn, Michael Grade and Martyn Lewis – for a decade.

1 Why do organisations such as Eden Vale take on the responsibility of supporting a charity?
2 It has been suggested that all organisations should make a minimum annual charitable donation. Comment upon this.
3 Describe how the Ski contribution will help the brand in:
   a the short-term
   b the long-term.

Using the marketing mix

As we have seen, the marketing mix is a carefully constructed combination of techniques, resources and tactics which form the basis of a marketing **plan** geared to achieve both marketing and corporate **objectives**. Whenever objectives or external influences change, so the blend of ingredients will have to be varied. No two mixes in similar types of organisation will ever be the same. Each will represent a unique approach to developing a strategy for the resources available.

In **undifferentiated marketing**, a single marketing message is offered to the total market-place. This is unlikely to be successful as markets are made up of buyers with different wants and needs.

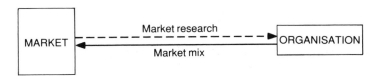

Figure 6.13 Undifferentiated marketing

Differentiated marketing is the strategy of attacking the market-place by tailoring separate product and marketing strategies to different sectors of the market. For example, the car market may be divided into an economy segment, a luxury segment, a performance segment etc.

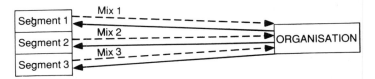

Figure 6.14 Differentiated marketing

Concentrated marketing is often the best strategy for small organisations. This involves choosing to compete in one segment and developing the most effective mix for this sub-market. Jaguar, for example, concentrates on the luxury segment of the car market.

Figure 6.15 Concentrated marketing

Although companies try to select and dominate certain market segments, they find that rivals are engaged in similar strategies. They therefore try to create a **differential advantage** over rivals. A positioning strategy will involve selecting a market segment and creating a differential advantage over rivals in that area.

Task

Look at two similar products. Comment on the similarities and the differences of their marketing mixes. To what extent are these due to positioning strategy? What are the differential advantages each product has over its rival?

The product life-cycle

An important aspect of the marketing mix is its use in managing the life-cycle of a product or brand. The **product life cycle** is an essential mechanism for planning changes in marketing activities. It recognises that products have a finite market life and charts this through various phases. The sales performance of any product introduced into the market will rise from nothing, reach a peak, and at some stage decline.

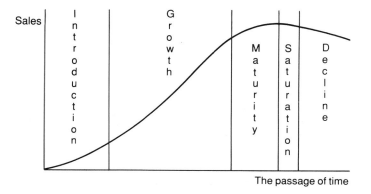

Figure 6.16 Stages in the product life-cycle

The life-cycle can be broken down further into distinct stages. In the **introductory phase**, growth is slow and volume is low because of limited awareness of the product's existence. Sales then rise rapidly during the period of growth. It is during this phase that the profit per unit sold usually reaches a maximum. Towards the end of this phase, competitors enter the market to promote their own products, which reduces the rate of growth of sales of the first product. This period is then known as **maturity**. Competitive jockeying – such as product differentiation in the form of new flavours, colours, sizes etc. – will sift out the weaker brands. During **saturation**, some brands will drop out of the market. The product market may eventually **decline** and reach a stage when it becomes unprofitable.

The life-cycle may last for a few months or for hundreds of years. To prolong the life-cycle of a brand or a product an organisation needs to readjust the ingredients of its marketing mix. Periodic injections of new ideas are needed – product improvements, line extensions or improved promotions.

A readjustment of the marketing mix might include:

- changing or modifying the *product*, to keep up with or ahead of the competition
- altering distribution patterns, to provide a more suitable *place* for the consumer to make purchases
- changing *prices* to reflect competitive activities
- considering carefully the style of *promotion*.

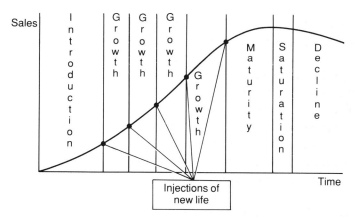

Figure 6.17 Periodic injections into the product life-cycle

The product portfolio

Most large organisations produce a range of products, each with its own life-cycle. By using life-cycles, companies can plan when to introduce new lines as old products go into decline. The collection of products that an organisation produces is known as its **product portfolio**.

In Figure 6.18, T_1 represents a point in time. At that point product 1 is in decline, product 2 is in maturity, product 3 is in growth and product 4 has recently been introduced.

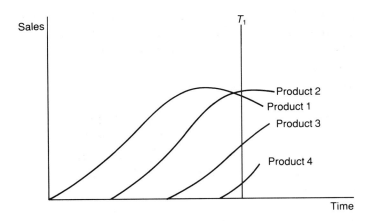

Figure 6.18 A product portfolio

Task

The organisation you work for or attend will have a portfolio of products or services. Identify the elements of the portfolio and try to determine where they stand in their life-cycles.

If an organisation's products are launched at just the right time, it is likely to benefit from a continuous period of growth. Most organisations today are multi-product and provide a portfolio of products *at different stages in their life-cycles*. This helps to avoid serious fluctuations in profit levels and ensures that the most profitable products provide support for those that have not yet become quite so profitable.

Case Study – Using market segmentation techniques to create defined services for different types of customer

Businesses of all kinds need efficient financial services, but the right financial package for one type of business may be the wrong type for another. The banks are aware of this and have started a process of market segmentation to

ensure that the right company gets the right service at the right times.

An example of this is the division by Midland Bank of its UK business customers into Enterprise (organisations with annual revenues of up to £250 000) and Corporate (revenues of between £250 000 and £250 million). Companies larger than this are handled by the bank's international and investment banking wing, Midland Montagu.

The idea was to enable the bank to concentrate its specialist resources on clearly defined groups of customers, which would then allow branch managers to spend more time on personal customers.

Whichever category a business falls into, it has access to a business centre, staffed by bankers especially trained for that particular field of industry. The idea of segmentation is one which complements that of 'one-stop-shopping' – the customer's needs can all be met under one roof. Both segmentation and one-stop-shopping are weapons in the bank's armoury against competition. Businesses today, more than ever before, want to deal with a bank that understands their needs and provides them with the services they want.

1 Explain why Midland Bank segments its market for business customers.
2 Identify other organisations that segment their products. Show how they apply market segmentation.
3 How might segmentation complement one-stop-shopping?
4 How do you as a bank customer respond to segmentation?

Case Study – Bringing Kettle Chips to Britain

Kettle Foods is Britain's newest and, arguably, most fragile potato crisp maker. In just two years the organisation has obtained a

£5 million slice of Britain's £1.4 billion snacks market. At the start it was told the situation was hopeless, but with luck, a neat distribution deal and hard work it has established itself as the UK's fastest growing food business.

The big manufacturers long ago realised the benefits of premium-priced snacks aimed at adults rather than children. Despite a continually large advertising spend by the larger organisations the premium sector of the market had begun to flatten out. Nirbhao Khalsa and Tim Meyer, the founders of Kettle Foods, perceived there was a real opportunity for something different. Kettle Chips are made from potatoes with a high natural sugar content so that they turn brown during frying; they are cooked in batches on a conveyor and flavoured with natural

ingredients. Larger companies would be horrified at the hand-cooked processes, the labour content of the crisps and the price of the ingredients (the potatoes cost three times as much as those used in traditional crisps).

Kettle Foods has neither a sales force nor an advertising budget. Instead, distribution deals have taken the product into all the big retail chains. The company knows that such deals are essential if it is to survive.

The managers at Kettle Foods feel that new ideas and quality will help to secure the company's future. They have recently launched Kettle Poppins – popcorn flavoured with white cheddar cheese and packaged in black bags.

1 *Using an example, explain what is meant by a premium priced product.*
2 *How important is distribution for the future of Kettle Chips? Does this mean that the company should have invested more in other ingredients in the marketing mix?*
3 *Working in groups, suggest new product ideas to extend the Kettle range. Comment briefly on the ingredients in the marketing mix you would emphasise for your new products.*
4 *Comment on whether it is possible for Kettle Foods to establish itself over a long period in the adult snack market.*

7
Communication

In administering any activity there is a need to organise, control and make decisions. An administrator has to take responsibility not only for his or her own actions, but also for the activities of others. Most administrative tasks require a range of talents in addition to a knowledge of the work, experience and judgement. Central to all administrative functions is the need to be able to communicate effectively, both inside and outside the organisation.

This chapter looks at the nature of communication in the context of administration. Various types of communication are studied – both verbal and non-verbal. Internal and external communication are contrasted.

Theories of management

Over many years, considerable efforts have been made by theorists to develop a clearer understanding of how managers and administrators can spend their time most efficiently. This work has contributed to the development of management theories as a science. For such theories it is possible to identify four broad functions that characterise all **administrative activity**. These are:

● **planning** – deciding what provisions need to be made in the future
● **organising** – making sure that all resources are available at the right moment
● **controlling** – making sure that things happen as they were planned
● **doing** – becoming actively involved in the task at hand.

Having identified these four functions it is possible to relate each to a specific level of management responsibility (see Figure 7.1). **Senior** or **top** managers in an organisation tend to spend a lot of their time planning, some time organising, a lot of their time controlling but very little time actually involved in the tasks. **Middle managers** spend less time planning, more time organising, more time controlling and more time doing the work. **First-line**

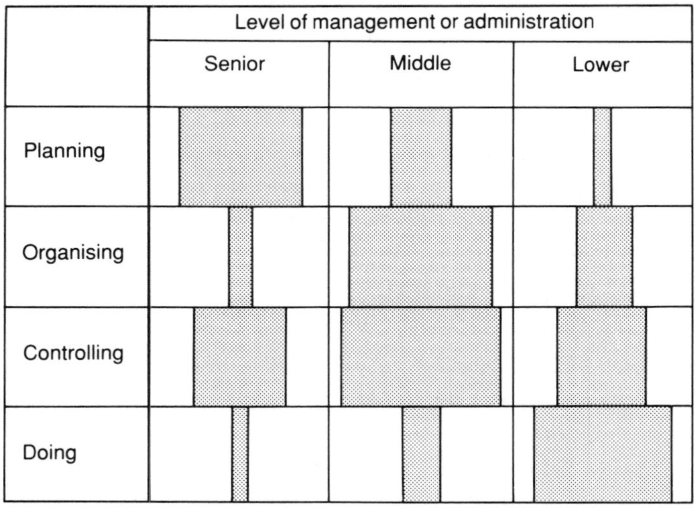

Figure 7.1 **The activities of managers at different levels**

or **lower managers** contribute little to planning, are involved in some organisation and some control, but spend most of their time actively involved in the task at hand.

Case Study – Transforming EMI

Jim Fifield joined EMI Music in May 1988, while in his mid-forties, and became President and Chief Executive Officer a year later. With an impressive career background in one of the largest US consumer product groups, he quickly gave new impetus to the substantial investment already being made in the business. EMI had a worldwide presence, but overall profitability was held back by its relatively small share of the crucial US market. This also limited the availability of US artists with international 'superstar' potential to help develop the strong businesses elsewhere in the world.

Working with his team of executives he set out to instil a 'winning culture' among EMI's 8000 employees worldwide. EMI's regional businesses, covering over 35 countries, were set challenging performance targets. Their ability to respond rapidly to new trends and to develop the all-important artist and repertoire base was aided by strategic acquisitions and partnerships with leading independent record companies. These added powerful new stars to EMI's global galaxy. Compact disc and cassette manufacturing and distribution were consolidated into major regional resources, as a separate, specialised operation. This allowed substantial cost savings. In parallel, a series of acquisitions built EMI's music publishing business into the world leader in its field. This business now contributes a significant share of total profit.

EMI Music ranks as one of the world's 'Top Three' music companies, with annual sales of over £1 billion. But, to Jim Fifield, the continuing goal is to be 'Number One'.

1 What sort of role should a chief executive like Jim Fifield have in a large organisation like EMI?

2 To what extent should the actions of Jim Fifield influence middle and lower managers? How important is it that he should be able to communicate easily with other managers and staff?

The nature of administration

When someone first starts to work for an organisation in a 'junior' position, his or her role is usually limited to a series of clearly defined tasks. As the employee begins to understand more about the functioning of the organisation, his or her duties can develop so as to include a range of simple administrative tasks. The employee's ability to be able to **organise**, **control** and **make decisions** will be crucial to many of these tasks.

Just as you have to organise and control your social activities, the success you have with your work role will depend on how well you can develop your organisational and administrative skills. Imagine you are arranging a party for a group of friends. You might have to

- identify a mutually convenient date
- check that a suitable venue is available
- decide who to invite
- make sure everyone knows when and where the party is taking place
- arrange for the food and refreshments
- borrow some records, tapes and CDs.

Each of these tasks involves you in *organisational* activity. If you had an offer of help from a friend, you might ask that person to sort out the invitations, order some glasses from the off-licence and buy and prepare some food. At the same time you have to oversee all the activities to ensure that the preparations are running smoothly: you are involved in *administration*. You have to monitor the completion of the tasks, providing guidance and help where necessary. You have to make decisions. As the administrator of the event – the party – you set out the plan, work out what needs to be done, work on many of the arrangements yourself, delegate, monitor the preparations; and finally, on the night you make sure that everything runs smoothly.

Task

Make a list of all your work activities. If you are not working, interview someone who is and then make a list of his or her work activities. In either case, indicate which activities involve *organisational* skills and which involve *administrative* skills (some may involve both). Explain briefly the essential difference between organising something and being an administrator.

Responsibility and skills

There is clearly a difference between carrying out day-to-day routines and identifying tasks which require some administration. Administrative tasks involve someone taking on **responsibility**. This responsibility means that someone has to ensure that whatever is meant to happen does actually happen. Administrators must therefore develop **managerial skills**. Whereas routine jobs can be undertaken by virtually anyone given the right background and training, most administrative tasks require an understanding of people and how they work together, a knowledge of the work of the organisation, experience, good judgement and the ability to make decisions.

Task

State which of the following positions involve managerial skills:

a nurse
e farmer
b teacher
c production-
line worker
d sales representative

f chief inspector
of police
g pub landlord
h gardner.

Most people require some form of managerial skill; the type and extent depend on the *degree* of responsibility they want to accept. For example, someone delivering milk to households has to take responsibility for a milk-float, make decisions about what products to carry on it, collect correct money, try to sell customers new products, cater for all of their dairy requirements and generally keep customers happy. To do this well clearly involves some managerial skills.

The need for communication

At the heart of management at all levels of responsibility lies a fundamental requirement to be able to **communicate**. A manager must be able to communicate effectively with all people within his or her span of control. In fact, managers and administrators tend to spend by far the majority of their time communicating with others. If communication as a basic business skill takes up so much time, a knowledge of how to communicate well has to be viewed as a vital requirement for all managers and administrators.

Communication is the two-way process of passing on ideas and information. All organisations need good, clear paths of communication. In Chapter 2 we saw how systematic lines of communication help to create a structure which coordinates the activities between different parts of an organisation. Effective communication in an organisation, however, goes further than this. It enables an organisation to make everyone aware of what they can achieve. It also helps employees solve problems through the use of technical language referring to the more scientific aspects of their work. Finally, by providing a uniform way of giving people information and an opportunity to put their ideas across, communication can be used to avoid misunderstandings, save time, resolve conflicts and provide all employees with a tool to express as clearly as possible what they really mean.

We all have to communicate. To communicate well requires the development of the basic skills of speaking, listening, reading and writing. In addition it involves an awareness and an understanding of the subject, the audience and the environment. Successful communication requires not only that information should be transmitted, but also that it should be fully received and understood. Listening and reading skills are therefore just as important as speaking and writing skills.

Task

Form small groups. Each member of the group should prepare a talk lasting for about one minute and then deliver it to the other members of the group. Analyse the problems encountered by both the speakers and the listeners.

Transmitters and receivers

The process of communication involves a **transmitter** (or sender) sending **messages** to **receivers**. A transmitter should put information into a form the receivers can understand, and this might involve oral, written or visual messages. This process is

known as **encoding**. The transmitter chooses a particular medium to use to send messages to the receivers – letter, report, fax etc. The receivers then interpret the messages through a process of **decoding**.

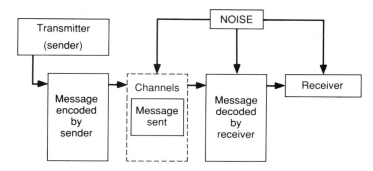

Figure 7.2 The communication process

Though a message flows from the sender to the receivers, there is no guarantee that the receivers will either receive the full message or even understand it. This is because the process may be subject to some form of interference or barrier to communication which affects the smooth flow of information. Communication problems of this nature are known as **noise** and may lead to the downfall of the message. Noise can take the form of any barrier acting as an impediment to the smooth flow of information. Here are a few examples:

- *Language problems* – The language used may not be fully understood, particularly if a receiver comes from a different background from the sender or has considerably less knowledge, technical or otherwise.
- *Jumping to conclusions* – The receiver might read into the message what he or she expects to see, rather than what is really there.
- *Lack of interest* – The receiver may not be prepared to listen to the message. The message has to be designed to appeal to the listener.
- *Competing environment* – Background sounds (real noise) or interference from other activities in the work environment may influence the message, particularly if it is long or complicated and requires concentration by the receiver.
- *Channels of communication* – Effective communication will be hampered if the means

chosen to pass the message is poor.
- *Cultural differences* – We all have different perceptions of the world according to our background and experiences, and this may result in our interpreting a message in different ways.
- *Steps in the message* – If there are too many stages in the message (i.e. if it is too complicated) it may not be properly understood.

Task

Identify at least one situation in which a barrier to communication has affected your interpretation of a message.

Basic communication skills

Communication skills must cover listening, speaking, reading, writing and information technology (IT).

Listening

We tend to think of **listening** as easy. However, we converse with quite a few people during an average day and 'listen to' so much information that it is very easy to forget what we have heard. Sometimes people try to listen to several conversations (i.e. messages) at the same time and only ever pick up snippets of information and never the full picture of events.

Listening involves:

- the process of physically hearing a message
- interpretation of the message
- evaluation, when decisions are made on how to use the information.

A problem with listening to messages can be that, unless you are making notes at the same time, much of the information received is forgotten and not followed up.

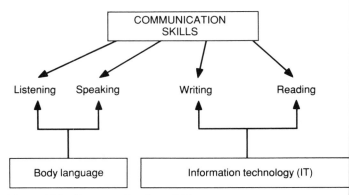

Figure 7.3 Communication skills

Task

Form small groups. Starting with the statement 'When Paul went out of the house he met Sarah', each member of the group should in turn add a simple item of new information; for example, 'When Paul went out of the house he met Sarah and John'. Continue to go round the group like this, without taking notes. At the end, write down as much information as you can remember. Were other group members easy to listen to? Did anyone use non-verbal communication? Was the exercise affected in any way by *noise*? How would taking notes transform this exercise?

Speaking

Speech takes place between people in close proximity to each other. Provided the listener (i.e. receiver) is attentive, ambiguity can be removed by **questioning**. Questioning is a very important process because it can clarify meanings and points of view.

For speech to be an effective means of communication it is important that an individual be aware of:

- his or her own role as a communicator
- the receptiveness of the listeners
- the listeners' own knowledge of the subject.

Writing and reading

Written messages vary from the very simple to the very complex. The following are some examples of situations where written communications are appropriate:

- the information needs to be received by several people in different places
- the information is highly complex, requiring extensive study
- the information needs to be referred to over a period of time.

The written word in some circumstances can be open to **ambiguity** if the receiver is not immediately able to question the sender. For this reason, even informal notes need to be accurate, clear in their meaning and easy to read. Documentation systems are widely used in industry to reduce elements of ambiguity and, very often, drawings and sketches are used to support the written text.

Some types of written communication are more easily read than others. For example, company accounts and other financial and quantitative information may be complex and require the reader to have specialist background knowledge. The target audience and the nature of the information are very important factors to take into consideration when deciding how to present data.

Information technology skills

IT skills are the 'penmanship' of the future. The revolution in information technology has transformed the way in which information is handled, processed and distributed – using desktop computer terminals. The result is that information quality can be improved. It can be accessed more quickly, sent more effectively and can contribute to more effective decision making and subsequent competitive advantage.

Body language

It is possible for some messages to be transmitted even without using the spoken or written word. Non-verbal communication or **body language** can be used on its own or to reinforce the spoken word. We all use physical gestures and show our feelings with facial expressions. Sometimes a gesture or expression on its own can say more than a verbal message – a nod or frown can convey its own special meaning. Being able to observe such signs is an important communication skill.

★Shaking hands	★Folding your arms	★Placing yourself in relation to others
★Shrugging your shoulders	★Leaning backwards or forwards in your chair	★Clenching your fists
★A slap on the back	★An arm around the shoulder	★Nodding your head
★Body posture		

Figure 7.4 Examples of physical gestures

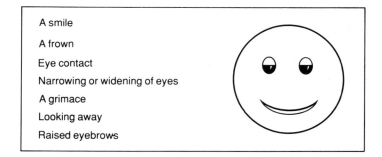

A smile

A frown

Eye contact

Narrowing or widening of eyes

A grimace

Looking away

Raised eyebrows

Figure 7.5 Physical gestures may be supported by facial expressions

Non-verbal communication can provide strong support for any message – it goes beyond the words themselves and gives a clearer view of what the sender really means.

Task

During your next group task, make a point of observing body language – the physical gestures and facial expressions of members of the group.

Explain how the use of such body language helped (or hindered) them in communicating their messages.

Case Study – A man of influence

Jean Peyrelevade is chairman of the Union des Assurances de Paris (UAP), France's biggest insurer and cornerstone of the country's *mixed economy*. A banker by background, he was made chairman in the summer of 1988 by France's newly elected socialist government. Monsieur Peyrelevade is perhaps best known for having been economic advisor to President Mitterand's first Prime Minister in 1981.

A journalist of the time characterised Jean Peyrelevade's role: 'In the socialist party . . . he adopted the habit of expressing, in a very strong and serious voice, certain simple truths which often provoked uproar.'

Since those times M. Peyrelevade has continued to be viewed as an influential figure. Many feel that there is a certain refreshing directness about him. He always takes pains to explain his position clearly and he does not evade questions but tackles them head on.

There are two ways of reading Jean Peyrelevade's mind. The first is to listen carefully to what he *says*

and the second is to look at what he *does*. Instead of looking at takeovers and acquisitions to expand UAP, he would like to see the creation of large groups of European insurers – he feels that co-operation would help to provide expansion for all those involved in such an operation. Given the nature of his approach there is good reason to believe all that he says.

1 *Identify certain key communication skills used by Jean Peyrelevade.*
2 *How important is it for influential figures to have such skills?*
3 *Explain why a good speaker can make listening easy.*

Communicating the message

Before communicating any information the sender needs to think clearly about what is to be achieved. The objective or goal should influence the way the message is communicated. The sender should therefore ask himself or herself a few simple questions:

- What do I hope to achieve by the message?
- With whom am I communicating and how will they react to my message?
- What is my relationship with the receivers, and will this influence the way they react to my message?
- What information should be included in the message?
- What techniques should I use to communicate this particular message?

Task

Imagine that the assignment you intended to hand in this week has not yet been completed. Write a short note to the appropriate member of

the staff explaining why it is late and what you are going to do about it. Use the questions in the text to help you to complete the message.

Feedback

Most messages generate some form of response. For example, a verbal message may provoke a non-verbal shrug or a frown, or another might lead to either a long-winded verbal response or a more formal written answer. These responses to the message are known as **feedback**. Feedback generally indicates how the recipient has interpreted the original message and whether the information has been understood.

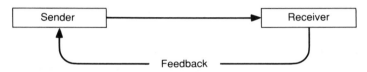

Figure 7.6 Feedback from a message

The nature of the feedback can reflect the *type* of organisation in which the message is directed. In an **authoritarian** structure the sender may not expect a response from the receivers. Managers may issue commands or instructions or make statements to subordinates. This communication is a one-way process. The sender does not expect instructions to be questioned and, as a result, misunderstandings may occur. Conversely, in a **democratic** structure, managers will want to avoid misunderstandings and will positively encourage feedback. By examining the response to a message the manager can assess how it has been received and more closely monitor the feelings of employees.

Internal communications

Internal communications are communications **within** an organisation. The purpose of most forms of internal communication is to transfer information or to initiate some action. Figure 7.7 explains this is more detail.

★ **To present facts/information** – Informing employees may affect their responses to day-to-day decisions or keep them aware of changes in procedures connected with health and safety, breaks etc.
★ **To give instructions** – These may influence how employees carry out their duties.
★ **To provide a basis for negotiation** – Conflict exists in all organisations and internal communication may provide a basis for resolving disputes.
★ **To present findings** – These may be the result of a piece of research.
★ **To motivate employees** – Communication may be used to increase the involvement of employees in the organisation's activities.
★ **To improve teamwork** – It allows employees to work more closely together.

Figure 7.7 Objectives of internal communication

Internal communication may flow:

- downwards – from higher to lower levels
- upwards – from lower to higher levels
- horizontally – between people and departments at the same level
- multi-directionally – in all directions.

A **grapevine** will throw information out in all directions to all interested parties.

Task

Analyse the internal communication methods in an organisation known to you. What sorts of internal communication can you identify (provide examples)? What do these internal communications try to do? How do they flow?

Verbal communications

Verbal communications involve the transmission of information effectively by word of mouth. Speaking is often a vastly underrated skill. It can be used to communicate ideas, reasons and conclusions. A good speaker is likely to have a far greater impact on the receiver of a message than a poor speaker and can provoke a far better response (see Figure 7.8).

1. Express your ideas clearly, using language that is appropriate for your listeners

2. Say exactly what you mean – speak accurately using reliable information and never generalise with statements that go beyond the facts

3. Show empathy with the listeners, and convey enthusiasm

4. Try to be sincere and not put on an act – relax and talk naturally

5. Use tone, expressions and some body language (not too much)

6. Use appropriate pitch and volume

7. Articulate and enunciate well – a regional accent does *not* affect good diction if you speak clearly

Figure 7.8 How to be an effective speaker

Task

Think of anyone you know with good speaking ability. What makes him or her a good speaker? Make a complete list of the qualities of a good speaker. Discuss your conclusions with others in a group situation.

For many people at work, verbal communications tend to be **face-to-face exchanges** for the purposes of relaying messages, personal discussion, giving advice, providing instructions and guidance etc. Such exchanges are particularly appropriate for discussing personal matters and for conveying feelings or confidential facts where information should not be divulged further. Face-to-face contact can create a less formal relationship and allow communicators to get to know each other. Feedback can be instant, so that disagreements can be sorted out quickly. The main disadvantage of face-to-face contact, however, is that it is a time-consuming exercise which usually provides no permanent record of the message unless notes are written. Discussion may lack precision, and this can lead to misunderstandings.

Another area where verbal communications are important is in **meetings** (see Chapter 9). Nearly all employees at all levels in an organisation will spend some time attending meetings; administrative staff and managers will use a large proportion of their time in this way. Meetings are held to deal with issues, problems and areas of concern for an organisation. They provide an opportunity for a group of people to use their specialist backgrounds, experiences and knowledge to contribute to a range of matters.

Perhaps the most frequently used means of verbal communication, after face-to-face contact, is the **telephone**. Telephones are involved in both internal and external communications – they make it possible to communicate directly with people within the organisation, and throughout the country and internationally. Over recent years there has been a massive expansion in telecommunications services which have provided a global connection/highway provided by a single organisation (Cable & Wireless). There are information services (e.g. Prestel), video-conferencing, mobile phones and a very extensive range of other specialised business services.

The massive expansion of **telecommunications** over recent years is not just about new services. An employee's time costs an organisation money. Letters and memos are time-consuming – and therefore expensive – to write; they often then have to be processed before being despatched, and after that a reply must be awaited. With the use of a telephone a reply can be obtained in the shortest possible time – and in fact many systems will allow a number of users into the conversation simultaneously.

It does not always follow, however, that a telephone call saves time. According to one recent estimate, more than a half of all telephone calls fail simply because they do not result in direct communication with the person intended. Another possible drawback of using the telephone is that once a conversation starts it is all too easy for the parties to become sidetracked, and then forget some of the reasons for the call.

Task

Comment upon your own experiences using a telephone. How effective is your telephone style? Are there any situations when you find conversation difficult? How could you improve your technique?

Case Study – Darlo Holdings

John Hoskins is Group Personnel Manager for Darlo Holdings, a company which owns and coordinates the activities of a range of subsidiaries in the rapid-transit parcel and courier industry.

At the group's headquarters in the North East of England, over 200 staff are employed in a modern well-equipped office block in Newton Aycliffe. Over the last 12 months there have been a massive number of changes within the group office. Five directors, including the managing director, have retired and there have been a number of consequential managerial movements – including John's appointment.

The 'new blood' in the boardroom are concerned that their approach to the running of the organisation should be identifiably different from that of their predecessors. They are acutely aware that for a long time the organisation operated as a *power culture*, under the authoritarian rule of the former MD. Their view is that during the early development phase this type of management was successful. However, over recent years the organisation has grown considerably by acquisition, and some managers now feel that such a regime is leading to a lack of motivation and high staff turnover.

At the heart of proposed changes designed to motivate staff at Darlo is the perceived need to create a mechanism which allows staff to be listened to and have their views and contributions taken account of. With these objectives in mind, the directors want to create more face-to-face contact between managers and employees at all levels. *Quality circles* and working groups/meetings have been suggested (see Chapter 9). There is confidence from the new management that, once developed, the system will help to generate new ideas and create an improved atmosphere within the organisation. John Hoskins has been entrusted with the responsibility of introducing these proposals.

1 Advise John Hoskins in detail on the likely advantages and disadvantages of the new proposals.
2 Explain the importance of staff training to help employees to develop verbal skills at meetings if the proposal is to be a success.

Written communications

Written communications are used within an organisation to convey information and ideas to others. They are also used to confirm important verbal messages.

For many people, putting pen to paper implies creating something rather permanent, and there can be fear of being misunderstood, particularly if the document is directed 'upwards' or is to be viewed by a number of other colleagues. Confidence is important, as is the need to read through the message to make sure that you get the message right.

The word **memorandum** (nearly always shortened to 'memo') derives from the Latin *memorare* which means 'thing to be remembered'. Today memos have a wider business use than just as memory aids, having become the most frequently used form of written communication within organisations. They are used to communicate information, instructions and enquiries. Though they are the internal equivalent of letters, there are one or two minor differences. An organisation's name does not normally appear on a memo for internal use, and it is not necessary to have a salutation or complimentary ending. Memos should be kept as short as possible and ideally deal with only one item. Copies of the same memo are often distributed to a number of recipients.

The style of memoranda varies considerably. Instructions from senior management are likely to be written in relatively impersonal language, while a quickly scribbled message on a memo sheet to a close colleague may be in conversational English. It is often necessary to be more careful and diplomatic when writing memos up the ladder, rather than down. On all occasions it is important to take account of people's sensitivities and the position you hold.

```
                    MEMORANDUM


To:   All staff        Ref:  BW/JK
From: B Watson         Date: 12 April 199_
      (Personnel Manager)


     REVISED HEALTH AND SAFETY REGULATIONS


It has come to my attention that there have
been a number of minor accidents in the last
few weeks which have gone unreported. May I
remind you that all accidents involving members
of staff and occurring on company premises must
be recorded in accordance with the guidelines
in the Staff Handbook.

Would all staff please re-read the section
"Safety Procedures" on pages 81 to 84 of their
Staff Handbook. Please also study the copy of the
letter showing how to fill in a safety report.

BW
```

Figure 7.9 A specimen memorandum

Task

Imagine that you are a college administrator. Write a short memo addressed to the relevant personnel, indicating the term-time college dates for the coming year.

Reports are another form of internal written communication. In simple terms, a report is a written communication from someone who has collected and studied some facts to a person who has asked for the facts (and possibly a recommendation) because he or she needs them for a particular purpose or to help with making a decision. It is therefore a basis for some form of action.

Reports may, for example, supply information for legal purposes (e.g. as a result of an incident or accident) or may be presented to shareholders. A report may attempt to assess the consequences of changes in company policy.

A well-written report is concise and does not contain anything the reader does not need to know. It should be clear and logically arranged but, at the same time, should not exclude anything that the reader needs.

Informal reports may be most suitably written or typed on a memo form, as in Figure 7.9. It is important to start with a title, and possibly a brief introduction, before going on to the body of the report. Recommendations for action should be clearly identified if these have been requested.

Formal reports will have many of the features listed below:

- Title page (subject matter, name and position of writer, date etc.)
- Contents page

- Terms of reference (explaining the reason for the report)
- Procedure (how the task was completed)
- Findings
- Conclusions and/or recommendations

When preparing a formal report, decisions have to be made on aspects such as language and style, circulation, and the presentation (including whether the report should have a cover and binding).

Task

Imagine that you are asked by the National Union of Students to write a formal report on the facilities available for students at the college or other place of tuition you are attending.

Your report should be based on *research* covering areas such as library and IT facilities, recreational and social facilities, guidance and counselling, refectory etc., and the strain (if any) put on these facilities by the numbers of students at the college.

Your conclusions and recommendations, clearly identified, should refer to the way in which the availability of facilities affects the working patterns of students at the college.

Minutes are a detailed record of a **meeting** and are often used as a form of internal communication. Such details, displayed on noticeboards or sent to key staff, inform people about decisions taken in various parts of the organisation. For example, in a school, copies of minutes of departmental meetings provide a useful guide to the headteacher on how staff might react to certain decisions. The same headteacher might put details of his or her meetings with deputies on a noticeboard so that other staff are kept up-to-date with developments. The minutes usually state who is responsible for specific actions arising from the meeting.

Before a meeting takes place, an **agenda** will list the items of business to be discussed and the order in which they will be taken. If an agenda is displayed on a noticeboard, a member of the organisation who is not invited to attend the meeting – and who might be concerned about a particular issue – will have the opportunity to have a prior word with someone who is invited.

Notices are another common form of written communication. They are placed in prominent positions and used to publicise any changes in policy, dates to be remembered, functions, events taking place etc. Notices are usually short and related to a single subject. They might be supported by artwork to catch the attention of staff.

House magazines, journals and newspapers are a useful way of communicating policies, information, events and public relations activities to employees throughout an organisation. They are a particularly useful form of internal communication in large organisations where they can be used to help staff to develop their identity within the group and feel a sense of belonging.

Case Study – St Michael News

Marks and Spencer is a company that has always attached great importance to the care and training of its staff. According to Lord Rayner, Chairman of M & S from 1984 to 1991, 'the continued development of our business depends upon the calibre of our people'. The company provides training, personal development and motivational packages which recognise the contributions of all the employees.

The senior management believes that the commitment of staff is greatly enhanced when they feel involved and consulted. Communications groups have been operating in stores for some time. Training encourages staff to use their communication group as an effective vehicle for two-way communication. Another aspect of partnership is the suggestions scheme – called the 'Good Ideas Scheme' – which produces many contributions designed to improve efficiency and save money. A further device to keep employees informed is the staff newspaper called 'St Michael News'.

St Michael NEWS THE STAFF NEWSPAPER OF MARKS & SPENCER

St Michael News is a bi-monthly glossy newspaper made available to all Marks and Spencer staff. It provides an opportunity for senior managers to communicate overall group strategy, successes and achievements and economic matters of interest to all employees – such as profits, store expansions, new systems and company policies. As well as this the newspaper acts as a forum for other events in the group – for example, the introduction of new collections of clothes, new food ranges, homeware products, financial services etc. Other articles cover information on the group's overseas activities, staff profit sharing, community involvement, long-service awards, retirements, and competitions such as crosswords and 'Young Environmentalist of the Year'.

The newspaper helps to reflect the changing culture of the organisation from paternalism to partnership to ensure that values within the organisation are shared and not imposed. With more than 75 000 employees working for Marks and Spencer worldwide, it is generally felt that good communications will improve involvement and help to create a working environment in which everyone wants to contribute.

1 *Comment upon why the Marks and Spencer management today places so much emphasis on partnership with the employees.*
2 *How important is a good internal communication system for creating such a partnership?*

3 *What methods, other than those indicated in the study, could be used to enhance internal communications in a large organisation?*

Visual communications

Visual communications within an organisation may take many forms. Presenting data by means of charts, graphs, drawings or photographs helps to reinforce a message. It also enables complex information to be communicated in a way that is readily acceptable to more people and easier to take in.

Although some visual information within an organisation will have a place on its own, most will be used to support verbal and written communications. For example, during an oral presentation various types of visual aid can be used to support the talk – flip-charts, magnetic boards, overhead projectors, videos, closed-circuit televisions etc.

Charts and diagrams can also be used to support internal written communications, as in a report or house magazine. The graphics in Figure 4.10 on page 87 are examples.

Task

Walk through the school or college you are attending. Make a list of the different types of visual communications.

External communications

External communications are concerned with how an organisation is viewed by others. All of the actions of and communications from an organisation are encompassed. Every organisation has a public face or image, and this conveys a message which affects or influences everyone who has dealings with the organisation – customers, shareholders, suppliers, competitors, governments, communities, international agencies, environmental groups. Providing a positive image through external communication creates a better external environment for the organisation. Successful manipulation of **public relations** convinces others that the organisation is worth dealing with, and might provide it with a considerable strategic and competitive advantage.

Task

Collect a range of external communications from a number of organisations. Comment briefly upon the image created by each item.

As with internal communications, external communications can be divided into verbal, written and visual.

External verbal communications

The most frequently used form of **external verbal communication** is the **telephone**. Its great benefit is that it is fast and allows people who would find it difficult to meet to converse.

A telephone call may be the first point of contact an outsider has with an organisation. If a bad impression is created through this first call, it may be difficult to correct. Developing a telephone technique which makes the caller feel at ease and which creates the impression of efficiency is always important. There are, therefore, basic rules for answering the telephone (see Figure 7.10).

★ Answer calls promptly
★ Greet the caller with 'Good morning' or 'Good afternoon'
★ Be courteous – your tone of voice is crucial
★ Be brief but not abrupt
★ Speak clearly and slowly
★ Be resourceful and *think* of ways you might be able to help
★ Remain calm, even when under pressure
★ Have pencil and paper handy in case you have to take a message (don't forget to record the date and time of the call)

Figure 7.10 How to answer the phone

If you have to make a telephone call yourself, make sure that:

● you have all the necessary information to hand
● you know who you want to talk to
● you are prepared to leave a message on an answering machine if necessary
● you speak clearly.

It may be necessary to have a **face-to-face exchange** with somebody from outside the organisation. In many administrative jobs employees are constantly in situations where they are meeting customers, members of the public, representatives from suppliers, visitors, candidates for jobs etc. Dealing with people on a daily basis requires a degree of sensitivity. It is a bit like being an ambassador – no matter what the response of the person you are dealing with, you need to remain in control of the situation and resolve any dispute or problem using common-sense. In fact, many organisations insist that their employees should conduct themselves in all their dealings with the public as if they were rendering a service.

Task

Imagine that you work for a government department as a civil servant. Make out a list of rules for dealing verbally with the public on a daily basis.

Another form of external verbal communication is an **interview** with somebody from outside the organisation, who may be interested in something the organisation has done (e.g. press, radio or television). Part of a public relations strategy in such circumstances is to build up a positive perception and image of your organisation. Your response should therefore be designed to improve public understanding of your organisation's actions.

Business letters

The **business letter** is still the most widely used form of external communication. It may be used, for example, to:

- make arrangements without the need for parties to meet
- provide both parties with a permanent record of such arrangements
- confirm verbal arrangements.

A well-written business letter conveys its message while maintaining goodwill. If a letter is sent promptly, is well set out and conveys its message accurately, the recipient will develop a favourable impression of that organisation, and is more likely to want to have further dealings than if the letter is tardy and inaccurate.

Task

Make a list of the advantages of using written communications outside the organisation, rather than some other means. Draw up another list covering the disadvantages.

To write an effective letter requires adequate **preparation**. It might be necessary to investigate the background to the letter by searching through previous correspondence, which may be stored in a file. As you research your letter, its necessary contents will become apparent to you. For example, you might have to:

- seek information as the result of an enquiry
- express an opinion
- deal with a problem or a fault
- place an order
- confirm an order
- seek references
- check creditworthiness
- obtain quotations
- quote a price
- seek payment for a debt
- convey a personal message.

Task

Collect examples of business letters you or your family have received from a variety of different organisations. What was each letter for? Comment upon the impression conveyed by each letter.

The layout, style and appearance of business letters – and even the envelope – varies from organisation to organisation. Most will endeavour to create a good impression, particularly by giving attention to the heading and layout. Organisations often have a **house style** which they encourage all clerical staff to follow. Business letters are usually typed on A4 or A5 paper, and a fully blocked open-punctuated style is now the most common form of display.

A typical business letter will have the following features:

- a heading or **letterhead** (Heinemann Educational in Figure 7.11)
- a **reference** – enabling the letter to be filed and traced later

Our ref: PJ/bw

HEINEMANN
EDUCATIONAL

Halley Court, Jordan Hill
Oxford OX2 8EJ

12 April 199

Telephone Oxford (0865) 311366
Telex 837292 HEBOXF G
Facsimile (0865) 310043

Mr J Saunders
18 First Close
Sutton Coldfield
West Midlands
B73 7DH

Dear Mr Saunders

Manuscript for BTEC publication

Thank you for sending me the BTEC manuscript so promptly. I read it over the weekend and was impressed with its content.

Over the next few weeks the manuscript will be out for review, after which I may have some suggestions for amendments.

Could you please send us a list of acknowledgements, and any photographic materials you may wish to include. If there are any further requirements I shall be in touch.

Yours sincerely

Peter James
Editorial Assistant

A division of Heinemann Educational Books Limited.
Part of Reed International Books
Registered Office: Michelin House, 81 Fulham Road, London SW3 6RB
Registered in England No: 677944

Figure 7.11 An open-punctuated fully blocked business letter

- a **date**
- the **inside address** – which is that of the recipient
- the **salutation** (Dear Mr Saunders)
- the **subject heading** (Manuscript of BTEC publication)
- the **body** of the letter
- the **complimentary close** (Yours sincerely . . .)

There is a convention about pairings of salutation and complimentary close. When the name of the recipient is not known, so that 'Dear Sir/Madam' is used, this should be paired with 'Yours faithfully'. When the name is known and 'Dear Mr/Mrs . . .' is used, this should be paired with 'Yours sincerely'. If the recipient is addressed by his or her first name,

this may be paired with 'Kind regards . . . Yours sincerely'.

When a letter is sent with **enclosures**, this is denoted by the letters 'Enc' or Encs' at the foot of the letter to alert the recipient to this fact.

When writing a business letter always plan what you are going to say beforehand. Organise your information into a logical sequence and try to keep your language simple. Be courteous yet direct. After you have written the letter, check it for spelling mistakes and grammatical errors.

Task

You have just received a batch of 50 reams of headed stationery from Monsons Press Ltd. Unfortunately the printer has used the wrong size paper and has used an out-of-date heading. It is generally unsuitable for office use. You have checked that the printer was given the correct information.

Draft a letter of complaint, open a file on a word-processor, type in your letter and print a copy.

A form of external communication which has experienced massive expansion over recent years – and which is capable of sending both written and visual information – is **facsimile** ('fax'). Fax machines send information electronically over telephone lines.

As an alternative to writing letters, organisations today may occasionally use **electronic mail**. The 'mail-box' is a computer terminal linked to a telephone network; it can put messages into the system and store messages that have been sent through the system. Every user has a password to allow him or her to use the system. A message can be sent to several recipients at once. The message is stored in a terminal's memory until the mail-box is 'opened'. There are now a number of subscriber-based systems, such as Telecom Gold. The main advantage over ordinary mail is speed of transmission.

Case Study – Interruptions to electricity supplies

1 *Why was it important for the Managing Director – Power to write this external communication?*
2 *How difficult would it have been to write such a letter?*
3 *Have you any criticism of this communication?*

NORTHERN ELECTRIC

NORTH YORKSHIRE REGIONAL OFFICE
DUNDAS STREET
THE STONEBOW
YORK
NORTH YORKSHIRE
YO1 2PQ
TELEPHONE: (0904) 628941

19 Dec 90

Dear Customer,
INTERRUPTIONS TO ELECTRICITY SUPPLIES – December 1990

I am writing personally to you, a valued customer of Northern Electric, to apologise for any inconvenience caused when there were widespread interruptions of electricity supplies following the severe winter weather during the weekend of 7/8 December 1990.
I am aware of the hardship and distress that has been endured by many of our rural customers in North Yorkshire and I felt that it was appropriate for me to express the concern which the Company had for all during this emergency.
Weather conditions were extremely severe and a combination of high winds, low temperatures and wet snow caused a large build up of ice on the conductors of overhead power lines. The weight of the ice on the line caused conductor breakages and pole failures. The damage was extensive throughout North Yorkshire and some 30,000 customers were off supply for varying periods ranging from a few hours to in excess of one week in some isolated rural locations.
The substantial task of repairing the damage and restoring supplies was given top priority and additional resources were drafted in from other Regions of Northern Electric. Some 350 linesmen and engineers worked long hours in the field and in the Depot Control Centres co-ordinating arrangements for the major repair operations.
They were supported by Customer Information Staff who manned telephones around the clock to deal with customers' calls and to provide the best information available at the time. Up to 9 helicopters were brought in to assist in repair work as soon as flying conditions were possible and the Army provided valuable assistance in flying in men and materials to troubled areas.
The extent of the disruption caused by the storm in respect of electricity supplies was the most severe that we can recall in North Yorkshire and I was surprised to see the degree of devastation when I visited the Region and toured some of the affected areas after the storm. As always in occurrences such as this there may be lessons to be learnt and action will be taken if appropriate to improve the service to our customers and our ability to deal with extremes of weather.
I have written in general terms because although all rural customers were not directly affected by supply interruptions you may have found other services disrupted as a result of loss of electricity supply. May I take the opportunity to thank you for your patience and tolerance in these difficult circumstances.

Yours sincerely

R Dixon
Managing Director – Power
Northern Electric plc. Registered Office: Cariol House. Market Street. Newcastle upon Tyne NE1 6NE
Registered in England Number 2366942

Figure 7.12 A letter of explanation and apology

Other means of communicating externally

Advertising is a form of external communication. At the heart of advertising lies the knowledge of how consumers will respond to different strategies and how these strategies might affect the image of the organisation. Assessing the effectiveness of advertising is difficult because it goes beyond just selling products.

Many large organisations send out an **annual report** to shareholders and the news media. The document, as well as publishing information required under the Companies Act, often contains non-financial reports covering overall strategies, social and environmental objectives etc. Some of these documents are lavish, with coloured illustrations to enhance the image and help to convey information.

Magazines, publicity literature and educational services, in both the public and private sectors, provide strong informed links between organisations and their various publics. For example, organisations send out brochures in response to enquiries in order to indicate what their activities, functions, beliefs and objectives are. Large organisations such as BP, the banks, British Rail, Shell and the Inland Revenue have their own educational services which supply packs of information and resources to schools and colleges on request.

Corporate videotapes have become increasingly popular over recent years as a method of providing a variety of interested parties with visual information about an organisation's activities. **Visits** and **open days** are another popular method of giving people a 'window' into an organisation – the Sellafield Visitors Centre claims to provide a 'window into a nuclear world' and has become a top tourist attraction in the North West of England. By means of **exhibitions**, organisations provide outsiders with a clearer understanding of their activities.

Point-of-sale displays and demonstrations attract the attention of consumers, generate interest and encourage them to approach and inspect a product before making a decision to purchase.

Videoconferencing allows organisations to hold face-to-face meetings between groups of people at two or more locations, nationally and internationally. Everyone can see and hear what is going on. British Telecom has eleven videoconferencing centres in cities and towns through the UK, and over 100 rooms are presently available worldwide with new locations being added all of the time. They can be booked in advance on a half-hourly basis. Videoconferencing can be used for meetings, product launches, press announcements and training sessions.

Case Study – Videoconferencing coming of age in the Gulf war

While the Gulf war crucified the airline industry, it provided a real boon to other businesses. Videoconferencing saw its prospects improve. People still had to meet and, if travel was too risky, an interactive TV link would be just as good. Said Steve Gaudy, marketing and sales manager for BT's Visual and Broadcast Services arm: 'The Gulf crisis was a watershed. Turnover has doubled since the Gulf conflict and revenue is now growing at 30–40% year-on-year.'

Videoconferencing

While the technology for videoconferencing and corporate TV networks has been around for almost thirty years, it is only in the last ten that it has begun to take off. The UK is catching up fast. There are now ten permanent networks in Britain, seven using British Aerospace's Satellite Management International (SMI) and three with BT. The total figure is expected to double soon.

Recent reports suggest that the videoconferencing market worldwide will grow ten-fold by 1995. Last year the market was worth around £121 million. A two-hour videoconferencing call from London to New York with six people at both sides costs about £1500.

BT is aiming to further develop its facilities through product innovation. On the drawing board is the 'videophone' – a miniature camera and screen attached to the telephone system and a personal computer. This would turn videoconferencing into desktop conferencing.

1 *How might videoconferencing save organisations money? (Hint: Consider the costs of time and travel.)*
2 *Comment briefly on the other benefits provided by videoconferencing.*
3 *How might such benefits provide organisations with a competitive advantage?*

Case Study – British Nuclear Fuels PLC

Nuclear energy now accounts for about one-fifth of the electricity produced in Britain; in Scotland the proportion is almost one-half. Fuel for all the nuclear power stations in Britain is produced by British Nuclear Fuels PLC (BNFL), which offers the complete nuclear fuel cycle service from uranium enrichment, through fuel manufacture and transport to spent fuel reprocessing and waste management. To counter adverse public images, the company encourages understanding of its operations by providing a range of publications and by offering a variety of public relations functions and activities.

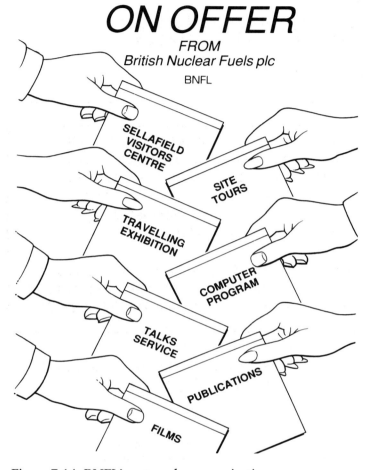

Figure 7.14 BNFL's external communications

1 Why are external communications of fundamental importance to BNFL?

2 Comment on the range of communications available. In each case, state whether it is verbal, written or visual.

8
Using Information Technology in Organisations

In this chapter we look at ways of handling information in the office of a modern organisation. All organisations process a great deal of information, so information systems lie at the heart of effective data management. The chapter therefore looks at different types of information, and the processes involved in handling it.

We go on to explore many important features of modern information technology (IT), including word processing, databases and spreadsheets – as well as more elaborate packages such as 'expert systems' and some of the very latest developments. The emphasis is on using *appropriate* technology rather than using technology for its own sake.

The activities are designed to encourage you to think about your own IT competence, and what **you may need to do to improve your existing skills.**

A few years ago the '**electronic office**' was regarded as a radically new idea. Today most organisations include some elements of the electronic office, and indeed in many organisations such developments have been steadily upgraded to new levels of 'hi-tech'.

The range of office activities that can be automated is increasing all the time, as is the number of ways of automating them. On the computing side – as opposed to telephony, photocopying and other elements of the electronic office – word processing, electronic message handling, financial modelling and computerised personal organisers are commonplace.

Task

What elements of the electronic office are used in your college, or in another organisation with which you are familiar? Draw a diagram like Figure 8.1 to show the range of applications.

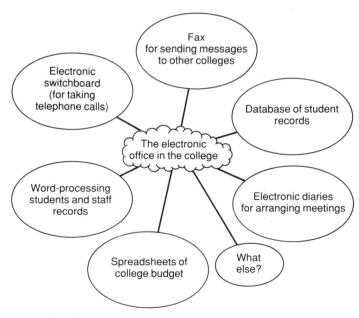

Figure 8.1 Some IT inputs

- Fax for sending messages to other colleges
- Electronic switchboard (for taking telephone calls)
- Database of student records
- The electronic office in the college
- Word-processing students and staff records
- Electronic diaries for arranging meetings
- Spreadsheets of college budget
- What else?

Many people working during the 1980s felt that **information technology** (IT) was adopted by many companies for the sake of appearing 'with it'. The organisations that were really successful with their office automation were those that implemented the product rather than simply installing it. When installing new information technology it is best to look at the needs of the organisation first. It may be most appropriate to gear the IT towards the existing physical and human systems in the organisation.

At the end of this chapter there is a task that asks you to look at your own IT skills. Perhaps there will be some areas you would like to improve upon.

Information technology skills

Information technology is now so widespread that it is useful to distinguish between:

- **general IT skills** needed across a range of jobs
- **specialist IT skills**, mainly at the professional level, needed for the development of sophisticated technology software and systems.

General IT skills

Very few jobs have been unaffected by information technology. Virtually all types of employees need some familiarity with the technology and its application in their particular working environment.

- *Managers* need sufficient understanding of the latest developments to spot new business opportunities and to carry out changes.
- *Technicians, maintenance and craft workers* need to deal with IT components in plants and vehicles of all types.
- *Clerical workers* have to be familiar with a variety of word-processing, spreadsheet, database and similar applications.
- *Professionals* need to use specialist IT applications – including 'expert systems' – as an aid to their decision-making.

Over the past decade at least, the rapid spread of

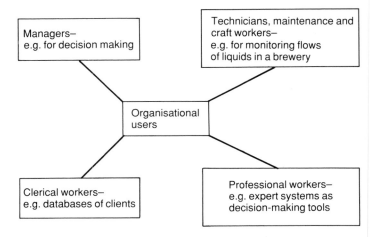

Figure 8.2 Users of IT in the workplace

microcomputers – and more recently of computer networks – has been matched by a good level of competence by a large proportion of the country's workforce. Over the next ten years, many organisations will be trying hard to catch up with the 'leading-edge' businesses of the 1980s.

People in the leading-edge businesses will in turn be developing their IT skills to work effectively with increasing integration between separate IT systems. They will be finding effective ways of using 'expert systems' and searching out the new opportunities and products from major telecommunications advances and new uses for robotics. We will be describing many of these changes in this chapter.

Specialist IT skills

Many of the readers of this book will become (if they are not already) generalist users of IT. In particular you will make use of the range of IT skills (as well as others) shown in Figure 8.3.

Some of the readers of this book may also become **specialist users** of IT skills. About one per cent of the working population (approximately a quarter of a million people) are in one of the IT professions. The numbers have grown by about 20 per cent since 1985. Despite the slowdown of the British economy in the early 1990s, numbers of recruits to this

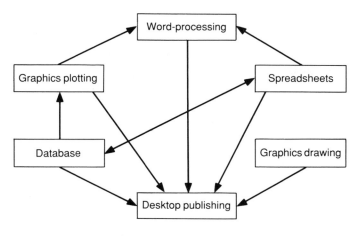

Figure 8.3 General IT skills

industry are expected to continue growing by up to 5 per cent a year for the rest of the century. The growth of this job sector is therefore one of the fastest in the country.

How IT can change the running of an organisation

A traditional business is often organised into **functional specialisms**. Each person in the organisation carries out one step before passing the job on to someone else. Often a job is passed from one department to another. Figure 8.4 shows this sort of flow – work starts on the left of the diagram. For example, market research is carried out by a few

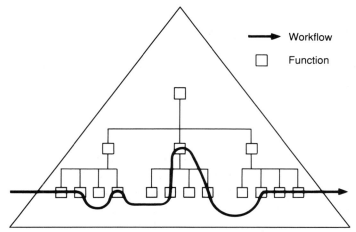

Figure 8.4 In a functional organisation the work flows step by step

people in the marketing department, who pass the results to the technology department. The technology department comes up with some proposals which are passed to production . . . and so on.

The departments shown in the diagram have worked together in a flow on a particular '**business process**', which is simply a set of work activities arranged logically to realise a business objective.

Task

Can you identify a business process in an organisation with which you are familiar? How are tasks passed on in a flow from one department to another?

Transformed businesses

Today many business writers use the term '**transformed business**'. Such an organisation is run according to business processes rather than functional specialisms. The business processes are handled by teams of people from different functions, working together to achieve the aim of the process.

In a 'transformed business' people involved in particular processes are given more freedom to make decisions and have more information at their finger-tips by virtue of information technology. Instead of having to get permission from their line manager, they are allowed to make important decisions. Senior managers then become more concerned with external matters than with running the internal system.

Organisations based on business processes put a high premium on information and on sharing IT facilities. IT has a very important role to play. Groups working together in a team will need to share information, and computer terminals of different specialists are linked so that information is available to all.

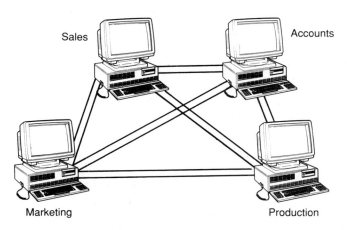

Figure 8.5 A network of information can be made available to the process team

One major benefit is a cost reduction as a result of simplifying the work flow. A job stays with one individual or team instead of passing in batches from specialist to specialist. The team is given the authority to make decisions, as well as the information and tools needed.

Another benefit is the improved responsiveness to customers' needs. Front-line staff are given powers to act rather than pass problems up to line managers.

Improved job satisfaction can be a result. Staff can share customer satisfaction with a job well done. They are more challenged and more fulfilled. The staff are part of a learning, adapting organisation focused on the customers' requirements.

Task

Study an organisation which uses IT widely. To what extent is information shared in the organisation? What

are the effects on decision-making? Can decisions be made more easily by individuals, or do they still need to be passed to supervisors or senior managers?

Make lists of what you consider to be the major advantages and disadvantages of

a *traditional functional organisations*
b *process-based transformed organisations*.

Computer usability

It is not long since a high proportion of the population was frightened by computers. The machines appeared to be highly complex, came with daunting manuals, and seemed to stop co-operating at the most inconvenient times. Modern computers have become more consumer-orientated, and a lot of thought has gone into making sure that they are '**user-friendly**' and that they meet organisational needs.

Computers rely on end-users to tell them what to do, but the biggest problem many new computer owners face is discovering how to get the equipment to do what it is asked.

A major breakthrough came with the development of **graphical user interfaces** (GUIs, or 'gooies'). GUIs are making the technology easier to understand and to use – they are literally changing

Figure 8.6 Icons

the face of computers. Instead of sitting there with a blank screen, a GUI presents you with a series of small pictures, called **icons**, which represent the various options available to you. A pointing tool, such as a 'mouse', is used to move an arrow around the screen and to select the icon for the desired action. At the press of a key the screen then redraws itself to show the next set of options. If the user has selected 'word-processing', for example, the screen will change to show him or her a second series of options; each option chosen leads to a further series of choices.

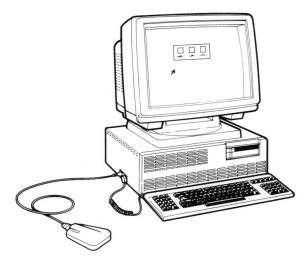

Figure 8.7 Selecting an item from the menu

Windowing systems go one stage further, giving the same type of graphical **interface** but allowing the user to carry out several tasks simultaneously. He or she can be writing a document in the word-processing window, while an address list, stored in the system, can be sorted at the same time. As with everything else in the computer industry, a variety of different windowing systems is available, depending on the machine type.

Task

Design icons which would help a computer user to identify the following facilities:

a word-processing *c* spreadsheet
b database *d* drawing and artwork.

What can be done with data?

In a modern office a number of operations make use of **data**. One way of looking at an organisation is as an 'information processing system'. As in any system there will be a means of transforming **inputs** into **outputs** by a number of processes. Today many of these processes are carried out with the support of information technology.

Here are a number of processes which take place in modern organisations, all involving data:

- recording
- checking
- classifying
- sorting
- summarising
- calculating
- storing
- retrieving
- reproducing
- communicating.

An example

We will demonstrate the kind of things we might want to do with data by using an example. An electricity company keeps records of customers and their outstanding accounts. It may keep a record of the amount owned by the Patel family who live at Greenlawns.

The company will keep a regular **record** of amounts owing for electricity used, the amounts paid by the family and the balance owed. Every now and then it will want to **check** on this information – for example, when the Patels have a query on their account.

The company may want to **classify** the information about the Patel's account into various subheadings – for example, into totals of electricity used at peak and off-peak times.

The information can be **sorted** in many ways – for example, into date order to show how much electricity the Patels used at different times of the year. The electricity company can sort out which customers have unpaid balances; and at the end of a quarter all the figures can be **summarised** to show the total amounts outstanding.

Calculations can be done with figures – for example, adding amounts owed and subtracting payments made.

All of the details relating to the Patel's account can be **stored** on files and **retrieved** from these files when required. This information can be **reproduced**, perhaps by making a copy of the Patel's records to send to them as a statement of account. This information can then be quickly **communicated** to them.

Simply by looking at one account we have been able to point to a wide range of **data-processing** activities.

Task

1 Describe how each of the data-processing activities outlined in the text can be related to:
   a your own student records
   b your bank or building society statement.
2 Show how you use data processing to keep personal records – for example, in budgeting or keeping a diary.

Word-processing, databases and spreadsheets

The most common information processing in modern offices carried out using information technology are word-processing, databases and spreadsheets.

Word-processing

Word-processors are used to manipulate text. They display on a screen and record in memory the text that a person enters on a keyboard. However, the word-processor can do far more. For example:

- New text can be put on to the screen while existing text moves to create space for it.
- Blocks of text can be moved around on the document that is being created.
- The text can be spaced out to fill the whole line.
- A word or phrase can be searched for, and if necessary it can be removed or replaced by another word or phrase.
- A header or footer (a piece of text that is printed at the top or bottom of each page) can be added.

You will know from your own use of word-processors that there are many other exciting features. For example:

- Different printing styles (such as italics, underlined text and so on) can be shown on screen either as different colours or as they would appear when printed. This is referred to as WYSIWYG (pronounced 'wizzywig'), which stands for 'what you see is what you get'.
- Text can be written in more than one column, as in newspapers.
- Graphics can be put into the text.
- A number of similar letters can be produced, with information added from a database on each letter. For example, if a company has a database of its suppliers and wishes to contact the local ones, the

database can be used to select all suppliers who are situated in the same county. The word-processor will then print a letter for each supplier, adding the individual information such as the name and address and salutation. This is called 'mailmerge'.

- A spelling checker can be used. This checks all the text against a dictionary and points out any word that it does not recognise, perhaps because it is spelt incorrectly. However, if you have used a technical word that the computer is not aware of, you can enter the new word into the computer's memory.

Desktop publishing

The improvements in word-processing systems and their ability to produce graphics and to operate with great efficiency, has made **desktop publishing** (DTP) possible. Special **computer programs** (also called **software packages**) make it possible to produce pages of text and graphics combined, to a very high quality of finish.

Different typefaces can be used, diagrams can be placed on pages with text flowing around them, and so on. Pictures can be introduced into the document and stretched or shrunk to fit a space. DTP is being used to produce items such as reports, company newsletters, training books and advertisements.

Task

Using a word-processor, draft a letter to the person responsible for your work experience placement, thanking him or her for the help and support you have received. Print the first draft and discuss it with your tutor. Then do several redrafts of the letter until you are happy with the final format. Save and print the document at each stage so that you can discuss progress with your tutor.

Task

If you have access to a desktop publishing system, use it to produce a cover sheet that can be adapted for each of your Business Studies assignments. The cover should be designed so that you can quickly amend it to word-process the new title of each assignment.

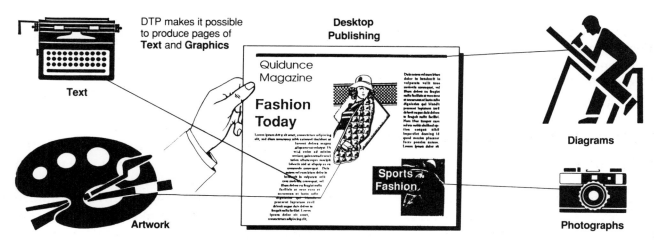

Figure 8.8 **A layout produced by DTP**

Databases

A **database** is a store of facts that can be called upon to provide information. A database may be used, for instance, in a bank or building society to store information on the state of all accounts. A database may be kept by a church to keep a record of all members of the congregation and their addresses. One may be used by a football club to keep a record of all tickets sold to various matches, and so on. Data (that is, information) is fed into the base in a clear form.

For example, a supplier might have a record of the account of Amin Stores. It would store the information in a number of fields – such as address, value of goods supplied, payments received, and balance of the account. If Mr Amin rings up asking for the state of his account, the supplier can simply order the computer to produce the appropriate information and display it on the screen.

Under the provisions of the **Data Protection Act,** companies wishing to store any personal information on a computer system must register with the government-appointed Data Processing Officer. It is necessary to indicate the type of data being stored and the use made of it. Individuals have the *right* to request (on payment of a small fee) details of any information held about them by *any* firm, and to require mistakes to be corrected.

Task

The students in your group may need to work together from time to time. If you were to compile a database of information about members of your group, what would you include in it? Bear in mind that the database should make it easier for the group to work together, and the data will be available for all students to consult at any time. Is there any information you should definitely *not* put in?

Using a database

Any work with a database needs careful **planning**. Once you have decided what you want to investigate you need to think:

- What questions do I want to ask?
- What information needs to be collected to answer the questions?

When using a database it is important to be **consistent**. For example, when entering figures you should not put 1.50 metres in one place and 150cm in another place (they are of course the same thing). If you use NAME, decide whether you mean first or second name. If you use GENDER, decide whether you will use male/female or man/woman, and so on.

Figure 8.9 shows a **printout** of information collected from one particular respondent to a market research questionnaire.

NAME	:	JONES
GENDER	:	MALE
BOVRIL	:	YES
CHEESE	:	NO
SALT/VIN	:	YES
ONION	:	NO
PLAIN	:	YES
TOMATO	:	NO
FAV	:	SALT/VIN

Figure 8.9 A section of printout

When information is extracted from a database you can present it in a variety of different forms, including pie-charts and bar-charts (see Figures 4.10 in Chapter 4). A database can be a very useful means of doing research, particularly if you are working in a group. You can work together to enter information into the base. However, make sure that you are aware of the purpose of the database and how to enter information consistently.

Spreadsheets

A **spreadsheet** is a table of numbers which can be organised and altered on a computer. A spreadsheet is used when making forecasts and doing calculations – the computer does the work for you. Spreadsheets are used extensively in financial forecasting.

For instance, a firm will make a forecast of all the money that will come in and go out of the firm over a 12-month period. The person using the spreadsheet can then alter the inputs to calculate the effect, for example, of lowering a heating bill by a certain amount each month. The computer will automatically recalculate the columns to change the heating figures, total cost figures and profits for each month. It will also recalculate the total profit figure.

In this way a managing director, accountant or any other user of a spreadsheet can quickly carry out business calculations – such as working out the effects of minor changes.

Task

Imagine that you are responsible for the financial management of a service station, and you need to plan your *budget* for the coming year. A budget is a series of figures indicating the possible income of your business (i.e. the money that you expect to take) and the outgoings (the money you have to spend). You think that the possible *sales income* for the year of your service station may consist of the following:

	£
Petrol	1 440 000
Lubricants	15 600
Confectionery	48 000
Fast foods (sandwiches and drinks)	8 400

Groceries	10 800
Accessories (such as torches, batteries)	14 400
Newspapers/magazines	12 000
Toys/greetings cards	3 600
Books/tapes	4 800
Cigarettes/tobacco	78 000

You estimate *outgoings* for the year to consist of the following:

	£
Staff wages	36 000
Insurance	1 500
Heat/light/power	4 500
Security charges	1 200
Rent/rates	4 200
Maintenance/repairs	2 100
Office supplies	5 400
Depreciation (estimated amount by which your assets decline in value during the year	3 600
Petrol	1 080 000
Lubricants	12 000
Stock for the shop	150 000

Your first task is to prepare a computer spreadsheet to cover a 12-month period, assuming that incomings and outgoings are spread evenly over all months of the year. Figure 8.10 on page 162 can be used as a guide.

When your spreadsheet is completed, you can experiment with some 'what if?' situations:

a *What if petrol sales were twice your original estimate – How would that affect overall profit? You would obviously have to pay more for your stocks of petrol from the depot, but would you also have to spend more money on wages?*

b *What if wages increase by 10 per cent in June? How does this affect the end-of-year profit figure?*

c *What if rent and rates on the site are increased by 20 per cent from 1 March?*

d *What if the cost of petrol and lubricants rises by 10 per cent in November with no corresponding increase in prices to motorists?*

INCOME	JAN	FEB	MAR	APR	ETC.
Petrol					
Lubricants					
Confectionery					
Fast food					
Groceries					
Accessories					
Newspapers/magazines					
Toys/greetings cards					
Books/tapes					
Cigarettes/tobacco					
TOTAL INCOME					
OUTGOINGS					
Staff wages					
Insurance					
Heat/light/power					
Security charges					
Rent/rates					
Maintenance/repairs					
Office supplies					
Depreciation					
Petrol					
Lubricants					
Stock for shop					
TOTAL OUTGOINGS					

Figure 8.10   The spreadsheet

Using the right technology

Changes in information technology go on at a tremendous rate. Today's growing product may next year be in decline. One way in which a small business can get an edge on bigger companies is through the appropriate use of technology. **Personal productivity** is one key to small business profitability. The link between time and money is very strong.

Two current methods of increasing productivity are through portable computers and cellular telephones. There is hardly a plumber, electrician, gardener or carpenter who can afford to miss a telephone call from a prospective customer. Employees on the move can now take a cellular phone with them. For a travelling office worker a portable microcomputer can make time spent in airport lounges and hotel rooms productive. Some portable machines are now just as powerful as desktop computers.

Hot competition in the personal computer market has produced a wide variety of products at low prices. These include easy-to-use word-processors, coupled with inexpensive but sophisticated laser printers which can make the correspondence of a small business look as slick as that from a large organisation with an inhouse typesetter. Nowadays paperwork from a number of modern personal computers can be sent by facsimile (faxed) directly to offices around the world.

The typical small business office will have a telephone, photocopier, fax machine, computer printer and telephone answering machine. Today there are many new products that combine all or just some of these functions.

Communications

The telephone network and other telecommunications networks make communication between computers possible in a number of ways. Here are some examples:

- Direct communication of data between organisations or between branches of the same organisation.
- Use of an 'email' (**electronic mail**) service such as Telecom Gold. To use this, a subscriber sends a message using the telephone line addressed to another subscriber; when the other subscriber calls the service he or she receives the message. The advantage over ordinary mail is speed.
- Using **remote databases**. Several large computer databases have been set up for specialist use, covering rapidly changing areas like case law, information on companies and medical knowledge. For a fee, individuals can call up and do a **search** on specific topics. Searches can specify a combination of factors. For example, an enquiry can be made for medical information referring to 'Aids' and 'Cardiff' to find only those items referring to both – the information is found rapidly and should be up-to-date.

Up-to-the-minute information is of tremendous benefit to a wide range of organisations.

Task
Describe how up-to the-minute database information helps the following organisations:

a the police
b hospitals
c oil companies.

Networking

If an organisation is using a number of personal computers, it is likely that some of the information on one will be useful to another user. It is possible to connect the machines together using a **local area network** (LAN), and this allows data to be transferred between machines.

There are two basic ways of using a LAN. In one, the computers work using their own programs and their own data, but can exchange data when required. In the other, the program and data are held on one machine, called a **file server**, and the others act as '**terminals**', updating the data on the file server.

Further important IT applications

As well as the more general uses of IT we have outlined, we should consider some of the more specialist uses that aid decision-making.

Project planning

Computers and their databases can be used to assist in *project planning*. Packages are used to plan and monitor a project consisting of a number of interrelated stages called **activities**. First the activities are defined and the time taken by each is estimated. Then the way in which the activities depend on each other is defined. The computer calculates the total time for the project and shows the activities which must be completed on time for the project not to be delayed.

A very simple example is the building of a new office. The activities and times may be:

1 Prepare land and build foundations	30 days
2 Build walls	30 days
3 Build roof	15 days
4 Install equipment	30 days
5 Equip office	20 days

Activity 1 must be done first, then 2, then 3. However, 4 and 5 – although they must come after 3 has finished – can be done at the same time. Therefore the total time for the project is only 105 days (30 + 30 + 15 + 30), not 125 days. The computer output will also tell you that activity 5 is not critical; that is, it can start late or take longer than planned without delaying the project.

This IT tool helps the project manager to determine the tasks that must be given top priority.

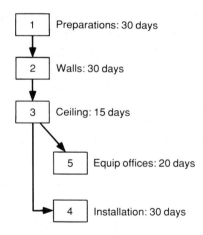

Figure 8.11 Planning the building of an office

Most versions of this computer program can also plan the use of resources on activities, record costs and produce a variety of reports. While this example would be too simple to require a program, we can see how useful such a facility could be in developing a project involving, say, 1000 or more activities.

Expert systems

Expert systems are becoming increasingly popular. They are computer programs consisting of a set of **rules** based on the knowledge of experts. These rules can be used to form conclusions on information the program is given. Imagine, for example, that you feed into the computer all the rules that experts know about a particular field – geology. Geologists could feed in all the information they know about conditions in which particular minerals are likely to be found. The program can then be used to support researchers looking for new mineral fields. One oil exploration company's geological experts have formulated the rules they use in deciding whether a certain area is likely to contain oil deposits. Data on different areas can then be fed in to the program and it will assess the chances of oil in a similar way to a human expert.

These programs are of particular use where a human expert is not available at the time. One interesting use is in medicine where a program is being tested to aid diagnosis. It is used by the patient, not the doctor, the idea being that for personal and intimate problems a patient may answer questions more easily from a machine than from a person. It also means that trivial problems can be diagnosed without using the doctor's time.

One big problem with setting up expert systems is that it is often surprisingly difficult for experts to define exactly how they reach decisions.

Task

Describe three situations in which you think an *expert system* would assist decision-making.

Ergonomics, health and safety

Office systems are the subject of a European Commission directive to be implemented by the end of 1992, and attention to safety aspects is increasing.

Enlightened self-interest makes this subject important to all organisations. Attention needs to be paid to **ergonomic factors** in offices if key personnel are not to be lost through injury or illness. Also, injured parties may make claims against organisations.

The main difficulty facing employers is that many of the ills associated with office technology are not well understood. For example, it used to be thought that orange characters on a brown screen were the last word in comfort for the eyes of a computer operator; now black on paper-white is widely favoured. Ergonomics in this context is still an imprecise science. Screen flicker is clearly harmful in the long run, and flicker-free monitors are becoming available. The reaction of the body to electromagnetic fields and to extra-low-frequency radiation is poorly researched. Employers have also to consider the environment in which equipment is used – the lighting, heating, ventilation and use of space – and the working practices followed.

Away from the computerised side of office automation, **conservation** is gaining ground. The **paperless office** is no more realistic a prospect than it ever was, but the nature of the paper is changing – many companies are now promoting recycled paper.

Case Study – The arrival of book computers

A new generation of computers, designed to be as simple to use as a notebook and pen, has arrived in 1992. Users operate a book computer with an electronic pen and pad and enter data or commands in their own handwriting.

The main advantages of book computers are portability and ease of use, and so the new machines are initially being targeted at mobile workers such as sales representatives, doctors, accountants, solicitors and the police, who often make notes or fill in forms away from their base. Book computers could be used in almost any situation where data is recorded.

Two further advantages of the book computer are:

- the ease with which it can be used in a meeting without offending other people (in contrast to the laptop computer) – it is a bit like bringing in a notepad and pen
- privacy – the flip-up screen forms a barrier to prying eyes.

Files can be selected by simply pointing the electronic pen at them. Most devices also include 'gestures' – shorthand-type symbols that can be used to alter or manipulate text.

Their key feature is the ability to recognise and store clear handwriting. This involves the user writing a series of words and then checking to see whether the computer has learnt them. At present, handwriting recognition is the main weakness of book computers. Each letter needs to be clear if the computer is to be able to decipher it.

1 *What do you consider to be the main advantage of book computers.*
2 *How widely are they being used?*
3 *How do you think they can be used in the modern office?*

The changing face of office technology

In the 1960s, big and expensive **mainframe computers** were introduced by large organisations to handle major data-processing operations – such as payrolls, stock and inventory control. These machines were housed in large, spotlessly clean (dust-free) rooms, and were managed by computer experts using systems that were difficult to operate. Keying in data was a monotonous task performed by semi-skilled staff, requiring accuracy and concentration but no knowledge of computers.

There have been great changes in the last 25 years. The development of **integrated circuits** led to the smaller, cheaper but equally powerful **minicomputer**. Hard on its heels came the tiny silicon-chip **microprocessor** carrying a vast number of electronic circuits. These chips make it possible to build sophisticated electronic control systems into very small spaces.

By 1990 personal computers (PCs) with equivalent power to the 1960s mainframes were to be found on desktops throughout the land, in offices large or small. These machines, costing sometimes less than a thousand pounds, can be used to run a range of software. Non-specialists can use PCs for many essential clerical and administrative tasks – word-processing, stock control, accounts, planning and so on. **Software** is widely available and becoming increasingly easy to use.

As we have seen, these machines become even more useful when linked together in networks. These range from three or four machines within the same office, to networks of several hundreds of computers across the country connected to each other by the existing telephone system.

Changes in the organisation of clerical and administrative work

When mainframe computers were introduced they led to **centralisation** of functions. As networking and PCs take over, **decentralisation** is following. Now different departments can use their own terminals to call up and update centrally held records. Typing is no longer carried out in the 'typing pool' – today word-processing can be carried out in any part of a building.

Low-cost microcomputers with user-friendly interfaces (keyboards, menus, mouses . . .) mean

that staff can routinely work on **word and number crunching** (electronic textual and numerical processing), information storage and retrieval (database applications) and manipulating and analysing information (spreadsheets).

PCs are invaluable for a lot of management functions including data analysis and forward planning. It is unfortunate that too many senior managers rely on 'chauffeured' use of this vital business tool, content that junior staff – often their secretaries – operate the computer terminal for them.

Trends in office automation in the next decade are likely to lead to a reduction in keyboard data entry, resulting in fewer junior clerical jobs.

IT in finance and service industries

Senior clerks are starting to take over some functions of managers. This could lead to an increase in senior clerical jobs and a reduction in the junior or middle managers.

Bank clerks have become 'personal bankers', using **on-line computers** to enable them to answer questions on financial services.

Expert systems can permit insurance clerks to answer questions formerly the province of expert underwriters.

Building society clerks have become adept at using spreadsheets to provide customers with instant details of financial options.

Database marketing

Marketing is clearly an area of business life that needs the use of IT competence. **Electronic marketing** is already well established.

Information technology is used to improve the marketing of many products, even if there is no 'electronic link' with the customer. For example,

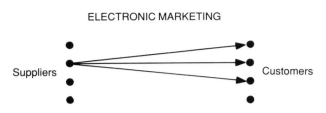

ELECTRONIC MARKETING

Suppliers   Customers

Figure 8.12 Electronic marketing

precision marketing is a form of direct mail which targets customers using computerised databases; this is more selective than **carpet bombing** with so-called junk mail. Sites for new supermarkets are chosen using maps which show areas by type of housing, average household income, propensity to buy certain type of products, and lifestyles. This is all part of **database marketing**.

American airlines pioneered electronic marketing – they gave travel agents terminals which provided access to their computerised reservation systems. This meant that seats could be booked without the travel agent having to make several phone calls to check if seats were available. Simulations of travel agent operations are now available from many **software houses** and are a useful way of learning about database marketing.

In the UK, the Bank of Scotland pioneered 'Hobs' – a home and office banking system. This enables users with simple videotext terminals to do their own banking by dialling into the bank's computers; and it meant that the bank could reach customers outside its geographical stronghold, without opening lots of expensive branches. The Midland and other banks now make similar software available to colleges and schools that want to set up their own students' banks.

Task

As a group, undertake a piece of research using *database marketing* to find out about consumer

preferences in relation to cinema attendance in your area. Collect data about age, frequency of visits, type of films favoured, mode of transport used, and other details. Use the evidence from your research to make recommendations about whether the cinema should invest in a new screen, what sort of films should be shown, how the cinema service could be improved in other ways.

Conclusions

A modern office lies at the heart of any organisation's information system. Like any system it needs to run well; in fact it needs to run in the best possible way. Inputs of raw data and semi-finished data need to be converted into finished information by using the most effective processes that are appropriate. It would be ridiculous for a small company to make a computer database out of sparse data relating to just three customers. It would be equally ridiculous nowadays for a large company to rely purely on pen and paper records for dealing with thousands of orders. Organisations therefore need to use **appropriate technology** to meet their needs. This often means obtaining specialist advice about systems available to solve the problems. No two organisations are alike – every one has its own needs for an effective information system.

When you develop your own IT competency it is important that you think about how new knowledge, skills and attitudes will help you. Get advice from your tutor, supervisor or careers adviser to find out what new areas you need to master. There is nothing more pointless than learning skills which are not required, or in using IT to do things that could be done more quickly in other ways. We have all heard of colleges where students are provided with elaborate computer timetables only to find that the rooms are all wrong, the times given are incorrect, and that the named lecturer left three years ago.

In short, make sure you know why you are learning new information skills, use the most appropriate information processing methods, and use them well!

Case Study – IT at use in a service station

A modern service station can be viewed as a complex office administering a range of buying and selling operations. This case study looks at the range of IT applications used by a service station.

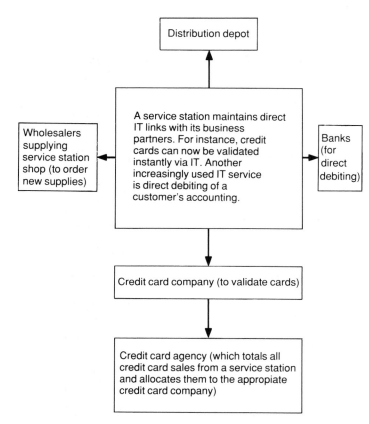

Figure 8.13 IT links between a service station and its business partners

Figure 8.13 illustrates the IT links between a service station and its business partners. Information technology facilities in a service station can carry out all the following procedures:

- transfer details of fuel withdrawals from the pumps to the central console
- monitor the amount of fuel left in the underground storage tanks

- issue the correct payment request and receipt
- accept cash, cheques or credit cards
- check and process the credit card transactions
- record the credit card transactions for daily 'polling' by a bureau acting for the credit card companies
- debit a customer's bank account directly
- record shop sales and monitor remaining stocks (broken down into product and package size)
- provide screen or printed management reports on sales and stock levels.

Some service stations have IT facilities to carry out every one of these procedures – and integrate them on to one database. Others have IT facilities that can carry out only some of them.

1 *Produce a database of information about the range and variety of IT facilities in use at service stations in your local area. The database should include basic data about each service station, including address, brands and types of fuel available, number of pumps, and facilities such as car-wash, shop and toilets.*
2 *Use the database to list the IT procedures that are carried out at each service station in turn.*
3 *Word-process a report on the range of IT facilities in use at the service stations in your area.*

Task

Looking at your own IT skills

In this chapter we have looked at a range of IT skills which you might be asked to use in a modern office. Now use the profile printed here to chart your own IT skills. Discuss with your tutor or supervisor ways of upgrading your skills.

IT SKILLS CHECKLIST

Indicate by a tick in the appropriate boxes what, in your opinion, is your level of **experience** with respect to the skills mentioned:

1 *I am experienced at this.*
2 *I have some experience of this.*
3 *I have no experience of this.*

Indicate by a tick in the appropriate boxes what you feel to be your **success** with the skills mentioned:

1 *I was successful at this.*
2 *I was reasonably successful at this.*
3 *I was rarely successful at this.*

	Experience 1 2 3	Success 1 2 3
Using a microcomputer in any way		
Using a simple word-processing package		
Using a more complex word-processing package		
Using a drawing/painting package		
Using a desktop publishing program		
Using a multimedia program (sound/animation/graphics)		
Using a data-retrieval system		
Using a spreadsheet		
Using a printer		
Using a colour printer		
Using a plotter		
Other experiences (specify)		

9

People in their Working Environment

In modern organisations managers are becoming increasingly aware of the requirement to place great emphasis upon understanding the needs of people in their working environment. Valuing the workforce also helps to defuse problems caused by changes in the employment market – the 'demographic time-bomb'. Ways of achieving co-operation and improving contributions from the workforce include teamwork, meetings, quality circles and extensive training and development.

In this chapter we look closely at the roles of these areas and assess how each contributes to improving the quality of life in the working environment.

If an organisation's activities seem to run smoothly it is easy to take the employees for granted. If something goes wrong, it is equally easy to blame them. Such an approach ignores the **needs** of employees and fails to take into account *why* something is or is not taking place. All organisations must plan for and manage effectively the people they employ to achieve the most from the skills and experiences they possess. An organisation's most valuable asset is its people and the work they do; each is indispensable to the other.

Think what might happen if a certain manager failed to manage his or her employees and organisation effectively. Initially, this might cause bottlenecks, inefficient procedures, possibly poor communication channels. Staff would be put in difficult and uncomfortable situations. They might lose time, not know what to do, be put under pressure unnecessarily, have to apologise to customers, and so on. How would employees react to these events?

In the early stages many would put up with the inefficiencies of management in the hope that things would improve. If the weak management remained, morale would start to wane, some employees might become resistant to events taking place, and become more time-conscious about the hours they worked. After a period many might leave, and some of those leaving might be key members of staff with important functional responsibilities – for which they have never been properly recognised and rewarded. Replacing them with staff of an equal calibre could be impossible without extensive delay and training costs. The organisation would, therefore, have suffered an **own-goal**.

Over recent years the concept of **human resource management** has become increasingly recognised. Human resource management places more emphasis upon people in the working environment and how their activities and needs should be understood, provided for, maintained and satisfied.

170

Case Study – Using the workforce properly

Using the workforce properly is a key to Australian industry becoming truly competitive, according to Dr Michael Deeley, the chief executive of ICI Australia.

Dr Deeley believes that improved competitiveness requires a fundamental shift in direction in relationships with employees: 'We need to move from seeing employees as an undesirable and variable cost, to seeing them as an important investment; as the key to improving performance through fully utilising their talents.' Dr Deeley thinks that this can be achieved by moving away from a workplace where employees are controlled, to a workplace designed to encourage them to become more committed: 'This is where employees are trusted and empowered, where management provides support and motivation by focusing on performance and outcome.'

This idea would create a workplace based upon commitment. An individual would have a job that was flexibly defined within a career structure and with opportunities for further advancement and training. Dr Deeley feels that 'where people have control over their jobs, where they have freedom to act and an ability to influence their working environment, they have job satisfaction and an outlet for their creativity. This in turn leads to more committed employees with secure and satisfying jobs.'

In support of these views is the Institute of Personnel Management of Australia (IPMA), which launched its annual Human Resources Week with the theme 'Our Workforce – Use It or Lose It', designed to raise public awareness of the importance of people to Australia's future. During the week the role of human resource management in Australia was discussed and debated.

1 How will using the workforce more effectively help Australian industry?

2 What fundamental shift in attitudes did Dr Deeley suggest?
3 Why did Dr Deeley suggest more participation by the workforce?
4 How might a Human Resources Week improve the ways in which organisations manage people?

The demographic time-bomb

Over recent years organisations have been hit by recession, shortages of people with suitable skills, increasing competition as well as a massive range of changes requiring them to manage their human resources more effectively. Never before has the requirement to recruit, train and retain suitable staff been quite as important.

As we move through the 1990s, however, these challenges will not only continue, but will also become more intense as the pace of change increases even further and the **demographic time-bomb** affects the availability of skilled labour.

The demographic time-bomb refers to changes in the employment market. It is estimated that the numbers of young people entering the employment market will fall drastically by the end of the century. By 1999 the number of people between 16 and 19 years of age will fall by a quarter, or 850 000. Organisations will therefore face growing problems recruiting suitable young people and trainees. There will be too many organisations competing for too few people with the right skills. The solution to this problem seems to be for organisations to reassess completely the whole range of their recruitment, retention and training policies.

Consider what happens if an employee leaves:

- Skills are lost to the organisation and may take a long time to replace.
- Specialist knowledge of how the organisation operates leaves with the employee.
- Those who leave may join a competitor.

171

- Quality of the organisation's output can be adversely affected.
- Pressure can be put on other employees to do more work.
- The recruitment, induction and training of another team member can be expensive.
- There can be a demotivating effect upon those who remain with the organisation.

The demographic time-bomb can be defused by maximising the contributions from existing employees through efficient human resource management designed to improve retention, and by looking to groups such as women who have previously stayed at home, the disabled, the over-50s and the long-term unemployed, who can be re-trained.

Task

Explain in detail how you might feel if you worked in a small section with four staff, and within a six-month period the other three staff left. (Your answer will obviously depend on whether all or any of the three people were replaced!)

Achieving co-operation

The successful organisation in the 1990s will be the one which has a **clear vision** of the future and of the resources it requires to take it there. This vision must relate to the future of employees and emphasise their role in achieving corporate goals. To attain such goals an organisation's:

- culture
- structure and communications system
- management
- policies and actions

must all be in line with this mission.

At the heart of reaching stated goals is the co-operation of all employees. Most want to do a good job, be recognised for what they do, feel adequately rewarded for their skills, learn more, develop their skills and be able to contribute their ideas and efforts. Managers achieve co-operation by providing a **secure environment** for employees. This involves them in having to make decisions and solve problems, but at the same time they must elicit commitment from employees by treating them with respect, providing them with a flow of information and a sense of involvement with the organisation. The remainder of this chapter looks in detail at ways of achieving this.

Teamwork

Teamwork and the development of a **team spirit** can go a long way towards increasing the sense of satisfaction people obtain from their working environment, and to providing them with a sense of purpose. For example, imagine what it would be like if you played in a rugby team in which the scrum-half did not like passing the ball, or if you were in a play in which the actors were competing with each other to impress the audience. In both situations confusion would arise. The group or team would not perform well because individuals would be working against each other – teamwork would be lacking.

Task

Choose one example of a team or group situation in which you operate. How important is it that you co-operate with other members of the group to perform the activity? What would happen if you did not?

At work, lack of teamwork might lead to a job not being completed or, if it is completed, it might be finished badly. Working relationships might be fractious. People might not listen to each other or respect others' views. They would be working as individuals and not heeding advice or providing suggestions. Group values, pride and purpose would not exist.

A team can be defined as 'a collection of people with a common purpose who communicate with each other over a period of time'. In a team the contributions of individuals are complementary. At the very centre of team operations is **collaboration**.

Figure 9.1 **Working together for a common purpose**

Whenever a team undertakes a task, there are three elements involved in making decisions about its completion:

- The **task** is the content of the work. For example, the team may be involved in a project or in the provision of a good or service.
- The **process** is all of the interaction which takes place between the different members of the group. It involves people working together, the relationships they establish and the feelings they generate within the group. One test of a good team is how well its members can contribute to a sequence of activities when they work apart.
- The **action schedule** is how the team is organised to undertake a particular task. It will set out who does what and all the procedures necessary for completing the task.

Outward Bound is one organisation which enables people to discover what they can achieve by teamwork, mutual support and co-operation with others. Their courses provide opportunities for people to learn by actually doing rather than simply watching or listening. Lever Brothers sends apprentices on Outward Bound courses to teach

them about themselves and each other – by learning about self-reliance, assertiveness, consideration and the ability to think, the company feels that the trainees will be able to contribute more to a team and therefore be of greater value to the company.

Task

In *Making It Happen*, Sir John Harvey-Jones says: 'When I took over as chairman of ICI one of my first actions was to arrange for the executive directors and myself to spend a week away together in order to discuss how the board should lead the company, and how we should organise our work.'

How does this statement by Sir John relate to the *task*, *process* and *action* schedule discussed in the text?

Case Study – Howtown Outdoor Education Centre

Early in 1991, three members of the business studies staff at Darlington College of Technology took a group of twenty-five BTEC National students in Business and Finance away to Howtown Outdoor Education Centre by the side of Lake Ullswater. The education centre, run by Durham County Council, is staffed and managed by teachers with expertise in outdoor activities.

The main reasons for taking the students to Howtown were to find out (1) how practical problem-related activities could relate to the BTEC National course, (2) whether working away from college would help the students to work together more closely, and (3) if it would be possible to build an assignment around the activities.

Upon arrival at the centre students were divided up into groups/teams and introduced to their instructors. Almost immediately the emphasis was placed upon allowing each group, wherever possible, to take responsibility for its actions. The groups were presented with a timetable of activities with the only criterion being that they had to spend a night away from the centre. Wherever possible, with any of the activities chosen, students would be encouraged to develop skills and be provided with feedback and support not only from staff but also from the group.

The key concept underlying the process was that, by putting students through a series of challenges, the experience would help them to understand their own strengths and this would show them how to relate more closely to others. It was hoped that building such awareness would assist them to develop personally in areas such as:

- self-confidence
- developing trust in others
- leadership
- independence
- working with others
- tackling problems as a group
- taking into account the feelings of others
- making decisions.

Whereas some of the activities were specifically for outdoors (e.g. skiing and climbing), others could be developed with a business application. For example, the raft-building exercise involved classroom work in which students were provided with a budget; they then designed and later built a raft with the materials they could afford. Quality control involved testing the raft – and the inevitable ducking!

Throughout the course activities were supported by good humour. Wherever someone struggled, others in the group were quick to respond with help, guidance and encouragement. Friendships and support for each other characterised the week. Given a purpose, a team and a problem to solve or

a task to undertake, each of the groups responded well. In fact many of the students were surprised at how they could work with others and just what they could do if they belonged to a team. The course seemed to make them more aware of themselves and built up their self-confidence. Back at college it was felt that the programme of activities had helped the group to interact better and this was borne out by other members of staff.

1 Why was it important to allow each group to take responsibility for it's actions?
2 Imagine you are a member of a group building a raft. Identify:
   a the task
   b the process
   c the action schedule.
3 What importance would an employer attach to staff being able to work effectively in a team?

Forming teams

The ability to work in a team is an important element in the learning process. When employers look for new staff, they do not just concentrate upon those with the right qualifications, important though these are. They look for people with the right personality for the job, who can cope with the work involved and also work with others. Smith Kline Beecham Pharmaceuticals recently advertised a management post in a daily newspaper. As the following extract from the advertisement shows, the company was looking for someone with both technical and business skills who could work well with others:

'You will lead a small team which is involved in all stages, from negotiation with key suppliers to the provision of first-class user support services. The implementation of new technology in the scientific environment presents special challenges, and you will need to combine a confident and persistent approach with tact, diplomacy and excellent communication skills. We are looking for someone whose high level of technical expertise is matched by business and management skills.'

The success of any project usually depends upon all the members of the team. For example, imagine a group of workers building a house. The completion of the project and the quality of the final product depends upon when each specialist turns up and how well they carry out their task. If anyone fails to pull their weight the success of the project is affected. Or imagine a group of people putting up a marquee: if they do not work together and pull on the ropes at the same time, it is not possible to erect the tent.

In an organisation, groups or teams may be formed by people who share workstations, who have a similar specialism or who work on the same project. This sometimes involves working with others from different departments or from other areas.

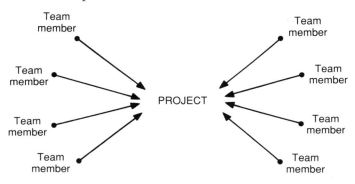

Figure 9.2 Working together as a team

Before any team can be put together a number of issues have to be addressed. These include:

- the size of the team
- the nature of the project
- the requirements of the group
- the roles of members of the team
- the abilities of the group members
- the norms of the group.

Case Study – Ignore teamworking at your peril

Heslegrave Gill, a Yorkshire-based consultancy, recently claimed that UK companies are ignoring one of their greatest assets by failing to harness the talents of the people

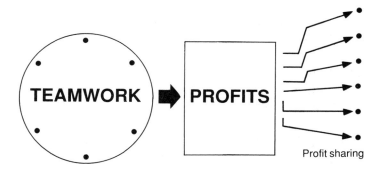

Figure 9.3 Benefiting from teamwork

working for them. They feel that giving more attention to teamworking would enable UK firms to emulate the success of the Japanese and they point to several examples to prove the case.

Teams of shift workers at the Scunthorpe Rod Mill in South Humberside were looking at ways of achieving greater levels of productivity. Team leaders were instructed in skills such as time management, identification of training needs and problem solving. The teams were given scope to manage their own work and introduced initiatives to improve both product quality and customer service.

At Penine SCS, a small Halifax firm supplying pneumatic equipment to British Steel and British Coal, the teamworking approach was used to involve employees in the running of the business. Mel Westwood, the company's Managing Director, commented: 'We have now installed what we call profit centre managers. These are people from the workforce who are in charge of each department. They are provided each month with a profit and loss report and have set up their own budgets. We have introduced a profit-sharing scheme and they know exactly what the financial position of the company is. We don't hide anything.'

The employees at Penine SCS became so committed to the best interests of their company that they insisted on postponing the profit-sharing scheme for a year so that a reinvestment programme could lay a solid foundation for the future. They showed that they wanted rewards in the future and not in the short-term.

1 Why do you think that many UK companies have ignored the talents of their workforce?

2 What are the benefits of teamworking?

3 Comment briefly on how teamworking has helped:

   a Scunthorpe Rod Mill

   b Penine SCS.

A **strong team** is one having a sense of purpose, with clear objectives and goals. Within the group there will be norms of attitude, behaviour and discipline. Individual team members will be open about their views, be prepared to confront where necessary but will be prepared to co-operate with decisions made by the group. Support and trust are important in a team, as are good relationships across the whole group.

Task

Work in teams of four to design and build a spaghetti bridge to span a gap of half a metre and be capable of supporting the weight of a boot. The bridge should be supported at each end by a tower constructed from a sheet of cardboard. Glue and sticky tape may be used. Summarise the following:

a how you planned the bridge

b how the team worked together

c the role undertaken by each member of the team.

Team roles

Within every team, various roles can be identified. In general there are four types or functions:

● leaders
● doers
● thinkers
● supporters.

A **leader** is someone who influences others with his or her actions or words in order to pursue the goals of the organisation. Many leaders have great strength of personality or charismatic qualities, while others are quietly forceful or persuasive.

A **doer** is a more practical person who gets things done and wants to get on with the job once decisions have been taken. A doer will quite often side-step problems rather than spend time trying to find the best solution.

A **thinker** inspires others by providing solutions to problems. A thinker is capable of deep thought, is inventive and can be a constant source of ideas.

A **supporter** is somebody who creates harmony in the team by looking for ways to overcome any problems or destructive undercurrents. A supporter can be particularly useful in a crisis.

Task

Imagine that you have been asked to form a small team consisting of yourself and a few of your friends. The team must contain a leader, a doer, a thinker and a supporter. What role would you give yourself, and which friends would you ask to fill the other roles? What leads you to believe that they fall into the categories you have assigned to them?

Group dynamics

For members of a team to work together effectively it is vital that they understand the corporate objectives of their organisation and how the tasks they are undertaking serve to fulfil such objectives. In the modern world people at work need to feel involved and informed about processes and decisions that affect them. Being in a team provides a **sense of belonging** and enables employees to establish friendships which help to make the workplace a more attractive place.

Advantages of groups

Teams are capable of carrying out a far wider range of activities than is an individual. Where some form of division of labour is required, teams can work better by allocating separate tasks or components of tasks to each member. Teams, properly organised, are also better at tasks requiring creativity and judgement as 'several heads are better than one'.

Another aspect of teamwork is greater impartiality. Humans, by their upbringing, have a certain bias in their opinions and outlook, whereas in a group such views are offset by a wider range of backgrounds and experiences.

Groups also seem to be able to make more courageous decisions than individuals alone. A risky decision is difficult for an individual to make, whereas group members sense that the overall responsibility will be shared.

Disadvantages of groups

There are several possible disadvantages of groups. One is **time-wasting** – groups require careful coordination, without which time is wasted. For example:

- time can be wasted pursuing just one issue
- members may persist with discussion about irrelevant points
- members may repeat statements made by others.

The presence of others sometimes inhibits group members and makes them feel that they ought to go along with what the others say rather than express their own views, particularly if a dominant character seems to be influencing the group. This is called **group-pressure**.

Another drawback to groups is delays. An organisation may not be able to make decisions quickly because of the need for group discussion, and so delays may ensue in dealing with an important issue.

Finally, groups may talk too much and do too little. A group may discuss a problem but not actually do anything about solving it – there is then **lack of action**.

Task

Weigh up the advantages and disadvantages of groups. Make lists of issues you feel that groups would be:

a good at dealing with
b bad at dealing with.

Factors affecting group dynamics

Many factors affect the way in which a group operates. All are interconnected and therefore influence each other.

Figure 9.4 Factors affecting group dynamics

The **size** of the group affects members in different ways. Some feel confident speaking to a large group, while others may find it difficult to contribute unless they know the group members well. With groups of under five people, often there is insufficient breadth of experience; whereas with a group of more than ten people, low participators stop talking, the group becomes more formal and discussion is stifled. The ideal size of a group is often between five and eight.

Task

What size of group do you prefer to belong to? Explain your answer.

The **physical location** of the group meeting affects interactions. A large room, or seating arrangements which separate members of the group from others according to status, both discourage interactions. If the group meets in the office of a senior member of staff the status relationships are likely to be reinforced, whereas if it meets on neutral ground members will tend to feel less inhibited.

Leadership style affects the way the group functions. If the leader is **democratic** and only guides where needed, members will tend to make extensive contributions to decisions. If, on the other hand, the leader is **autocratic**, then the group will be driven to agree to the beliefs and goals of the leader – and dissatisfaction of the other members.

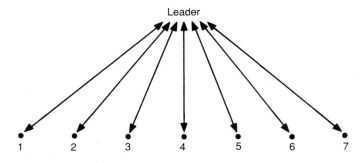

Figure 9.5 Autocratic leadership style

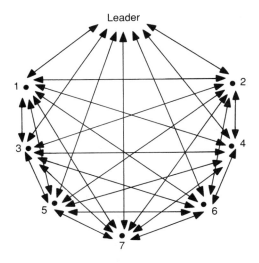

Figure 9.6 Democratic leadership stlye

Interaction will largely depend upon the style of leadership. With an autocratic style interaction will be centralised (see Figure 9.5), and with a democratic style it will be decentralised (see Figure 9.6).

The nature of the **task** will affect the way in which the group works. A group may be expected simply to share information or to sanction some suggested action. On the other hand, the activities of the group may be more creative, in which case it will be expected to come up with ideas designed to solve problems, or to work together to complete a defined task.

The **behaviour of group members** will depend upon factors such as:

- perceptions of the leader
- atmosphere
- morale
- the need for recognition
- influence
- conflict/consensus
- competition.

In order to overcome any problems caused by the above factors, it may be necessary for the group leader to indulge in group-building. This can involve:

- encouraging contributions, recognising and praising them
- making it possible for all members of the group to make a contribution

- providing the group with a direction designed to avoid conflict
- constantly summarising the feelings of the group.

Each member of a group is there for a reason, which determines the **role** they will undertake. For example, he or she may be there because of expertise or because of seniority. The individual's behaviour will be determined by these parameters.

Finally, members of the group will approach the task with **different beliefs**. Some might come with preconceived values, while others will come with no notion of what contribution they can make. Some may come simply to defend the area they represent or to cover up errors or even to use the platform for amusement. As a generalisation, groups where members have similar beliefs tend to be more harmonious and satisfying for their members, whereas groups where members have widely differing beliefs tend to be more productive.

Task

This task will only be possible if you are studying in a class. Form a circle of eight people in the centre of the room, and elect a group leader. The rest of the class should sit outside the circle as observers. The task of the central group is to design a student magazine. The observers should look at the process and make comments under the following headings:

a How did the appointed leader control the activities of the group?
b Did the group work well together?
c Who tended to lead the discussion?
d Was everyone involved?
e Did anyone block progress?
f Who seemed to listen and who did not listen?

You should allow ten minutes at the end of the session for comparison of notes.

Meetings

Meetings provide one type of opportunity for organisations to consult employees. They bring together interested parties who can express their views and help to develop a common policy designed to achieve the organisation's objectives.

Meetings are therefore an important administrative activity; information can be exchanged, ideas passed and opinions expressed. They also play an important part in communicating information, providing a forum where problems can be solved and where decisions can be made.

Aims of meetings

People tend to be more committed to a decision if they are **consulted** and are involved in some way in the decision-making process. If they understand why a decision is necessary, they are more likely to accept all that it entails.

Some meetings are called to generate ideas. Individuals have different backgrounds and the number of ideas being put forward tends to increase with group size. One popular problem-solving technique is **brainstorming**, which was originally used in the advertising industry with the object of coming up with new ideas. In a brainstorming session, the problem is stated and participants to the meeting are encouraged to produce as many ideas as they can, out of which the best can be selected.

Meetings can be called to give people **information** or spread **knowledge**. These are particularly important if a lot of people need to be informed or if the information is confidential.

Meetings allow parties from both sides of an issue to **negotiate an agreement**.

Often meetings are used to get **collective decisions** from members by democratic means. If an individual does not have the authority to make a decision, he or she might call a meeting so that others can agree to some proposals. Sometimes when a decision is made by a senior member of staff, it then needs ratification (confirmation) by others in a meeting.

Finally, meetings can be called to **investigate** something that has happened – for example, an accident or a series of thefts.

Task

Working with a group of others, try a *brainstorming session* to come up with an idea for a new garden tool.

Informal and formal meetings

Meetings range from **informal** unstructured gatherings between a few people to **formal**, heavily structured meetings controlled by rigid rules and procedures.

Informal meetings involve the gathering together of individuals, often at short notice and without any set procedures. Informal meetings are flexible and can be called to respond to any issue, or can be used to share responsibility for a decision.

On the other hand, the rules and procedures for a formal meeting may be contained in a company's Memorandum and Articles of Association or in an organisation's standing orders or written constitution. The features of a formal meeting are:

- The meeting is called by a **notice** or **agenda.**
- Conduct in the meeting depends on the formal rules of the organisation.
- Decisions are reached by voting.
- Formal meeting terms are used.
- The proceedings are recorded in **minutes.**

Task

Give some examples of formal meetings and informal meetings.

Procedures for formal meetings

Formal meetings must be properly conducted according to legal requirements or a written constitution. It is usual to give **notice** of the meeting to every person entitled to attend according to the rules and regulations. The notice should be signed by the issuer and should specify the date, time and place of the meeting.

NOTICE OF MEETING
CROWTHORNE FOOTBALL CLUB

The Annual Meeting of the Selection Committee will be held in the upstairs room of The Buckshot Inn on Monday 18th August 199_ at 7.45 pm. Any items for inclusion in the Agenda should reach me no later than 18th July 199_.

Secretary:

Figure 9.7 A notice of meeting

AGENDA
CROWTHORNE FOOTBALL CLUB

Annual Meeting of the Selection Committee
to be held on Monday 18th August 199_ at 7.45 pm in The Buckshot Inn

1 Apologies for absence
2 Minutes of the last meeting
3 Matters arising from the minutes
4 Reports: Treasurer's report
       Team Secretary's report
       Chairperson's report
5 Proposal to redecorate clubhouse
6 Proposal to increase match fees
7 Any other business
8 Date of next meeting

Secretary:

Figure 9.8 An Agenda

A notice of a meeting will be accompanied or followed by an **agenda,** which is a list of topics to be discussed at the meeting. It will normally be sent to all those entitled to attend the meeting so that they can consider the topics in advance of the meeting.

Task

In your role as Secretary to the Richmond Squash Club, prepare an agenda of a meeting to be held next Friday in the clubhouse at 8.00 pm. As well as the regular items, include the following: entry fees; bar takings; redecoration of the clubhouse.

A **chairperson** has certain duties and powers in a meeting. He or she makes sure that the meeting is properly constituted, preserves order, works through the agenda preventing irrelevant discussion, and ascertains the views of the meeting by putting **motions** and amendments to those attending.

Often a chairperson will have a special copy of the agenda known as the **chairperson's agenda.** On this, further information is provided for the chairperson's guidance, and space is provided on the right-hand side for notes to be made.

Shortly before the time a meeting is designated to start the chairperson makes sure that there is a **quorum** – this is the minimum number of people required for the meeting to go ahead according to the rules. He or she will also ensure that everybody has an agenda and that all new members are introduced.

The **secretary** then states whether any apologies have been received for absence, and reads through the official record – the minutes – of the last meeting. If the minutes have already been circulated, it will be assumed that they have been read! Members are asked to approve them as a correct

record of the last meeting and, if necessary, the secretary will amend them before they are signed by the chairperson.

At this stage any **matters arising** from the minutes will be discussed. For example, if the last meeting suggested that certain individuals undertake certain actions, these may be mentioned.

The chairperson then works through the business of the meeting according to the agenda. If **reports** are to be read (again, circulated reports are assumed to have been read) the writers may be asked to speak briefly about their reports. If a **motion** is proposed the chairperson will ask for a proposer and a seconder, allow for discussion of the motion making sure that all sides are heard, and then call for a vote. The chairperson usually has a casting vote if the voting is tied.

Any other business is normally limited to non-controversial issues, because if it is felt that something deserves further attention it must be put on the agenda for the next meeting. At the end of the meeting a decision may be made about the date, time and place of the next meeting.

While a meeting is taking place, the secretary records the proceedings with a series of notes – the minutes. These should provide an accurate and clear record of what has taken place at the meeting. They are usually written up immediately after a meeting and are in the past tense.

- **Narrative minutes** include details of discussion and the decisions reached.
- **Resolution minutes** record only details of the decisions agreed.
- **Action minutes** have a column which indicates who is to follow up and take action upon any decision reached.

Whichever version is produced, the secretary only summarises the main points.

The secretary will usually have a folder containing agendas and minutes from previous meetings. It is important that such documents be kept as they provide a permanent record of issues that have been discussed and decisions that have been sanctioned.

CROWTHORNE FOOTBALL CLUB

Minutes of the Annual Meeting of the Selection Committee held on Monday 18th August 199_ in The Buckshot Inn at 7.45 pm.

Present
Mr A James (Chairperson), Mr D Smith (Team Secretary), Mr R Pitt, Mrs H Johnson, Mr N Rees (Secretary), Miss E Walters (Treasurer)

1 Apologies
Apologies for absence were received from Mr R Cook and Mr S Turner.

2 Minutes
Minutes of the last meeting were taken as read, approved and signed.

3 Matters arising
Mrs Johnson reported that, since last season she had taken on the task of writing the press releases and match reports that had regularly appeared in local newspapers.

4 Reports
Miss Walters presented the Treasurer's report. The club had a good season and finances were healthy. A copy of the audited accounts were distributed.
   Mr Smith presented the Team Secretary's report. The first team squad last season was strong and this was reflected in performances. The second eleven, however, struggled to attract players, and this was reflected in several dismal performances.
   Mr James thanked everybody for their hard work last season. Sponsorship had increased for the season ahead, and they had received a record number of enquiries from new players.

5 Clubhouse redecoration
Mr Rees said that this was long overdue and was conveying a poor image of the club to visiting teams and supporters. After further discussion it was agreed that this was a priority and the secretary was asked to obtain quotations and to bring these to the attention of the committee as soon as possible.

6 Match fees
Miss Walters pointed out that match fees had not increased over the last 3 years. Mr Smith expressed that if match fees increased too much this might deter new players from joining the club. It was agreed to increase match fees by just 50p per game.

7 Any other business
Mrs Johnson expressed that a small gift should be sent to Jim Robinson for running the line last season. Mr Pitt volunteered to visit local businesses to increase sponsorship.

8 Date of next meeting
It was decided to hold a short meeting of the committee on 5th September 199_ at 8.00 pm at the same location to discuss clubhouse redecoration.

Chairman
21st August 199_

Figure 9.9 Minutes of a meeting

Case Study – The entertainments committee

Peter Jones, Dawn Williams, Tony Peters, Alison Sharpe, Donna Thomas, Alison Piper, Michael Sherbourne and Roger Hanson are all interested in setting up an entertainments committee at their local Community Centre. The centre's administrator has agreed to their request to set up a committee and has indicated that they can use the centre's hall on a trial basis on the last Friday of each month. He has, however, set certain conditions:

- Events should not make a loss.
- There will be no hire fee for the hall but half the profits from each event must be contributed to the centre's funds.
- Events must not disturb local residents.
- Events should attempt to cater for as wide a range of residents as possible.
- The entertainments committee must have a chairperson, a secretary and a treasurer.
- All meetings of the entertainments committee must have a proper notice of meeting and an agenda, and minutes must be taken.

1 Consider whether you feel that the committee could be successful.

2 Have a preliminary meeting of the committee with seven colleagues. Make arrangements for a notice of meeting, agenda and items for inclusion to appear for the next meeting. Stage the meeting and take minutes.

3 Analyse your role in the meeting. What sort of contribution did you make? How could it be improved?

Contributing to meetings

At the majority of meetings you attend you will be a participant rather than the chairperson, secretary or treasurer. In such circumstances the sort of contribution you wish to make will rest on your shoulders. Raising a point at a meeting is something that many people do not feel comfortable about doing. The following might act as a useful guide:

- Scrutinise agenda items before you attend the meeting to see if there are any areas that may be of interest to you.
- Research such areas of interest and obtain any associated reading materials.
- Plan out, either in your mind or by making notes, what you might wish to say.
- Listen to what others have to say before speaking yourself.
- Timing is important – make sure the point you make fits into the discussion.
- Do not ramble on.
- Be tactful, and do not deliberately upset someone.
- Be assertive.
- Make your contribution coherent.
- Be ready for some sort of opposition by trying to anticipate the response you might receive to the points you are making.

Quality circles

Making the most of what employees have to offer and valuing their contributions is becoming increasingly important for industries wishing to remain competitive today. The old-fashioned notion that employee involvement was about collective bargaining through trade unions is steadily disappearing. Today's ideal form of consultation tends to be by means of groups or teams of employees in **quality circles**.

Quality circles originally came from Japan in the early 1960s. They were developed in order to improve quality and productivity in manufacturing. It was not, however, until the early 1980s that they started to appear in Western industry. Originally they captured the attention of management specialists as they brought together workers in a **consultative process** which involved group dynamics.

As a result, over recent years quality circles have attracted a lot of attention and thousands of companies have established them. To coordinate the diverse activities of quality circles, the International Association of Quality Circles has been formed.

Quality circles comprise small groups of employees engaged on any sort of problem affecting their working environment – for example, safety, quality assurance, efficiency. They are a medium for employees to improve their working life by bringing forward their points of view on day-to-day issues. They are therefore a form of indirect consultation designed to meet both employee and management needs. They also allow employees to identify their actions more closely with the success of the organisation and this increases their degree of job satisfaction.

Like many management theories the quality circle is easy to understand. A typical circle consists of between eight and twelve people from similar working backgrounds. They meet perhaps once a week, usually during working hours, and each circle has a leader. Figure 9.10 indicates what a quality circle does.

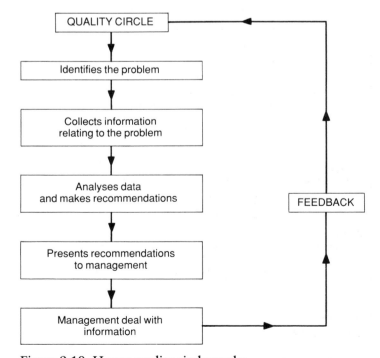

Figure 9.10 How a quality circle works

Task

Form a quality circle of between eight and ten people. You have been asked by management to suggest practical ways of improving the quality of your course.
Discuss your ideas and make recommendations.

A great benefit of quality circles is that an organisation can use line specialists, who know their jobs and understand how they work, to resolve problems without having to call in management consultants. Furthermore, the management's support of quality circles implies that the employees are trusted to solve problems and their contributions are valued. This helps to develop stronger links between managers and employees and improves morale, as well as the quality of performance.

Case Study – Quality circles in management accounting

Managements are beginning to realise that the principle of quality circles can be applied to accounting personnel as well as to production workers. Quality circles offer accountants an opportunity to identify areas of working which could be improved and made more productive.

A quality circle consultancy exercise was carried out by a major UK manufacturer with the establishment of a quality circle management accounting group. The group broke down its activities into two main areas: quantitative and qualitative.

The quantitative areas were capable of measurement:

- The production of management reports to time schedules improved from 86 per cent to 94 per cent over a two-year period.
- The accuracy of accounting data being entered into the computer improved. Whereas in the past 2 per cent of entries had errors, as a result of the quality circle errors fell to 0.4 per cent. Fewer miscodes into the computer reduced overtime by 45 per cent.
- There were reduced errors in inventory records from 30 per cent average error to 1.7 per cent.
- Late payments to suppliers were reduced from 5 to 0.027 per cent.

Savings made by such improvements were thought to be substantial.

On the qualitative front, the quality circle had a major impact on the suggestions scheme. The numbers of suggestions increased by a half and the number of people participating by a quarter. Savings resulting from suggestions went up by three-quarters.

It was also felt that improved quality had raised morale. An opinion survey revealed that employees felt their general satisfaction with the company had improved, their skills were being better utilised, and they had developed personally from the experience.

1 *What degree of improvement took place in accounting data input after the introduction of a quality circle?*
2 *Why did the establishment of a quality circle improve morale?*
3 *To which other parts of the organisation could quality circles be applied?*

Training and development

Training is an investment in the workforce. It is used not only to meet short-term organisational objectives but also to develop employees personally and create a long-term future for them. This can help them to achieve their ambitions, undertake responsibilities and, at the same time, increase their sense of belonging to the organisation.

In **on-the-job training,** an individual is placed into a job position and trained to perform the task under close supervision. This is training for a specific function, but an increasing amount of training today is directed towards improving employees' understanding of how the organisation operates. **Induction training** also fulfils this aim.

Staff development provides skills and qualifications for promotion. This is often off-the-job training acquired by attending courses.

Some training is directed towards developing employees personally so that they can fulfil personal needs. This type of training is based on the belief that it will benefit the organisation in the long-term.

Certain questions arise when considering training requirements. Training is a **cost,** and while staff are being trained, unless the training is on-the-job, they are absent from the workplace and not contributing to output. Another consideration is who should undertake the training – should an organisation train in-house or should it use an external agency?

The immediate tangible benefit of training is improved standards or work. However, there are other benefits and these are usually not quite so visible. As a result of training employees generally feel more involved, so that morale should improve and labour turnover be reduced. Also, staff who are developed and prepared for promotion become motivated to undertake further responsibilities; indeed, some would argue that without preparation for higher levels of responsibility employees could become promoted beyond their true level of competence.

Though many organisations today still direct their attention primarily towards organisational training needs, there is an increasing recognition of the need for genuine employee development.

Case Study – Management discovers training

The tendency of management in the UK to regard training simply as a cost rather than also as an investment is well-known. When a recession occurs it tends to be one of the first areas to suffer cutbacks. This weakens the ability of organisations to hold and recruit staff and undermines their ability to cope with problems. For example, a recent study by the Small Business Research Trust suggested that lack of management training was a significant factor in the reluctance of small firms to pursue a growth policy.

Professor David Ashton from Lancaster University believes there has been a significant change in attitude in recent years by larger companies, though the old weaknesses persist amongst smaller companies. Among larger businesses he has seen increasing interest in management qualifications rather than training alone. This has led to a provision by business schools of a range of programmes tailored to the requirements of business, such as the Master of Business Administration. Projects on which managers work in such programmes are often viewed as key to future business success. Companies themselves have also responded to the demands of managers and seem to view management development as a valuable strategy for retaining personnel.

Professor Ashton's findings are supported by a survey carried out by Harbridge Consulting Group. This indicated that today a more thoughtful approach is taking place in management development. More organisations feel that training should take place entirely on individual needs, and management development is also being discussed more frequently at board level than ever before.

Management development is, however, usually planned on a one-year basis in most companies. The Harbridge report indicates a need to bring an understanding of long-term issues into the process of planning for management development. This will enable organisations to cope with demographic changes in the structure of the workforce.

1 Why is training sometimes regarded simply as a cost rather than as a benefit?
2 How might training help to retain personnel?
3 Express your views as to whether or not training should be based upon organisational needs or individual needs.

Case Study – Gaps in training threaten growth

In some circles there is a strong feeling that training in the United Kingdom for too long has been regarded as a second-rate activity. Some statistics suggest that competitor countries spend between three and ten times as much on training as we do in the UK. France and Germany, for example, produce two to three times the number of craftsmen and ten times the number of individuals obtaining middle-ranking vocational qualifications.

The recent White Paper, 'Education and Training for the 21st Century', is an attempt to pull together education and training. Yet despite the passing on of responsibility to Training Enterprise Councils (TECs), the Construction Industry Training Board recently reported a 10 per cent drop in craft trainees.

The real problem is trying to encourage employers and individuals to take part in training. Unfortunately, many employers have in recent years been under pressure to cut back. Individuals may be more willing to pay for training if they can see a tangible reward, leading to a vocational qualification which will enhance their job prospects.

Over recent years the National Council for Vocational Qualifications has developed NVQs. An NVQ is a statement of competence relevant to work which is intended to facilitate entry into or progression further in employment, education and training. The hope is that the new qualifications will be quickly understood by teachers, pupils and parents and that employers use the qualifications as a basis for recruitment and view them as an essential way of motivating their employees. If employers fail to take on this responsibility, there is a strong likelihood that Britain's economic fortunes may take a further downward decline.

1 Do you feel that the case study exaggerates the plight of training in Britain?
2 Who do you feel should pay for training?
3 How should NVQs help to simplify vocational qualifications?

Case Study – Problems as opportunities

The following is an extract from an article by Tony Colman published in *Purchasing and Supply Management*.

'As a manager it always seemed to me that it was a good thing to be surrounded by problems. After all, I tried to convince myself, perhaps one reason for my continued employment was that my boss (poor misguided chap) rated me an effective problem-cracker. Far from it in reality, although it would have been wonderful to have been endowed with near-infallible "over the horizon" anticipation of the oncoming problem.

'Of course my mistake was not seeing problems as opportunities. Eventually, persuaded by academics and management gurus to "think positive", I finally came to see the profound truth underlying this concept.

'Soon I was able to welcome disasters. A sudden supplier bankruptcy became an opportunity to find a better source, a demand from Sales to double next month's output appeared as a welcome challenge, while a late engineering design change offered scope to develop one's persuasive power with disgruntled suppliers.'

1 *How does the author of the article approach problems?*
2 *To what extent should being able to deal with problems be part of a training programme?*
3 *Do you agree with the author that problems should be viewed as opportunities?*

10

Financial Resources

The performance of every organisation is in some way related to its stated objectives. In order to review performance and assess whether such objectives have been achieved an organisation needs to control, manage and interpret financial information.

In this chapter we look at the need to plan the activities of a business. This planning includes the construction of a basic business plan, forecasting of financial requirements, and assessing various sources of finance. We also look at the importance of the accounting function and at the necessity for accurate recording procedures.

What is performance?

Whether we are at school, at college, in an interview or meeting the parents of a new friend, we are concerned, to a greater or lesser extent, with how we get on, and how we might get on or perform in the future. In order to measure the results of such experiences we rely on **information** and **feedback**. Some of the information we receive might be precisely measured – for example, perhaps you achieved 64 per cent in an examination or took 2 hours 50 minutes and 25 seconds to run a marathon. This sort of information is described as **quantitative**. Other information may not be capable of precise measurement but may nevertheless support a view or a considered judgement – for example, somebody saying 'I liked that jacket', 'that colour is nice' or 'that car seems fast'. This sort of information is described as **qualitative**. Whether we like the information we receive will largely depend upon our **objectives** or **goals**. If, as above, you achieve 64 per cent in an examination and you expected or hoped to get 50 per cent, you would have exceeded your objectives. If you hoped for 70 per cent you would have been disappointed and not achieved your goal.

In the same way, organisations must be concerned with their performance and with what they are likely to be doing in the future. As we saw in Chapter 1, organisations do have goals and objectives which they strive to achieve. Just as we have to use quantitative and/or qualitative information to indicate a standard by which we can judge our success or failure, organisations are in exactly the same position.

Case Study – The world of British Airways

The following edited extracts are from a recent statement by Lord King, Chairman of British Airways:

'British Airways is not only the world's largest international airline – it is also the world's leading airline, and one of the most profitable.

'Our corporate statement of objectives lists seven goals, and we have new information systems to track our progress in achieving them.

'First of all, we must be safe and secure. Safety has always been our paramount concern, and it must remain so. Safety and security are areas of no compromise.

'Our second goal is another overriding objective: to deliver a strong and consistent financial performance. As any business person knows, you must make profits if you are to maintain and expand your business. *The airline business is often regarded as cyclical.* We have to prove that we can produce good profits consistently.

'We aim to secure a leading share of air travel business worldwide with a significant presence in all major geographical markets. *Hence our global strategy.*

'We seek to provide overall superior service and *good value for money in every market segment* in which we compete, and we are out to excel in anticipating and quickly responding to customer needs and competitor activity.

'Any service industry's real strength is its staff. Our policy is to sustain a working environment that attracts, *retains and develops committed employees* who share in the success of the company.

'Finally, our intention is to be a good neighbour, concerned for the community and the environment.

'Overall, our aim is to be the best and most successful company in the airline industry. It is an objective that we are in no doubt we can achieve.'

1 *Identify British Airways' seven goals.*
2 *Why do organisations require goals?*

3 *Explain the following:*
   a *'The airline business is often regarded as cyclical.'*
   b *'Hence our global strategy.'*
   c *'good value for money in every market segment'.*
   d *'retains and develops committed employees'.*
4 *Comment briefly upon how the BA information systems might measure the company's success in achieving its stated goals.*
5 *What is an overriding objective?*

Organisations use information to cover as wide a range of activities as possible. The more thorough and accurate the information, the more successful decision-making is likely to be and the better the performance. On the other hand, misleading information may result in poor decisions and poor performance.

Every level of management within an organisation has different information requirements for improving performance. For example:

- **Strategic** level managers deal with policy decisions and matters concerning the future of their organisation. They need summarised information from all parts of the organisation, as well as from outside.
- **Tactical** level managers make decisions based upon strategic policy decisions. They are invariably concerned with analysing issues *within* the organisation and often require information relating to time periods.
- **Organisational** decision makers deal with the 'grass roots' – the day-to-day running of an organisation. They need information which helps them to solve short-term practical problems.

How does a manager know what information to concentrate on to achieve the organisation's objectives? Remember Coloroll, the home furnishings group. Coloroll collapsed in June 1990 with debts of around £400 million. The company's objective had been to build a solid base for expansion, and by 1988 the group had annual sales of around £300 million. The target set for 1995 was £1 billion, but this it was destined to miss: poor management, over-emphasis on market-share figures and neglect of cash income contributed to the group's downfall.

The lesson to be learned from Coloroll is quite clear. All organisations, whether large or small, in the private or public sector, have a common feature – they all have to deal with **financial information**. If an organisation wishes to pursue its objectives in order to improve performance, it must not neglect its management of **financial resources**.

Sources of finance

An organisation has to engage in a **planning** process to consider what its financial requirements are and how they are going to be met. This financial planning process involves looking at present financial resources, **forecasting** changes likely to take place in the future, and then ensuring that the plans match the organisation's objectives.

Usually, in order to obtain finance, an organisation has to draw up a **business plan**. As we shall see later in this chapter, a business plan provides essential information to the people whose support is needed.

The first important decision about any finance is for how long a period you require it. Though **short-term** funds tend to be the most expensive, they are also more flexible – and this benefit can offset the lower cost of **long-term** funds, which might not be fully employed if fluctuations take place in business activity.

Many organisations expand by using short-term finance and then replace this type with long-term finance through a **funding operation**. Funding in this situation therefore raises long-term finance to pay off short-term finance, so that further short-term finance is then made available for the organisation to expand again.

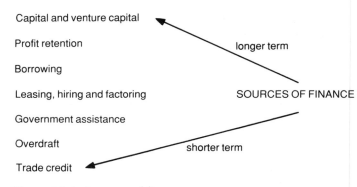

Capital and venture capital

Profit retention

Borrowing

Leasing, hiring and factoring

Government assistance

Overdraft

Trade credit

longer term

SOURCES OF FINANCE

shorter term

Figure 10.1 Sources of finance

Capital and venture capital

The type of capital available varies according to the make-up of the organisation.

A **sole trader** business is easy to set up and is the most common form of business ownership. Though a sole trader has considerable flexibility, this type of business carries a lot of risk. As a result a sole trader often relies on finance from personal sources and additional sums can be difficult to raise.

Sole traders frequently look to expand by taking in **partners**. Partners can bring in further capital together with greater expertise. They are particularly suitable for the professions, but limitations on numbers can restrict capital-raising opportunities.

Task

List the possible drawbacks of bringing in a partner to develop a sole trader business.

Share capital

In order to achieve the benefits of **limited liability** and extend their capital-raising opportunities, many partnerships transform themselves by a legal process into a registered company, and issue shares.

As we have seen in Chapter 1, companies can be either **private** or **public**. A **private limited company** has certain restrictions on the rights of members to transfer shares, and there are limits on the ability of the public to subscribe for share ownership. Membership of the **Unlisted Securities Market** (USM) is often seen as a half-way stage between a small company and a company that is fully listed on the London Stock Exchange. The USM, which was created in 1980 by the Stock Exchange, has enabled many smaller companies to become public and raise finance for expansion before progressing to a full Stock Exchange listing. A fully listed **public limited company** has almost endless opportunities to raise fresh capital from the financial markets.

of investors through an intermediary (a share dealer).

In a public limited company most capital is held usually in the form of **ordinary shares**. An ordinary share is a fixed unit of ownership and gives the holder the opportunity to share in the profits or losses. Most ordinary shares carry voting rights at shareholders' meetings. Shareholders elect the Board and sanction the level of dividends proposed. **Authorised capital** is the maximum amount of share capital a company is empowered by its shareholders to issue, whereas **issued capital** is the nominal amount of share capital issued to shareholders.

Task

Obtain a prospectus from a public company.

For example, a public limited company can create a **public issue by prospectus.** An issuing house (probably a merchant bank) organises the issue of shares by compiling a prospectus (a brochure), accompanied by an advertisement and an invitation to buy shares. This can be expensive – something like 7 per cent of the money raised by the issue can go to meet the costs.

Another method for a public company to raise finance is to make an **offer for sale**. The public company issues shares directly to an issuing house, which then offers them for sale at a fixed price. This too is an expensive method and is best used when the size of the issue is too small to need a public issue by prospectus.

A **rights issue** is a cheaper method of obtaining finance – existing shareholders are offered shares directly at an advantageous price. Another method which avoids the expense of 'going to the market' is a **placing**, whereby shares are placed with a number

---

Case Study – Burton wins approval for cash call

THE BURTON GROUP PLC

Sir John Hoskyns, Chairman of Burton Group, had to ride out a bumpy shareholders meeting. He had to resist calls for the sacking of the entire Board, and in doing so won overwhelming approval for the Board's £161 million cash call.

Sir John defended the group's strategy, controversial pay rises for senior directors and a one-for-one rights issue. Questioners at the meeting were mostly hostile. One called for the entire Board to be replaced. To applause, another said: 'It looks like the Board is looking after the interests of directors at the expense of shareholders.'

Several complaints were made about the directors' contracts signed just before the group announced the rights issue. The chief executive earned £375 000 and other directors more than £200 000 a year. Sir John rejected some analysts' suggestions that the group was close to ruin. In the end the rights issue was approved by the shareholders present by 108 votes to 10.

1 How does this case illustrate a division between the loyalties directors have to the company, the shareholders and to themselves?

2 Explain what is meant by a 'one-for-one' rights issue.

3 How would you feel about this rights issue if you were a Burton shareholder?

Another class of shares is **deferred shares** (or **founders shares**). These are issued to members of the family which built the business, and they sometimes carry enhanced voting rights so that a small group of people can maintain control of a family business.

Task

Identify the founders of some large companies. Comment upon how the organisations they founded have developed.

Preference shares are a less flexible class of share. Owners of these shares are not, strictly speaking, part owners of the company and their exact rights will be found in the company's Articles of Association. However, they do have preferential rights to receive dividends if profits exist and, in the event of a company winding up, will receive the face value of their shares before the ordinary shareholders are repaid. On the other hand, dividends on preference shares are limited.

Some companies issue **cumulative preference shares** and this avoids the difficulty of having to pay preference shareholders if profits are too small. The holder of the cumulative preference share will receive arrears of dividends accumulated from the past in later years. **Redeemable preference shares** are

such that the company can buy back the shares from the shareholders. Redemption can be made from profits or reserves or it may be financed by a fresh issue of more shares. **Participating preference shareholders** receive dividends above the fixed rate when ordinary shareholders have been paid and if the company has done well in a particular year.

It should be noted that organisations in the **public sector** are publically owned and – unless they are going through the process of privatisation – cannot go to the Stock Exchange for capital. They can, however, use the financial markets for loans.

Venture capital

Venture capital is capital available from non-banking commercial organisations who offer investment for private customers for specific projects. The provider of the finance usually demands a strong element of control over the borrowing company.

Profit retention

A very important source of capital for British industry is **profits** that have been 'ploughed back'. Initially profits are subject to Corporation Tax payable to the Department of Inland Revenue. Then a proportion of the remaining profit is paid as dividends to shareholders. The directors recommend how much profit should be allocated as dividends. Whatever is left over is retained in the business as reinvested profit, and is shown in the balance sheet

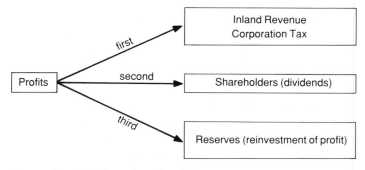

Figure 10.2 Order of profit allocation

as **reserves**. The funds represented by the reserves are spread out amongst the assets of the business.

Borrowing

Financial institutions today try to provide a package of lending facilities designed to meet the needs of the market. **Borrowing** is considered an acceptable feature of commercial activity. The charge for borrowing is **interest**, and a crucial element in calculating the interest charge is the amount of **risk** involved in the loan.

An organisation may negotiate a loan from a **high-street bank** such as National Westminster or Barclays. With these loans, repayments are usually credited to a separate loan account held by the organisation and are repaid in equal instalments. Alternatively, the **merchant banks** provide specialist business and financial services.

A long-term loan obtainable through the Stock Exchange market is called a **debenture**. This is an acknowledgement of a debt taken up by a company for a fixed rate of interest. A debenture is transferable – that is, it can be bought and sold like a share.

Other sources of finance include the government's small-firms Loan Guarantee Scheme, and loans from the Rural Development Commission.

Lenders always try to minimise the risks of loan finance. When providing finance for a limited company, it is possible for the lender to demand a **personal guarantee** of repayment from the main shareholder, and this effectively removes that shareholder's limited liability and puts him or her in a similar position to a partner or sole trader. Lenders also frequently ask for **security** or **collateral** against a loan. In this way certain assets are 'secured' and, if the business has to be wound up, the lender has priority over other creditors in claiming any money raised from the sale of these secured assets (office furniture and equipment, vehicles, machinery etc.)

Case Study – Japanese borrowers

The Japanese have had a reputation for being very careful and wise savers. However, a report from the Economic Planning Agency has raised many eyebrows, for its shows that Japanese consumers now owe more than Americans! Japanese consumers now tend to borrow 20 per cent against their disposable

income compared with 19 per cent for American consumers. The Japanese, who have only recently learned to spend, have certainly learned how to borrow.

1 *To what extent has borrowing today become a way of life for individuals and organisations?*
2 *What might happen if an organisation borrows too much in comparison with its income?*

Leasing, hiring and factoring

One way in which an organisation can obtain the *use* of an asset without having to pay for it outright is through **leasing**. The *lessee* uses the asset and makes regular payments to the *lessor* who owns it. An **operating lease** is for a small amount and a **capital lease** is for a large amount over an extended period. The procedure for leasing is for the lessee company to choose the exact equipment it requires, and this is then purchased and supplied by the lessor company. A contract determines the rent payable, maintenance, conditions and so forth.

Task

What are the advantages to an organisation of leasing equipment rather than purchasing it outright from profits, from a bank loan or from any other source of finance?

Finance houses, which often have links with banks, provide a variety of schemes which enable customers to receive goods immediately and make payments over an agreed period of time. Goods on **hire-purchase** remain the property of the finance company until the customer has made all of the payments, whereas other **credit purchasing schemes** permit the goods to belong to the customer from the time of the first payment.

Factoring can provide finance for an organisation by making use of the amounts of money owed to the organisation by its own **debtors**. Factoring companies 'take over' the debts – they invoice the customers, collect the money due and pursue any slow payers; in the meantime the organisation has the benefit of the payments from the factoring company.

Government assistance

A range of schemes is made available by central and local government to help organisations requiring finance. Many of these schemes are directed specifically at small organisations. Examples are

Regional Selective Grants, Regional Enterprise Grants, and the government's Loan Guarantee Scheme.

Overdraft

A bank **overdraft** is the most frequently used form of short-term finance and is often used to ease a cash-flow problem. An arrangement is made between the customer and the bank to agree a limit up to which a customer can draw funds over and above what is deposited. Interest is calculated on the level of overdraft on a daily basis. Since overdrafts are repayable on demand, organisations must make sure that they are in a position to pay back the money owed.

Trade credit

A useful form of finance for all organisations is that of **trade credit** allowed by suppliers. The credit period is the time between receiving the good or service and being obliged to make payment for it. Credit periods are usually governed by the type of business and the relationship between the purchaser and the supplier. Although no rate of interest is attached to trade credit, cash discounts may be forfeited if payments are not made within the agreed time. Organisations trying to extend trade credit in order to improve their short-term cash situation endanger their reputation with suppliers.

Case Study – Late payers deal the fatal blow

This account is now overdue for payment

The UK recession has claimed many casualties. Among the victims are many small and medium-sized businesses, many of which blame their plight on more than economic downturn and high interest rates. They claim that having supplied goods or services to large companies, late payments by those customers are often the final fatal blow.

It is a common accusation that, by deliberately withholding payments for months on end, many well-known public companies greatly enhance their own cash positions, but at the same time squeeze the life out of weaker, more vulnerable suppliers who find it difficult to fight back – and might lose business if they did.

A nationwide survey of 250 financial directors of large, small and medium-sized companies by accountant Pannell Kerr Foster found that 70 per cent believed that late payment was making the recession worse, and an overwhelming 96 per cent said it was adding to their business problems. Nine out of ten companies said that small firms were hit hardest by late payments. The survey also revealed that 76 per cent of firms had to wait a staggering three months or more for their bills to be paid, while only 14 per cent received their money within the widely accepted contractual credit period of 30 days.

Richard Pearson, the Chairman of Pannell Kerr Foster, commented: 'The message we have to get across is that companies – small, family-run firms – need to adopt a much tougher attitude towards credit control and take active measures to ensure that they are paid what they are owed on time.'

Various other surveys show that, on average, companies take 75 working days to pay suppliers' invoices. Late paying seems to have become a culture in the UK. Companies seem to think it is common sense for them to delay payment for as long as possible, but many feel that late payments are putting certain categories of business organisation at a considerable competitive disadvantage with foreign businesses. It seems likely, however, that the little organisation at the end of the payment chain will continue to suffer the brunt of late payments.

1 Explain why late payments by debtors may cause a fatal blow to a business.
2 How might withholding payments improve an organisation's cash flow?
3 In your opinion, what is a reasonable credit period?
4 What is meant by credit control?
5 Why is late payment causing a competitive disadvantage?

Forecasting financial requirements

Whereas profit is a **surplus** from trading activities, **cash** is a liquid asset which enables an organisation to buy the goods and services it requires in order to add value to them, trade and make profits. It is therefore possible for an organisation to be profitable while at the same time creditors have not been paid and liquid resources have not been properly accounted for.

On the other hand, an organisation must look carefully to see that its use of cash is to its best advantage. For example, if it holds too much cash in the bank it might be sacrificing income it could otherwise earn.

An organisation must therefore ensure that it has sufficient cash to carry out its plans, and ensure that the cash coming in is sufficient to cover the cash going out. At the same time it must take into account any cash surpluses it might have in the bank. The organisation is said to have a certain **cash-flow** position. Looking carefully at the availability of liquid funds is essential to the smooth running or any organisation. With cash planning or budgeting it is possible to forecast the flows into and out of an organisation's bank account so that any surpluses or deficits can be highlighted and any necessary action can be taken promptly. For example, overdraft facilities may be arranged in good time so that funds are available when required.

Case Study – When the numbers fail to add up

Every year thousands of businesses fail as a result of cash-flow problems. The root cause of these problems seems to be weak financial management, which is frequently identified when the businesses are wound up. Today it has become one of the key reasons for business failure.

The paramount importance of effective cash management is touted again and again in booklets, guides and starter packs. For example:

'Finance . . . is where your numbers stand up and be counted.' (Price Waterhouse)
'The banker is far more concerned by the cash flow that trading generates.' (Ernst & Young)
'Many businesses fail to make profits or to have enough cash at the right time, because the management has not planned ahead.' (National Westminster Bank)
'The big question in cash flow is: what would happen if … …? (Barclays Bank)

Despite these points being made in every booklet and guide, the message concerning weak financial management seems slow to penetrate.

Lee Manning, a senior manager at Buchler Phillips, says that 'weakness in company management and the information available to it' is a common theme running through reports of business reviews carried out for lenders. He identifies five principal components within that theme:

● Most companies which suffer long-term financial difficulties are victims of inadequate and insufficient management information, with particular emphasis on up-to-date cash-flow information.
● Cash-flow forecasts are generally prepared at the start of the business period and not reviewed again until the period has elapsed, thus defeating the object of cash-flow analysis.
● Cash-flow forecasts are generally highly optimistic.
● Management tends to ignore the quality of debtors and tends to look at the face value of invoices rather than how easy it is to get the money in.
● Companies are often brought down by large speculative projects which represent a move away from their core business.

According to one firm of accountants, businesses often reach crisis conditions before thinking about their cash flow. The major lesson to be learnt from accounting is that 'cash is king'.

1 *Explain why an organisation's cash flow is considered important by its bank.*
2 *What does Barclays Bank mean when its representative says 'The big question in cash flow is: what would happen if … …?'*
3 *Why, in your opinion, do so many businesses ignore cash flow?*

Preparing a cash-flow forecast

In order to prepare a cash-flow forecast, it is necessary to know or to estimate what receipts and payments are likely in the future and when they will happen.

Let us imagine, for example, that C. Moon Ltd has £500 in the bank on 1 January. The owner, Christine Moon, anticipates that her **receipts** over the next six months are likely to be as follows:

JAN	FEB	MAR	APR	MAY	JUN
£2300	£1400	£5300	£6100	£4700	£1400

She has also worked out what her **payments** are likely to be over the next six months:

JAN	FEB	MAR	APR	MAY	JUN
£1400	£4100	£5600	£5000	£3100	£900

Christine Moon is concerned about whether she needs an **overdraft facility** and, if so, when she is likely to need it. Her cash-flow forecast for the six months would look like Figure 10.3. It is possible to match receipts to payments to forecast her expected cash position at the end of each month. Note that whenever the cash balance is a negative, brackets are put around the figures. C Moon Ltd therefore requires an overdraft from February to the start of May.

	JAN £	FEB £	MAR £	APR £	MAY £	JUN £
Cash balance	500	1400	(1300)	(1600)	(500)	1100
Add receipts	2300	1400	5300	6100	4700	1400
	2800	2800	4000	4500	4200	2500
Less payments	1400	4100	5600	5000	3100	900
Balance carried forward	1400	(1300)	(1600)	(500)	1100	1600

Figure 10.3 The cash-flow forecast of C. Moon Ltd

Task

In the example in the text, what would be the consequences if C. Moon Ltd's actual receipts for January, February and March were each £1300 higher than expected? Assuming that all other receipts and payments remain the same, how would this affect the overdraft requirements, and the cash position at the end of June?

Task

Prepare the cash-flow forecast of S. Todd Ltd. The business has £250 in the bank and the owner anticipates that his *receipts* over the next six months are likely

to be as follows:

JAN	FEB	MAR	APR	MAY	JUN
£1400	£1600	£1500	£1000	£900	£700

He has also worked out his *payments* and expects these to be:

JAN	FEB	MAR	APR	MAY	JUN
£1100	£700	£900	£1400	£1000	£900

The cash-flow forecasts we have considered so far have shown monthly totals. In real life, however, the information is likely to be broken down into specific components. It is useful to ascertain when each of these components needs to be applied and what the effect of each is. It is therefore possible to modify the cash-flow forecast by making it more detailed.

For example, Andrew Nut sets up in business as a manufacturer of string vests by putting £28 500 into a business bank account on 1 January. For the first six months of the year he anticipates or **budgets** for the following situations.

- His forecasts for the purchase of raw materials and sales receipts for finished goods, based upon extensive market research, are as follows:

	PURCHASES (£)	SALES (£)
January	6 500	5 500
February	7 000	7 100
March	7 300	8 000
April	7 500	14 000
May	6 100	17 000
June	6 500	14 300

- Andrew Nut has arranged one month's credit from suppliers, so raw materials purchased in January will have to be paid for in February.
- He expects one-half of sales to be for cash and the other half on credit. He anticipates two months on average to be taken by credit customers; i.e. sales made in January on credit will not be settled until March.
- Wages are expected to be £1000 per month, paid in the same month.
- Machinery must be purchased for £15 500 on 1 January and must be paid for in the same month.

197

- Rent for his factory is £6000 per annum, payable in equal instalments at the start of each month.
- Other costs (**overheads**) are £1500 per month, and these are assumed to be paid in the month following that in which they are incurred.
- In April, Andrew Nut expects to receive an inheritance from his Auntie Kitty of £8000, which he will put straight into the business bank account.

Andrew Nut's cash-flow forecast for the first six months would therefore be as in Figure 10.4.

	JAN £	FEB £	MAR £	APR £	MAY £	JUN £
RECEIPTS						
Sales – cash	2 750	3 550	4 000	7 000	8 500	7 150
Sales – credit	0	0	2 750	3 550	4 000	7 000
Other receipts	0	0	0	8 000	0	0
Total receipts	2 750	3 550	6 750	18 550	12 500	14 150
PAYMENTS						
Raw materials	0	6 500	7 000	7 300	7 500	6 100
Wages	1 000	1 000	1 000	1 000	1 000	1 000
Machinery	15 500	0	0	0	0	0
Rent	500	500	500	500	500	500
Other overheads	0	1 500	1 500	1 500	1 500	1 500
Total payments	17 000	9 500	10 000	10 300	10 500	9 100
Opening balance	28 500	14 250	8 300	5 050	13 300	15 300
Add receipts	2 750	3 550	6 750	18 550	12 500	14 150
	31 250	17 800	15 050	23 600	25 800	29 450
Less payments	17 000	9 500	10 000	10 300	10 500	9 100
Balance carried forward	14 250	8 300	5 050	13 300	15 300	20 350

Figure 10.4 The cash-flow forecast of A. Nut Ltd

Amending the forecast

We have seen that it is essential for any organisation, particularly one starting up in business, to prepare a cash-flow forecast. It is also important for the organisation to amend the forecast as events take place. It is possible for a business, as we mentioned earlier, to be quite profitable but still not have sufficient cash for its needs. To be in a position to draw up an accurate forecast an organisation must be able to predict the flows of cash coming into and leaving the business and the **timings** of these flows.

Task

Albert Spanner sets up as a manufacturer of machine tools by putting £17 400 into the business bank account on 1 January. For the first six months of the year he anticipates or budgets for the following:

- His forecasts for the purchase of raw materials and sales receipts for finished goods, based upon market research, are as follows:

	PURCHASES (£)	SALES (£)
January	3 200	2 000
February	3 350	4 000
March	4 185	6 200
April	5 500	7 000
May	5 700	8 200
June	5 900	8 400

- Albert Spanner has arranged two months' credit from suppliers.
- He expects one-quarter of sales to be for cash and the other three-quarters to be on credit. He anticipates two months credit on average to be taken by credit customers.
- Wages are expected to be £800 per month, paid in the same month.
- Machinery is to be purchased in January for £2 500 and in April for £3 500. On both occasions the owner anticipates making payments in the month following purchase.
- Rent for his factory is £3 000 per annum, payable in equal instalments at the start of each month.
- Other overheads are £1 000 per month, to be paid in the month following that in which they are incurred.
- In May, Albert Spanner will take out a loan for £4000, which he intends to put straight into the business bank account.

Prepare A. Spanner's cash-flow forecast for the first six months of the year.

Task

Construct a cash-flow forecast, on a week-by-week basis, of your own receipts and payments for the next six weeks.

The business plan

A **business plan** is a key requirement of any successful enterprise, no matter how big or well established. If you want to start a business, the business plan is vital as it helps you to anticipate problems and make arrangements to deal with them. It also gives essential information to the people whose support you need – particularly anyone lending money.

In order to construct a business plan it is necessary to have the answers to several questions, of which the following are the most important:

- Will people or organisations wish to buy the good or service you intend to provide?
- What competition exists?
- What will be the objectives of the business?
- What premises, equipment etc. will be required?
- Will you need to employ staff?
- Where will you need to locate the business?
- How much finance will be required over a certain period?
- What sources of finance are available?
- What will be the cost of borrowing?
- What other forms of assistance may be available?
- How successful is the enterprise likely to be?

The answers to all of these questions should be put together in an organised plan. This will then take into consideration almost all areas of concern and **integrate** them into a single document. The business plan is intended to be a vision of what the organisation is likely to achieve and how it is likely to perform.

A typical business plan might have the following headings:

- **Introduction.** This will explain the objectives of the business and how it is intended they should be achieved.
- **Details of the business.** This will be the name and address of the business and a detailed description of the product or service being offered.
- **Business organisation.** This will state whether the organisation will take the form of a partnership, private limited company etc.
- **The market.** The plan will indicate the nature and likely size of the market, whether it is static, expanding or in decline, how many competitors there are, and any special features of the product or service on offer.
- **Marketing.** The plan may also indicate the marketing mix.
- **Costs.** Details of premises, machinery, equipment, vehicles etc. will be given, with an estimate of their life spans.
- **Costings.** All the financial details will be brought together to show the cost of producing the product or service, the price it is proposed to charge, the projected profit, and the cash-flow forecast.
- **Finance.** This will show how it is intended to raise the money – how much should come from personal sources, how much should be borrowed etc.

Task

Look at the suggested headings and contents for the business plan. Comment briefly on how each area would be of interest to an organisation providing some of the finance for the enterprise.

The importance of accounting

Cash-flow forecasting and business planning are not the only requirements for an organisation wishing to manage its activities successfully. It also has to set up an **accounting system**, which may be simple or complex.

The accounting process is concerned with measuring, recording, communicating and analysing all of the financial aspects of an organisation's activities. Accounting acts as an information system by processing business data so that interested parties can be provided with the means to understand how well or badly the organisation is performing.

Business data is the input into the accounting system, and the output is valuable **financial data**. Such information can then be passed to those who need it for decision-making and record-keeping purposes (see Figure 10.5).

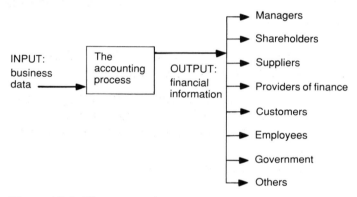

Figure 10.5 The accounting process

For example, managers require information in order to run the organisation efficiently by monitoring the results of their decisions. Shareholders want to assess the performance of managers and need to know how much profit or income they can expect to take from the business. Suppliers need to know whether the organisation can pay its debts, and customers may wish to ensure that supplies will be forthcoming. Any provider of finance for the organisation – such as a bank – will wish to know about the organisation's ability to make repayments of a loan. The tax authorities (Inland Revenue and Customs & Excise) require information so that they can make accurate assessments for tax. Employees have a right to know how an organisation is performing and how secure their jobs are. Financial advisors and brokers need to know about an

organisation's activities so that they can advise their clients accurately.

Financial accounting

The process of accounting can be divided into two broad areas. **Financial accounting** is primarily concerned with the recording process and the information that can be extracted from such a process. It ensures that an organisation's accounts give a **true and fair view** of its activities and that they comply with the provisions of the Companies Acts.

At the end of a certain period, accountants prepare summary statements – called **final accounts**. By studying these, shareholders know how the directors or managers have performed on their behalf. From the final accounts, **ratios** and other figures can be extracted which provide fairly precise **indicators of performance**.

Financial accounting involves auditing, bookkeeping, advice on taxation, insolvency and many other areas.

Management accounting

Though the information from financial accounting is important, it deals only with the past and tends to view the organisation as a whole. **Management accounting** is concerned with providing information for managers so that they can plan, control and make decisions about future activities. It involves guiding an organisation in a particular direction so that it can achieve its objectives. Business operations can be closely monitored to ensure that processes, products, departments and operations are managed efficiently.

The accounting profession

The accounting profession is represented by a number of different bodies. For somebody to call themselves a **qualified accountant,** he or she must have passed examinations to have become a full member of one of these professional bodies. They include:

Institute of Chartered Accountants in England and Wales
Institute of Chartered Accountants in Ireland
Institute of Chartered Accountants in Scotland
Chartered Association of Certified Accountants
Chartered Institute of Management Accountants
Chartered Institute of Public Finance and Accountancy

Standards

If a number of accountants were presented with the same data and asked to present the accounts for an organisation they might well come up with different figures or arrive at different conclusions. This happens because estimates have to be made about future events, and this involves an element of opinion and guesswork. For example, in calculating depreciation – how an asset loses its value over time – estimates have to be made for the useful life of each asset; accountants will have different estimates.

The 1970s saw the appearance of the first Statements of Standard Accounting Practice (SSAPs), designed to ensure consistency and comparability between the financial statements of companies. These **standards** describe the approved methods of accounting which should be applied to all final accounts so that a 'true and fair' view is obtained.

own right. Creation of the Accounting Standards Board is a progressive step designed to produce a better world of accounting.

In the 1960s the growth of the accounting profession had gone unnoticed. However, this quiet progress was brought to an abrupt halt following the hostile takeover of Associated Electrical Industries (AEI) by General Electric Company (GEC). In 1967, AEI had forecast a profit of £10 million, and GEC based its takeover bid partly on this expected profit. But the actual results for 1967, revealed after the takeover had been completed, showed an AEI loss of £4.5 million. In the ensuing controversy it became clear that much of the difference arose because of different subjective judgements. This led to the formation of the Accounting Standards Committee and SSAPs.

In more recent years there have been further concerns about the ASC; for example:

- a general failure to respond to emerging issues
- a lack of timeliness in setting standards
- doubts over the independence of the standard setters
- concern over the flexibility of their pronouncements.

There is a feeling today that the Accounting Standards Board will have greater independence.

1 Why are SSAPs needed?
2 What were the criticisms of the ASC?
3 What are the benefits of an independent Accounting Standards Board?

Case Study – The Accounting Standards Board

On 1 August 1990 the Accounting Standards Board took over from the Accounting Standards Committee. Unlike the ASC which was a joint committee of the six major accounting bodies, the new Board is independent of the professional institutes and will set accounting standards in its

A good example of one of these standards is SSAP2 which refers to the four fundamental concepts that should underlie financial accounts (see Figure 10.6). The **going concern** concept assumes that an organisation will persist with its current activities into the foreseeable future. The **accruals/matching** concept recognises that costs are incurred as soon as their liability is taken on, and not later as money is paid. Thus as the end of an accounting period all

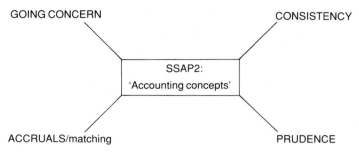

Figure 10.6 Accounting concepts

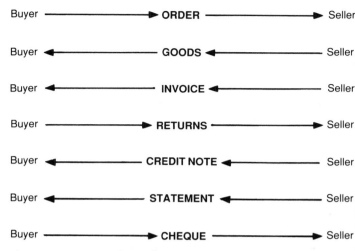

Figure 10.7 Recording a business transaction

transactions relating to that period will appear in the accounts whether payments have been made or not.

The **consistency** concept is that the accounting treatment of similar items should be consistently applied within each accounting period and from one period to the next. Finally, the concept of **prudence** (or **conservatism**) is that businesses should not lay claim to profits unless they are sure they have been earned.

Financial record keeping

As we have seen, the recording of business transactions provides accounting information. The first stage of any transaction generates a business document known as a **prime document**, which serves as the basis for an entry to be made in the books of accounts.

On receipt of an **order** for goods, a seller will send the goods required to the buyer and issue an **invoice**. The order and the invoice are important documents and have details of vital aspects of the transaction. If the goods are unsatisfactory and have to be returned to the seller, the latter may issue a **credit note** to reduce the invoice total.

If a buyer engages in several transactions with a particular seller, invoices may not be paid as and when received – the buyer will wait for each monthly **statement**, which is a record of all the transactions. As the majority of transactions taking place between organisations are on credit, it is essential that proper documentation is used. These documents then provide the basis for recording financial information by both the buyer and the seller.

Case Study – Electronic data interchange

Electronic data interchange (EDI) has the objective of simplifying and speeding business transactions between trading partners. It achieves this by allowing data, messages or documents to be transferred directly from one company's computer to another's.

The obvious benefits are savings on paperwork, time, and the elimination of data re-keying. It follows that the more paperwork an organisation handles, the more apparent will be the potential benefits.

Although the early initiatives for EDI originated with the large manufacturers, retailers and distribution companies, increasingly the benefits of electronic trading are being experienced through the mid-range and smaller companies.

In the 1990s, there is really no reason for trading with regular partners through the postal service. Now that communications software suppliers can deliver simple, automated systems for communicating EDI messages, electronic trading should rapidly become an accepted and preferred method of conducting business.

1 *What benefits other than reduced paperwork might EDI provide?*
2 *Will EDI make a supplier more responsive to the market?*
3 *Can you see any dangers in using EDI?*
4 *How might EDI affect a small supplier with a wide client base in a horizontal market?*

Double-entry bookkeeping

Accounting transactions are recorded in **ledgers** using the process known as **double-entry bookkeeping**. This system recognises that there are two elements to every transaction. For example, if you buy a bar of chocolate you *give* (i.e. pay) cash and *receive* chocolate. Under this system every transaction necessitates an entry into two accounts: one account is **debited** because it receives value and another account is **credited** because it has lost value. A separate account is held for each element of each transaction and every debit entry is always matched by a credit entry.

Most organisations divide their double-entry accounting systems into four main areas:

- The **sales ledger** comprises the individual accounts of debtors, being people or organisations to whom goods or services have been sold on credit. They become debtors until they pay for the goods or services they have received or, if they fail to pay, until their debt is declared to be a bad debt.
- The **purchases ledger** comprises the individual accounts of creditors, being people or organisations from whom goods and services have been purchased on credit. Creditors remain in the ledger until they have been paid.
- The **cash book** records the organisation's receipts and payments.
- The **general ledger** comprises all of the other accounts – for example, expenses, assets such as land and buildings and machinery, sales and purchases accounts, an account recording the owner's capital, loan accounts etc.

Ledger accounts at one time were held in large leather-bound volumes which were then meticulously looked after. Today computer systems are extensively used to deal with the recording of ledger transactions. Changes brought about by information technology have improved the way in which information is captured, stored and processed.

Case Study – Information technology and accounting

Information technology has had an impact on many of the functions carried out in accounting offices. For example, it assists in the capture and identification of information. More rapid capture helps to make an organisation more efficient. Another benefit is that data can be processed more quickly and in a range of ways. Users of an accounting system can decide what they need, how they want the information and then gain direct access to it.

Through IT, the users of an accounting system come from a wide range of areas in an organisation. Accounting information has developed a wider clientele, who are able to use the information to make better decisions across the organisation.

1 *Make a list of the benefits of using information technology in the accounting process.*
2 *What demands might the use of IT in accounting put upon staff training and development across the organisation?*

Books of prime entry

As it is generally not practicable to enter each and every transaction individually into ledgers, books of **prime entry** tend to be used. These are used to record details of all business transactions, and then similar transactions are added together to provide *totals* which are entered into the ledgers at regular intervals.

Books of prime entry include:

- the sales daybook which is prepared from invoices issued and which gives sales totals
- the purchases daybook which is prepared from invoices received and which gives purchases totals
- returns books prepared from credit notes issued and received
- the cash book (which as we have seen is also a division of the ledger) which records receipts and payments.

The sales daybook

The **sales daybook** records all the credit sales made by the organisation from the invoices issued for each transaction made. It therefore provides a total for the credit sales made over a period, and this total is transferred at regular intervals to the **sales account** in the general ledger. Information for individual customer accounts is also transferred from the sales daybook, but this time to the sales ledger to list the organisation's **debtors**.

SALES DAYBOOK			
DATE	NAME	INVOICE NO	£
199_			
4 June	B. Hicks Ltd	10237	451.20
7 June	Gem Stones Ltd	10238	54.85
15 June	B. Sting PLC	10239	368.85
21 June	R. Donald	10240	21.50
27 June	J. Lowry	10241	82.25
30 June	Transferred to Sales Account		978.65

Figure 10.8 Part of a sales daybook

The purchases daybook

The **purchases daybook** records all the credit purchases made by the organisation and is prepared from all the invoices received from suppliers. It is used to provide a total made for credit purchases over a period, and this is transferred at regular intervals to the **purchases account** in the general ledger. Information about individual **creditors** is transferred to the purchases ledger.

PURCHASES DAYBOOK			
DATE	NAME	INVOICE NO	£
199_			
3 June	R. Thompson Ltd	B3456	34.50
18 June	M. Pillings Ltd	A789	78.40
21 June	E. Murphy Ltd	44544	125.70
28 June	A Donkey Ltd	R567	35.75
30 June	Transferred to Purchases Account		274.35

Figure 10.9 Part of a purchases daybook

Returns books

Often when goods are bought and sold **returns** are made – perhaps because the goods are faulty, or because the wrong goods have been delivered.

Goods that have been sold by the organisation and returned back from a customer are known as **returns inwards** or **sales returns**. Credit notes are issued when the returns are received, and these notes are used to compile the **returns inwards daybook**. The total from the returns inwards daybook is transferred to the **returns inwards account** in the general ledger. All of the accounts of each customer/debtor returning goods are also adjusted in the **sales ledger,** and the amounts they owe are reduced to cater for the returns.

RETURNS INWARDS DAYBOOK			
DATE	NAME	CREDIT NOTE NO	£
199_			
12 June	B. Hicks Ltd	CN525	10.00
19 June	B. Sting	CN526	18.50
30 June	Transferred to Returns Inwards Account		28.50

Figure 10.10 Part of a returns inwards daybook

On the other hand, goods that have been bought by the organisation but sent back to the suppliers are known as **returns outwards** or **purchases returns**. Credit notes are sent by suppliers when the goods are returned to them, and these are used to compile the **returns outwards daybook**. The total from the returns outwards daybook is transferred to the **returns outwards account** in the general ledger. All of the accounts of each supplier/creditor to whom goods have been returned are also adjusted in the **purchases ledger,** and the amounts owed to them are reduced to cater for the returns.

RETURNS OUTWARDS DAYBOOK

DATE	NAME	CREDIT NOTE NO	£
199_			
21 June	M. Pillings Ltd	X33	21.00
28 June	E. Murphy Ltd	A21	5.00
30 June	Transferred to Returns Outwards Account		26.00

Figure 10.11 **Part of a returns outwards daybook**

Task

Imagine that you work as a clerk for A. Corn Ltd, which is a small electrical business in which all purchases and sales are on credit. You have just returned from holiday and find a boxfile on your desk containing invoices received from suppliers, copies of invoices sent out to customers, credit notes received from suppliers, and copies of credit notes sent to customers. From the detailed list which follows, enter the transactions into the appropriate daybooks.

01 August Invoice 1345 sent to R. T. Electronics Ltd for £45.40
02 August Invoice A230 received from Breman PLC for £1250.25
03 August Invoice 1346 sent to M. P. Electrics Ltd for £82.25

04 August Invoice X217 received from P. Thompson Ltd for £95.34
05 August Credit note P254 received from Breman PLC for £90.10
06 August Invoice 1347 sent to R. Bingley for £20.00
07 August Credit note CN121 sent to R. T. Electronics Ltd for £10.00
08 August Invoice 14279 received from A. Bognor Ltd for £324.76
09 August Credit note H20 received from P. Thompson Ltd for £12.30
10 August Invoice 1348 sent to R. T. Electronics Ltd for £27.59
11 August Credit note CN122 sent to R. Bingley for £5.00
12 August Invoice 18948 received from H. Charlton Ltd for £345.99
13 August Invoice 1349 sent to R. T. Electronics Ltd for £675.45

The cash book

The **cash book** is used for recording receipts and payments of both cash and cheques. The most common form is the **two-column cash book** which has two columns on the left-hand side of the page and two columns on the right-hand side. The first left-hand column is for the receipts of cash and the second left-hand column is for the receipts of cheques. The first right-hand column is for the payments of cash and the second right-hand column is for the payments of cheques. The cheque columns are usually labelled 'bank'.

Often there is a need for a transfer between the bank columns and the cash columns – for example, when putting cash into the bank. This is known as a **contra** transaction and requires two entries (a withdrawal or payment of cash and a receipt of money into the bank account – see Figure 10.12).

In Figure 10.12, note that the contra entry is indicated by the letter 'C' and, in the situation indicated, requires £100 to be taken from the cash

CASH BOOK

		RECEIPTS					PAYMENTS		
DATE	DETAILS	CASH	BANK	DATE		DETAILS		CASH	BANK
199_		£	£					£	£
1 Jun	Balances brought down	200	1200	2 Jun		Rent			50
3 Jun	Sales	50		3 Jun		SMP Ltd			200
7 Jun	Sales	150		4 Jun		Purchases		200	
16 Jun	R. Peters		430	17 Jun		Bank	C	100	
17 Jun	Cash **C**		100	21 Jun		Wages			500
22 Jun	Sales	200		23 Jun		R. Smith			125
				24 Jun		Electricity			50
				30 Jun		Balances carried down		300	805
		600	1730					600	1730
1 Jul	Balances b/d	300	805						

Figure 10.12 Entries in the cash book

column on the payments side and then paid into the bank account on the receipts side. Note also that, at the end of the month, the balances left in cash and in the bank account are calculated by adding up the columns and taking the columns with the least from the columns with the most. The balances are then **brought down** for the start of the new month.

Task

Imagine that you are working for I. M. Lucky Ltd as a cashier, and one of your duties is to maintain the two column cash book. Prepare the cash book from the details below and balance it at the end of the month:

- 01 Aug Balances cash £265, bank £1657
- 02 Aug Received £278 cash from sales
- 03 Aug Payment of motor expenses £44 by cheque
- 04 Aug Received £125 cheque from A. Bennett
- 07 Aug Payment for stationery £10 cash
- 08 Aug Received £400 cash from sales

- 10 Aug Payment to R. Sid Ltd £76 by cheque
- 17 Aug Put £350 cash into the bank
- 22 Aug Received cheque from A. Pridgeon for £65
- 25 Aug Pay B. Nasty Ltd £322 by cheque
- 27 Aug Received £30 cash from sales
- 28 Aug Pay wages £476 by cheque
- 29 Aug Payment for stationery £33 with cash

Checking the cash book

At the end of every accounting period the **closing balances** in the cash book should be checked. The actual **cash in hand** should be counted and checked to ensure that if agrees with the figure in the cash column. If it does not, this may be due to one of the following:

- an incorrect entry into the cash book
- figures totalled incorrectly
- loss or theft of cash
- loss of a source document such as a receipt.

The bank reconciliation statement

Checking the bank columns of the cash book is not quite so easy since the money is deposited with the bank. It is therefore important that the cashier always checks the cash book records against the organisation's **bank statements**. This matching of the cash book balances with the balances shown in the bank statements involves the preparation of a **bank reconciliation statement**. Preparing such a statement is vital to ensure that mistakes have not been made either in the cash book or in the bank statement.

However, it is quite common – *even if a mistake has not been made* – for a bank statement balance to differ from the balance in the bank column of the cash book. This may be due to items that have appeared in the cash book but which do not yet appear on the bank statement. These are known as **timing differences**. Timing differences may result from:

- cheques that have been issued and been recorded in the cash book, but which have not been paid into the recipient's bank account

- cheques that have been received, recorded in the cash book and paid into the bank but, because they have not yet **cleared**, have not been recorded in the bank statement.

Furthermore, items may appear on the bank statement but not appear in the bank columns of the cash book. These may include

- payments such as standing orders, direct debits and bank charges
- receipts such as interest, dividends received by the bank, and bank giro credits or credit transfers received by the bank.

Stages in preparing a bank reconciliation statement

- Tick (in pencil) all the entries appearing in the cash book against those appearing in the bank statement.
- If items appear on the statement but do not appear in the cash book, then the bank columns of the cash book should be brought up to date. The bank columns of the cash book should be balanced with the new figure.
- Timing differences which appear in the bank columns of the cash book and which do not appear in the bank statement should now be used to prepare the bank reconciliation statement.

Let us look in detail at an example. The cashier of A. Jones Ltd needs to reconcile the bank columns of the cash book and the bank statement shown in Figures 10.13 and 10.14.

RECEIPTS			PAYMENTS		
DATE	DETAILS	BANK	DATE	DETAILS	BANK
199_		£			£
1 Aug	Balance b/d	525	8 Aug	J. James Ltd	65
12 Aug	P. Jamieson	16	17 Aug	R Nettle Ltd	20
21 Aug	R. Tree	122	22 Aug	P. Green	38
28 Aug	N. Bell	165	28 Aug	J. Smith	15
			31 Aug	Balance c/d	690
		828			828
31 Aug	Balance b/d	690			

Figure 10.13 Cash book bank columns of A. Jones Ltd

DATE	DETAILS	PAYMENTS	RECEIPTS	BALANCE
199_		(£)	(£)	(£)
01 Aug	Balance b/d			525
03 Aug	Standing order P. Proby	50		475
11 Aug	J. James Ltd	65		410
13 Aug	Credit		16	426
14 Aug	Credit transfer		85	511
15 Aug	Direct debit	34		477
19 Aug	R. Nettle Ltd	20		457
23 Aug	Credit		122	579
28 Aug	Bank charges	4		575

Figure 10.14 Bank statement of A. Jones Ltd

Having checked all the entries appearing in the cash book against those appearing in the bank statement, and vice versa, the cashier will amend the cash book so that it looks like Figure 10.15.

RECEIPTS			PAYMENTS		
DATE	DETAILS	BANK	DATE	DETAILS	BANK
199_		£			£
31 Aug	Balance b/d	690	3 Aug	Standing order	50
14 Aug	Credit	85	15 Aug	Direct debit	34
	transfer		28 Aug	Bank charges	4
			31 Aug	Balance c/d	687
		775			775
1 Sept	Balance b/d	687			

Figure 10.15 Amended cash book bank columns of A. Jones Ltd

The amended cash book balance would then be used to draw up the bank reconciliation statement, as shown in Figure 10.16.

```
                    A Jones Ltd
        Bank Reconciliation Statement as at 31 August 199-

                                                           (£)
Balance at bank as per cash book (amended)                 687
Add: cheques drawn but not yet presented for payment
        P. Green        38
        J. Smith        15                                  53
                                                           740
Less: cheques deposited but not yet cleared
        N. Bell                                            165
Balance as per bank statement                              575
```

Figure 10.16 The reconciliation statement

Task

Imagine you are the cashier of C. More Ltd. Prepare a bank reconciliation statement from the bank columns of the cash book and the bank statement in Figures 10.17 and 10.18.

RECEIPTS			PAYMENTS		
DATE	DETAILS	BANK	DATE	DETAILS	BANK
199_		£			£
1 Sep	Balance b/d	931	2 Sep	R, Joyce Ltd	54
7 Sep	N. Smith	25	9 Sep	H. Fawcett	338
8 Sep	R. Peterson	15	18 Sep	N. Ray	55
20 Sep	N. Jones	30	21 Sep	P. Bryan	82
27 Sep	R. Mink	58	27 Sep	J. Jewel	151
			30 Sep	Balance c/d	379
		1059			1059
30 Sept	Balance b/d	379			

Figure 10.17 **Cash book bank columns of C. More Ltd**

DATE	DETAILS	PAYMENTS (£)	RECEIPTS (£)	BALANCE (£)
199_				
01 Sep	Balance b/d			931
04 Sep	Credit transfer		25	956
07 Sep	R. Joyce Ltd	54		902
08 Sep	Credit		25	927
09 Sep	Credit		15	942
15 Sep	H. Fawcett	338		604
16 Sep	Bank transfer	12		592
18 Sep	Credit transfer		39	631
21 Sep	N. Jones		30	661
24 Sep	Standing order	50		611

Figure 10.18 **Bank statement of C. More Ltd**

The trial balance

At the end of each accounting period the bookkeeper will produce a **trial balance**. This is a summary of all the balances in the ledger accounts. It is drawn up to check the accuracy of all the double entries made in the ledger accounts. An accountant will prepare the **final accounts** of an organisation from the trial balance.

Case Study – Beating the cash flow crisis

When banks pull in the reins on lending, such as in a time of recession, many organisations look to factoring companies to control their flow of cash. Factoring companies will often allow up to 80 per cent of the face value of invoices to become immediately available. The remaining 20 per cent of the invoice (less charges) will become available when the customer pays.

There are some powerful advantages for companies who use factoring in preference to other forms of funding. For example:

- Clients gain a flexible form of finance geared to current levels and needs. It means they can avoid having to take out an overdraft.
- Organisations do not have to surrender shares or a form of ownership to another (e.g. venture capital) company.
- Factoring companies offer benefits to terms of credit management, such as expert collection of debts. This will, in turn, mean reduced working capital needs.
- It can save on time and administration costs, as companies can do without a credit controller.
- Part of the factoring service involves advice on customers who might be potential bad debts.

The cost of factoring is competitive with other forms of financing. A service fee is typically 1.5 – 2 per cent of turnover. Clients also pay a base rate plus 3 per cent which compares favourably with rates charged by banks. According to the director of one company: 'The finance charge is very similar to running a bank overdraft, but the real benefit is in time and money spent employing a credit controller, paying for calls and postage and spent preparing

statements. The cost of the service is far
outweighed by the benefits to the company.'

In today's business climate more and more
organisations are coming to the conclusion that
factoring can ease cash flow difficulties.

1 *Examine the importance of cash flow to an
   organisation.*
2 *What advantages does factoring have over other
   forms of finance?*
3 *Suggest other methods of improving an
   organisation's cash flow.*

11
Understanding Financial Statements

> With the increasing complexity and diversity of information available to managers and administrators across the working environment, it has become important today for more employees to be able to read and understand financial statements. Such statements help to provide the basic information necessary to make decisions.
>
> In this chapter we look first at the basic financial statements of a sole trader and then at those of a company. We consider what these statements mean and how they can be interpreted. The chapter provides a series of tasks related to each area to enable users to develop basic accounting skills.

What sort of statements do you know about? You have probably seen a bank statement, and some readers may have been asked to give a statement to the police about an event they have witnessed or have been involved in. While these statements are quite obviously different in kind, they do have some things in common. Each provides a summary of events, and it may be possible to use these to find out:

- about something that has happened
- the current state of events
- likely developments in the future.

Final accounts

As we saw in Chapter 10, accountants use information from the **trial balance** to draw up an organisation's **final accounts**. Final accounts are the summary financial statements produced at the end of each year's trading. Different types of organisations will need different types of financial statements. We start by looking at the financial statements of a sole trader, and then look at those of a limited company.

Final accounts of a sole trader

The basic financial statements of a sole trader include:

- a trading account
- a profit and loss account
- a balance sheet.

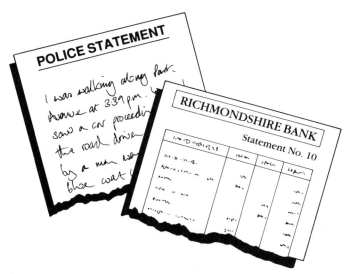

Figure 11.1 Two kinds of statements

The trading account

The **trading account** can be likened to a video giving ongoing pictures of an organisation's trading activities. For many businesses trading involves buying and selling stock. The difference between the value of the stock sold (sales) and the cost of producing those sales – which is the production costs of manufactured goods for a manufacturing company, or the cost of purchasing the supplies for a trading company – is known as **gross profit**. The trading account simply shows how gross profit is arrived at:

Sales – cost of sales = gross profit

'Cost of sales' has to take into account the value of **stocks**. 'Opening stocks' is effectively a purchase as these will be sold in the current trading period. On the other hand, 'closing stocks' must be deducted from purchases as these will be sold next year. The true cost of sales is therefore found by applying the following formula:

Cost of sales = opening stocks PLUS purchases LESS closing stocks

The profit and loss account

The **profit and loss account** may be drawn up beneath the trading account and covers the same period of trading. The gross profit figure from the trading account becomes the starting point for the profit and loss account.

Net profit = gross profit PLUS income from other sources LESS expenses

Some organisations receive income from sources other than sales. There may be rents received, commission received, discounts received, profits on the sale of assets etc. As these are **extra income** they are added to the gross profit. In addition, every organisation incurs **expenses** and a range of **overheads**, and these are deducted to show the true net profit of the business. The expenses might include:

- rent of premises
- gas
- electricity
- stationery
- cleaning costs
- insurances
- business rates
- depreciation
- bad debts
- interest on loans
- advertising costs
- sundry expenses
- motor expenses
- accountancy and legal fees.

Figure 11.2 shows how the final account might look. The part of the account up to and including the gross profit is the trading account, while the remainder is the profit and loss account. Net profit is the final profit in the business and will belong to the owner.

	(£)	(£)
Sales		27 500
Less cost of sales:		
Opening stock	9 000	
Add purchases	15 000	
	24 000	
Less closing stock	3750	
		20 250
Gross profit		7 250
Add other income:		
Profit on sale of plant		2000
		9 250
Less expenses:		
Electricity	510	
Stationery	125	
Business rate	756	
Interest on loans	159	
Advertising	745	
Depreciation of motor vehicles	1000	
Insurances	545	
Sundry expenses	124	
		3 964
Net profit		5 286

Figure 11.2 Trading and profit and loss account of E. Blyton for year-ended 31 May 199_

Responsibility for the accounts

Most sole traders employ an accountant to draw up their accounts. Nevertheless, whoever prepares them, it is the sole trader who remains responsible for their accuracy and for correctly declaring the amount of the profits. The **tax authorities** will need to be satisfied that the accounts supplied to them represent the true results of the business.

It is essential to keep full and accurate records from the start of a business. Well-kept books make the preparation of the annual accounts easier, and save the accountant's time (so keeping down the fee charged).

Case Study – Assessments and payments of tax

The following is an edited extract from a booklet *Starting in Business*, issued by the Inland Revenue (IR28).

'If you cannot give your Inspector an accurate statement of your profits, they will have to be estimated and you will then have to pay tax on the basis of this estimate. If you consider the estimate is too high, it will be up to you to prove it. So it is in your own interests to keep accurate records.

'You are required by law to make a true return of your income each year. This, of course, includes your business *profits*. If possible you should send in a copy of your business accounts, either with your return form, or – if your accounting year ends some time before the return is due – in advance of the return.

'If your business makes a *loss* there are four main things you can do with it, and it is up to you to decide which of the various alternatives to adopt. You can:

- set the loss against future profits from the same business, starting with the earliest profitable year first
- claim relief for the same income tax year as the year of the loss
- claim relief for the income tax year following the year of the loss
- claim relief for the three income tax years before that in which you make the loss.

'The Small Firms Service is an information and business counselling service to help managers of small businesses with their plans and problems. It also acts as an advisory service to those thinking of starting their own business.'

1 Why do sole traders need to inform the Inland Revenue of their activities?
2 How important is it for sole traders to keep accurate records? What might happen if they did not?
3 Briefly explain what might happen if the business makes a loss.
4 Why does the Inland Revenue provide a Small Firms Service?

Task

A business sells £100 000 work of goods during 1992. Its stock at the beginning of the year is worth £10 000. During the year it makes purchases worth £50 000 and its stock at the end of the year is worth £20 000. It has three main expenses: rent of £5000, rates of £5000 and advertising costing £10 000. Show a trading/profit and loss account for the year-ended 31 December 1992.

The balance sheet

Whereas the trading account gives an ongoing picture, a **balance sheet** is a snapshot of what an organisation owns and owes *on a particular date*. It is a clear statement of the assets, liabilities and capital of a business at a particular moment in time (normally the end of an accounting period).

Looking at the balance sheet can thus provide valuable information because it summarises a business's financial position at that instant in time.

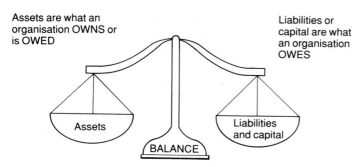

Assets are what an organisation OWNS or is OWED

Liabilities or capital are what an organisation OWES

Assets

Liabilities and capital

BALANCE

Figure 11.3 Assets equals capital plus liabilities

The balance sheet does balance simply because the accounts record every transaction twice. For example, if you give me £100 we can say that:

- I *owe* you £100 (a liability or debt)
- I have now got £100 (an asset, something I *own*).

Look at Figure 11.3. Does it seem odd to you that 'capital' is *owed* by the organisation? This will become clear when you have read page 215.

At the end of a trading period a business will have a number of assets and liabilities. Some of these will be for short periods of time, while others will be for longer periods. Whatever the nature of the individual assets and liabilities, *the balance sheet will balance*.

Task

Make lists of six probable assets and six probable liabilities of a small corner-shop. Do the same for a public house.

The parts of a balance sheet

Every balance sheet has a **heading**, which contains the name of the organisation and the date at which the snapshot is taken. You will find it helpful to refer to Figure 11.5 on page 215 as you read this section.

Assets

The **assets** side of the balance sheet is normally set out in what is called an **inverse order of liquidity**. This means that items which may be difficult to convert into cash quickly (and are therefore **illiquid**) appear at the top of the list of assets. By looking down the order it is possible to gauge the ease with which successive assets can be converted to cash, until we come to the most liquid asset of all, cash itself.

Task

A small bakery has the following assets. Try to put them into an *inverse order of liquidity* with the most illiquid at the top and the most liquid at the bottom:

- cash in the tills
- a bakery van
- bread in the shops
- the bakery oven
- supplies of flour
- money in the bakery's bank account
- money owed to the bakery by firms
- the baker's premises

Assets can be divided into fixed assets and current assets. **Fixed assets** tend to have a life-span of more than one year. They comprise items that are purchased and generally kept for a long period of time. Examples of fixed assets are premises, machinery and motor vehicles. When a business buys fixed assets it does so by incurring **capital expenditure**.

Case Study – Brand accounting

Some of the most valuable assets owned by many organisations are the brands they have developed and nurtured. Despite this, the Market

213

Accounting Research Centre at the Cranfield School of Management discovered from a survey that a majority of businesses do not place a price on their portfolio of brands. It could well be argued that an accountant cannot create a 'true and fair view' of the business if they are not included.

The survey found that brand support and other marketing costs are rarely treated as an *investment* to achieve competitive advantage in the long-term. Furthermore, the strategic benefits of including brands in the accounts are not recognised by managers.

1 *Using examples to support your analysis, comment on whether a brand could be included in a balance sheet as an asset. What sort of asset might it be?*
2 *What are the advantages and the disadvantages of including brands within the balance sheet?*

Current assets are sometimes called 'circulating assets' because the form they take is constantly changing. Examples of current assets are stocks, debtors, money in the bank, and cash in hand.

A manufacturing business holds **stocks** of finished goods in readiness to satisfy the demands of the market. When a credit transaction takes place, stocks are reduced and the business gains **debtors**. These debtors have bought goods on credit and therefore *owe* the business money; after a reasonable credit period payment will be expected. Payments will have to be made on further stocks, so that the business has a **cash cycle**. 'Cash' or 'bank' changes to 'stock', then to 'debtors', back to 'cash' or 'bank' and then to 'stock' again.

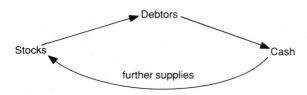

Figure 11.4 **The cash cycle**

Task

Identify (giving reasons) which of the following items should be considered as a current asset of a newsagent:

● the fixtures and fittings of the shop
● cash in the tills
● money in the bank
● money owed by the newsagent to the suppliers.

● money owed by customers for newspaper bills
● the delivery bicycle
● stocks of newspapers in the shop

Current liabilities

Current liabilities are debts which a business needs to repay within a short period of time (normally a year). Current liabilities include **creditors**, who are suppliers of goods on credit for which the business has been invoiced but not yet provided any payment. They might also include a **bank overdraft** which is arranged up to a limit over a time period and is, technically, repayable on demand. Other current liabilities might include any short-term loans and any taxes owed.

Working capital

The balance sheet is set out so as to show **working capital** because this is always an important calculation for an organisation. The working capital is the current assets less the current liabilities. The **working capital ratio** is the ratio of current assets to current liabilities:

> Working capital ratio
> = current assets : current liabilities

It is important for an organisation to maintain a sensible ratio. The level of ratio necessary depends on the type of business, and the likelihood that funds will be required quickly to meet liabilities (e.g. creditors demanding repayment quickly). For most businesses a ratio of 2:1 is regarded as a sign of careful management, but some businesses have lower ratios.

Working capital is important because it provides a buffer to 'keep the wolf from the door'. Many businesses have suffered the consequences of having too many of their assets tied up as illiquid assets.

Long-term liabilities

A **long-term liability** is sometimes called a **deferred liability** as it is not due for payment until some time in the future. By convention, in a set of accounts, this means longer than one year. Examples for a sole trader might include a bank loan or a mortgage.

	(£)	(£)
Fixed assets		
Land and buildings		80 000
Machinery		13 200
Motor vehicles		8 700
		101 900
Current assets		
Stocks	9 700	
Debtors	3 750	
Bank	2 100	
Cash	970	
	16 520	
Less **Current liabilities**		
Creditors	9 000	
WORKING CAPITAL		7 520
		109 420
Less **Long-term liabilities**		
Bank loan	9 000	
Mortgage	30 000	
		39 000
		70 420
Financed by:		
Capital		70 000
Add net profit		5 286
		75 286
Less drawings		4 866
		70 420

Figure 11.5 Balance sheet of E. Blyton at 31 May 1992

Capital

Capital is provided by the owner of the business and is therefore deemed to be *owed to the owner by the business* (look again at Figure 11.3). The balance sheet keeps an updated record of the amount owed by the business to the owner.

During a year's trading the owner's capital may be increased by the inflows of **profits** and decreased by outflows of **drawings** (money or other assets taken out of the business for personal use). Having taken these into consideration a new capital figure is calculated at the end of the year. So the balance sheet shows how the capital has increased (or decreased) since the last balance sheet was prepared.

Using the trial balance to prepare final accounts

Accountants make use of the trial balance to prepare the final accounts. The trial balance contains a list of all the business's accounts (see Chapter 10). Accounts will have either a **debit balance** or a **credit balance**. Debit balances will generally comprise the assets of the business, expenses and the totals of purchases and costs. Credit balances will comprise any liabilities such as capital and creditors, as well as income from sales.

Each item in the trial balance will appear once in the final accounts. It is useful to tick each item in pencil as it is entered, so that none is missed. The **closing stocks** figure taken at the year end is not listed in the trial balance but is shown as a note underneath the balance. The closing stocks will appear twice, once in the trading account and then again in the current assets in the balance sheet.

Task

From the following trial balance of J. O. Nory draw up her trading/profit and loss account for the year-ended 31 December 1992,

215

together with her balance sheet at that date. The closing stocks at 31 December 1992 were valued at £10 300.

	(£)	(£)
Stock @ 1 Jan 1992	12 700	
Sales		81 250
Purchases	18 325	
Electricity	1 451	
Stationery	1 526	
Business rate	1 845	
Loan interest	3 955	
Advertising	2 150	
Sundry expenses	1 205	
Land and buildings	161 000	
Machinery	4 900	
Motor vehicles	18 300	
Debtors	12 100	
Bank	4 250	
Cash	325	
Bank loan		10 000
Mortgage		20 000
Creditors		4 300
Drawings	9 350	
Capital @ 1 Jan 1992		137 832
	253 382	253 382

Final accounts of a limited company

It will help our understanding of the accounts of a limited company if we first go over some of the essential features of this type of organisation. As we have already seen in earlier chapters, in limited companies:

- the company has a legal identity separate from that of its owners
- the owners are known as shareholders
- shareholders have limited liability
- management is delegated to a board of directors, who may or may not be share-holders
- corporation tax must be paid on profits made.

Companies must comply with the Companies Acts, and the Companies Registration Office controls their formation. There are two types of limited companies: public, which have their shares traded on the Stock Exchange, and private, for which there are restrictions on the trading in their shares.

To set up a limited company it is necessary to go through a number of legal procedures. This mainly involves the presentation of various documents to the Registrar of Companies. All limited companies must produce a **Memorandum of Association** and **Articles of Association** to receive a Certification of Incorporation.

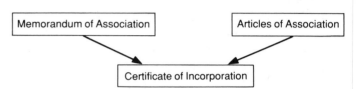

Figure 11.6 Documents required by a limited company for corporate status

The Memorandum spells out the nature of the company when viewed from the outside. Someone reading the Memorandum should be able to gain a general idea of what the company is and the business with which it is concerned. The Memorandum sets out:

- the name of the company
- its address
- its objectives (i.e. what types of activities it will engage in)
- its capital.

The Articles spell out the rules which govern the inside working of the company. In particular they set out the details of how accounts will be kept and recorded.

Once a private company has lodged these documents with the Registrar and had them accepted it can start to trade. The Certificate of Incorporation sets up the company as a legal body *in its own right*. The company (not the individual shareholders) enters into contracts and can sue or be sued in a court of law.

A public company, however, must take further steps before being granted a Certificate. A **Prospectus** has to be issued and shares have to be allotted.

One clause of the Memorandum of Association states the **share capital** of the company and indicates how it is to be divided into separate shares. **Authorised share capital** is the amount the shareholders have authorised the directors to issue. **Issued share capital** is the amount that has actually been issued by the directors.

There are a number of types of shares. For example, there are **ordinary shares**, for which **dividends** are normally expressed as a percentage of the nominal value of the shares or as a monetary value per share. There may be **preference shares**, which carry a preferential right to receive a dividend. Companies can also issue **debentures**, which are split into units in the same way as shares; they are in effect loans made to the company and secured by specific assets of the company.

The trading/profit and loss accounts

The **trading account** of a limited company is similar to the trading account of any other type of organisation. However, in the **profit and loss** account:

- directors' fees or salaries may be included, because these people are employed by the company and their fees and salaries are an expense
- debenture payments, being the same as loan interest, also appear as an expense.

The appropriation account

Beneath the profit and loss account of a company will appear the **appropriation account**. This is designed to show what happens to any profit and how it is divided.

Corporation tax is the first charge on profits and has to be paid to the Inland Revenue. For example, the tax rate was 33 per cent for the tax year 1991/92 for company profits over £1 250 000. **Shareholder**

dividends are the portion of the profits paid to shareholders.

Reserves are the portion of the profit which the directors and the shareholders prefer not to distribute as dividends. This money is set aside for another purpose.

Any profit left over at the end of the year, after taxes and shareholders of all kinds have been paid, is added to the balance of profit from the previous year, to give the new **retained profit**.

Balance of profit at end of year = net profit from this year PLUS retained profits from previous years LESS corporation tax LESS dividends LESS transfer to reserves

An example of an appropriation account for a company with a net profit of £250 000 is shown in Figure 11.7.

	(£)	(£)
Net profit		250 000
Less Corporation Tax		100 000
Profit after taxation		150 000
Less proposed dividends:		
Ordinary shares	70 000	
Preference shares	20 000	90 000
		60 000
Less transfer to General Reserve		40 000
		20 000
Add retained profit from previous year		30 000
Balance of retained profit		50 000

Figure 11.7 An appropriation account

Task

Workhard Ltd has just announced a net profit of £300 000. Prepare the appropriation

account from the following details:

a The taxation rate is at 25 per cent.
b There are 500 000 ordinary shares of £1 each, fully paid. A dividend of 10 per cent is proposed.
c There are 300 000 10% preference shares of £1 each, fully paid. The 10 per cent dividend is to be paid.
d £50 000 is to be transferred to General Reserve.
e Retained profit from the previous year was £125 000

The balance sheet

In the **balance sheet** of a company the **fixed** and **current assets** are presented in the same way as in any other balance sheet.

The **current liabilities** are the liabilities due to be paid within 12 months of the date of the balance sheet. In addition to those which normally appear in this section, limited companies also have to show the Corporation Tax which is due to be paid during the next 12 months, as well as the ordinary and preference share dividends due to be paid. **Long-term liabilities** may include debenture payments.

At the beginning of the 'Financed by:' section of the balance sheet, details will appear of the **authorised capital**, specifying the type, value and number of shares that the company is authorised to issue. These are in the balance sheet for interest only and their value is excluded from the totals. The item on **issued share capital** contains details of the classes and numbers of shares that *have* been issued (obviously the issued share capital cannot exceed the authorised).

Reserves are shown beneath the capital. Reserves and **retained profits** are the amounts the directors and shareholders decide to keep within the company.

Example

From the trial balance of Wargrave Ltd shown below and the notes that follow it, we can prepare the trading account, the profit and loss account, the appropriation account and the balance sheet for the year-ended 31 December 1992:

	(£)	(£)
Stock @ 1 Jan 1992	21 300	
Sales		118 100
Purchases	35 000	
Electricity	8 000	
Stationery	5 000	
Business rate	1 300	
Loan interest paid	1 000	
Debenture interest paid	800	
Advertising	3 200	
Sundry expenses	1 350	
Directors' salaries	12 000	
Land and buildings	320 000	
Machinery	24 000	
Motor vehicles	12 000	
Debtors	7 100	
Bank	23 200	
Cash	500	
Bank loan		10 000
10% debentures		8 000
Creditors		500
General Reserve		4 000
Retained profit @ 31 Dec 1991		35 150
Issued share capital:		
200 000 ordinary £1 shares		200 000
100 000 10% £1 preference shares		100 000
	475 750	475 750

Further information:

- The closing stock is £12 250.
- Corporation Tax is charged at 25 per cent of profits.
- There will be a 6 per cent dividend on ordinary shares.
- The 10% preference share dividend is to be paid.
- £2000 is to be allocated to the General Reserve.
- Authorised share capital is 400 000 ordinary shares of £1 each and 100 000 10% preference shares of £1 each.

The accounts and balance sheet based on this data are shown in Figures 11.8 and 11.9. Relate each item to its corresponding entry.

	(£)	(£)	(£)
Fixed assets			
Land and buildings		320 000	
Machinery		24 000	
Motor vehicles		12 000	
		356 000	
Current assets			
Stocks		12 250	
Debtors		7 100	
Bank		23 200	
Cash		500	
		43 050	
Less **Current liabilities**			
Creditors	500		
Proposed dividends:			
Ordinary shares	12 000		
Preference shares	10 000		
Corporation Tax	10 350	32 850	
Working capital		10 200	
		366 200	
Less **Long-term liabilities**			
Bank loan	10 000		
10% debentures	8 000		
		18 000	
		348 200	
FINANCED BY:			
Authorised share capital			
400 000 ordinary shares of £1		400 000	
100 000 10% preference shares of £1		100 000	
		500 000	
Issued share capital			
200 000 ordinary shares of £1 fully paid		200 000	
100 000 10% preference shares of £1 fully paid		100 000	
		300 000	
Reserves			
General Reserve	6 000		
Balance of retained profit	42 200		
		48 200	
		348 200	

Figure 11.8 Balance sheet of Wargrave Ltd for the year ended 31 December 1992

	(£)	(£)
Sales		118 100
Less cost of sales:		
Opening stock	21 300	
Add purchases	35 000	
	56 300	
Less closing stock	12 250	
		44 050
		74 050
Gross profit		
Less expenses:		
Electricity	8 000	
Stationery	5 000	
Business rate	1 300	
Loan interest paid	1 000	
Debenture interest paid	800	
Advertising	3 200	
Sundry expenses	1 350	
Directors' salaries	12 000	
		32 650
Net profit		41 400
Less Corporation Tax		10 350
Profit after tax		31 050
Less proposed dividends:		
Ordinary shares	12 000	
Preference shares	10 000	22 000
		9 050
Less transfer to General Reserve		2 000
		7 050
Add retained profit from previous year		35 150
Balance of retained profit		42 200

Figure 11.9 Trading, profit and loss and appropriation account of Wargrave Ltd for the year ended 31 December 1992

Task

From the following trial balance of Twyford Ltd and the attached notes, prepare the trading account, profit

and loss account, appropriation account and balance sheet for the year-ended 31 December 1992.

	(£)	(£)
Stock @ 1 Jan 1992	7 300	
Sales		123 400
Purchases	12 500	
Electricity	4 100	
Advertising	3 200	
Business rate	800	
Salaries	16 000	
Director's salaries	18 000	
Loan interest paid	4 400	
Debenture interest paid	1 000	
Land and buildings	124 000	
Motor vehicles	16 000	
Debtors	7 000	
Bank	15 000	
Cash	1 000	
Bank loan		25 000
10% debentures		10 000
Creditors		4 000
General Reserve		3 000
Retained profit @ 31 Dec 1991		4 900
Issued share capital:		
50 000 ordinary shares (£1)		50 000
10 000 pref. shares (£1)		10 000
	230 300	230 300

You have been informed that:

- The closing stock has been valued at £3400.
- Corporation Tax will be charged at 25 per cent of profits.
- The 10 % share dividends are to be paid.
- £3000 is to be allocated to the General Reserve.
- Authorised share capital is the same as issued share capital.

Statements of cash flow

The profit and loss account provides information which matches sales and costs, and a balance sheet is a static statement showing a business's financial position. Neither of these shows how a business has *used* its funds and cash.

In 1975 the tenth Statement of Standard Accounting Practice (SSAP) was issued which required a business with an annual turnover of £25 000 or more to provide a statement to fill this gap, as part of its final accounts. This was called a **funds flow statement**.

Funds flow statements were prepared through a process of comparison. If a company's balance sheets for two successive years were listed alongside each other, then clearly the changes during the year could be seen. Differences between the two years were then listed and grouped together either as sources or as applications of funds.

Sources of funds included profits, new loans, share issues and profits on the sale of assets. **Applications of funds** included purchase of fixed assets, tax paid, dividends paid, and loans repaid.

	(£)	(£)	(£)
	31 Dec 1990	31 Dec 1991	Comparison
Premises	3 000	3 000	0
Stocks	8 000	10 000	+2 000
Bank	3 000	3 000	0
	14 000	16 000	
Capital	14 000	14 000	0
Creditors	–	2 000	+2 000
	14 000	16 000	

Figure 11.10 Two balance sheets for B. Regis

The example in Figure 11.10 shows how an increase in stocks could have been financed. Clearly this increase in stocks has been financed through the credit provided by suppliers, and this fact is shown in the form of a statement (Figure 11.11).

Sources of funds – creditors	£2000
Application of funds – increasing stocks	£2000

Figure 11.11 Funds flow statement for B. Regis

Another way of presenting this sort of statement was to have a section which analysed *working capital changes*. The reason for this was to enable managers to exert a firmer grip upon these changes. The change in working capital between the two balance sheets would then equal the difference between the sources and applications of funds. This is illustrated in Figure 11.12.

```
Balance sheets
                         (£)      (£)      (£)
                       31 Dec   31 Dec  Comparison
                        1990     1991

Fixed assets            450      550      +100
Long-term investments   500      450       -50
Current assets less
   current liabilities  150      200       +50
                      ------   ------
                       1 100    1 200

Capital                 360      400       +40
Profits                 300      500      +200
Loans                   440      300      -140
                      ------   ------
                       1 100    1 200

Funds flow statement
                                 (£)      (£)

Sources of funds:
  Capital                         40
  Profits                        200
  Sale of investments             50      290
Application of funds:
  Fixed assets                   100
  Loan repayments                140      240

Increase in working capital               50
```

Figure 11.12 Balance sheets and funds flow statement for H. O. Gate

The new way: cash flow statements

As we saw in Chapter 10, in 1990 the Accounting Standards Board took over from the Accounting Standards Committee and this heralded a new era in accounting standard-setting. All accounting standards (SSAPs) now come under the authority of the ASB and are to be subject to scrutiny and change.

In September 1991 the ASB set out the first **Financial Reporting Standard** (FRS1) on **cash flow statements.** The standard supersedes SSAP10 on sources and applications of funds, discussed above. The new standard FRS1 will change the nature of the third

statement in a company's accounts. The aim is for the cash flow statement to be viewed as just as important as the balance sheet and the profit and loss account.

The problems with funds flow statements were that:

● companies drew up their statements in different ways
● they were difficult to use to compare one business with another
● they looked at funds or profit rather than at cash
● the meaning of funds was not very clear.

The new cash flow statements focus on something which all business managers can identify with – the need for a steady cash flow. Figure 11.13 shows an example. The bottom line is the change in what is called 'cash and equivalents'. The cash flow statement explains the movement by placing all cash flows into five categories. Note that in this example

```
                                          (£m)     (£m)
Net cash inflow from operating
activities                                          6

Returns on investment and servicing
of finance
  Interest received                         2
  Interest paid                            (4)
  Dividends paid                           (4)
Net cash outflow from returns on
investment and servicing of finance                (5)

Taxation
  UK corporation tax paid                          (4)

Investing activities
  Purchases of tangible fixed assets      (4)
  Purchase of subsidiary undertakings
    (net of cash and cash equivalents
     acquired)                           (18)
  Sale of plant and machinery              4
Net cash outflow from investing activities        (18)
Net cash outflow before financing                 (22)

Financing
  New secured loan repayable in 1995       17
  Repayment of amounts borrowed           (2)
Net cash inflow from financing                     15
Increase in cash and cash equivalents               7
```

Figure 11.13 A cash flow statement for the year ended 31 March 1992

221

we have adopted the more usual convention of putting outflows of cash in parentheses, rather than using a minus sign as we have been doing. Further information is given in notes, in particular a reconciliation of operating profit to operating cash flow.

The idea is that a user can see at a glance the extent to which, for example, cash flow from operations has or has not paid for dividends, tax and new investments, or the extent to which those items had to be financed by the raising of new capital. The statement should expose more quickly than before those companies that are not generating cash – even though they may be reporting profits.

The statement in Figure 11.13 shows that:

- the operations provided cash inflow of only £6 million
- £6 million was used up in dividends and interest
- £4 million was used up in paying tax
- £18 million was used up in new investment
- the cash balance *decreased* by £7 million
- to make all of this possible, £15 million had to be obtained by way of new finance.

It is clear immediately from the example that the operations were not even supporting the dividends and the tax payment. The company is using up cash without even considering further investment. This is exactly the kind of thing a cash flow statement is intended to bring out. This sort of information should help to provide readers of accounts with clearer warnings of business failures.

Task

If you were an investor in a company, what sort of information would you require about your investment? Make a list.

Case Study – King cash

SSAP10 on sources and applications of funds has formed an integral part of final accounts for all but the very smallest of businesses for many years. However, today it is replaced by a cash flow statement. The change has been:

- to improve the *quality* of information provided in published accounts
- to bring the UK accounting procedures into line with international practices.

The monitoring of cash flow is probably the most significant aspect of the successful operation of any organisation. It is one thing to have a 'theoretical' profit reported in the profit and loss account, but another matter – and probably more important – to have the physical resources available to meet payments to short-term creditors.

This need for businesses to have short-term liquidity and long-term profitability is illustrated by today's emphasis upon cash flow. Particularly in times of recession many firms strive to report a book profit figure but ignore the need to meet short-term creditors.

Many criticisms have been levelled at funds flow statements over recent years. These concentrated upon funds as movements in working capital at the expense of examining in more detail general changes in funds. Also, their format and content varied considerably between companies and this caused difficulty with interpretation and comparison. Cash flow statements will provide more information on the connection between liquidity and profitability. They will also actually record the cash flow generated by an organisation over its financial year. Cash flow statements will therefore assist in emphasising to investors the risks they are undertaking.

FRS1 should now be adopted by all organisations as their standard in respect of financial statements relating to reporting periods on or after 23 March 1992. SSAP10 was withdrawn as of that date.

1 *Why is it important to improve the quality of information in published accounts?*
2 *Why is it necessary to bring UK accounting practices into line with international practices?*
3 *Explain the difference between profit and cash.*
4 *What might happen if a business fails to pay creditors?*
5 *Write a short report explaining why cash flow statements will improve the quality of final accounts.*

Auditing

All registered companies in the United Kingdom are required to have their final accounts **audited** (i.e. checked) by a professional accountant. The purpose of the **audit report** is to testify that the accounts show a 'true and fair view' of the affairs of the company. The audit report, placed usually at the end of the final accounts, will indicate that the accounts have been produced in accordance with the law and other rules and regulations laid down. Figure 11.14 shows a typical example.

I have audited the above financial statements in accordance with Auditing Standards. In my opinion the financial statements give a true and fair view of the profit and the state of affairs of the Company at 31 December 1992 and of the source and application of funds for the year then ended, and have been properly prepared in accordance with the Companies Act 1985.

PARKER & PARKER
CHARTERED ACCOUNTANTS

Figure 11.14 The audit report

As well as having their accounts audited, all companies must send the accounts to the Registrar of Companies. Companies must also supply:

- details of subsidiary companies
- group accounts if there is a group of companies
- a summary of their activities in the form of a directors' report
- the audit report.

Task

Study the annual report and accounts of a major public company. Find the accounts section, details of operations, details of subsidiaries, the directors' report and the audit report.

Interpretation of final accounts

An organisation's accounts can be analysed to pick out information that gives an indication of its performance and structure. The four major areas of interest are:

- profitability
- liquidity
- asset usage
- capital structure

and we shall look at each of these in turn.

Taken in isolation, figures in accounts have limited value. For example, what does it mean to say that a company has a profit of £6 million? It is better to look at how profits have risen or fallen since the previous year, how other similar companies have fared, how much the company has invested to make a profit of £6 million, and so on.

By reducing financial information to **ratios**, we can compare the performances of different companies and performances from year to year. However, ratios must be used with care and a good understanding of the sorts of questions they can answer effectively. Before using a ratio always ask yourself *why* you are using it and *what* it is likely to tell you.

Profitability

To assess the profitability of an organisation one can turn to the published accounts. We have seen that the balance sheet gives a snapshot view of the organisation; alternatively one can take the video view from the profit and loss account or look at the cash flow statement. If it is a public limited company (PLC) one can look at the Stock Exchange valuation – this reflects the stock market's view of how the company is doing, based on expert study of the accounts and other snippets of current information.

Return on capital employed (ROCE)

A good indication of profitability is the relationship between the capital employed in the business and the profits the business has generated. This ratio is expressed as a percentage and is calculated in the following way:

$$\text{Percentage return on capital employed} = \frac{\text{net profit for year}}{\text{capital employed}} \times 100\%$$

The figure for capital employed is usually taken as the figure at the beginning of the year as this is the capital that generated the profit in the following year. The best way to think about the percentage return is to compare it with other investments. For example, if you invest £100 with a building society and receive £10 a year in interest (before tax), then you can see that you are getting a return on your capital of 10 per cent. This is a good measure of how effective your investment is. ROCE is therefore a quick and useful way of calculating the effectiveness of an investment in the business: it relates profitability to other investments.

Gross profit percentage

The *gross* profit percentage is a ratio that is extracted from the trading account. It relates gross profit to sales revenue:

$$\text{Gross profit percentage} = \frac{\text{gross profit}}{\text{sales revenue}} \times 100\%$$

For example, if sales of £100 000 produce a gross profit of £25 000, then the gross profit percentage is 25 per cent. In terms of buying stock and selling it, this means that every £1 worth of sales gives a 25p gross profit.

The gross profit percentage should be calculated at regular intervals, and if it rises or falls the reason should be investigated. If the percentage falls this may indicate that stock is being stolen or damaged. Alternatively, it could mean that the cost of stock is rising and the increase has not been passed on to the consumer.

Task

Why might a small business constantly check its stock and keep a close eye on its gross profit percentage?

Net profit percentage

The *net* profit percentage is calculated as follows:

$$\text{Net profit percentage} = \frac{\text{net profit}}{\text{sales revenue}} \times 100\%$$

It should be similar from year to year and should be comparable with the ratios of other enterprises in the same field of business. It takes into account business expenses.

If the *gross* profit percentage is consistent from year to year, any changes in the *net* profit percentage could indicate an increase in overheads (costs) as a proportion of sales revenue, and a need to make economies or to adjust prices.

Liquidity

Liquidity defines the ability of an organisation to convert its assets into cash. Cash is *perfectly liquid*.

Assets such as money in the bank and debtors are *highly liquid*, while assets such as buildings and machinery are clearly *illiquid*. It is always important to have a range of assets to meet the demands of any short-term creditors if required.

Current or working capital ratio

The **working capital ratio** is something we have met before in this chapter (see page 214). It is the ratio of current assets to current liabilities.

Clearly some assets are more liquid than others and the time factor involved in transferring them into cash is something an experienced manager should be able to estimate. A prudent ratio is sometimes said to be 2:1, but this might not necessarily be the case if stocks form the bulk of the value of the current assets. Companies have to be aware that bank overdrafts are repayable on demand and that figures extracted from a balance sheet might reflect the position of the current assets and liabilities at the time but not over the whole year. In practice most businesses operate with a slightly lower ratio than 2:1.

Quick ratio

The **quick ratio** (also called the **acid-test ratio** or the **liquidity ratio**) is the ratio of current assets to current liabilities *when stock value is taken off the current assets*.

The quick ratio is a tougher test than the working capital ratio because it excludes stocks, which as we have seen may not be immediately available as cash to meet short-term liabilities. A rule of thumb for the quick ratio is that it should be greater than 1.0. This will, however, depend upon the type of business, the relationship with suppliers and several other factors.

Debtor's collection period

This is calculated by the formula:

$$\text{Debtor's collection period} = \frac{\text{debtors}}{\text{average daily sales}}$$

It may be possible to improve a company's liquidity by reducing the debt collection period. Customers who are late in paying their debts are receiving free finance for their own activities. This ratio indicates the average number of days of credit received by customers before they provide a payment.

The average sales are calculated by dividing yearly sales by 365. The normal period of debt is between 30–60 days.

Period of credit taken from suppliers

This is calculated by the formula:

$$\text{Credit period} = \frac{\text{creditors}}{\text{average daily purchases}}$$

Now we are looking at the other side of the coin. Just as liquidity can be analysed by looking at the debt collection period, it could also be helpful to look at the average credit period taken from suppliers.

Task

The table shows a set of ratios calculated from the final accounts of a small laundry for 1991 and 1992. What might the figures indicate about the business? What questions would you want to ask to find out more about the changes that have taken place?

	1991	1992
Gross profits as a percentage of sales	10%	12%
Net profit as a percentage of sales	11%	10%
Net profit as a percentage of capital employed (ROCE)	12%	10%
Current ratio	2:1	1.5:1
Acid-test ratio	0.5:1	0.5:1

Asset usage

Asset usage ratios can be used to assess how effectively an organisation is using its assets and how its performance might be improved by using the assets more efficiently. Comparisons can then be made with similar companies.

Stock turnover

An organisation does not want to have its stock hanging around. **Stock turnover** is the average period of time an item of stock is held before it is used or sold. The adequacy of this ratio depends upon the type of business an organisation is in. For example, a jeweller may hold the same items of stock for a long period of time. It would be unwise for a fashion clothes retailer or baker to hold stock for the same period of time. Stock turnover can be calculated by the formula:

$$\text{Stock turnover} = \frac{\text{cost of sales}}{\text{average stock}}$$

In this formula the average stock is calculated by adding together the values of the opening stock and the closing stock and dividing the result by 2.

Many organisations today hold smaller stock levels than in the past. Often they operate a 'just in time' system – this means that they keep just enough stock to meet current demand. Consequently they have a higher stock turnover ratio.

Task

List six types of business which need to replace existing stock regularly. List six which would probably need to keep the same stock for a considerable length of time. Identify the problems associated with having a low rate of stock turnover.

Asset utilisation

This ratio shows how effectively fixed assets are used to generate sales revenue. It is measured by:

$$\text{Asset utilisation} = \frac{\text{sales}}{\text{fixed assets}}$$

This is really an efficiency ratio designed to show how well managers are using fixed assets to generate sales. However, as with all ratios we must be careful. Some businesses need only limited fixed assets (e.g. a market trader). Other businesses require substantial fixed assets (e.g. an oil company). The level of the ratio will depend upon the type of organisation.

Capital structure

Companies are financed by share capital, loans and funds from several other sources. The shareholders or owners receive dividends on their investments, and people or organisations which lend money receive interest. Both investors and suppliers of loan finance will want to ensure that their money has been invested wisely and that it brings in a secure return. In particular they might be interested in the ratio of share capital to loan capital.

Gearing

Gearing makes a direct comparison between the capital in a business provided by ordinary shareholders and that provided in the form of long-term loans and preference shares. It is calculated from the formula:

$$\text{Gearing} = \frac{\text{interest-bearing capital}}{\text{risk capital}} \times 100\%$$

It can also be represented by:

$$\frac{\text{prior charge capital (long-term loans and preference shares)}}{\text{equity (ordinary shares plus reserves)}}$$

A company is highly geared if the gearing is more than 100 per cent, or low-geared if the gearing is less than 100 per cent.

The higher the gearing, the higher the proportion of a firm's revenue that must be used to pay interest. This means that fixed costs are higher and, therefore, average costs are higher. Higher average costs put the firm at a competitive disadvantage when compared with rivals. Highly geared companies are more likely to fail particularly when there is a recession, or when high interest rates need to be paid.

If a highly geared company wishes to raise extra finance it may find it difficult to raise a loan. The great attractions to a company of raising money through loans are that loans do not carry voting rights, interest payments attract tax relief, and the reward to debt holders is generally lower than that required by shareholders.

A company may be highly geared because:

- it has just started up
- it is in a capital-intensive industry with many fixed assets which are secured against loans
- it has owners who wish to maintain control and so do not want outside shareholders
- the owners are not fully aware of the dangers of being highly geared
- the owners are optimistic about returns on capital and do not view interest payments as a problem.

Gearing levels vary from organisation to organisation and from industry to industry. If a firm has a stable background, high gearing may be safer.

Case Study – The Maxwell legacy

The Maxwell publishing empire was created by the drive of Robert Maxwell, who died suddenly in November 1991 whilst on a yachting holiday. Robert Maxwell controlled many businesses around the world, including *The European* and *The Daily Mirror* in the UK. Finance for the various enterprises was raised not only through the sale of shares, but also on the basis of large-scale loans. Many of these loans were secured against shares in the companies.

Despite the recession of the early 1990s the businesses continued to expand their interests.

At the time of Robert Maxwell's death, the Maxwell Communications Corporation (MCC) owed banks £1.4 billion. Though the businesses were mainly sound they borrowed at a time when money was not cheap to borrow and there was a general climate of recession. The general feeling in the industry was that the businesses had become too highly geared and had over-traded.

1 *Make a list of the dangers of relying too heavily on loan capital.*
2 *Explain what you think is meant by 'over-trading'.*

Interest cover is a measure of the risk of gearing. This ratio is calculated by the formula:

$$\text{Interest cover} = \frac{\text{profit before interest and tax}}{\text{interest paid in the year}}$$

If the ratio is less than 1:1 a company has not earned enough to cover interest charges. Some people argue that a sensible ratio is 3:1.

Dangers of using ratios

People studying an organisation's financial statements have to be careful when using ratios. Making comparisons can sometimes be unrealistic, particularly when so many organisations vary so considerably in size, structure and management style. For example, they may value their assets using different methods, and financial information may be distorted when we compare one year with the next because of the way in which inflation distorts prices.

Furthermore, financial information only provides a partial picture of what a business is trying to achieve. For example, it ignores the human relations aspects.

However, ratios are a useful means of spotting problems in a business and can provide a constructive guide as to profitability and financial strength.

Accounting policies

When you look at the accounts of any major public company you find a reference to the basis upon which the accounts have been put together. This reference is likely to be a statement of the policy on:

- inflation accounting
- stock valuation
- depreciation.

Inflation accounting

For most companies, the main statements of account are based on **historical costs**. This means that, unless a company has *revalued* any of its assets, they will appear in the balance sheet at the original cost (less depreciation), no matter when they were bought. Other transactions will also appear at their original values.

> **Accounting convention.** The accounts are prepared under the historical cost convention and in accordance with Accounting Standards.

Figure 11.15 A statement in the accounts

At times when prices are quickly changing, historical cost accounts can lead to distortions. For example, if a company bought a machine last year which then cost £500 000 and, because of price rises, the same machine now costs £700 000, it will still appear in the accounts as being worth under half a million pounds – say £350 000 (after depreciation is taken into account). Is this an accurate reflection of the *true* value of the asset?

Some companies produce a second set of accounting statements which show **current costs**. These statements are prepared using *replacement* costs rather than historical costs (in other words, the assets are *revalued*). In the annual report they are often referred to as 'current cost accounts', although in everyday language they are often known as 'inflation accounts'.

Task

What do you think gives the best reflection of the real worth of a company – assets measured in historical or in current cost terms? Look at some reports of public companies. How do they value their assets?

Stock valuation

When an accounting statement is set out, a value has to be put on the **stocks**. This value will obviously have a direct influence upon what the company declares to be its profits. For example, with a high valuation of stocks the profit will be high, and with a low valuation the profit will be lower. This is illustrated in Figure 11.16.

	High valuation (£)	(£)	Low valuation (£)	(£)
Sales		50 000		50 000
Less cost of sales:				
Opening stock	25 000		25 000	
Add purchases	40 000		40 000	
	65 000		65 000	
Less closing stock	20 000		40 000	
		45 000		25 000
		5 000		25 000

Figure 11.16 How the stock valuation affects profit

The **prudence concept** rules out the use of selling prices in the stock valuation process, as profits should only be recognised when they are actually made – after the goods are sold. The Standard **SSAP9** indicates that stocks should be valued either at their original cost or at their **net realisable value** – whichever is the *lower*. The net realisable value of the stocks is their selling price less the cost that would be incurred in getting them ready for sale and actually selling them.

Depreciation

Fixed assets do not last for ever. Organisations have expectations about the lifetimes of all their assets. They will wish to show a true asset value in the balance sheet, and charge the cost of its declining value (its **depreciation**) to the profit and loss account.

SSAP12 defines depreciation as 'the measure of the wearing out, consumption or other reduction in the useful economic life of a fixed asset, whether arising from use, time or obsolescence through technological or market changes'.

Case Study – Comparing financial statements

The following details have been taken from end-of-year financial statements prepared by two sole traders who own similar businesses:

	Jane (£)	Alan (£)
Sales	320 000	292 500
Less cost of sales	240 000	234 000
Gross profit	80 000	58 500
Less expenses	32 000	23 400
Net profit	48 000	35 100

The *average* stocks held by each business during the year in question were £12 000 (Jane) and £13 000 (Alan).

1 Work out:
  a the gross profit for each sole trader as a percentage of sales
  b the net profit percentage.
2 Comment on the differences between the two accounts.
3 Alan feels that his working capital is unusually small. Advise him upon how he could increase his working capital.

Case Study – What about quality?

An unfortunate trait within working groups is to start blaming someone else when anything goes wrong. As long as it is not our fault, all is well! This sort of conflict often exists in an organisation, and when such disputes start to affect profits the first thing the organisation may do is resort to cutting costs. This tends to make customer/supplier relations worse, and the situation deteriorates. However, there is an increasing feeling today that improving *quality* across the organisation is perhaps a better way of improving its performance.

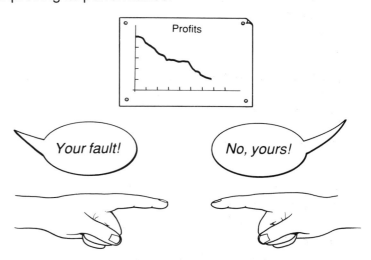

Figure 11.17 The allocation of blame

One of the tasks of management is to find ways of involving employees in all aspects of their jobs. In this age of IT, this means giving them plenty of information and asking their opinions. Quality thus rises throughout the organisation.
Reducing waste by elevating the status of employees, consulting them more frequently and allowing them to take further responsibility for their decisions, all help to add revenues as well as reduce costs.

1 Why do organisations seek to cut costs if profits start to fall?

2 How would the techniques suggested in this passage reduce the need to cut costs in the traditional way?

3 How does quality improve performance?

12

Using Information for Forecasting

In the business world, organisations constantly monitor the risks involved with each of their activities. In order to minimise these risks, organisations can use financial information to help them to forecast the effects of their actions. Management accounting provides many of the techniques which enable them to do so.

In this chapter we look at how organisations use investment appraisal, marginal costing and break-even analysis and budgetary control to forecast their activities. The chapter concludes by looking at the reasons for business failure. Though accounting information reduces unpredictability it will never eliminate it.

Think about your shopping experiences. To get the best value for money you have to research the market by exploring catalogues and visiting shops to find out as much product **information** as possible. You then weigh up all of the alternatives before making a decision.

Organisations also need information, but the **stakes** are much higher. If you make a poor decision when shopping all you end up with is a poor-quality or faulty product, but if an organisation makes a poor decision or repeatedly makes poor decisions its very existence can be threatened. The quality of information influences decision-making and will ultimately affect the **risk** involved in an organisation's activities. The law of the business world is often said to be 'the survival of the fittest'.

Making decisions is rarely an easy process, and the extent of the information required to take decisions can be immense. Information may be generated internally from departments or divisions throughout the organisation. At the same time, external variables in the business environment will be constantly changing. If an organisation is to succeed

it must make use of all of this information to **forecast** future events, and **plan** for them.

Case Study – The need to forecast

● **Denver's giant new international airport** could turn out to be one of the biggest white elephants ever. The airport is a huge project, covering an area twice the size of Manhattan Island and big enough to allow several aircraft to take off and land simultaneously. Denver already has the usual internal traffic, but the present airport, Stapleton International, only just lives up to the 'international' tag by attracting two direct overseas flights each week. The two billion dollar project faces considerable criticism. Many argue that, outside the skiing season, nobody is keen to fly to Denver. They also point out that the airport is 17 miles out of town and that the plans for a rapid transport system are both long-term and vague. Those in favour of it

231

argue that, by operating in all weathers, it will ease air traffic problems over a vast area from Chicago to Los Angeles. The whole project seems to point towards an uncertain future. If the planners are right the city of Denver could become the aviation hub of America; but if they are wrong, and there is a massive lobby who think this is so, they could be like the gold prospectors before them, just shovelling dirt to no avail.

- **Glaxo's explosive growth** in the pharmaceutical industry has been largely due to one product, its anti-ulcer drug Zantac, now the world's top-selling drug. Analysts expect cheaper anti-ulcer treatments to be available by 1995. But Glaxo seems to have prepared itself well. In addition to building one of the largest marketing departments in the industry, the company has come up with two new drugs which promise to be huge money-spinners just when Zantac's profit margins come under pressure. Sumatriptan, a migraine treatment now being considered by regulators worldwide, could bring in annual sales of two billion dollars by the mid-1990s. Salmeterol is the first breakthrough in asthma treatment since Glaxo's own Ventolin became available in 1969. It offers round-the-clock protection against asthma.

- In 1990 **Bass**, Britain's leading beer baron and publican, paid £1.03 million for the icon of the US roadside, Holiday Inn, gaining control of about 1400 hotels in America. It was the highest price ever paid for a hotel chain. Shortly after acquisition, Bass's shares dropped, their corporate debt increased and their profits fell. Many believe that Bass not only paid several hundred million dollars more than the brand was worth – purchased just before the market 'collapsed' – but that the hotel group will struggle with meagre returns for many years to come.

- In 1991 **Joseph Dooley III** arrived in the former East German town of Ahlbeck. The 27-year-old Bostonion with an undisclosed fortune plans to turn what was formerly a quiet seaside town catering for trade unionists and members of the Communist Party into one of reunited Germany's premier seaside resorts. The news has come as quite a shock to Ahlbeckers. The town, which lies close to the Polish border, was remote under communism. According to Dooley, 'the Mediterranean is overcrowded and overpolluted and the West German coast is over-developed'. He feels that there could be no better place for summer vacations in the reunited Germany than Ahlbeck.

1 Comment on the degree of risk involved in each of the four projects mentioned and then list them in order of risk.

2 What sort of information would each of the projects have required before going ahead?

3 How would the information you have identified have helped those involved to forecast the outcome of each project?

4 Would it be possible to eliminate completely the uncertainties of each project?

What is management accounting?

Whereas **financial accounting** is concerned with transactions recorded from a former accounting period and with financial statements representing past events, **management accounting** is concerned with planning, and advising on how to manage an organisation and its activities in the future. Management accounting therefore provides managers with recommendations which help them to make not only short-term day-to-day decisions but also longer-term decisions affecting the whole future of the organisation.

At the heart of management accounting is the requirement for information. This comes not only from within the business – such as information on costs and the market – but also from outside. Managers need to know what might influence the environment in which the organisation operates.

Investment decisions and the appraisal of capital

Nearly all the decisions made within an organisation involve **risking funds** in the hope of returns later. A good decision will bring in a good return while a poor decision may result in few benefits. Managers must try to make decisions which maximise returns and provide the shareholders with the best possible investment.

In order to make the right decisions, organisations have to choose the ones likely to benefit them most from all of the available alternatives. This means gathering information in order to **appraise the alternatives**. Where decisions involve non-financial matters this can be difficult – for example, how a project might affect the overall image of the organisation.

The decision-making process will be primarily concerned with weighing up the likely benefits of each decision against the costs, and then comparing the results with alternatives. Criteria such as the initial outlay, financial returns and the length of time the project is expected to last can be examined. This process is known as **capital appraisal**. There are three main methods:

- payback
- accounting rate of return
- discounted cash flow (or net present value).

Payback

The purpose of the **payback** method is to establish how quickly the investment cost can be repaid in full. In general, the shorter the payback period the better the project. For example, if we have two investment possibilities which both have an initial cost (outlay) of £18 000 and with expected receipts as shown in Figure 12.1, we can use the payback method to appraise these alternative plans.

Both of the projects will have brought in £25 000 at the end of six years. Project A, however, pays back

	Project A (£)	Project B (£)
Initial outlay	−18 000	−18 000
Year 1 receipts	+3 000	+2 000
Year 2 receipts	+5 000	+3 000
Year 3 receipts	+7 000	+4 000
Year 4 receipts	+5 000	+6 000
Year 5 receipts	+3 000	+6 000
Year 6 receipts	+2 000	+4 000

Figure 12.1 Data to illustrate the payback method

the initial cost in year 4 whereas project B does not repay the initial cost until year 5. Using the payback method, project A would be chosen.

The essential feature of the payback method is that it takes **timing** into consideration. Many organisations will attach primary importance to the early return of invested funds, particularly if **liquidity** might be a problem for them. For organisations in 'hi-tech' industries where equipment is constantly being changed, it may provide a rough guide to the extent of the risk.

Task

Projects I, II and III each involve an investment of £30 000. Project I is expected to bring in £12 000 in year 1, £15 000 in year 2, £13 000 in year 3 and £5 000 in year 4. Project II is expected to bring in £16 000 in year 1, £15 000 in year 2, £9 000 in year 3 and £5 000 in year 4. Project III is expected to bring in £8 000 in year 1, £13 000 in year 2, £18 000 in year 3 and £6 000 in year 4. Use the payback method to choose the 'best' project.

The payback method usually involves simple calculations and is easy to understand. One benefit is that it places more emphasis upon the earlier cash receipts, and these forecasts are more likely to be accurate than later ones. A criticism of the payback method, however, is that it does not take sufficient account of actual cash flows. In Figure 12.2, for example, the payback method does not reveal any differences between project C and project D because both pay back the initial outlay in three years. In this example the method also ignores cash receipts after the payback period, and because no attention is placed upon subsequent years the final profitability of each of the ventures cannot be judged.

	Project A (£)	Project B (£)
Initial outlay	−15 000	−15 000
Year 1 receipts	+13 000	+1 000
Year 2 receipts	+1 000	+1 000
Year 3 receipts	+1 000	+13 000

Figure 12.2 Two projects with identical payback periods

Accounting rate of return (ARR)

This method is concerned with expressing profitability as a **rate of return** on an investment. It is generally considered to be a quick and convenient guide for assessing the profitability of alternative projects. Profit is expressed as an **average** over the life of the project, and capital is usually considered to be the **initial outlay** or the capital invested. It is therefore calculated by:

$$ARR = \frac{\text{average annual profit}}{\text{initial outlay}} \times 100\%$$

For example, imagine that we have to choose between the two projects shown in Figure 12.3. For these projects we have:

$$\text{ARR for project E} = \frac{4000}{20\,000} \times 100\%$$
$$= 20\%$$
$$\text{ARR for project F} = \frac{10\,000}{40\,000} \times 100\%$$
$$= 25\%$$

Project F would therefore be chosen in preference to project E because the accounting rate of return is greater.

	Project E (£)	Project F (£)
Initial outlay	−20 000	−40 000
Year 1 receipts	+8 000	+18 000
Year 2 receipts	+10 000	+18 000
Year 3 receipts	+10 000	+24 000
Year 4 receipts	+8 000	+20 000
Total cash receipts	+36 000	+80 000
Profit over four years	+16 000	+40 000
Average annual profit	+4 000	+10 000

Figure 12.3 Data to illustrate the ARR method

The accounting rate of return method is cricitised for basing figures on book values, and so it fails to take heed of changing price levels. Though it overcomes one of the weaknesses of payback – by taking into account all earnings – it still does not take sufficient account of actual cash flows.

Task

In what ways is the accounting rate of return method similar to and different from the payback method?

Discounted cash flow (or net present value)

The benefits of any investment are reaped over a number of years, and so the **real values** of all future returns have to be assessed. However, the value of money, too, alters with time – £1 today will not be **worth** quite so much in five years.

Interest rates provide a rough guide to the future value of an investment. They also enable one to compare the present value of an investment with what it was worth in the past.

If an investor has £1000 in a bank account where it is earning 10 per cent interest, the balance will stand at £1100 at the end of the first year. By **compounding** this annually we discover the following:

- at the end of year 2 the balance will be £1210 (£1100 + £110)
- at the end of year 3 the balance will be £1331 (£1210 + £121)

At the end of this time (three years) the investor can say that his or her £1331 *was worth £1000 three years ago.*

This can be shown the other way around. For example, what would a present £1000 have been worth three years ago, at a 10 per cent annual rate of interest over that period? The above calculation showed us that a present £1331 would have been £1000 three years ago; and so, by taking simple proportions we have:

$$\frac{1000}{1331} \times £1000 = £751.30$$

Thus, assuming a constant rate of interest of 10 per cent, £1000 now would have started off as £751.30 three years ago; and it will be £1331 in three years' time. The £1000 is called the **net present value** (NPV). In this way the time element has been taken into account.

Published tables enable future cash to be made equivalent to present time values in a simple way, without having to do several calculations. These are called **discounted cash flow** (DCF) tables, an example of which is shown in Figure 12.4.

As an example we shall look at the returns for two projects which both have an initial capital investment of £300 000 (see Figure 12.5). Figure 12.6 shows the discounted cash flows for these two projects at a rate of interest of 10 per cent. Note that the third columns have factors read from the DCF table in Figure 12.4. From an initial investment of £300 000, project G therefore earns £453 995 whereas project H earns £462 400. Clearly project H is the project to opt for as, *at today's value,* returns will be higher.

	Project G (£)	Project H (£)
Year 1 receipts	95 000	110 000
Year 2 receipts	105 000	140 000
Year 3 receipts	200 000	150 000
Year 4 receipts	105 000	160 000
Year 5 receipts	95 000	40 000
Total earnings	600 000	600 000

Figure 12.5 Data for example

If the net present value of the total receipts comes out at less than the original investment, it may not be worth considering the project at all.

The clear advantage of the NPV method is that it takes into consideration the time element of money value and is easy to calculate with a little practice. The **danger** of depending upon it is that both interest rates and cash flows are subject to uncertainty.

Future years	1%	2%	3%	4%	Annual percentage 5%	6%	7%	8%	9%	10%
1	0.990	0.980	0.971	0.962	0.952	0.943	0.935	0.926	0.917	0.909
2	0.980	0.961	0.943	0.925	0.907	0.890	0.873	0.857	0.842	0.826
3	0.971	0.942	0.915	0.889	0.864	0.840	0.816	0.794	0.772	0.751
4	0.961	0.924	0.888	0.855	0.823	0.792	0.763	0.735	0.708	0.683
5	0.951	0.906	0.863	0.822	0.784	0.747	0.713	0.681	0.650	0.621
6	0.942	0.888	0.837	0.790	0.746	0.705	0.666	0.630	0.596	0.564

Figure 12.4 DCF table

Year	Earnings (£)	Discount factor from Figure 12.4	NPV (£)
Project G			
1	95 000	0.909	86 355
2	105 000	0.826	86 730
3	200 000	0.751	150 200
4	105 000	0.683	71 715
5	95 000	0.621	58 995
			453 995
Project H			
1	110 000	0.909	99 990
2	140 000	0.826	115 640
3	150 000	0.751	112 650
4	160 000	0.683	109 280
5	40 000	0.621	24 840
			462 400

Figure 12.6 Comparison of projects G and H

Case Study – West Brighton Engineering PLC

West Brighton Engineering PLC is in the process of considering two alternative projects which each involve an investment of £45 000. You have been called in to advise the company on the merits of each project using techniques of capital appraisal.

Project I involves equipping a production line to increase automation in the production process. This will result in substantial savings in production line labour and servicing costs, and should increase receipts in year 1 by £18 000, in year 2 by £23 000, in year 3 by £28 000 and in year 4 by £12 000.

Project II entails increasing the spending on the company's marketing activities. It is estimated that this should increase receipts in year 1 by £6000, in year 2 by £12 000, in year 3 by £25 000 and in year 4 by £25 000.

1 Using the three techniques of capital appraisal discussed in the text, advise the company on each of the projects proposed. Assume a constant rate of interest of 6 per cent.

2 Comment briefly on any other information that might be useful and have an influence on the decision as to which project to follow.

More about costs

The word **cost** has several meanings, even in everyday language. The cost of items we purchase is something we come across daily – it is a money sacrifice we have to make for the things we want. Organisations frequently refer to calculating the cost of an event or an activity – managers talk about **costing an activity**. Within this context they are using a knowledge of costs together with a knowledge of revenues to determine whether or not something they are planning will ultimately reap the rewards they desire. Today **cost accounting** and the use of costing techniques provides a useful source of data for management accountants.

Nearly all of an organisation's activities involve some sort of cost. A sound knowledge of these costs and their influence is fundamental for assessing profitability, as profits are only a reflection of income over and above such costs. Costs from the past – which therefore have already been incurred – often provide a guide to likely costs in the future.

There are two broad areas into which costs can be allocated. **Fixed costs** are those that *do not increase as the total output increases*. For example, if an organisation has the capacity needed it might increase its production from 25 000 units to 30 000 units. Its rent, rates and heating bills will be the same, since they also had to be paid when the organisation was producing 25 000 units.

Variable costs are those that *increase as the output increases*, because more of these factors need to be employed as inputs in order to increase the output. For example, if you produce more items you will need more raw materials.

Marginal costing

Marginal costing is a commonly used technique which uses costs to forecast profits from the production and sales levels expected in future periods. The great benefit of marginal costing over other costing methods is that it overcomes the problem of allocating fixed costs – only variable costs are allocated, as we shall see.

The difference between an item's selling price and the variable costs needed to produce that item is known as the **contribution** (that is, its contribution to the whole profit).

Contribution = selling price per unit LESS variable costs per unit	

By producing and selling enough units to produce a total contribution that is in excess of the *fixed* costs, an organisation will make a profit.

For example, Penzance Toys Ltd manufactures plastic train sets for young children. It anticipates that next year it will sell 8000 units at £12 per unit. Its variable costs are £5 per unit and its fixed costs are £9000. From the above formula we can deduce that the contribution is £12 minus £5, which is £7 per unit. Therefore – for each unit made – £7 will go towards paying off fixed costs. We can also show this using totals to show how much profit will be made if the company sells 8000 units (see Figure 12.7).

	(£)
Sales revenue (8000 × £5)	96 000
Less marginal costs (8000 × £5)	40 000
Total contribution	56 000
Less fixed costs	9 000
Net profit	47 000

Figure 12.7 Profit statement for Penzance Toys Ltd

The problem can also be looked at by constructing a table as in Figure 12.8.

Task

Rovers Medallions Ltd produces a standard size trophy for sports shops and clubs. It hopes to sell 2000 trophies next year at £9 per unit. Its variable costs are £5 per unit and its fixed costs are £4000. Draw up a profit statement to show how much profit it will make in the year. Also construct a table to show how much profit it will make at each 500 units of production up to 3000 units.

Marginal costing is particularly useful for making short-term decisions – for example, helping to set the selling price of a product, or deciding whether or

Units of production	Fixed costs (£)	Variable costs (£)	Total costs (£)	Revenue (£)	Profit (loss) (£)
1 000	9 000	5 000	14 000	12 000	(2 000)
2 000	9 000	10 000	19 000	24 000	5 000
3 000	9 000	15 000	24 000	36 000	12 000
4 000	9 000	20 000	29 000	48 000	19 000
5 000	9 000	25 000	34 000	60 000	26 000
6 000	9 000	30 000	39 000	72 000	33 000
7 000	9 000	35 000	44 000	84 000	40 000
8 000	9 000	40 000	49 000	96 000	47 000
9 000	9 000	45 000	54 000	108 000	54 000
10 000	9 000	50 000	59 000	120 000	61 000

Figure 12.8 Profit table for Penzance Toys Ltd

not to accept an order. It might also help an organisation to decide whether to buy in a component or whether to produce it themselves.

Break-even analysis

Break-even analysis is an extension of marginal costing. Breaking-even is the unique point at which an organisation makes neither profit nor loss. If sales go beyond the break-even point profits are made, and if they are below the break-even point losses are made. In marginal costing it is *the point at which the contribution equals the fixed costs.*

To calculate the break-even point there are two stages:

- Calculate the unit contribution (selling price less variable costs).
- Divide the fixed costs by the unit contribution:

$$\text{Break-even point} = \frac{\text{fixed costs}}{\text{unit contribution}}$$

For example, in Penzance Toys Ltd (see above) the contribution per unit is £7 and the fixed costs are £9000. The break-even point would therefore be:

$$\frac{9000}{7} = 1286 \text{ units (to nearest unit)}$$

The **sales value** at the break-even point can be calculated by multiplying the number of units by the selling price per unit. For Penzance Toys this would be:

$$1286 \times £12 = £15\,432$$

Penzance Toys has covered its costs (fixed + variable) and broken-even with a sales value of £15 432. Anything sold in excess of this will provide it with profits.

If an organisation has a **profit target** to aim at, break-even analysis can be used to calculate the number of units that need to be sold and the value of sales required to achieve that target.

For example, we can imagine that Penzance Toys wishes to achieve a target of £15 000 profit. By adding this £15 000 to the fixed costs and dividing by the contribution, the number of units can be found which need to be sold to meet this target. Thus:

$$\frac{£9000 + £15\,000}{£7} = 3429 \text{ units (to nearest unit)}$$

The difference between the break-even point and the selected level of activity designed to achieve the profit target is known as the **margin of safety.**

Task

B. Hive Beehives Ltd is a small business selling hives to local keepers. Each hive is sold for £25. Fixed costs are £18 000 and variable costs are £13 per unit. The company wishes to achieve a profit of £18 000.

a *Calculate the break-even point in both units and sales value.*
b *Calculate both the units and sales value necessary to achieve the stated profit.*

Cost/volume/profit analysis

Cost/volume/profit (CVP) analysis is a term sometimes used to show changes in the relationship between costs, production volumes and various levels of sales activity. This sort of information can be shown in the form of a break-even chart. This is the procedure to construct a **break-even chart** (you may find it helpful to look forward to Figure 12.9):

- Label the horizontal axis for units of production and sales.
- Label the vertical axis to represent the values of sales and costs.

- Plot fixed costs. Fixed costs will remain the same over all levels of production, so plot this as a straight line parallel to the horizontal axis.
- Plot the total costs (variable costs + fixed cost). This will be a line rising from where the fixed-cost line touches the vertical axis. It is plotted by calculating total costs at two or three random levels of production.
- Sales are plotted by taking two or three random levels of turnover. The line will rise from the intersection of the two axes.

The break-even point will be where the total-cost line and sales line intersect. The area to the *left* of the break-even point between the sales and total-cost lines will represent *losses*, and the area to the right of the break-even point between these lines will represent *profit*.

As always, an example will make this clearer. Eddie Bowen plans to set up a small restaurant. In doing so he knows that he will immediately incur annual fixed costs of £10 000. He is concerned about how many meals he will have to sell to break-even. Extensive market research indicates that a typical customer will pay £8 for a meal, and Eddie knows that variable costs – such as cooking ingredients and the costs of serving customers – will amount to about £3. Eddie has set himself a profit target of £14 000 for the first year of operation. Our task is to advise Eddie on the number of meals he has to sell and to indicate to him his margin of safety.

Eddie's unit *contribution* is:
£8 − £3 (selling price − variable costs)=£5 per meal

His *break-even point* in units will be:
£10 000 (fixed costs)÷£5 (unit contribution)
=2000   meals

The *sales value* of the meals will be:
2000 meals × £8 (selling price) = £16 000

His *profit target* will be achieved by:

$$\frac{£10\ 000\ \text{(fixed costs)} + £14\ 000\ \text{(profit target)}}{£5\ \text{(unit contribution)}} = 4\ 800\ \text{meals}$$

The *margin of safety* will be the difference between the selected level of activity and the break-even

point. It will be between 4800 meals with a turnover of £38 400 and 2000 meals with a turnover of £16 000.

The three random levels of variable costs and sales chosen for the purpose of plotting the break-even chart are at 1000 meals, 3000 meals and 5000 meals:

	1 000 meals (£)	3 000 meals (£)	5 000 meals (£)
Variable costs (£3/meal)	3 000	9 000	15 000
Fixed cost	10 000	10 000	10 000
Total cost	13 000	19 000	25 000
Sales	8 000	24 000	40 000

We can now plot the break-even chart (Figure 12.9) which shows graphically the break-even point of 2000 meals with a sales revenue of £16 000. The margin of safety can be seen on the chart if we identify the selected level of profit (at 4800 meals) and the targeted turnover (of £38 400), and compare this point with the break-even point.

The break-even chart is a simple **visual tool** enabling managers to anticipate the effects of changes in production and sales upon the profitability of an organisation's activities. It emphasises the importance of earning revenue and is particularly helpful for those who are unused to interpreting accounting information.

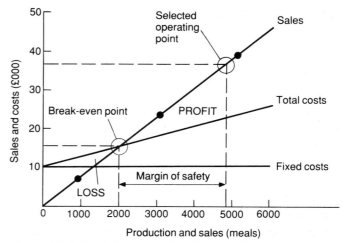

Figure 12.9 Eddie Bowen's break-even chart

Case Study – Taking over the family business

John Smith had a visit from an aged relative who wanted advice. For many years she had run a small hotel in a market town in the Thames valley. After careful consideration she had decided to 'call it a day' and retire, but she was keen to see the business continue and wished to retain her ownership in it.

John is interested in a proposition she has put forward, which involves running the hotel on her behalf. The hotel has been allowed to deteriorate over the years and, in John's opinion, it is obvious that extensive refurbishment is necessary before he could realistically consider her proposal. The hotel is, however, in a prime spot, was extensively used little more than ten years ago, and John feels that with hard work it has the potential to become successful again.

He arranged for a number of quotations to be made for building works. The most favourable quotation received was for £180 000, which involved extensive interior redecoration and refurbishment as well as completely reorganising the reception and kitchen areas.

John's intention is that the finance for the building work should come from a five-year bank loan with a fixed annual interest rate of 10 per cent, payable each calendar month, and based upon the original sum. The loan principal would be paid back in five equal annual instalments.

He has estimated the following fixed and variable costs:

Fixed
Annual loan repayment (£36 000)
Annual interest on loan (£18 000)
Business rate and water rates (£7000 p.a.)
Insurance (£4500 p.a.)

Electricity (£1300 per quarter year)
Staff salaries (£37 000 p.a.)

Variable
These include direct labour such as cleaners and bar staff, as well as the cost of food, bar stocks etc. After careful research John has estimated these to be £2000 for each 100 customers who visit the hotel.

John has had a local agency conduct an extensive market research survey and feels confident that the hotel will attract about 100 customers per week, who will each spend on average (including accommodation, food and drinks) about £70 in the hotel.

1 *Work out the break-even point for the hotel in both numbers of customers and value.*
2 *Work out the number of customers required to make a gross profit of £35 000.*
3 *Draw a break-even chart showing the break-even point, the profit target and the margin of safety.*
4 *Use ONE method of investment appraisal to further consider the project.*
5 *What other information might John Smith require before deciding whether to go ahead with the project?*

Limitations of marginal costing

Marginal costing is often considered to over-simplify organisational behaviour by reducing it to an equation: how to generate sufficient contribution to cover fixed costs and provide a surplus (profits). Its limitations are several:

● It can be argued that, in real situations, fixed costs actually vary with different activity levels, and so a stepped fixed-cost line would provide a more accurate guide.
● Many organisations fail to break-even because of a limiting factor restricting their ability to do so (e.g. shortage of space, labour or orders).

- The variable-cost and sales lines are unlikely to be linear (i.e. straight). Discounts, special contracts and overtime payments mean that the cost line is more likely to be a curve.
- Break-even charts depict short-term relationships, and forecasts are therefore unrealistic when the proposals cover a number of years.
- Break-even analysis is (like all other methods) dependent upon the accuracy of forecasts made about costs and revenues. Changes in the market and in the cost of raw materials could affect the success of the technique.

Task

Think about a business activity you might like to engage in. Describe the activity and what it involves. Anticipate the selling price you would expect to set and then work out your variable costs per unit and your overall fixed costs. Use the marginal costs technique to work out whether your project could be successful. Comment in detail on the outcome.

Budgetary control

Budgetary control is the technique of looking into an organisation's future in order to anticipate what is going to happen and then trying to make it happen. It is considered to be a system of **responsibility** accounting because it puts an onus upon managers to perform in a way that has been outlined for them, and its success will depend upon the quality of information provided.

In Chapter 10 we looked at how to forecast financial requirements with a cash budget or cash flow forecast. We saw that a cash budget ensured that an organisation would have sufficient cash to cater for any **plans** it might have, and that it would help the organisation to highlight any problems at an early stage so that managers could take the necessary action.

Organisations that fail to produce a budget are likely to be uncertain about what is happening. When their financial accounts are drawn up and presented the owners or managers may be pleased or upset with the results. This is uncertain and undisciplined. Management should not have to wait for the financial statements to understand how they have performed. Budgeting helps them to understand how they are performing as well as how they are likely to perform in the future. Budgets can cover every aspect of an organisation's activities – production, cash, overheads, labour, purchases, debtors, creditors etc. Information drawn from these separate budgets can then be used to forecast the final accounts for the end of the following year.

Case Study – The born-again IBM

The UK subsidiary of IBM, the world's largest computer manufacturer, has been shaken to the core as drastic measures to improve efficiency and effectiveness have been put into action. These include:

- the loss of many jobs
- a pay-incentive scheme which depends upon customers' opinions
- a futuristic plan to manage individuals' workloads through a computerised control system.

There is scarcely an employee left at IBM at any level who has been unaffected by the changes. IBM is going through this corporate transformation as it fights with increased competition, declining profit margins and overweight bureaucracy. Mr Nick Temple, IBM UK's general manager, who was recently appointed for planning and overseeing the shakeup of the UK operation, describes it as 'a renaissance: a rebirth of a local company'. His mission was to create a blueprint for a lean, flexible organisation able to respond to its customers' requirements speedily and efficiently.

The 'Temple Plan' involved a powerful attack on expenses – with an across-the-board 8 per cent reduction. It also involved measures which not only change people's jobs but also their careers and ideas. To measure the success of the renaissance IBM UK today has a series of criteria, such as:

- a computer model of the company which shows how successfully resources are deployed and the extent to which overheads are being reduced
- an accreditation process which measures the level and variety of skills acquired by IBM staff
- opinion surveys to measure whether the corporate culture is changing fast enough
- quality surveys against both US standards and customer opinions
- business performance measured by sales and pre-tax profits.

1 Given the problems at IBM UK, how important is forecasting to the company?

2 How might budgeting help IBM UK to become a 'lean, flexible organisation'?

3 Comment on the prospect of a pay-incentive scheme dependent upon customers' opinions.

4 How might the computer model manage the company's budgetary activities?

We all budget to some extent. Our short-term budget is probably our plan to survive the month, meet all our commitments and do all the things we intend to do. Our longer-term budget might involve planning for Christmas presents or for how we are going to pay the car insurance. In exactly the same way organisations try to dig deep into their future, to plan ahead and forecast their commitments. Budgets enable an organisation to prepare for the year ahead and include all activities as part of a longer plan, perhaps over three or five years.

The budgeting team

An organisation may appoint a **budget controller** to coordinate the budgetary activities, and the **budgeting team** then consists of representatives from various areas of activity within the organisation. The task of the team can be considered under headings (see Figure 12.10):

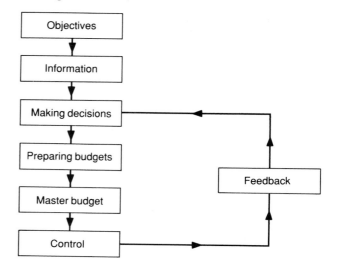

Figure 12.10 Preparing a budget

- *Considering objectives.* The team will undertake activities designed to enable the organisation to meet its objectives (e.g. profit maximising, improving market share, improving product quality).
- *Providing information.* The team will also look at figures from previous years so that new budgets can to some extent be based on past results. A clear knowledge of the environment in which the organisation is competing is also important.
- *Making decisions.* Whenever forward planning takes place it will highlight the need to make decisions.
- *Preparing budgets.* Detailed budgets are then prepared for all areas of the organisation's activity.
- *Preparing a master budget.* The individual budgets, when linked together, can be used to forecast a set of final accounts.
- *Controlling.* Even though budgets are drawn up, this does not always mean that such plans are

successful. Managers try to use their budgets as a guide to achieving certain results. If there is a difference between actual performance at the end of a year and budgeted performance, action can be taken.

Variance analysis

Variance analysis can be used to quantify the difference between the budget and the actual outcome, and feedback from such an analysis can affect decision-making in subsequent years. Variance analysis detects problems and enables managers to take prompt action to improve efficiency and profitability. For example, there could be a sudden upturn in expenditure on raw materials, caused perhaps by one of the following:

- increased wastage
- inefficiency by operators
- materials damaged in transit
- inefficient buying.

The list is not exhaustive, but the variance analysis has indicated a problem and the manager can use experience to find out the cause.

What a budgetary system can do

Each year the way the organisation functions is reviewed by the budgeting team, and this provides a **better understanding** of the organisation as a whole. In addition, budgeting increases co-operation between various parts of an organisation and lowers departmental barriers.

When a budget is drawn up, non-accountants from various parts of the organisation become more aware of the **importance of costs**. This helps them to work to achieve the budgeted targets. It also helps individuals across the organisation to become aware of **profitability**.

Sometimes, however, these are problems with a system of budgetary control:

- If the actual results are completely different from the targets, the budget can lose its significance as a

means of control. Whereas a **fixed budget** is not able to adapt to such changes, a **flexible budget** will recognise changes in behaviour and can be amended to fall into line with changing activities.
- Following a budget too rigidly can restrict an organisation's activities. On the other hand, if a manager realises towards the end of the year that his or her department has *under*spent, he or she might go on a spending spree.
- If budgets are *imposed* upon managers without sufficient consultation, they may be ignored.

Task

Interview someone who has responsibility for a budgeted area of activity. Find out how the budget helps and hinders the ways in which the person supervises his or her area of operations.

Preparing a budget

Budgets are prepared for a set time period known as a **budget period** (quite often a year). Sometimes the budget period is broken down into shorter **control periods**, such as months. Each part of the master budget is the responsibility of an individual manager, and the part of the organisation for which each budget is prepared is known as a **budget centre**.

In looking at budgets we shall start by drawing up **cash budgets**, and take them through to final accounts. Then we shall look at budgets for other activities.

Example 1 – P. Rogers (sole trader)

Peter Rogers has recently been declared redundant by a large industrial component manufacturer in the

North East of England. However, he had been worrying about the prospect of redundancy for some time and had been making plans for such an eventuality. In his spare time he had been repairing cars for friends, and this led him to decide to use his redundancy money to start a garage business locally. Peter has found a suitable site.

Drawing up the opening balance sheet

The purchase price of the existing garage is £130 000. It comprises a small filling station with two pumps, a small office, toilets and a service area of 200 square metres containing an inspection pit and other facilities. This has been valued at £100 000, and the remainder of the selling price is for equipment and tools valued at £25 000, and petrol and oil stocks of £5000.

Peter received £40 000 redundancy money. He has surrendered two life insurance policies for a further sum of £30 000, and has remortgaged his house and obtained £30 000. He intends to borrow another £40 000 from a local bank. Hence, when he has paid the £130 000 purchase price he will have £10 000 left in the bank account.

His **opening balance sheet** will therefore be as shown in Figure 12.11.

	(£)	(£)
Fixed assets		
Land and buildings		100 000
Equipment and tools		25 000
		125 000
Current assets		
Stocks – petrol and oil	5 000	
Bank	10 000	
Working capital		15 000
		140 000
Less **Long-term liabilities**		
Bank loan		40 000
		100 000
FINANCED BY:		
Capital		100 000
Capital employed		100 000

Figure 12.11 Opening balance sheet of P. Rogers' garage at 1 January 1992

Drawing up the cash budget

Peter has put together estimated *sales figures* for the first six months based upon the records of his predecessor. In the list below, the left column shows Peter's projected sales of petrol and oil, and the right column shows expected income from repairs and servicing:

Jan	8 000	3 100
Feb	9 800	2 100
Mar	12 300	1 700
Apr	11 200	1 800
May	8 100	2 300
June	8 300	3 100
	57 700	14 100

All *sales* of petrol and oil will be for cash, with immediate payment. It is anticipated that one-half of the receipts for repairs and servicing will be in cash, received immediately, and one-half will be on one month's credit terms.

Deliveries for January to March inclusive will involve £8000 of petrol and oil delivered on each occasion, and from April to June will involve £7000 of petrol delivered each month. One month's credit is given by the supplier.

Other *expenses* each month will be £200 for wages, £90 for insurance, £100 for the business rate, and £30 for advertising. These are all to be paid at the end of each month.

Peter *draws* £800 from the business each month for personal use. It is estimated that the *stocks* of petrol and oil at the end of the six-month period will be valued at £4400. Peter intends to *purchase* a pick-up truck in March for £21 000 and a van in June for £10 000.

Peter's **cash budget** (the cash-flow forecast) for the first six months will therefore be as shown in Figure 12.12.

Drawing up the master budget

Debtors for repairs and servicing are £1550 at the end of June, and *creditors* for petrol supplies are

	Jan (£)	Feb (£)	Mar (£)	Apr (£)	May (£)	Jun (£)
Receipts						
Sales – cash	9 550	10 850	13 150	12 100	9 250	9 850
Sales – credit	–	1 550	1 050	850	900	1 150
Total receipts	9 550	12 400	14 200	12 950	10 150	11 000
Payments						
Petrol and oil	–	8 000	8 000	8 000	7 000	7 000
Wages	200	200	200	200	200	200
Business rate	100	100	100	100	100	100
Insurance	90	90	90	90	90	90
Advertising	30	30	30	30	30	30
Drawings	800	800	800	800	800	800
Motor vehicles	–	–	21 000	–	–	10 000
Total payments	1 220	9 220	30 220	9 220	8 220	18 220
Opening bank	10 000	18 330	21 510	5 490	9 220	11 150
Add receipts	9 550	12 400	14 200	12 950	10 150	11 000
	19 550	30 730	35 710	18 440	19 370	22 150
Less payments	1 220	9 220	30 220	9 220	8 220	18 220
Balance c/f	18 330	21 510	5 490	9 220	11 150	3 930

Figure 12.12 P. Rogers' cash budget

expected to be £7000 at the end of June. From this information, and the totals in the cash budget, the **financial operating statement** for the six months ending on 30 June 1992 can be drawn up as shown in Figure 12.13. The **forecasted balance sheet** at 30 June is shown in Figure 12.14. These two documents constitute P. Rogers' **master budget** for the first six months of operation.

	(£)	(£)
		71 800
Sales		
Less cost of sales		
Opening stock	5 000	
Add purchases	45 000	
	50 000	
Less closing stock	4 400	45 600
Gross profit		26 200
Less expences:		
Wages	1 200	
Business rate	600	
Insurance	540	
Advertising	180	2 520
Net profit		23 680

Figure 12.13 P. Rogers' financial operating

	(£)	(£)
Fixed assets		
Land and buildings		100 000
Equipment and tools		25 000
Motor vehicles		31 000
		156 000
Current assets		
Closing stock –		
petrol and oil	4 400	
Debtors	1 550	
Bank	3 930	
	9 880	
Less **Current liabilities**		
Creditors	7 000	
Working capital		2 880
		158 880
Less **Long-term liabilities**		
Bank loan		40 000
		118 880
FINANCED BY:		
Capital		100 000
Add net profit		23 680
		123 680
Less drawings		4 800
		118 880

Figure 12.14 P. Rogers' forcasted balance sheet

Task

Rachel Salt set up in business as a grocer on 1 January 1992. She spent £100 000 on land and buildings and £5000 on fixtures and fittings. She started with stocks of £1000. She also put £14 000 from her bank account into the business. Rachel has forecast the following figures:

- She expects sales over the next six months to be:

	(£)
Jan	2100
Feb	1800
Mar	1800
Apr	2100
May	1800
June	2000

All sales are for cash with immediate payment.
- Deliveries of stock to her shop from January to June will be made monthly. She expects to purchase:

	(£)
Jan	1400
Feb	1200
Mar	1700
Apr	1800
May	1200
June	1200

Two months credit is given by suppliers.
- Other expenses each month will include:

	(£)
Wages	400
Business rate	70
Insurance	30
Transport	20
Advertising	20

- Rachel draws £600 each month for her personal use.
- It is estimated that stock at the end of June will be worth £4300.
- Rachel intends to purchase a new till in March for £400.

a Show Rachel's opening balance sheet.
b Forecast her likely cash flow over the first six months.
c Produce a financial operating statement, and a forecasted balance sheet for the end of the period.

Example 2 – Meashams Ltd

In this example we look at an exercise which produces:

- a **raw materials budget** showing figures for each month
- a **production budget** showing figures (in units) for each month
- a **production cost budget** showing cost figures for each month
- a statement showing total **debtors** and **creditors** at the end of a six-month period
- a **cash budget**
- a **forecasted operating statement**
- a **forecasted balance sheet.**

	(£)	(£)	(£)
Fixed assets			
Premises			90 000
Plant and machinery			105 000
Office equipment			9 000
Motor vehicles			50 000
			254 000
Current assets			
Stocks – finished goods		26 000	
Stocks – raw material		2 000	
Debtors		87 000	
Bank		4 000	
		119 000	
Less **Current liabilities**			
Creditors for fixed expenses	3 000		
Creditors for raw materials			
(Mar 28 500, Apr 25 500)	54 000	57 000	
Working capital			62 000
			316 000
FINANCED BY:			
Share capital: Ordinary shares			250 000
Preference shares			46 000
Reserves			20 000
			316 000

Figure 12.15 Balance sheet of Meashams Ltd at 30 April 1992

Alison Bicknell, the accountant of Meashams Ltd, has been asked to set up a budgetary system to forecast the next six months' activities. As budgetary controller she has met representatives from various departments before putting together her budgetary estimates. On the 30 April 1992, Meashams' balance sheet was as shown in Figure 12.15.

The plans

Measham's plans for the next six months are as follows:

- After lengthy consultations, a sales price of £15.00 per unit has been agreed. By carefully analysing the market the *number* of sales are expected to be:

May	June	July	Aug	Sept	Oct
6500	7750	8000	8200	8550	9000

All of the sales are on credit, and debtors usually pay their outstanding balances one month after they have received the goods.

- In order to satisfy production requirements it has been agreed that purchases of raw materials will be:

May	June	July	Aug	Sept	Oct
£23 700	£24 300	£24 500	£27 500	£28 250	£24 750

All raw materials are bought on credit, and the creditors for raw materials will be paid two months after purchase.

- It has been decided that production will be 8000 units per month from May to August and 9000 units per month in September and October.
- Production costs will be (per unit):

	(£)
Direct materials	3.00
Direct labour	4.00
Variable overheads	6.00
	13.00

- Fixed expenses average £3000 per month and these are always paid one month in arrears.

To forecast the sales income the selling price of £15.00 is multiplied by the number of units for each

month. For example, in May the value of sales is expected to be £97 500, June £116 250, July £120 000, August £123 000, September £128 250 and October £135 000. The total sales figure for the six months is therefore £720 000. As debtors pay one month after they have received the goods, the debtors from the balance sheet in April will pay in May; May debtors will pay in June etc. When Alison produces her cash budget these will be entered as *receipts*.

The raw materials budget

The **raw materials budget** is intended to ensure that there is always an availability of resources to move on to the production line and that levels do not dwindle. Decisions about minimum stock levels have already been taken. The raw materials budget involves adding purchases to the opening stocks materials for each month, and then deducting those used in production each month (see Figure 12.16).

	May (£)	June (£)	July (£)	Aug (£)	Sept (£)	Oct (£)
Opening stock	2 000	1 700	2 000	2 500	6 000	7 250
Add purchases	23 700	24 300	24 500	27 500	28 250	24 750
	25 700	26 000	26 500	30 000	34 250	32 000
Less production materials	24 000	24 000	24 000	24 000	27 000	27 000
Closing stock of raw materials	1 700	2 000	2 500	6 000	7 250	5 000

Figure 12.16 Measham's raw materials budget

It must be remembered that creditors for raw materials are paid two months after purchase. This means that those for March (as shown in the balance sheet in Figure 12.15) will be paid in May, those from April in June etc. In the cash budget these will be *payments*.

The production budget

The **production budget** links production volume with sales volume. The production budget is therefore normally produced in units. The opening stock of finished goods is added to anticipated production levels for each month, and then the monthly sales are deducted. This is shown in Figure 12.17.

	May	June	July	Aug	Sept	Oct
Opening stock						
(finished goods)	2 000	3 500	3 750	3 750	3 550	4 000
Add production	8 000	8 000	8 000	9 000	9 000	9 000
	10 000	11 500	11 750	11 750	12 550	13 000
Less sales	6 500	7 750	8 000	8 200	8 550	9 000
Closing stock						
(finished goods)	3 500	3 750	3 750	3 550	4 000	4 000

Figure 12.17 Meashams' production budget (in units)

The closing stock of finished goods is therefore 4000 units at the end of October. As stocks are valued at their cost price, the value of the closing stock of finished goods – to be transferred to the balance sheet – will be 4000 units × £13 production cost, which is £52 000.

The production cost budget

The **production cost budget** supplies the costs of production on a month-by-month basis and gives the total cost of goods completed, which can then be transferred to the trading section of the forecasted operating statement. It involves multiplying the unit production costs of direct materials, direct labour and direct overheads by the number of units produced month by month. This is shown in Figure 12.18.

Debtors and creditors

Alison now works out the **debtors** figure for the end of October. As debtors pay their outstanding balances one month after they have received the goods, the debtors figure for the end of October will be the sales figure for *September*, that is £128 250. She knows that **creditors** for raw materials are paid two months after purchase. The creditors figure for the end of October will therefore be made up of *September's* and *October's* purchases of raw materials of £28 250 and £24 750, totalling £53 000.

The cash budget, forecasted operating statement and balance sheet.

Alison now has sufficient information to work out the **cash budget**. This is shown in Figure 12.19. With all sectional budgets completed, she can finally draw up a **master budget** in the form of a forecasted operating statement and balance sheet. These are shown in Figures 12.20 and 12.21.

Information from the sectional budgets and master budget can now be fed back into departments. The budgetary system has coordinated the revenue and expenditure areas and organised them into an overall plan.

	May (£)	June (£)	July (£)	Aug (£)	Sept (£)	Oct (£)	Total (£)
Materials cost	24 000	24 000	24 000	24 000	27 000	27 000	150 000
Labour cost	32 000	32 000	32 000	32 000	36 000	36 000	200 000
Variable cost	48 000	48 000	48 000	48 000	54 000	54 000	300 000
	104 000	104 000	104 000	104 000	117 000	117 000	650 000

Figure 12.18 Meashams' production cost budget

	May (£)	Jun (£)	Jul (£)	Aug (£)	Sept (£)	Oct (£)
Receipts						
Sales	87 000	97 500	116 250	120 000	123 000	128 250
Total receipts	87 000	97 500	116 250	120 000	123 000	128 250
Payments	*March*	*april*	*may*	*June*	*July*	*Aug.*
Raw materials	28 500	25 500	23 700	24 300	24 500	27 500
Direct labour	32 000	32 000	32 000	32 000	36 000	36 000
Variable o/h	48 000	48 000	48 000	48 000	54 000	54 000
Fixed expenses	3 000	3 000	3 000	3 000	3 000	3 000
Total payments	111 500	108 500	106 700	107 300	117 500	120 500
Opening balance	4 000	(20 500)	(31 500)	(21 950)	(9 250)	(3 750)
Add receipts	87 000	97 500	116 250	120 000	123 000	128 250
	91 000	77 000	84 750	98 050	113 750	124 500
Less payments	111 500	108 500	106 700	107 300	117 500	120 500
Balance c/f	(20 500)	(31 500)	(21 950)	(9 250)	(3 750)	4 000

Figure 12.19 Measham's cash budget for May–October

	(£)	(£)	(£)
Fixed assets			
Premises			90 000
Plant and machinery			105 000
Office equipment			9 000
Motor vehicles			50 000
			254 000
Current assets			
Stocks – finished goods (4000 units)		52 000	
Stocks – raw materials		5 000	
Debtors		135 000 ← *Oct sale,*	
Bank		4 000	
		196 000	
Less **Current liabilities**			
Creditors for fixed expenses	3 000		
Creditors for raw materials			
(Sep 28 250 + Oct 24 750)	53 000	56 000	
Working capital			140 000
			394 000
FINANCED BY: ~~Share capital~~ *ORDINARY SHARES*			250 000
~~Ordinary shares~~ *PREFERENCE SHARES*			46 000
~~Preference shares~~			98 000
Reserves (£20000 + retained profit)			394 000

Figure 12.20 Measham's forcasted balance sheet as at 31 October

		(£)
Sales		720 000
Less: cost of sales:		
Opening stock of	26 000	
finished goods	650 000	
Add cost of goods supplied	676 000	
Less closing stock of		624 000
finished goods	52 000	
Gross profit		96 000
Less overheads:		18 000
Fixed expenses		78 000
Net profit		

Figure 12.21 Measham's forcasted operating statement

Using accounting information for forecasting

The main problem with any information system is that is reflects data from the past and present, and will only enable *predictions* to be made about the future. At the same time, numerous pressures in their jobs may impose constraints upon managers which affect the quality of information they collect. The problems can be numerous. Clearly nothing can be forecasted with absolute certainty. No matter what financial and marketing research takes place, every organisation has to take **risks**. Though accounting information may reduce the unpredictability of events in the future, it will never eliminate it.

Case Study – The reasons for business failure

The economic recession of the late 1980s and early 1990s claimed some notable scalps. For example, within a short period in early 1991 receivers moved into Easthope, the 53-store jewellery chain, once part of Next. John Dee, one of the UK's largest road haulage companies, crashed and this was shortly followed by the double glazing company Stormseal. In fact business failures in 1991 were at their highest level for many years.

Many organisations found their forecasts completely out of line with their plans when they became sandwiched between a falling market for their products and high interest rates on debts they took on during the boom years of the mid-1980s. Companies which were highly geared – with a high proportion of loan capital to share capital – were often particularly vulnerable to the climate. Late payments by larger organisations, and tough action by the banks over loans and overdrafts, also contributed to many failures.

The early signs of a business's failure appear long before it crashes. Initially, profits start to fall, gearing starts to increase and then losses are reported. The beginning of the end is when trading in shares is suspended. **Liquidation** occurs when it is considered that a company can no longer pay its debts – liquidation is ordered by a court, usually at the behest of a creditor. In many cases the next step is **receivership** – this involves the appointment of an independent accountant to supervise the sale of the company. Over the whole period that the company is struggling to survive there is always the possibility of a **white knight** attempting to launch a rescue for it. For example, over the eleven years that the newspaper *Financial Weekly* existed, it had four different proprietors who collectively lost about eleven million pounds. It was rescued from extinction twice, had two management buyouts and was in a permanent state of crisis. Against the recent background of notable business failures, there always seem to be many thousands of budding business entrepreneurs willing to put their ideas into action – and many will undoubtedly do so with their redundancy money!

1 *List five possible causes of business failure.*
2 *What measures might an organisation take to avoid failure?*
3 *What are the various stages of a business failing?*
4 *Find examples of business failures reported in the national newspapers. Can you find a white knight?*

Case Study – Britain's twilight homes

At Tony Acton's elegant mews house there is nothing to betray his role as chairman of a conglomerate with products ranging from kitty-litter to nursing homes. Acton is one of a growing band of corporate executives who are keen to pursue demographic changes which will see Britain's over-85 population increase by 40 per cent by the year 2000. Welfare subsidies and the spur of the Community Care Bill have recently encouraged more development of nursing homes in the private sector.

However, according to the industry's trade associations, nursing and residential homes are closing at the rate of four a week, sunk by high interest rates, rising staff costs and falling occupancy rates. The nursing home sector, previously dominated by husband-and-wife teams, had become ripe for rationalisation and for large organisations to move in. One such organisation is Takare. Takare's blueprint is to build nursing homes to its own specifications. All except one are in single-storey 30-bed units built round a central management facility. The company believes it can benefit from greater economies of scale. The chairman feels that the company's proven formula enables it to 'give twice the care for half the cost'. Where others seem to be failing Takare seems destined for success.

1 Explain how larger organisations are able to run nursing homes more efficiently than smaller organisations.
2 If you were running a small nursing home, in the sort of market indicated here, how would you attempt to manage the finances of your business? What decisions might you have to make?

13
External Influences on the Organisation

Business life can be fully understood only when viewed against a background of inter-dependence and complex interrelationships. All organisations operate with many external influences on their activities, and in this chapter we examine a wide range of such influences.

Furthermore, the environment in which an organisation exists is in a constant state of change. People responsible for running the organisation must be fully aware of changes in the external influences if they are to respond positively with effective measures to meet the organisation's objectives.

The activities of organisations do not take place in books – they take place in the real world. In this world there are many **outside** influences that affect the ways in which an organisation as a whole can act, and which therefore affect the ways in which individual members of the organisation can behave. For example, you may need to make an urgent parcel delivery to the other side of town, but the speed with which you can get it there depends on the speeds of other motorists on the road, the ease with which you can get someone to carry your parcel, the speed limits on the roads, the direction taken – and many other factors.

The activities of any organisation are therefore affected by happenings outside itself, as well as being influenced by activities within the more controlled area of its own environment. The outside influences can be at a local level, a national level, and an international level.

What do these external influences really mean for the operation and running of a business organisation? In the real world some of the key influences of business activity are:

- the customers
- the suppliers of goods and services
- competitors
- people living near the business premises
- central and local government decisions
- European Community legislation
- trade unions.

Types of external influence

In studying organisations we usually classify external influences under the following headings:

- economic
- social
- political
- legal
- technological
- environmental

While this classification is useful in theory it is well worth remembering that in the real world these factors are all intermeshed.

Figure 13.1 The organisation in its complex intermeshed environment

Economic influences

These are the effects of decisions made in society as to how to allocate resources (see Chapter 1). Choices are made by individuals, groups, organisations, governments, countries, and international groups. Economic decisions are also made on a global level – for example, to reduce the emission of gases that create the 'greenhouse effect'.

Decisions are made by individual consumers to buy, for example, hamburgers rather than vegiburgers, quiche rather than steak, cheesecake rather than yoghurt and so on. Changing patterns of consumer spending clearly affect the fortunes of individual enterprises.

Decisions made by trade unions to attempt to increase wages influence business costs, and decisions made by businesses to close down an old plant (or open a new one) clearly influence the fortunes of members of a local Job Club.

Economic decisions made by groups of trading countries to reduce import taxes influence all the businesses that previously paid the higher levels of taxes.

Changes in the economy therefore have a major influence on organisations.

Social influences

Society is in a constant state of change, and organisations form just one part of it. Society expands and contracts, as the population changes, and social forces are dynamic. Values and attitudes in society frequently change – for example, we talk of attitudes becoming more or less permissive.

Society is made up of many systems, such as the education system, the health system, law and the justice system, and so on. Each of these systems is in turn made up of many sub-systems which interact with each other.

These social changes affect organisations in many ways. For example, membership of most of the main churches has fallen steadily throughout the twentieth century as people have become less interested in religion.

Political influences

Political pressure comes from both national and local government, and from the work of pressure groups. Governments spending less on defence and the health services has a direct impact on organisations working in these areas. Political decisions are made by groups with large powers vested in them to represent the wishes of the community.

Legal influences

National and international laws affect the running of organisations in many ways. Every organisation, and individuals working for them, must have a clear picture of their rights and responsibilities. Many larger organisations employ legal specialists whose job it is to be familiar with relevant laws and to communicate appropriate information to other members of their organisations.

Technological influences

Technological influences and changes have been with us since the dawn of civilisation. However, today the pace of technological change is very rapid. Innovation and change is the order of the day, and all organisations need to update their approaches continually.

Environmental influences

A major spinoff of economic and technological changes has been the threat to the environment that new developments present. Natural and man-made environments have always affected the ways in which organisations operate. Today, however, there is greater awareness of this influence, and for many organisations there is a fear that environmental deterioration can cause very real problems.

Task

For this task you should work in groups of three or four. You will be considering a specific outside influence on one large company, British Airports Authority PLC.

BAA is at present the world's largest international airport group. It owns eight UK airports, handling in total 70 per cent of UK passenger traffic and 85 per cent of air cargo. The airports owned by this group are at:

Aberdeeen   Stanstead
Edinburgh   Heathrow
Glasgow   Gatwick
Prestwick   Southampton

The following are some financial and other results for the company in the 12-month period up to 31 March 1991:

Revenue	£834 million
Profit before tax	£247 million
Earnings per share	37·8 pence
Tangible fixed assets	£2 875 million
Capital expenditure	£503 million
Passengers	72 million
of which on international flights	56.9 million
Air transport movements	791 000
Cargo	968 000 tonnes

A very important source of revenue for BAA is **duty free sales**, and nearly half of this revenue comes from customers travelling between countries in the European Community (EC).

However, the European Commission has proposed that in the year 1993 duty free sales in this category are to be abolished. Although to date no final decision has been made by the Council of Ministers on this important issue, BAA accepts that ultimately intra-Community duty free sales will cease, but that a lengthy transition period may be required to make the necessary adjustments.

Task
- You and your group make up a Working Party of senior BAA managers. You are all very busy but have managed to meet for 30 minutes.
- You are aware of the potential loss of revenue to BAA resulting from the European Commission's proposals. You have to produce an outline proposal or series of proposals to be considered by the BAA Board of Directors at their next board meeting.
- Try to agree on five major proposals. The proposals should be headed as follows: 'Suggested proposals to offset any revenue losses from the proposed abolition of intra-community duty and tax free sales'.

The economic framework

We can look at the effect of the **economy** on organisations at a number of levels. Organisations may be as directly affected by local changes as by national or international ones. For example, the closure of the American naval base at Doonray will hit local people harder than would the effects of a world recession. **Macroeconomics** is the study of large-scale economic changes that tend to affect the whole of a nation's economy. However, we should always remember that 'macro' trends affect different groups and individuals in different ways.

The national economy can be seen as a systems model (see Figure 13.2). Organisations use inputs such as labour and machinery to create goods and services. If the demand for goods is higher than the stock available, then organisations will employ more inputs to increase production. Prices may start to rise (scarcity) and unemployment to fall (more jobs). On the other hand, if supply is greater than demand there will be unsold stocks and companies may begin to discard workers, to invest less in new machinery, and to reduce prices. This is a simple model of the economy.

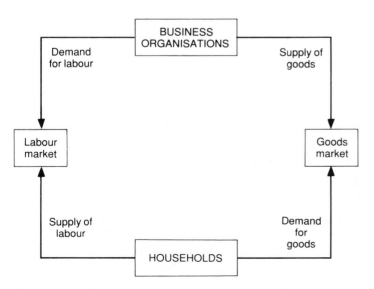

Figure 13.2 **Simple systems model of a national economy**

A more complex model of the economy

The simple model of the economy in Figure 13.2 shows that it is made up of two basic groups – **business organisations** and **households**. Households supply labour and other factors of production to organisations (e.g. funds for investment). In return households receive incomes for their services, which they then spend on the outputs produced by businesses. If the businesses supply products that households wish to purchase, then this system will work very well. Indeed, in a market economy led by market-conscious business units, although some goods will be temporarily unsold, new products will be developed to replace those that are outmoded. Firms employ labour and other factors. Firms supply goods and services to the market. Firms also purchase capital items (e.g. machinery), raw materials and partly finished goods in the market-place.

Task

Using examples of a household and a business organisation with which you are familiar, show that:

a the household (i) provides factor services to the market economy, (ii) earns income from these services, and (iii) purchases goods from producers
b the business organisation (i) buys factor services, (ii) buys raw materials, and (iii) buys capital equipment and semi-finished goods.

In the real world, economies are more complex. We need to add government and international transactions to our model. The government buys and sells goods. For example, the government buys armaments and health care in the market-place, and it sells products and services such as the outputs of its nationalised industries. The government is the major purchaser of goods in the United Kingdom.

Trading between nations is also significant. Finished goods, partly finished goods, raw materials and foodstuffs are imported and exported. The service sector (e.g. financial services) also accounts for a considerable volume of trade.

We therefore need to represent government activities and international trade in a more complex model. This is shown in Figure 13.3.

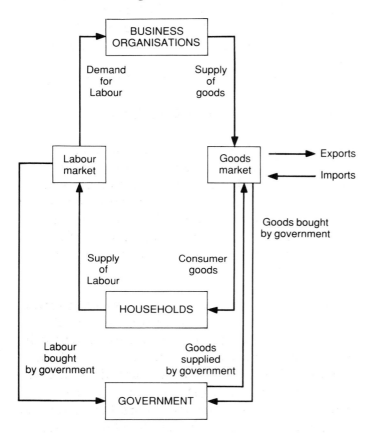

Figure 13.3 Labour and goods markets in an open economy with government

Aggregate demand

In Chapter 5 we looked at demand for particular goods and services. **Aggregate demand** is the total level of demand in the whole economy. Aggregate demand is made up of:

- demand by consumers for goods and services (call this C)

- demand by producers for goods that go into further production (call this I, for investment demand)

- government demand for goods and services (call this G).

Furthermore we need to *add* the demand from foreigners for our goods and services (exports, X), and *subtract* the demand (M) by our citizens for foreign goods and services, because money leaves the country. A useful measure of aggregate money demand is therefore:

> **Aggregate money demand = C + I + G + X – M**

We have said that the amount people spend in an economy will be received by the providers of goods and services. If we want to be absolutely accurate, however, we should account for indirect **taxes** and **subsidies**.

If you buy a packet of sandwiches in a bakery the owner of the bakery will not be able to use all this money in his business. Some of the revenue will be paid over to the government in VAT (value-added tax) and other indirect taxes. When measuring aggregate money demand, therefore, we should *subtract* indirect taxes. Furthermore, some sellers will receive more than the sales price of their goods, probably as a result of government subsidies. A subsidy should therefore be seen as an *addition* to consumer demand, provided by the government. A more comprehensive definition of aggregate money demand (AMD) is therefore:

> AMD = C + I + G + X − M + indirect taxes – subsidies

Aggregate demand and aggregate supply

When aggregate money demand in the economy *equals* aggregate money supply (AMS), then the economy is in temporary equilibrium. If this state of equilibrium remains then prices will remain steady, and so too will the level of production (see Figure 13.4).

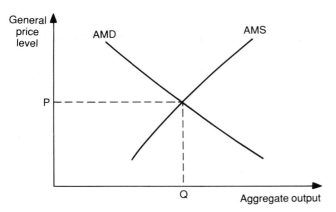

Figure 13.4 AMD = AMS

However, in the real world economic forces are continually changing. Conditions of aggregate demand and supply frequently alter, and economies tend to go through a **trade cycle** (see Figure 13.5). For a few years demand increases, prices start to rise, and unemployment to fall. This is followed by a period of slump when prices fall and unemployment increases again.

Indicators

During a boom, a number of **economic indicators** related to demand all tend to increase. The main indicators are:

- production
- employment
- sales.
- interest rates
- investment

During a recession these indicators then fall.

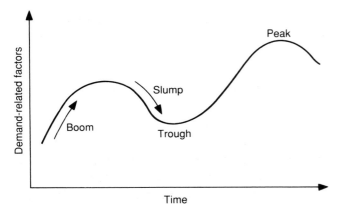

Figure 13.5 The trade cycle

Task

Study some economic reports in a national newspaper. Are the commentators talking about a period of boom or recession? Are we near to a peak or a trough? When is the economy expected to slow down or warm up? What problems are caused by the current position in the trade cycle?

Unemployment and inflation

Unemployment and inflation are economic problems which have repercussions for a large number of individuals and organisations. When **unemployment** is at a high level, the population as a whole has less money to spend, and this affects many firms and industries. In a period of **inflation**, rising prices are likely to affect everybody in one way or another.

There is always considerable disagreement over the exact number of unemployed people in the UK at any time, because only those receiving state benefits and registered for work are counted in the **official statistics**. This misses out most married women who, if their husbands are working, cannot receive benefit. People on various training schemes are also not included, nor are men over 60 who have been unemployed for a long time. The unemployment figures therefore depend very much on the way they are collected.

The RPI

Inflation is also measured in several different ways. To the government, inflation means a general increase in the level of prices. Statisticians use the **retail price index** (RPI), which is an average of price changes and shows the general change over a period of time. Some items in the index will rise, some will remain the same, others will fall.

The RPI is calculated in the following way. About 7000 households throughout the UK keep a record of all their spending over a two-week period. This gives a picture of the 'typical items' bought by an 'average household'. The items are recorded in the index. Each month, government officers make a record of about 150 000 prices of some 350 different items up and down the country. The average price of each of these items is calculated.

Using these data the average inflation rate can be calculated. Each individual price change is given a 'weight' which depends on how important it is in the typical household's spending pattern. For example, food makes up about one-fifth of a typical household's spending, so that a 10 per cent rise in the price of food would raise average prices by one-fifth of this – 2 per cent.

Price changes are measured over a definite period of time so that it is possible to compare the changes from one period to another. The matter of choosing a starting (or 'base') date for an index is important, the aim being to choose a time which is 'normal' – that is, when nothing abnormal or unusual is happening.

The base date is given an index of 100. We can then say, for example, that if in 1974 the RPI stood at 100 and today it is 350, prices *on average* have risen three and a half times over that time.

Calculating the RPI

In an imaginary country, Averageland, Mr Average spends half his income on food, a quarter on clothing and the remaining quarter on entertainment. We can thus give these items 'weightings' out of 10: food 5, clothing $2\frac{1}{2}$, entertainment $2\frac{1}{2}$. In 1974 (the base year) food cost on average £1 per unit, clothing £5 per unit, and entertainment £2 per unit. In 1990, food in Averageland cost £2 per unit, clothing £7.50 per

unit, and entertainment £3.00 per unit. We can analyse these changes in prices as follows:

	Original index	New index	Expenditure weighting	New index × weighting
Food	100	200	5	1000
Clothing	100	150	$2\frac{1}{2}$	375
Entertainment	100	150	$2\frac{1}{2}$	375

The total of the last column is 1750. In order to find out the new RPI in Averageland we must divide this total by the total number of weights (10), so:

$$\text{New RPI} = \frac{1750}{10} = 175$$

This shows that, *on average,* prices rose by 75 per cent. Food doubled in price, whereas the other two items increased by one-and-a-half times. Food was the most significant item in the index because Mr Average spends as much on food as on clothing and entertainment combined.

Task

Do Mr or Mrs Average exist in the real world? Is the answer to this question important either to individual families or to the government?

Task

- In Redland, the average consumer spends seven-tenths of his or her income on wine, two-tenths on bread and one-tenth on cheese. In 1974 (the base year) the price of all these items was £1 per unit. In 1989 wine had fallen to 50p per unit, bread had gone up to £2 per unit and cheese had risen to £4 per unit.

a What is the new index for 1989?
b Has it risen, fallen or remained the same?

C Give at least three reasons why the weighting might need to be altered in 1989.

- In Blueland, the public buy four items – eggs, cheese, bread and salt. Four-tenths of their income is spent on cheese, and two-tenths on each of the other three items. Between 1960 (the base year) and 1990, eggs doubled in price, cheese went up by 50 per cent, bread remained the same and salt went down by 10 per cent. Calculate the new index relative to the base year.

What causes economic boom or slump?

This is a very complex question, and in any good library there are shelves full of books devoted to the subject. The analysis that we give here presents a very simplified view.

Booms and slumps arise almost inevitably from changes in market **demand** and market **supply** on a grand scale. On the **demand side**, changes in demand are likely to come from:

- consumers
- investment decisions
- governments
- exports.

Consumer demand varies with incomes. When incomes are rising people are likely to spend more. When people have more **disposable income** they will spend more – for example when taxes are lowered. People are also likely to spend more when it is easier to borrow money, and the cost of borrowing (i.e. the interest rate) is low.

Investment demand is likely to be high when the economy appears to be booming. At this time business people will be optimistic – they can expect good returns on their investments. Investment by businesses will also be higher when interest rates fall, because loans are less expensive.

Government demand is likely to be higher when the government is trying to encourage a boom. This may be to reduce unemployment or to make people feel better before an election. A government will also spend more if it believes this to be the right thing to do. For example, a government may feel that it has an important role in securing high standards of health care and education.

Export demand is likely to be high when a country's products are relatively cheap on world markets. The volume of world trade is likely to be highest when there is a general world boom.

Demand will be lower in situations which are the opposite of those outlined above.

On the **supply side**, output is likely to increase when goods can be produced more efficiently. This may be because factors of production become more effective, there are fewer problems in the production process, or when technology improves.

The government's role in the economy

In the nineteenth century the UK government played only a small part in the control of the economy. Today, the most desirable role of the government in this sphere is open to debate, but most people accept that it should at least try to influence economic activity. Why has this change in attitude taken place? We shall look at some of the more important reasons.

Widespread unemployment in the 1920s and 1930s
In some towns in the 1920s, over half of the potential labour force were unemployed. Many people felt in the light of the terrible suffering during this period that the government should play a central role in **creating and sustaining employment**.

Rapid inflation in the 1970s
The 1970s was a period of rapid increases in prices. People felt the effects of inflation in different ways, depending amongst other things on how much power they had to raise their own incomes to cope with price rises.

The general effect of price rises is to distort the working of the price system. Trading ideally needs to take place in settled price conditions. If you expect to be paid £100 in three months' time you will be very disappointed to find that when you receive payment you can only purchase half of the goods that you would have been able to obtain today.

If people become reluctant to trade, then fewer goods will be produced to sell. If fewer goods are made, fewer people are employed in production. Price disturbances can therefore cause the whole economy to stagnate.

The Citizens' Charter
Many industries previously owned by the government – such as telecommunications, fuel and power – have been privatised (sold to shareholders). Other industries, such as rail and coal, may be privatised in the future.

Services such as health and education operate in the 1990s far more on the basis of local management. This means that local managers (such as headteachers and school governing bodies) are responsible for spending their own budgets in the way they see fit to use resources effectively in their own areas. However, the government still continues to play the major role in providing funds from taxes and other sources – government spending still accounts for nearly a half of all spending in the country.

The other side of this story is that there is far more emphasis on public accountability. Local managers need to be able to show how they are spending their funds. They need to manage their budgets wisely. Citizens are to be given far more right to complain. For example, under the government's **Citizens' Charter** rail-users will be entitled to refunds of their fares if trains fail to run on time, and motorway contractors can be fined for coning off sections of road when no work is taking place.

Task

Look at a copy of the Citizens' Charter at your local library. Outline some of the

major changes it sets out to make public servants more accountable for their actions. The Citizens' Charter was drawn up by a Conservative government, but the labour party has also published its own charter. How is this similar and different from the Conservative government's charter?

Main objectives of government economic policy

In an ideal situation there would be no price increase, no unemployment, a steady growth of national output, a healthy trading position with other countries, and a steady and predictable exchange rate between our currency and those of other nations. However, in the real world prices increase, there are unacceptable levels of unemployment, national output increases in stops and starts, there are frequent balance-of-payments problems, and the exchange rate goes through highs and lows.

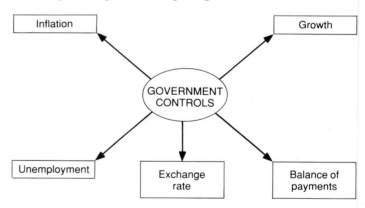

Figure 13.6 **Government controls on economic variables**

These five variables are the central focus for government economic controls. The way in which the government tries to influence these variables is very important. Government economic policies affect organisations in a direct way.

Government control of the economy

In this section we look at three different ways of

dealing with the economy. Each way is supported by people with different views as to how the economy works. The three policies we look at are:

- laissez-faire
- demand-side economics
- supply-side economics.

Laissez-faire policy

The French expression *laissez-faire* means 'leave it alone'. It therefore signifies government non-interference in the economy.

The theory behind laissez-faire is that free markets will lead to the best use of resources. If people want goods they will choose them by voting (with their money) for them to be produced. They will also make themselves available for work so that they can earn money to buy goods. Employers will employ labour so long as they can make a profit.

This theory was applied throughout the nineteenth century. The economy grew rapidly and many new products were invented and developed. When some goods become old-fashioned they are replaced by new goods. Wages fall in some industries and rise in other industries. Some people will temporarily be unemployed, but they will be taken up in the newer industries. The natural state of affairs for the economy is thus one of full employment.

The mass unemployment of the 1920s could be explained by the fact that trade unions and other groups did not allow wages to fall in a period of recession. If wages and other prices had fallen then employers would have been prepared to employ labour in the new growing industries.

Demand-side economics

Demand-side economics was developed to provide an alternative explanation of the massive unemployment of the twenties and thirties. Much of the early work in this field was carried out by the

economist John Maynard Keynes. Keynes argued that full employment was just one possible state for the economy.

Keynes maintained that the factors which create supply do not always lead to a demand for goods. Earners of money do not always spend it. This can lead to a fall in national expenditure, and to a reduction in output as suppliers are not able to sell stocks of goods.

We can illustrate this theory by using a circular flow diagram. In Figure 13.7, all income earned by households is re-spent by them on goods and services.

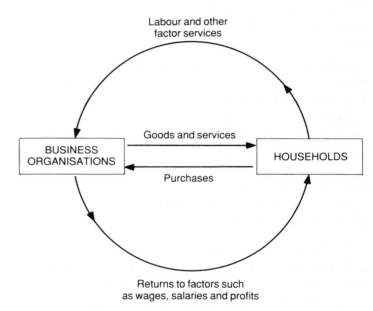

Figure 13.7 **The simple circular flow diagram**

In the real world, however, we do not re-spend all our incomes on domestically produced goods. Some of our money is *saved*, some goes in *taxes*, and some goes on *imports*. In other words, some money is *leaked* from the circular flow.

At the same time, money demand is injected back into the system in the form of *investment* by businesses in new equipment and machinery. Some money demand is injected by *government expenditure* and some money demand is injected by *export* sales (see Figure 13.8).

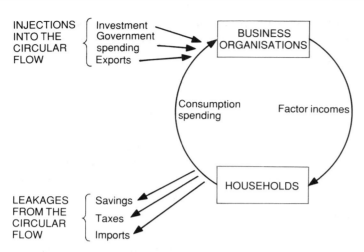

Figure 13.8 **The amended circular flow diagram**

If we look at the demand side of the picture, we can see that aggregate monetary demand is made up of consumers' expenditure, investment expenditure, government expenditure, and exports. In the real world there is no guarantee that the total of this demand will be sufficient to create full employment. Indeed, demand fluctuates from one month to the next.

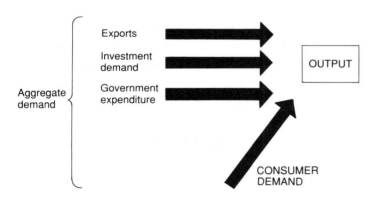

Figure 13.9 **The demand for goods and services**

In particular, investment demand is quite volatile. If business people are confident that the economy will boom for a period of time they will be keen to invest. However, when they are gloomy they will cut back heavily on investment projects. If you watch business news programmes you will frequently hear references to **business confidence**.

Task

What is the current state of business confidence in the economy? What are the likely effects for investment?

Changes in demand factors can have a dramatic impact. For example, when a building contractor loses a contract to build a new plant, he or she may have to lay off workers. These workers then forgo their wage packets. They buy less in local shops. The local shops then 'feel the pinch'. They buy in fewer stocks and reduce the overtime of staff. In turn these people have smaller incomes and they spend less.

The multiplier effect

The **multiplier effect** measures the change in total demand in an economy as a result of an initial change in demand. The size of the multiplier depends on the size of the leakages from the circular flow. If leakages are a high proportion of income, then the multiplier will be low, and if leakages are a low proportion of income then the multiplier will be high. The multiplier can be measured mathematically in the following way:

$$\text{Multiplier} = \frac{1}{\text{marginal propensity to leak}}$$

The **marginal propensity to leak** is the fraction of *extra* income earned by the average person which is leaked from the circular flow. It is obtained by adding together the marginal propensity to save, the marginal propensity to be taxed, and the marginal propensity to buy imports.

This sounds complicated but it is not. For example, if the typical citizen saves one-quarter of his or her extra income, is taxed one-eighth of his or her marginal income, and spends one-eighth of marginal income on imports, then the marginal propensity to leak is $\frac{1}{4} + \frac{1}{8} + \frac{1}{8}$, which is $\frac{1}{2}$. If the marginal propensity to leak in the economy is one-half, then the multiplier will be 2.

The multiplier is a useful tool in showing us that a change in aggregate demand will lead to further falls in demand.

The accelerator

The **accelerator** is another simple but useful tool. It shows us that if consumers' demand falls by a little bit, this may have a much bigger consequential effect on the machinery and capital-goods industries.

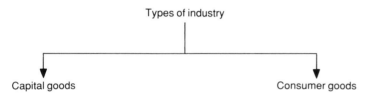

Figure 13.10 Classification of industry

One way of classifying industry is into companies that produce capital goods and ones that produce consumer goods. Consumer-goods producers buy machinery from the capital-goods industries. Each year they will need to replace machinery that is wearing out. For example, they may replace 10 per cent of their machinery. Now if the economy is in a slump they may not buy any new machinery at all. Just imagine the effect if all consumer-goods producers did the same thing. There would be little demand for capital goods. The capital-goods industry would have a massive down-turn in orders. Many capital-goods companies would be crippled. We can therefore say that a relatively small down-turn in orders for consumer goods will have a vastly *accelerated* effect on capital-goods companies.

It is not surprising, therefore, that capital-goods producers look carefully at the economic forecasts of booms and slumps. When they are gloomy they will start to make cutbacks, and these cutbacks may be *multiplied* into a slump in consumption which

feeds back into an *accelerated* slump in investment. The accelerator and multiplier effects therefore work together.

The impact of demand

Our demand-side analysis so far has shown the tremendous power of demand to influence the fortunes of the economy, and hence of organisations. Falling demand leads to recession, unemployment and wasted resources.

On the other hand, excess demand can lead to rising prices and the effects of inflation. Rising investment can have a multiplied effect on expenditure. The same is true of increases in exports, and government spending or indeed an increase in consumer spending. If demand rises and supply is not able to expand at the same rate, then inflation will result.

The Phillips curve

Most economists recognise that there is a trade-off between unemployment and inflation. If the government is worried about inflation then it will need to dampen down demand. It can do this by, for example, raising interest rates to reduce borrowing

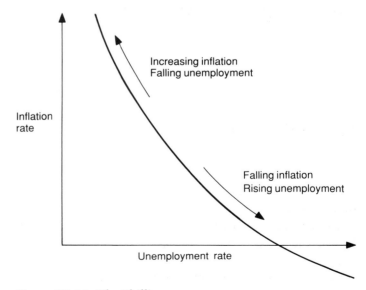

Figure 13.11 The Phillips curve

and cutting back its own spending. This will lead to a slow-down in the economy and to unemployment. If the government feels that the unemployment level is unacceptably high then it can increase demand, perhaps by lowering interest rates and increasing its own spending.

The **Phillips curve** is an attempt to show a statistical relationship between unemployment and inflation. When inflation is rising unemployment is falling, and when unemployment is rising inflation is falling. Today the notion of the Phillips curve is used to describe this trade-off. However, it is clear that the position of the Phillips curve moves from one period to the next.

Task

Up-turns and down-turns in the economy are frequently referred to in the media. When they occur they have dramatic impact – closures, or the opening of new organisations to meet new demand, the spread of unemployment or inflation etc. Every organisation will feel some of these effects. Find out from your work placement or work experience how these external economic influences are affecting the organisation you are involved with. Try to develop a series of statistics which help to describe the trends that you outline.

Supply-side economics

During the 1980s there was a big switch in economic policy away from demand-side to supply-side theories. Whilst demand management had worked very well after 1945, the policy eventually ran into trouble.

After the war most governments used Keynesian policies (i.e. the ideas of Keynes). To counteract

unemployment the government would use its own spending to pump up demand in the economy. However, a major fault of this policy was that outdated industries were artificially supported. Instead of inefficient units being cut out they continued to survive on government subsidies. This meant that the United Kingdom was losing its competitive edge in world markets.

The supply of goods in the economy rose very slowly in the 1960s and 1970s. Because supply was rising slowly, an increase in demand tended to lead to both rising prices and an increased reliance on foreign imports. Too many imports led to an increasing national debt, and the government was then forced to cut back on spending to reduce imports. Britain experienced **stagflation** – a stagnant economy that was not growing, coupled with inflation. Demand management did not seem to be working.

The cure came with new policies that the Conservative government began to introduce in 1979. These policies concentrated on increasing supply rather than increasing demand. A whole host of measures were introduced to get supply going. these included:

- reducing income tax to encourage people to work longer hours
- reducing taxes on profits made by companies
- reducing benefits to those out of work
- reducing subsidies to loss-making industries
- privatising rather than nationalising industries
- reducing the size of the civil service
- reducing government spending
- passing laws to reduce trade union powers
- measures against monopolies and restrictive practices
- encouraging competition amongst groups such as solicitors, opticians, and even in the health service and schools.

The emphasis of this policy was to use supply as the means to drive the economy forward.

Task

How effective do you think supply-side measures have been? Select two or three of the examples of supply-side measures in the text and try to find out what the effects have been of implementing these policies. Why are different groups and individuals likely to have different views as to how effective these policies have been?

Case Study – New plans

The table below outlines the Labour party's industrial and economic programme intended to replace that of the Conservative party.

Labour's industrial and economic plan

INDUSTRY:
NEW MANUFACTURING INVESTMENT PROGRAMME
■ additional capital allowances for plant and machinery
■ tax allowances for investment in new technology
■ tax incentives for individual investment in smaller businesses

CITY:
NEW RULES GOVERNING TAKEOVERS
■ bidders to prove that merger is in public interest
■ requirement to disclose bid intentions at early stage
■ workers to get statutory right to be consulted
■ wider public interest test for bids

INVESTMENT:
NEW NATIONAL INVESTMENT BANK
■ providing long-term funding for small and medium-sized businesses
■ mobilising private capital for long-term public infrastructure projects
■ British Technology Enterprise (to foster links between academia and industry)

INNOVATION:
■ New tax incentives for R & D
■ Technology Trusts formed by industry?City/academia/government
■ Government to spend 5 per cent of R & D budget with firms employing under 500

REGIONAL POLICY:
■ New regional development agencies For England
■ Strengthened role for Welsh and Scottish Development Agencies

■ Regional agencies to take on some of National Investment Bank's responsibilities

TRAINING:
■ New training schemes for 16–19-year-olds to replace YTS
■ Schemes to be based on qualifications and closer link between educational and vocational training qualifications
■ All school-leavers to receive training before entering employment
■ Legal obligation to firms to spend 0.5 per cent of payroll on training

INDUSTRIAL RELATIONS:
■ Statutory right to join union and take strike action
■ Secondary action allowed in certain circumstances
■ Creation of Industrial Relations Court

TAXATION:
■ Top rate of income tax to be raised to 50 per cent and greater number of bands
■ upper limit on national insurance contributions to be scrapped

PUBLIC OWNERSHIP:
■ National Grid to be taken back into public ownership
■ Return of water industry to public ownership a priority but no timescale
■ British Telecom to be renationalised if public stake still at 49 per cent

SPENDING:
■ Commitment to a "priority programme" costed independently at £20bn–£35bn
■ Labour's only costed commitment is to raise pensions and restore child benefit to 1987 value

1 *Which of the proposals seem to you to be demand-side and which supply-side policies?*
2 *Which of the plans are likely to be effective in your view?*
3 *What do you think will be the overall effect of the policies on the economy?*
4 *Explain how the plans are likely to effect one organisation you are familiar with.*

Today the trend seems to be to work with a combination of supply-side and demand-side ideas.

Fiscal policy

Fiscal policy is the government's policy with regard to public spending, taxes and borrowing. The government can try to influence the level of demand in the economy through directly altering the amount of its own spending in relation to its total tax revenues.

A **deficit budget** arises when the government spends more than it takes in taxes (see Figure 13.12). The government can then borrow money on the Stock Exchange or from banks and other sources in order to carry out its own expenditure policies. The difference between government spending and tax revenue is known as the **public sector borrowing requirement** (PSBR). The logic of the deficit budget is simple. If there is not enough spending in the economy to create enough demand for goods to give everyone a job who wants one, then the government can boost spending itself. However, as we have seen above this may have inflationary effects.

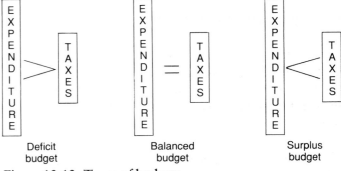

Figure 13.12 Types of budgets

A **balanced budget** describes a situation whereby the government matches its spending with taxes. The idea behind the balanced budget is that the government should not encourage price increases. There is also a belief that the government itself should spend as little as possible, because private individuals and groups are in a better position to make their own spending decisions.

A **surplus budget** arises when the government takes in more revenue than it spends. This is known as a **deflationary policy** because one outcome is a cut in inflation.

Monetary policy

Monetary policy is concerned with controlling:

- the quantity of money in the economy
- the price of money in the economy.

Monetary policy is felt to be important today. Most people now feel that there is a strong link between the amount of money in the economy and inflation. The view is that if people start spending money at a faster rate than new goods come on to the market, then prices will rise. **Monetarists** believe that it is essential to eliminate general price rises because of the way they destabilise industry and the economy. Uncertainty about prices means that industry cannot concentrate on its main task – producing goods. People become dissatisfied and the whole economic order starts to crumble – people fail to pay up on time, businesses are reluctant to invest, there is more industrial unrest, and so on.

Definition of money

There is more than one way to express the quantity of money in the economy.

If all people used only coins and currency notes to make their purchases, calculating the quantity of money would be easy. Instead, people use a variety of forms of money, the most obvious being coins and notes, cheques, credit cards, and other forms of credit payments. Today it is also common practice for people to draw money out of building society and other savings accounts to make purchases. A wide range of new facilities for making payments is developing. So, it is almost impossible for the government to know how much money is available to citizens to spend on goods at a particular moment in time.

In order to control the quantity of money, the government must decide on the definition of money which it thinks most accurately determines people's likely expenditure. It will then seek to control changes in the supply of money according to this chosen definition.

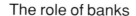

Task

Study recent newspaper articles and other sources to try to discover the commonly used definitions of money. These definitions change fairly frequently. Examples are M0 and M1.

The role of banks

The Bank of England has an important part to play in controlling the lending of high street banks and other financial institutions. The measures available to the Bank for limiting increases in cash and lending include giving advice and instruction to other banks on how much to lend and whom to lend to, and raising interest rates to discourage borrowing.

The lending institutions, such as banks, need to be carefully supervised by the government because of their tremendous powers of lending. They can grant **overdrafts** and **loans** and a wide range of other lending arrangements to customers.

A bank's customers carry out a relatively small number of their transactions using cash. Financial institutions, by creating credit instruments such as cheques and credit cards, make it possible for individuals and organisations to borrow money and make payments by means other than cash. The more these credit instruments are expanded, the more purchasing power there is in the economy. It is essential that the government does not let this spending get out of hand. It therefore sets targets and builds up a framework for controlling the financial system. The Bank of England plays an important part in policing this system – it licenses financial institutions and keeps a watchful eye on their lending practices.

Task

Find out from your local bank manager what limitations are currently placed on the bank's lending by government. How much are banks able to lend in a given period of time? What conditions do they establish for granting loans? Does the amount they can lend vary from time to time? In what circumstances are they likely to lend more money?

As well as controlling the quantity of money in the economy, the government can and does also control the **price of money**. Minimum interest rates can be quickly altered by the Bank of England, and the change will rapidly spread to all financial institutions such as banks and building societies. This is another way of controlling the quantity of money borrowed. If interest rates rise, people are more reluctant to borrow money.

Task

The following role play involves a union wage negotiation in the car industry. For this activity you will need to split into two groups. One group will represent management and the other group trade union officials.

You must negotiate a wage settlement to be operative from November. The two parties involved are the managers of the Foroyta Car Company and the union officials of the blue-collar workers of Foroyta. The negotiations cover 25 000 workers.

In recent years workers in few other companies have achieved the increases enjoyed by workers at Foroyta, but their pay package has set a target for union negotiators in the crucial two months after Christmas when most major settlements are struck. After an 'inflation-plus' increase last year of 13.4 per cent, the aspirations of union leaders should be more modest this time. Last year the deal was settled after a strike, but this year there is a lot of unemployment in the economy and the union is keen to protect its members' jobs. Recently the company has announced the redundancies of 1000 workers at one of its key plants. Car sales are down and the company is going through a difficult financial phase. There is little hope, however, of employee's representatives being happy with anything at or below the inflation rate, which stands at 4.1 per cent and is not likely to rise in the coming year.

Although pay settlements have been falling throughout the year, as the charts show, inflation has been falling even more quickly. And except in sectors particularly hard hit by the recession, workers will be expecting – indeed demanding – rises above the RPI. While in the second half of last year they settled for less than inflation rates that were at or near double figures, this year they are likely to achieve basic rate increases in excess of the RPI.

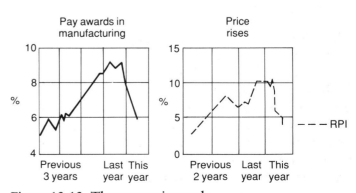

Figure 13.13 The economic trends

The table below shows percentage settlements for other groups of workers this year.

Already made

August	BBC	5.7 plus £50
	Rolls Royce	pay freeze (9 months)
	Johnson Wax	7.2
September	Police	8.5
	Local authority	6.4
	Vauxhall	5.0
	Kwiksave	7.0

To come (current demands)

November	FOROYTA	?
	Rover	7.5
	Jaguar	7.0
	British Coal	4.2
January	Nissan	7.0
	Michelin	6.0

Once you have carried out your negotiations and arrived at a settlement, discuss how external economic influences have affected members of the blue-collar trade union at Foroyta.

Social influences

The way in which society is organised and the social values the people have both influence the operation of organisations. In some countries people are prepared to work for very long hours, whilst in others they are not. In some countries great emphasis is placed on equal opportunities, but in other countries the idea is largely ignored. In some countries young people expect to have a say in how organisations should be run, in other countries older people have far more influence. These and many other social factors influence organisational behaviour.

Every society has its own **culture**, and culture affects attitudes and behaviour. Culture is a term used in many varied ways. Two anthropologists once studied 164 definitions of culture and wrote a book about the varying definitions. They concluded that it is not yet possible to find a satisfactory definition that can be used in every circumstance. Talcott Parsons defined culture as 'the complex of values, ideas, attitudes and other meaningful symbols created by man to shape human behaviour and the artifacts of that behaviour as they are passed down from one generation to the next'.

Ingredients of the cultural environment will clearly influence organisations, groups and individuals working within a society or operating in different societies. Some important cultural ingredients are listed in Figure 13.14.

MATERIAL	ABSTRACT
Architecture	Language
Painting	Religion
Music	Law
Sculpture	Folk-law and superstition
Jewellery	Attitudes to women
Gestures	Attitudes to family
Hairstyles	Attitudes to work
Cooking	Attitudes to bargaining
Tools	Attitudes to selling
Other products	Role models
Computers	Courtship
Games	Ethics
Dancing	Etiquette
Advertisements	Hygiene

Figure 13.14 Some cultural ingredients

When we explore cultural environments it immediately becomes obvious that societies differ in their cultural values. It follows that organisations wishing to operate in a different cultural setting must tread warily. We can bring this home by looking at a few examples:

Language. A literal translation of 'Coke adds life' informed Japanese consumers that Coke could raise their dead relative. GEC–Osram is a long-established lighting division of the British General Electric Corporation, but in Polish the word *osram* means excrement!

Attitudes towards women. In India and the UK, women have become national political leaders, whereas in some states in the Middle East some women wear black and walk behind their husbands.

Aesthetics. White is regarded as the colour of mourning in Japan, and purple is associated with death in many Latin American countries.

Superstition. Most US hotels have eliminated mention of the thirteenth floor.

Religion. Procter & Gamble was attacked in the 'Bible-belt' of the southern United States for spreading Satanism through its registered trademark – a crescent moon and thirteen stars. The rumour started in 1980 and by 1982 the company was receiving 15 000 calls a month to its customer services department. Eventually it had to discontinue use of the logo on packaging.

Personal hygiene. When American firm Helen Curtis introduced its Every Night shampoo line in Sweden, it renamed the product Every Day because Swedes usually wash their hair in the morning.

Population size and make-up

A major social influence on organisations is population. If a population is decreasing then organisations will find it more difficult to retain members, to recruit employees, to attract customers and so on. In times of increasing population the reverse may be true.

It is not just the size of the population that is important, but also the make-up of relevant sections of the population – for example, the ratio of the old to the young, male to female.

As the population structure of the UK changes over the next few decades there will be many major changes facing organisations. Study the shapes in Figure 13.15, which show the age/sex pyramids for the UK for 1970, 1990 and the projected forecast for 2010.

Task

What major changes in the population structure are highlighted by the pyramids in Figure 13.15? How might these changes affect:

a hospitals?   c banks?
b schools?   d manufacturing companies?

Task

In 1990 a major problem facing many companies was the shortage of young people entering the job market. It is estimated that in the first five years of the decade there will be 20 per cent fewer school-leavers.

1 *Explain how this problem might have been alleviated by a period of recession.*
2 *What strategies could companies employ to deal with the problem of fewer school-leavers? Write a report outlining three main strategies. A useful starting point might be to look at strategies employed by companies that you have worked for.*

Political influences

In politics, those who have power and authority decide on issues and courses of action. They decide whether to spend money on this or that thing; whether to carry out one course of action or another; whether to allow one thing or another.

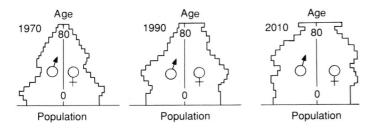

Figure 13.15 **Age/sex pyramids**

Since many of these decisions affect us and the organisations with which we are involved, it is in our interests to know how decisions are made.

Most modern Western governments are elected by the people. People's government is known as **democracy**. In Britain we have a system known as **representative democracy**, in which certain people – known as Members of Parliament – are chosen to represent their constituents (people who live in an area from which the MP is chosen). Members of Parliament typically represent about 60 000 people.

However, our democracy involves more than simply choosing people to represent us. We also have the freedom to express opinions that are critical of the government, other bodies and individuals. We also have uncensored media, free from the controlling hand of government, and an independent legal system.

Decision-makers can therefore be influenced by a wide range of individuals and groups, including political groups, the media, pressure groups and others.

Political groups

Political parties are organised groups of people who share similar sets of ideas and beliefs. These political parties publish **manifestos** setting out the sorts of policies they would like to see come into effect.

Task

Write to the head office of a major political party (or several) asking for a manifesto. How would the policies of this party (or parties) affect the activities of an organisation with which you are familiar?

Political parties can have an enormous impact on the decision-making within organisations. New laws are passed through Parliament, and it is the party with a majority vote in Parliament which will be able to see a wide range of its policies become laws. These policies will cover such issues as:

- how large the public sector should be
- who should manage the public sector
- national policy for transport
- how to control pollution
- how much money to spend on various services, such as education and defence.

Opposition parties can also influence the decision-making process by voting against the government, by canvassing support, and by making the public aware of a wide range of concerns.

National government

National decisions are made by Parliament. The government of the day presents proposals for **new laws** (Bills) which are discussed and voted on by Members in the House of Commons. It is still possible for some new laws to be proposed by individual Members, but only a few days are set aside for discussing and voting on such 'private bills' each year.

Once a new law has been discussed, amended and voted on in the House of Commons, it has then to be discussed in the House of Lords (unelected). The House of Lords can delay new laws and propose amendments to them, but these days does not have the power to veto them completely. Finally, a new law must receive the signature of the sovereign (queen or king).

Government **ministers**, chosen by the **Prime Minister**, have responsibility for running specific departments, covering areas such as health, defence, education and so on. Those ministers responsible for major issues work closely with the Prime Minister – they form the Cabinet and many of the key policies are shaped by this group.

Ministers are supported by **civil servants**. These people are not politicians; they are employed by the state to research new proposals and suggest possible courses of action that ministers might like to follow up. They are therefore concerned with collecting and processing information.

Task

Identify from a news-paper, the television news or elsewhere a new Bill going through Parliament. Keep a diary of how the Bill progresses. Is it, for example, opposed by any individuals or groups? Does it have to be altered? How does it fare in the House of Lords? Does it become a new law? How popular is the measure?

Case Study – The Children Act 1989

In October 1989 the Children Act became law. The law is an attempt to reform the rules relating to children's welfare in the light of a number of scandals which had resulted in children suffering from ill-treatment and lack of proper care. The main features of the new law are shown in Figure 13.16.

However, even despite these reforms and the tightening of regulations regarding children's homes, and improved complaints procedures, many experts feel that the changes are inadequate. They question the provisions for children leaving care, who often end up on the streets, sleeping rough, or in prison, with few educational or training opportunities.

The Act makes it much harder to remove children from their families. Taking a child into the care of a local authority becomes the last option and, even then, strictly time-limited.

Key elements

■ A new concept of 'parental responsibility' (the rights, duties, powers, responsibilities and authority given to parents by law)
■ New duties on local authorities to support families with children in need
■ A new framework for protecting children from the risk of harm and to ensure a proper education
■ New local-authority duties towards children living away from home or with foster parents or being looked after by childminders or nannies
■ New unified court system with specially trained judges and magistrates

Key principles

■ The welfare of the child is paramount
■ Families should bring up children wherever possible, with help where children are in need
■ Courts only to make orders where this is better than no order
■ Courts must avoid delay
■ Children should have a say in decisions about their future and will have certain rights to complain about local authority services
■ Parents must participate in decisions about their children even when they are no longer living with them.

Figure 13.16 Main features of the new Children Act

1 Study recent reports from the press to judge how well the Children Act is faring.
2 Are there fresh calls for reform, or is there generally a favourable press for the Act?

Local government

Local government is in the hands of **local councils**, who are elected. Over half of the funding for local councils comes from national government funds, in the form of **support grants**. In recent years there has been a lot of **privatisation** of local services, and local government officials are responsible for handing out contracts for such things as running leisure centres, maintaining parks, refuse collection and keeping the roads clean. Contracted firms that fail to meet quality standards have contracts removed.

On the one hand there has been a greater emphasis placed on giving powers to the local government, whilst at the same time some powers have been taken away (for example, the delegating of budgets to individual schools).

Task

Each year your local council puts a leaflet through your letterbox explaining local services. Make a list of these services and how they are funded. What powers does the local council have in your area?

Local authorities have considerable influence over the ways in which the organisations in their area are run. Taxes are levied on local businesses and individual citizens. The local authority also has considerable powers for granting or refusing permission for new buildings or businesses, and licences for particular activities. For example, if you were going to set up a 'fast food' business or a pub you would need permission from the local council. The council is also responsible for local roads and the supervision and licensing of car parks, as well as many other services.

The media

The media include all forms of written communication to the public, such as newspapers, magazines and books, and all forms of transmitted communication, such as radio, television and cinema. The media play an important part in a number of areas of industrial society:

- in the transmission of information
- in the shaping and reinforcing of opinions
- as large employers, and as parts of larger media groups.

Transmission of information

The **mass media** reach a wide audience. A single edition of a mass-circulation newspaper can reach up to 10 million people, and a popular television programme may be seen by 15 million viewers. It is estimated that 95 per cent of the population became

aware of the British Gas share issue through an expensive advertising campaign involving a fictitious character, Sid.

The obvious means of getting messages across to the general public is through television and national newspapers. Important public information can be communicated quickly to large numbers of people, as has been demonstrated by recent campaigns about the disease Aids.

Shaping and reinforcing opinions

There is a continuing debate as to how and to what extent the media influence people's behaviour. Advertisers are prepared to pump millions of pounds into promotions of their products in the media. These campaigns are often highly successful and similar adverts may be used for many years. Recently, even political parties have been prepared to pay huge sums, using advertising agencies, to promote a party image.

The media as employers

Apart from the BBC, which is a large employer in the public sector, most of the other mass media concerns are parts of large groups with a range of media and non-media interests. Many also have interests overseas. Hence the media are major employers.

Pressure groups

Pressure groups put **pressure** on organisations to modify or change their ways. They may be made up of just a few people – such as a group of parents demanding a public enquiry into practices in a hospital where their children appear to have had inadequate treatment. Alternatively they may be large international pressure groups – such as the environmental group Greenpeace.

Pressure groups do not fall readily into categories. Some are highly organised with paid officials, subscription charges and planned meetings – these groups may last for several years. Others may be 'three day wonders', being set up on the spur of the moment, lacking any real structure and vanishing as quickly as they arose.

Task

List eight pressure groups with which you are familiar. Try to find out more about the organisation of these groups. Are they highly organised or just a loose collection of individuals? What are the common characteristics of the groups that you have described?

Two main types of pressure groups are commonly recognised, protection and promotional.

Protection groups

These are set up to fight on a specific issue, such as danger on a local road threatening the lives of school-children. In other words, these groups seek to protect their interests against an outside threat. Other examples are a parents' protection group set up to oppose the planned closure of a local playgroup or nursery school, or rail commuters objecting to the threatened closure of a train service. A protest meeting will usually be called at which tactics are decided.

Promotional pressure groups

These are more formal groups which are sometimes highly organised and fight campaigns on a wide range of issues. Examples are Greenpeace and Friends of the Earth.

Such groups have clearly defined, long-term objectives. Their sustained pressure on various authorities helps to create radically new perspectives

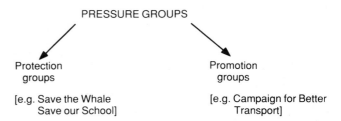

Figure 13.17 Pressure groups

from most organisations, including businesses, trade unions, schools and colleges. They use measures which vary from madcap adventurist stunts to high-profile media advertising campaigns.

Case Study – Library charges

Gotham City College of Arts and Technology has decided to make students pay to use the college library. Clearly this will disadvantage students who are not able to pay the charges. It may also discourage students who have rarely used the library from starting to do so. Moreover, the policy seems to go against the notion of making education accessible to everyone.

The business managers of the college argue that all college services should pay their way. They argue that charging for use of the library will improve the quality of the service offered, and will make it possible to buy many new resources.

1 *Do you think that the students should be made to pay for library facilities?*
2 *Imagine that, as a student at the college, you have decided to set up a pressure group to campaign for free library services. How would you go about organising a pressure group to have maximum impact?*
3 *How would you attract supporters and maintain the interest of these supporters?*

Legal influences

Laws are a major factor constraining the operations of organisations. This is true of a children's home, a charity, a church or a company. Laws in the United Kingdom come mainly from three sources: common law, statute law and EC law.

Common law is the term used to describe a set of laws that have developed over hundreds of years, through custom and practice. Their exact origin is unknown or uncertain, but they are accepted as true laws despite that. For example, some footpaths have existed since before the first land records were ever kept; today these paths belong to the public and nobody can build on them, plough them up or fence them in – they are 'public footpaths'.

Statute law is concerned with laws that come into being as a result of Acts of the UK Parliament. These can be amended or repealed if circumstances suggest that they no longer serve the intended purpose. As time passes, a number of laws become out of date, others become untidy. Every now and then new laws need to be passed to tidy up an existing law in a particular area – for example, laws about how companies should operate, laws about health and safety in organisations, and so on.

Most statutory laws run to thousands of pages. It is therefore sensible for an organisation to seek expert legal advice, both when it is first set up and when changing its existing practices.

Every new employee should find out about his or her rights and obligations in the context of the organisation. In Chapter 17 we look at a number of rights and obligations that you will have in your workplace.

The third source of laws in the United Kingdom is the European Community. This is the subject of a case study at the end of the chapter.

Case Study – The European Court of Justice

The European Court of Justice is run by judges from the 12 countries of the European Community. Sitting in Luxembourg, it settles arguments where community laws are concerned. These laws affect:

- individual people
- companies
- other organisations (e.g. hospitals, schools)

in all the countries of the EC.

In July 1991 the Court of Justice made a ruling which overturned part of the UK's Merchant Shipping Act 1988. Lawyers said that Britain had known since 1973 when it signed the Treaty of Rome that it must abide by Community law. The significance of this case was that it showed that the EC can invalidate laws even when dealing with matters which are traditionally associated with sovereignty.

The case stemmed from a conflict that arose in the early 1980s when Spanish vessels decided to re-register as British fishing boats, giving them access to British quotas of catches. In 1988, after widespread protests from British fishermen, the UK government brought in a rule that 75 per cent of the directors and shareholders of companies owning British vessels must be British citizens.

It was this piece of legislation that was challenged as discriminatory in the European court. Lawyers involved in the case said the decision came as no surprise – already in 1990 the court had made an interim judgement that the Merchant Shipping Act should be suspended until a final judgement could be made.

The ruling, which established for the first time that a UK law could be shelved on suspicion that it broke an EC law, proved a clear indication that the House of Commons now plays second fiddle to EC law.

The UK government had argued that it had a right under international law to decide whether vessels could be registered as British. This argument was dismissed by the European court, which decided that the Act discriminated against other EC countries. The judgement said that if a vessel was owned by a British company, and was operated out of the UK, then it was entitled to be registered as British.

1 *Why was this judgement important in setting out who makes laws in the European Community?*
2 *What are the likely knock-on effects of this judgement?*
3 *What are the implications for organisations in the United Kingdom? What should they do about it?*
4 *What are the implications for members of organisations?*

Technological influences

Throughout history, society has undergone change. The **industrial revolution**, for example, changed people's lives radically. It brought great **wealth** to the mill and factory owners, but it also brought **social upheaval** by throwing thousands out of work from their traditional occupations.

Today the **pace** and the **scope** of change is as fast and as varied as ever. To illustrate the speed and magnitude of technological change, consider the following facts. In 1950 the size of a computer with the same power as a human brain, using the technology of the day, would have been enough to occupy the whole of London. By 1960 a computer with the same capacity would have fitted inside the Albert Hall, and by 1970 inside a double-decker bus. By 1980 it could be carried in a taxi, and in 1990 it would fit inside a TV set.

This example gives some insight into the rate of change that has taken place in just one part of one industry. Change presents great challenges for businesses and other organisations. As we have seen,

organisations are part of society and they must change along with that society, or they run the risk of becoming irrelevant and outmoded. Change is therefore not only something that an organisation must learn to cope with, but also something that can be turned to advantage.

Case Study – Technology at Seiko

The commercial contest over the technology and accuracy of timepieces was settled in the 1980s. Seiko, the leading Japanese watchmaker – it makes 131 million watches a year, compared with the 89 million made by the entire Swiss watch industry – rose to international prominence in the late 1960s with its highly accurate quartz technology.

In the early days the competitive edge was gained through accuracy. In more recent years Seiko has concentrated on design and style. Each year a team of 150 designers launches 2000 new products. To succeed, Seiko has to keep up with the relentless pace of change of style in the clothes and jewellery people wear, how they furnish their living rooms and decorate their walls. Seiko watch 'collections' are rolled out twice a year in line with the practice in fashion houses.

Seiko's new design strength is still largely supported by technological strength. Its most recent developments (early 1992) are complex chronometers with several mini-dials set within the main dial. Until now such watches were only available from the most exclusive watch-makers. Seiko has managed to make them with a technology that can be applied to mass production.

It has also been able to develop a wide range of specialist watches of appeal to groups such as divers, swimmers, athletes, joggers and motor-racing enthusiasts.

275

When watchmakers were selling a technology rather than a style, it was easier to make products which would sell around the world. But with fashion and style becoming increasingly important, so design has to reflect local tastes in different markets. Seiko sets great store in 'area merchandising' to develop watches for regional markets. For example, Seiko employs specialists in France, the UK, the USA and Italy specifically to develop regional products in these areas.

1 List the various ways in which Seiko can be said to have been influenced by change.
2 How did Seiko manage to turn technological change to its advantage? What is the likely outcome of the company's actions?
3 For the staff of the company, what are the likely implications of the changes you have listed?
4 List what you believe to be the major advantages and disadvantages of technological change (do not restrict your answer to the company that creates the change).
5 What other forms of change can you think of that might affect a business?

Case Study – Change not always for the good

When you travel around any large city you cannot fail to notice the noise, the congestion and the pollution caused by road traffic. In this context the products of technology in transport have caused problems. The motor car, from being an expensive luxury enjoyed by the few, has now become a highly affordable item as a result of the technologies that have created modern low-cost manufacture. Alternative technologies are now needed to deal with the resulting problems.

In some cities the traffic congestion is so bad that local councils have realised the need to reduce the numbers of vehicles on their roads. They know that people will not stop using their cars until there is another suitable way for them to travel.

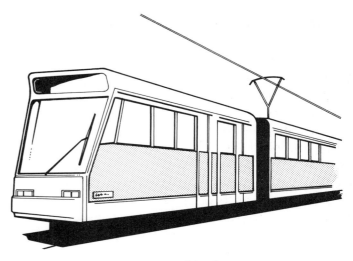

Figure 13.18 City transport of the future?

Nottingham, Manchester and Sheffield intend to introduce rapid-transport (RT) systems. Coaches will run along tracks laid in the road. The RT systems will derive their electrical energy from overhead cables. It is hoped that a clean, reliable and efficient RT service will encourage people to leave their cars and use public transport again.

1 You are the public relations officer with a council that is planning to build an RT system. Your remit is to design posters to tell people about the advantages of the new system. What messages would you try to get across?
2 As the public relations officer you have also been invited to give a talk to local people to tell them about the new RT system. Plan such a talk, which should emphasise the good things about the new way of travelling.
3 Will RT be good for everyone? Write lists of the advantages and disadvantages of the RT system.

Environmental influences

Organisations operate today in a world which increasingly has been forced to become aware of environmental concerns. Whether **environmental consciousness** has become a genuine concern by all organisations, or is being manipulated by some as a subtle **marketing tool**, remains to be seen. For example, it would appear that motor vehicle manufacturers are responding to environmental pressures, but the trend is still towards more and more in-car gadgets, which inevitably increase the weight and hence the petrol consumption. The producers would argue that they are responding to consumer demand. At the same time it is clear that the life-cycle of products is shortening in response to increased competition and change. Volkswagen, for instance, has recently reduced the expected life-cycle of its new products from 11 to 8 years.

With a shortening of the life expectancy of products it becomes easier to accommodate the **'green agenda'** if consumers vote with their money for 'greener' cars. Some companies are currently designing vehicles with totally recyclable parts.

As we shall see in Chapter 15, many customers are concerned by 'green' issues. Organisations therefore need to respond positively. This pressure clearly demands that organisations should make their employees more environmentally aware.

Case Study – Poison in the water

On 6 July 1988, at 4.30 pm, the driver of a tanker from a chemical supply company arrived at the Lowermoor water treatment plant in Cornwall, with a delivery of aluminium sulphate. The gate was locked and the plant deserted. However, the driver, who had never been to Lowermoor before, had been given a key by a colleague and so unlocked the gate and drove in. But where was he to put his delivery of aluminium sulphate?

He had been told that the tank was 'on the left', but he found that there were several tanks on the left. He came to a hatch set in the ground and found that he could open it with the gate key. Concluding that this was the correct tank, he poured in the chemical. The aluminium sulphate *should* have gone into a separate storage tank from which it would have been dispensed at a maximum of 50 parts per million to help cleanse the water supply. Inadvertently the

driver had poured it into a tank which allowed the undiluted chemical to join the water supply to be dispensed to consumers in the South West.

When the disastrous error was discovered, the water company blamed the chemical supply company. The water company said that the chemical should have been delivered on 4 July or 5 July, and that in any case it did not accept deliveries after 4pm. It queried how the driver had obtained the key. The water-workers union suggested that the key was one of a number handed out to contractors to help break the water-workers' strike of 1983.

1 Comment on the seriousness of this incident.
2 What general lessons does the case present for organisational responsibility towards the environment?
3 What are the lessons for employees working for organisations?
4 What experiences have you had of working in situations in which your actions or inactions were a potential threat to the community? How well trained were you to prevent risks?
5 How high on an organisation's list of priorities should be a responsibility towards the external environment?
6 Do you think that environmental concerns provide too much pressure on the way organisations operate today?

Case Study – Decision-making in the European Community

- The EC is an *economic* union – for example, it is a free trade area.
- The EC is a *political* union – for example, it has a parliament.
- The EC is a *social* union – people are able to travel freely between countries and the community has its own social policy.
- The EC is a *legal* union – it has its own community laws.

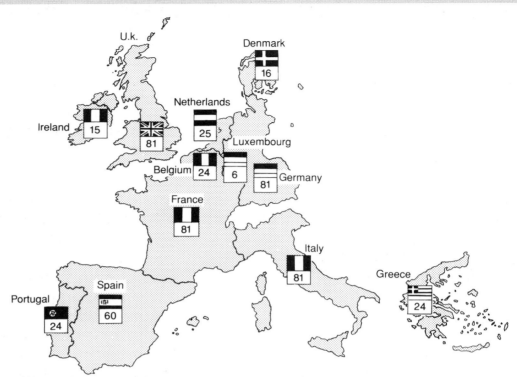

Figure 13.19 The number of MEPs in each country

- The EC is a *technological* union – with policies for the sharing of new technologies.
- The EC is an *environmental* union – with policies for dealing with the very real problems of pollution and other environmental matters.

The European Community is made up of 340 million people living in 12 member states. Those citizens with a vote choose the people they want to represent them in the European Parliament. There are 518 Members of this Parliament (MEPs). The number from each country is shown in Figure 13.19. The European Parliament meets in Strasbourg. The MEPs discuss European matters and any laws that are being suggested or changed – they do not themselves propose new laws. They do not sit in country groups, but in groups of people with similar ideas.

The community laws are made by ministers from the governments of each of the 12 countries. The Council of Ministers meets in Brussels. These ministers draft the new laws which will be discussed by the European Parliament. The Parliament can change the proposals for new laws if it does not like them.

There is also a Commission in Brussels made up of 17 Commissioners. Their job is to monitor the need for changes in the laws and to identify ways of making sure the laws are kept.

Some people want the EC to have more power to make more rules for the whole community. Other people think that countries should have more power to make their own laws without interference from the EC. Others think that things are just about right at the moment.

1 *Which do you think has the most power – the Council of Ministers, the European Parliament, or the Commission? Give reasons for your answer.*
2 *Which body do you think should have the most power? Again, give reasons.*
3 *What would be the advantages if all 12 countries were governed from the EC bodies? What would be the disadvantages? Would these advantages and disadvantages be the same for everyone?*

14
The Environment of Change

In this chapter we start by exploring ways of identifying and preparing for changes we might want to make as individuals. Making a change requires first the identification of needs, and then taking action to make sure that these needs are met.

Organisations too need to identify areas for change and to make appropriate plans. The remainder of the chapter concentrates on some major features of the modern changing environment, as they affect organisations. These include changes in the general industrial structure, the international trading position, technology, transport, communications, leisure patterns, and the outside environment.

All of these changes demand thought and planning. In particular they demand changes in the skills, knowledge and attitudes required by organisations and members of those organisations.

Changes take place all the time. Some are almost unnoticeable because they occur over a long period of time, and only when we look back is it clear that they have taken place. For example, many of the changes involved in growing up happen so slowly that they go unnoticed at the time. Other changes are dramatic and obvious – for example engagements or bereavements.

Task

First think of changes that happened as you grew up. Which of these were dramatic and obvious and which were almost unnoticeable?

Then think of changes that have taken place in an organisation with which you are familiar. Answer the same question about these changes.

Lastly, identify if you can which of the changes were of greatest importance in each case.

Of course, both slow and quick changes are important, and one should be aware that change is ever present. Any organisation that you work for will experience changes. People who work for the organisation will need to alter the ways in which they operate, the skills they use, and knowledge will need to be updated and attitudes adjusted. As a member of an organisation you will need to be flexible.

Managing personal change

Some of the changes we experience in our lives are **inevitable**, such as growing older. Others can be

279

controlled. For example, you can decide to go on a training course, to learn to drive a car, or to alter your appearance. Attitudes to change vary from one individual to the next. This is because individuals have certain driving forces within them, which we refer to as 'wants', 'needs', 'urges', and 'fears'. One person may feel the need to 'play it safe' all the time, while another may actively seek risky situations.

When we looked at Maslow's hierarchy of needs in Chapter 3, we saw that the needs of individuals are not always fixed. At certain times particular needs are all-important, but once these have been satisfied they may be replaced by new needs.

It is appropriate to start our discussion by looking at ways of **managing change**, particularly so that you can take responsibility for changing the way you operate in an organisation.

Force field analysis

Force field analysis is commonly used to look at problems that have restraining forces as well as driving forces (see Figure 14.1). Analysing a problem in this way helps you to arrive at a strategy for bringing about changes that deal with the problem.

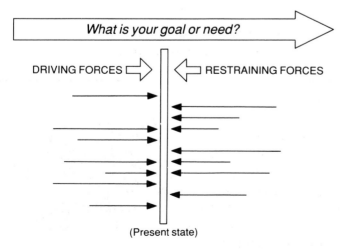

Figure 14.1 Force field analysis

Task

First think of a problem or difficulty that you are faced with at the moment. Copy Figure 14.1, and write a short title for the problem in the top (large) arrow. On the right side list all the forces (reasons) that are preventing the change from taking place – these are the restraining forces. On the left side list all the driving forces that are encouraging change (e.g. Maslow's motivational drives). After you have filled in your force field chart and thought about it, set out an action plan that will help you to:

a increase the driving forces
b reduce the restraining forces.

In planning for personal change you will need to:

> KNOW WHERE YOU ARE NOW

> KNOW WHERE YOU WANT TO BE

> HAVE SOME MEANS OF KNOWING IF YOU HAVE ARRIVED

In other words you will need to set out some clear **objectives**. At the same time you will need to decide on ways of measuring whether these objectives are being met.

Setting out objectives

When you write down your objectives, make sure that they are:

● worthwhile and consistent with your own values
● clear (not vague)

- realistic and attainable
- measurable
- time bound (e.g. to be achieved by the end of the year).

Here is an example of a possible format:

Objectives: To improve my performance when being interviewed
To appear more confident when being interviewed
To prepare answers to the questions I may be asked

Measurement: I can check on improvements in my performance by studying videos of my mock job interviews
I can ask advice from friends and tutors on how well I did
I will be able to judge how confident I feel as time passes
Ultimately I can see whether I am successful in being offered jobs

Time period: I will need to improve my skills by the end of May for interviews in June

Another way of setting out a framework for personal change is to use three categories:

Performance
Conditions
Standards

Performance is the actual objective, *conditions* are the environmental context your objectives need to be set against, and the *standards* are the ways in which you will measure success. Under the standards heading you should include the time scale and ways of measuring competencies. This is made clear by the example in Figure 14.2.

PERFORMANCE	CONDITIONS	STANDARDS
Study effectively for BTEC Business and Finance	Within the present course environment	Satisfy myself that I have learned, and obtained the necessary competencies

Figure 14.2 A framework for personal change

Task

Set out three of your major objectives for the coming year in a framework of performance, conditions and standards.

Self-assessment

When managing changes it is essential to know how successful we have been. We can more effectively develop these skills by looking at ourselves more critically.

The profile form in Figure 14.3 gives the opportunity for self-assessment in terms of the personal and social skills required to operate as a member of a group. The form can be adapted to self-assessment in other areas. The tick boxes are intended to be filled in according to the following pointers:

1 = I am experienced at this.
2 = I have some experience of this.
3 = I have no experience of this.

and

1 = I was successful at this.
2 = I was reasonably successful at this.
3 = I was rarely successful at this.

Task

Complete the questionnaire in Figure 14.3. Try to base your answers on specific experiences at school, college, in the family, at work or in voluntary organisations .

As a member of any group have you experience of:	Experience 1	2	3	Success 1	2	3
*Contributing ideas						
*Listening to other people's ideas and making use of them						
*Compromising when your opinion was not shared by others						
*Taking notes of what went on in the group						
*Carrying out an agreed task in co-operation with others						
*Carrying out part of a task assigned to you as an individual						
*Showing flexibility						
*Asking for things to be explained even though you could have looked silly						
*Getting the task finished						
*Choosing a person to do a particular task						
*Keeping a check on how far the group had got in carrying out a task						
*Chairing a meeting						
*Giving instructions to others						
*Trying to influence others in a group						
*Contributing ideas to a group discussion						
*Making a formal presentation to a group						
*Producing visual material as part of a presentation						
*Helping to organise a major event						
*Deciding on the best solution and planning a way forward						
*Encouraging people to carry on even when they were disinterested						
*Getting the group to finish on time						
*Sharing any praise						

Figure 14.3 A self-assessment questionnaire

When you have finished the questionnaire you may want to consider which aspects you would like to improve on. You could then set out some objectives (with your tutor) to develop realistic plans to improve on these areas as part of your course.

Organisational change

Like individuals, organisations need to monitor continually where they have come from, where they are and where they are going. The **planning process** lies at the heart of preparation for change.

The planning process
translates
PURPOSES
into
POLICIES
into
PLANS
to ensure
IMPLEMENTATION, FEEDBACK and REVIEW

Implementation is making sure that policies are carried out, *feedback* means that actions, successes and failures are recorded, and *review* entails looking at successes and failures with a view to planning future steps.

Responding to change: an example

A service station provides a good example of a working environment. There is always plenty of action to be seen at a successful station, with customers continually coming in for the products and services they want.

There is plenty of action behind the scenes too. The people working at the service station must:

- maintain stocks in good condition (and order more when necessary)
- keep all the equipment in first-class condition
- monitor and control the finances
- ensure that publicity is up-to-date and effective
- see that the whole site is kept clean and attractive
- adhere strictly to safety and security procedures.

This list shows that there is a lot of work to be carried out to keep the service station simply ticking over. Each day certain stocks need to be replenished, and this involves keeping track of what is going out and making sure that it is re-ordered in good time. Each day a lot of money comes in for petrol, oil, foodstuffs, the car wash, maps, and many other facilities and services. If an accurate record is not kept straight away, then the whole financial record-keeping system will become a mess.

Litter must be cleared from the site, water replenished in cans and buckets, spillages dealt with straight away, lights repaired and toilets cleaned. Activity within the station is therefore continuous, and change will continually be taking place (remember that many service stations are open 24 hours each day).

In addition to these daily fluctuations there are seasonal changes – more people take to the roads during holiday times, and fewer during bad weather. There are changes in response to the economy – for example, in a period of recession there are fewer vehicles on the roads, and before the Budget there may be a rush in demand for petrol if motorists think taxes will rise. Then there are legal changes affecting the way service stations operate – for example, in the late 1980s it became compulsory for all service stations to have toilet facilities, and health and safety laws have been considerably tightened up. Changes in social attitudes constantly affect people's expectations about the way in which service stations operate – for example, fewer people today expect attendant service, and most people have switched to lead-free petrol.

The pace of activity in a service station demands that many of the operations involve information

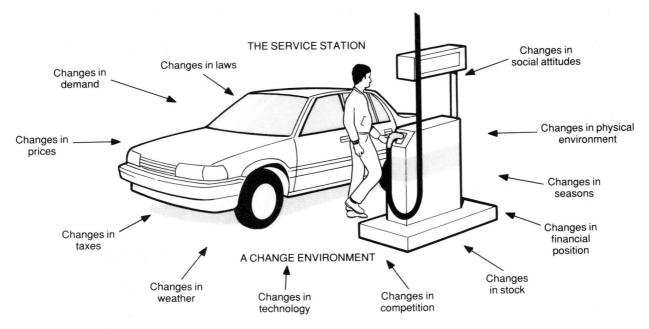

Figure 14.4 A change environment

technology. Staff need to be constantly updated in IT operations and in many other areas of running a dynamic business.

Working for such an organisation therefore involves an ability to respond to change. One day employees at a service station may have to respond to lengthy queues of motorists rushing to buy fuel before an expected price rise. The next day they may be working flat out to keep the station running smoothly in a snowstorm – keeping entrances clear, water mopped up from floors, dealing with stranded motorists and so on.

The changing industrial structure of the UK

In the nineteenth century the United Kingdom was known as the 'workshop of the world'. This is not surprising when one looks at the statistics. As a result of early **industrialisation**, Britain led the world in manufacturing. However, during the last quarter of the nineteenth century several other Western nations not only came to be core industrial

producers, they even overtook Britain. This process continued into the twentieth century with the rapid development of the United States, Germany and then Japan, and more recently many other countries. This change of world leadership in industrial production in the early part of the twentieth century is clear from Figure 14.5.

	1870	1913	Late 1920s
Britain	31.8	14.0	9.4
USA	23.3	35.8	42.2
Germany	13.2	15.7	11.6
France	10.3	6.4	6.6
Japan	0	1.2	2.5

Figure 14.5 Percentage share of world industrial output

Britain must now be considered an industrial dwarf compared with several other countries. Today manufacturing is concentrated largely among the big three (the USA, Germany and Japan), which account for about a half of all world manufacturing output. In the United Kingdom, many of the early pace-setting industries – coal, iron and steel, engineering and shipbuilding – are in an advanced stage of decline. Manufactured goods traditionally exported by Britain have declined as a proportion of all production in the country for a long time, and by 1984 Britain was importing more manufactured goods than she was exporting.

When manufacturing industry goes into relative decline and the service industries become more important, this process if often called **de-industrialisation**.

For statistical purposes industries are normally grouped together under a major heading or **division** in what is called the **Standard Industrial Classification** (SIC). The divisions are shown below, together with examples of groupings within divisions.

DIVISION 0 – AGRICULTURE, FORESTRY AND   FISHING
Farming and horticulture
Forestry
Commercial sea and inland fishing

DIVISION 1 – ENERGY AND WATER SUPPLY INDUSTRIES
Coal-mining and manufacture of solid fuels
Extraction of mineral oil and natural gas
Production and distribution of electricity, gas and other forms of energy

DIVISION 2 – EXTRACTION OF MINERALS AND ORES, MANUFACTURE OF METALS, MINERAL PRODUCTS AND CHEMICALS
Metal manufacture
Extraction of stone, clay, sand and gravel
Manufacture of non-metallic mineral products
Chemical industry (includes paints, varnishes and inks, pharmaceutical products, some perfumes, etc.)

DIVISION 3 – METAL GOODS, ENGINEERING AND VEHICLE INDUSTRIES
Foundries
Mechanical engineering
Electrical and electronic engineering
Manufacture of motor vehicles and parts
Instrument engineering

DIVISION 4 – OTHER MANUFACTURING INDUSTRIES
Food, drink and tobacco manufacturing industries
Textile industry

Manufacture of leather and leather goods
Timber and wooden furniture industries
Manufacture of paper and paper products, printing and printing products
Processing of rubber and plastics

DIVISION 5 – CONSTRUCTION
Construction and repairs
Demolition work
Civil engineering

DIVISION 6 – DISTRIBUTION, HOTELS AND CATERING, REPAIRS
Wholesale distribution
Retail distribution
Hotel and catering (restaurants, cafes and other eating places, public houses and hotel trade)
Repair of consumer goods and vehicles

DIVISION 7 – TRANSPORT AND COMMUNICATION
Railways and other inland transport
Air and sea transport
Support services to transport
Postal services and telecommunications

DIVISION 8 – BANKING, FINANCE, INSURANCE, BUSINESS SERVICES AND LEASING
Banking and finance
Insurance
Business services
Renting of movables
Owning and dealing in real-estate

DIVISION 9 – OTHER SERVICES
Public administration, national defence and social security
Sanitary services
Education
Medical and other health services, veterinary services
Other services provided to the general public
Recreational services and other cultural services
Personal services (laundries, hairdressing and beauty parlours)
Domestic services
Diplomatic representation, international organisations, allied armed forces

Task

Endeavour to obtain from your local Employment Office a breakdown of the numbers of people in your area who work in each of the divisions of the Standard Industrial Classification.

Alternatively, carry out some research of your own. You could, for example, work in groups to do street interviewing to find out the sorts of jobs people do. You would need to plan carefully how and when you would do this research. You would need to decide on which day of the week you would get a representative sample of people in your area on the high street. How large would your sample need to be to give a reflection of the typical population of your area? What problems would you be likely to encounter in setting up and carrying out the research?

Case Study – New jobs for old

If we look at 'who does what' in Britain today we get a picture of the types of job that are disappearing and new jobs that are growing in importance.

1 *Does the table tell us that more jobs will be created than lost in the period 1987–95?*
2 *What types of job are being created? What type are being lost?*
3 *What does the table tell us about the changing nature of employment in the UK?*
4 *Look at five categories of jobs that are in decline and five categories that are increasing. Try to explain why these trends are taking place.*
5 *How does the national picture relate to your local picture? What jobs are declining in your area?*

What jobs are expanding? What types of job are being offered in your local employment market? Carry out some research – look in the local press, Job Centre, Employment Office, etc.

	Employment in 1987	Net change 1987–95
	(thousands)	
Agriculture	558	−38
Mining	207	−34
Utilities	291	−22
Metals, minerals	443	−23
Chemicals	345	−17
Engineering	2239	−91
of which:		
Mechanical	737	−25
Electrical	567	−32
Motor vehicles	245	0
Food, drink, tobacco	581	−61
Textiles and clothing	563	−39
Other manufacturing	1102	+5
Construction	1569	+201
Distribution	5268	+414
of which:		
Distribution	3972	+97
Hotel and catering	1295	+317
Transport, communication	1500	+18
Business services	2631	+602
Other services	2420	+615
Manufacturing	5362	−230
All industries	19 807	+1523
Health and education	3001	+265
Public administration	2178	−66

Figure 14.6 Forecasted employment changes in the UK

Organisational response to changing markets

We have seen that there are some industrial divisions that are growing and some that are in decline. Some new products are being researched, others are in a period of infancy or growth, while still others are mature.

In Chapter 6 we looked at this in terms of **life-cycles.** The product life-cycle suggests that all products have a limited life. Of course, the rates at which their cycles proceed will vary. For some the life-cycle may last just a single year (e.g. a new fashion item such as 'loon pants' or 'hot pants'). For others the life-cycle is much longer (e.g. hearing aids, hot-water bottles, Ribena). There is, however, growing evidence that the lengths of product cycles are tending to become shorter. So, in order to continue to grow and to continue to make profits, businesses need to innovate on a regular basis. There are several ways of doing this.

Figure 14.7 illustrates three ways of maintaining sales. One way is to introduce a new product as the existing one becomes obsolete, so that there are **overlapping cycles**. This is a common practice with motor vehicles. A second alternative is to **modify** the existing product in order to extend its life-cycle. This is the case with many modern desktop computers – improved models with more memory, a wider range of applications and greater speed continually update old models. A third option is to change the production **technology** itself to make the product **more competitive** – for example, by employing better production technology in the textile industry.

In fact most business organisations today employ a mixture of three ways of extending product life-cycles.

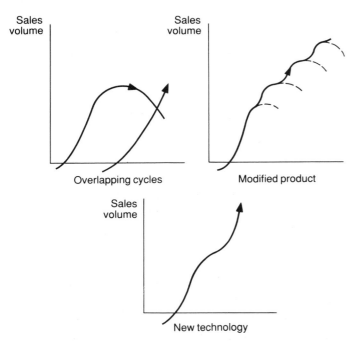

Figure 14.7 Three ways of extending product life-cycles

Product and process innovation

In modern competitive markets it is essential for businesses to be able to innovate. Freeman, in a book *The Economics of Industrial Innovation* (Penguin), argued that for a large business organisation, 'not to innovate is to die'. Indeed, such organisations are trapped on an 'innovation treadmill'. Inevitably, therefore, employees who work for these organisations need to be prepared for changing practices. They need to adjust to new styles of operation and management.

As industries become more mature the emphasis on change is placed on the **processes of production** as opposed to the products themselves. In their early days, new products can set their markets alight with their flair and product originality. As time passes other businesses will copy, so that if companies want to remain as market leaders they need to re-think their methods (see Figure 14.8).

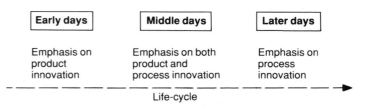

Figure 14.8 Moving the emphasis of innovation

Two major trends have become more noticeable in the production process in recent years. The first is **increasing specialisation** so that the processes can be split into many separate operations. The second is **increasing standardisation** of these separate operations so that they can be done by semi-skilled and unskilled labour. This is particularly so during the mature phase of a product's life-cycle.

Many of the declining industries are therefore characterised by more old-fashioned working practices, lower-paid workers and resistance to change.

Hirsch produced an interesting picture to show the relative importance of different factors of production during the life-cycles of products. This is presented as Figure 14.9.

Life-cycle phase			Factors of production
NEW	GROWTH	MATURITY	
2	3	1	Management
3	2	1	Scientific and engineering know how
1	2	3	Semi-skilled and unskilled labour
3	2	1	External economies
1	2=	2=	Capital

Figure 14.9 Relative importance of factors of production at different stages of product life-style

It is important to remember that different products have different production methods. Also, although many modern products are made in automated plant this does not necessarily mean that they have to be produced on a large scale. Traditional automation is geared to high-volume standardised production, but newer flexible manufacturing systems are quite different. With flexible manufacturing different products can be produced on the same line. Flexible manufacturing means that economies can be achieved for both large-scale and small-scale production. A flexible automation system can turn out a small batch or even a single copy of a product as efficiently as a line geared to producing a million identical items.

Task

Make a study of changing industrial processes in a local industry. What changes have taken place in recent years? Have the changes been in the products or the processes, or both? What new products have been developed? What new processes? How have the processes affected the organisation of work? How have employees in these organisations had to adjust? What have been the effects of these changes? What further new changes, if any, need to take place?

Case Study – Changes in the textiles industry

Figure 14.10 shows changes in employment in the UK textiles industry in recent years. During the 1990s there was a steady drip of closures which sapped the lifeblood of what is still Britain's fifth largest industry. The British textiles industry has been in decline for so long, people could be forgiven for thinking it no longer exists. In fact, it has an output of more than £13 billion and employs close on half a million workers. It was the country's first major industry.

During the 1980s the textiles industry seemed to be recovering from years of decline. Between 1980 and 1988 productivity rose by more than 40 per cent, and companies invested more than £4 billion in new plant and machinery. Exports rose by more than 50 per cent in this period, and the level of home demand increased with rising incomes and people spending more of their incomes on clothes. However, in 1988 the textiles industry was the first to slump into recession. It was hit by falling demand at home, particularly in household fabrics. The

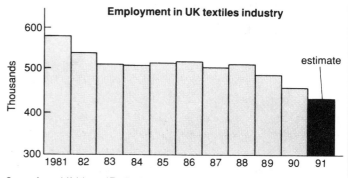

Source: Apparel, Knitting and Textiles Alliance

Figure 14.10 Employment in UK textiles industry

288

industry was hit again by a weak dollar – US and Far Eastern exports are priced in dollars.

A lot of the new investment of the 1980s has been wasted. Investments in cutting costs have been effective, but investments in increasing capacity have not.

Today the market for UK textiles rests around flexibility. As fashions change faster, and as shops look to sell a wider range of new products, manufacturers have had to deliver their products faster. UK manufacturers find it difficult to compete with Far Eastern suppliers, particularly on price. Their only main advantage is closeness to the market. UK manufacturers therefore have to concentrate on delivering products to the market quickly. Shortening lead times and being flexible require considerable managerial skills and the sort of machinery that can be quickly adapted to new products. It also needs a skilled and flexible labour force.

1 *Outline three major changes in the textiles industry in the 1990s.*
2 *What skills and attitudes are needed to respond to these changes?*
3 *What restraining forces can you identify that might hold back change?*
4 *How do you think change can be brought about in British textiles to give the industry a competitive edge?*

The changing pattern of international trade

Britain has a long history as a trading nation. In the nineteenth century the UK imported raw materials from all over the world and exported goods made from them. Since 1945, Britain has become even more dependent on foreign trade. Approximately 65 per cent of exports and imports are made up of trade in goods (**visibles**) and 35 per cent trade in services (**invisibles**). Figure 14.11 gives some details based on published figures for 1989.

	Exports	Imports
	(£ million)	
Food and live animals	4 228	9 762
Beverages and tobacco	2 326	1 667
Crude materials, inedible not including fuels	2 264	6 098
Mineral fuels, lubricants etc.	5 776	6 235
Animal and vegetable oils, fats and waxes	84	385
Chemicals	12 350	10 440
Manufactured goods	14 510	21 730
Machinery and transport equipment	37 690	45 900
Miscellaneous manufactures	11 773	17 058
Other items	2 256	1 512
Totals	93 257	120 787

Figure 14.11 **Britain's main trading items in 1989**

Task

Study the table in Figure 14.11. Identify one item in each category. According to the table, which of your chosen items are in trading surplus and which in trading deficit? Can you explain why they are in surplus or deficit?

What is the overall trading position in visible goods? Is this a problem for the UK? Give reasons for your answer.

The United Kingdom has become accustomed to running a **trading loss** with the rest of the world on visibles, but has continued to make a **surplus** on invisibles (i.e. services). Figure 14.12 shows the **balances** of each part of the invisible account in 1989 (that is, it shows invisible exports *minus* invisible imports).

	£ million
SERVICES	
General government	−1833
Private sector	
and public corporations	
Sea transport	−578
Civil aviation	−862
Travel and tourism	−2042
Financial and other services	9478
INTEREST, PROFITS AND DIVIDENDS	
General government	−837
Private sector	
and public corporations	6456
TRANSFERS	
General government	−3269
Private sector	−306
INVISIBLE BALANCE	**6207**

Figure 14.12 Invisible balance in 1989

Whilst visibles are fairly self-explanatory, the invisibles are not so obvious. *General government services*, for example, covers the amount spent by the government in looking after and keeping its embassies, consulates and other political activities abroad. It also includes the cost of maintaining armed forces abroad. *Sea transport* is money earned by UK-registered shipping and ferry companies, and by ports and harbours, from use of British services overseas. *Travel and tourism* is a major item in the UK invisible trade account. *Civil aviation* represents money earned by UK airlines from abroad, both for passenger and freight transport. *Financial services* covers the fees and commissions earned essentially by the City of London for the provision of insurance underwriting and banking. *Other services* are telecommunications and postal services, advertising, royalties on books, films and records etc. *Interest, profits and dividends*, which have always been of importance to Britain, are the returns to the government, businesses and individuals from money lent overseas, or dividends earned from shareholdings overseas. *Transfers* involve dealings where one of the parties involved does not receive a monetary return (e.g. aid to Third World countries). The government's

contribution to the European Community budget is another example.

The current account

The **balance of payments** account shows the whole country's trading with the rest of the world in a given time period. The **current account** is the most important part of the balance of payments account, and the one to which attention is mainly focused in the media and in parliamentary debate. The current account is in surplus if the country's exports are worth more than its imports, and in deficit if its exports are worth less than imports. These situations are illustrated in Figure 14.13.

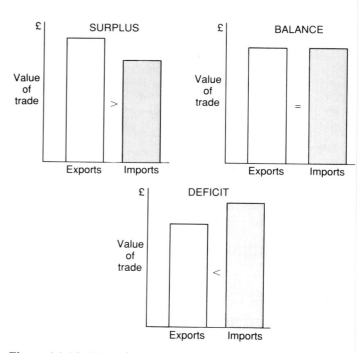

Figure 14.13 How the current account can vary

In the *short term* it is not a problem to have a surplus or deficit. Problems arise in the *long term* if a country runs a surplus or deficit year after year. Remember, exports earn money for the sale of goods or services, whereas imports lead to an outflow of money to buy goods or services.

The current account may be set out in the manner shown below: a plus sign (+) indicates money flowing into the country and a minus (−) money flowing out:

Visible exports (+)
Visible imports (−)
Visible balance = exports minus imports (+ or −)

Invisible exports (+)
Invisible imports (−)
Invisible balance = exports minus imports
(+ or −)

Current balance = visible balance plus invisible
balance (+ or −)

The state of the account is simply calculated by adding the total value of exports and subtracting the total value of imports.

Task

Find the latest current account figures for the United Kingdom. They are reported each month in national newspapers. What has been happening to the figures in recent months and years? What are the reasons given? How are these changes likely to affect industry and other organisations?

The exchange rate

The **exchange rate** expresses the amount of one currency that can be obtained in exchange for the currency of another country. At the end of 1991, for example, £1 in sterling could be exchanged for 1.7 US dollars, 1.4 ecus or 3.0 deutschmarks.

Exchange rates in recent years have been changing frequently and by quite large amounts. As a trading nation Britain is particularly interested in these changes in the exchange rate, because they affect what must be paid for imports and what is received for exports.

Changes in international markets.

When we buy and sell goods and services on the world market we may use other currencies. For example, when an organisation buys goods from Germany it may use D–marks (deutschmarks). As a result the exchange rates (in effect the prices of other currencies) depend partly on the demand for goods and services from those countries. In Chapter 5 we looked at how prices are determined through demand and supply. The same rules apply on international markets. If everybody wants to buy British goods they will want British pounds. If nobody wants British goods then the value of the pound (its buying power) will fall. If Britons want to buy a lot of imports, the importers will need to buy foreign money to make the purchases. The supply of pounds will rise and the price of the pound will fall.

In Figure 14.14, the value of the pound falls when Britain is selling fewer exports (there is less demand from foreigners for British pounds). At the same time Britons are buying more imports and supplying more pounds to international markets.

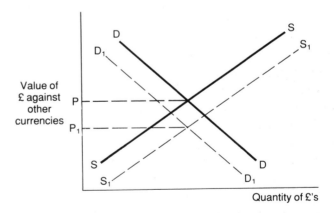

Figure 14.14 Demand and supply lines for the British pound

Task

Draw a demand and supply curve for British pounds. Then show the effect of:

a *a fall in demand for imports by Britons*
b *a rise in demand by foreigners for British goods.*

What happens to the value of the pound in these situations?

Changes in the quantity and value of exports affect the livelihoods of nearly everyone in a country. If you do not work for an organisation that exports, then you are likely to work for one that trades or deals with others that do export. When we sell fewer exports abroad there is less money available for people in our country, and everyone is likely to feel the effects.

Changes in the value of the pound can have quite a dramatic impact on livelihoods. If the pound's value rises, for example, then British companies find it difficult to export because their prices are **less competitive** (they are higher). This inevitably leads to cutback in production.

When exchange rates rise and fall according to international demand and supply, it is difficult for traders to predict **future prices**. For example, a British exporter who supplies £10 000 worth of goods, with payment expected in three months' time, may find that when he or she converts the foreign money back to pounds on payment day it is worth considerably less than £10 000 (it may, of course, be worth more).

In 1990, Britain joined the European Exchange Rate Mechanism, so that the value of the pound is now almost fixed in relation to the currencies of our European Community partners. This makes sense now that most of our trade is with the EC countries.

Change to a single European market

In 1986 the Single European Act was signed by the heads of government of the 12 member countries of the European Community. The Act aims to establish a **single market** by the end of 1992. In more specific terms this means the free movement of goods, capital, labour and services.

In manufacturing industry many of the trade barriers have already been lowered. However, by the end of 1992 the community should have achieved the complete abolition of frontiers and restrictions on unimpeded trade. The resulting effect will be the creation of a market containing 340 million people. By the end of the century it is likely that many of the Eastern bloc countries will have joined.

Figure 14.15 indicates what economic union actually entails.

	Removal of trade restrictions between members	Common external trade policy towards non-members	Free movement of factors of production between member states	Harmonisation of economic policies under supra-national control
Free trade area	✓			
Customs union	✓	✓		
Common market	✓	✓	✓	
Economic union	✓	✓	✓	✓

Figure 14.15 What economic union entails

After 1992, UK organisations will be operating in a competitive market where price, standard of service and product innovation will determine their success. European **regulations** and **standards** will mean that products approved in any one EC country may be freely sold throughout the EC. These conditions should create opportunities for businesses wishing to expand and develop their full potential.

The single European market has already encouraged companies to invest. The free movement of factors within Europe, capital in particular, has created better **investment opportunities**, with associated benefits of technological and managerial improvements. We are now more likely to see international collaboration on major projects like the Channel Tunnel, and tunnels through the Alps to improve road and rail networks.

The free movement of **people** will have major implications for UK organisations. European companies are today recruiting on a Europe-wide level and looking for modern skills such as familiarity with information technology, decision-making, problem-solving and language skills.

The breaking down of **technical barriers** may cut the costs of British companies operating on a Europe-wide basis. For example, the harmonisation of electricity power supply will mean that electrical goods can be built to one common European standard, allowing longer production runs and lower unit costs.

European businesses will be helped in their investment activities by the sources of **finance** made available by the European Investment Bank, and the Regional Development Fund as well as the European Social Fund in areas of deprivation. Financial services will increasingly be provided on a European as opposed to a national scale.

European businesses will also benefit from a more competitive **communications** and **transport** system. The 'red tape' involved in road haulage will be removed, shipping services between member countries will be provided on equal terms, competition on air routes will increase, and the Channel Tunnel will open. A far more competitive and efficient European service in telecommunications and IT will develop.

British companies that are more efficient than their European rivals will benefit in open markets as a result of their competitive edge. At the same time, less efficient businesses will be less successful. Government contracts (e.g. for defence projects) will no longer be given as a priority to domestic firms. As we saw in Chapter 13, monopolies and mergers will be controlled more by the community. The community will also play an increasingly important part in deciding environmental issues.

Task

Interview a manager from a local company to find out the implications of the single European market for that business.

Alternatively, find out how free labour mobility has affected local people. How many people can you find who have worked in other single market countries? What types of skill and qualifications did they need? How many people can you find who are now thinking of working in other EC countries? What special qualifications and training will they require?

An even larger market

At the end of October 1991, the European Community agreed to form, with the **European Free Trade Association**, a combined market of nearly 400 million people in 19 nations stretching from Iceland to the Mediterranean. The move cleared the way for free movement of goods, services, capital and labour between the 12 EC nations and the seven EFTA countries – Finland, Iceland, Norway, Sweden, Switzerland, Liechtenstein and Austria. The new combined area will be known as the European Economic Area (EEA).

Under the agreement, EC rules govern the free movement of goods, people and services. Competition, social and environment policies will apply to the EFTA countries, which in turn gain greater access to European markets.

The deal also involves writing some 1500 EC laws and regulations on to EFTA statute books, and will be policed by a specially created structure, to include a governing council, consultative bodies and an independent court of arbitration.

EFTA nations will be expected to implement policy decisions that they have had little or no opportunity to initiate or even influence – which may force them to press for full EC membership sooner rather than later.

Changes in transport and communications

We have already looked at some of the major changes that have taken place in recent years and their impact on organisations. Clearly two of the most significant changes have been in transport and communications.

Transport systems are the means by which people, materials, products and other things are taken from place to place. Transport is always an important cost which needs to be added to other production costs. For example, Ireland is somewhat disadvantaged in trading with the European Community because extra transport costs usually account for at least 10–20 per cent of total costs.

In terms of the time taken to get from one side of the world to the other today, the globe has certainly shrunk. The most important developments in this respect have been the introduction of commercial jet aircraft, the development of much larger ocean-going vessels, and the introduction of containers which enable loads to be transferred quickly from one mode of transport to another. The transport revolution has sped up the process of **concentration of production** into large plants. These plants can then serve extensive market areas – often global markets.

The basis of the **communications** revolution lies in electronics. Today information can be transmitted over long distances at great speed. If you have ever dialled a relative in Australia you will be aware that your voice travels there in a matter of seconds. Using a laptop computer you can communicate with other computers anywhere else in the world. During the Gulf war journalists were using sophisticated telephones which bounced messages off satellites, enabling instant communication with their

audiences around the world. Satellite technology has undoubtedly created a **global communications** network at the touch of a button.

Technological change

In this book we have looked at many of the technological changes that affect the way organisations operate today. Many large organisations employ **state-of-the-art** technology. Hospitals have electronic scanners for helping diagnosis, college and business organisations have sophisticated information technology equipment, and so on. However, many organisations still work with out-of-date equipment and with old-fashioned work practices. Many organisations do not operate in a 'hi-tech' way because, for them, the sheer cost of new technology may be off-putting. For others the scale of operations may not warrant investment in the most modern equipment.

Technology is the process of applying knowledge to the development of tools, products and processes. For example, we might want to improve the production of chocolate bars so that the process produces a consistent taste with a given recipe. A technologist would work out a solution to this problem.

A **production technique** is the way in which labour, equipment and other means of production are combined to make a finished product. Therefore we can change the technique of production by altering the way we combine the factors. For example, if we made a cake using an electric mixer rather than a spoon we have changed the production technique.

Technological change is concerned with adding new techniques to those already known.

Task

What technological changes are taking place in an organisation with

which you are familiar? How can you keep abreast of these changes? Make an action plan setting out appropriate objectives for you to keep abreast of the changes.

Case Study – Automatic identification: bar-codes

One major area where technology has revolutionised the way organisations operate in recent years is automatic identification. Today the market for products associated with automatic identification is worth between two and three billion pounds a year in Europe alone. Products and services based on bar-code technology, including sales of scanners and printers, bar-coded forms, labels, tags and other kinds of packaging, make up much of this market.

Bar-codes are to be seen on nearly all food packets, and on many other products such as records and books. The symbol can also be found on the boxes that are used to deliver goods to shops.

Figure 14.16 A bar code

The bar-code system is very simple and very clever. The bar-code itself contains a number of light and dark stripes of different widths, which represent a particular number. The one in Figure 14.16 represents 5 012345 678900. It is, therefore, just a way of writing numbers so that they are easy for a computer to read.

When a scanner reads the bar-code, it identifies the number contrast between the light and dark areas. The scanner is rather like a torch – it puts out a beam of light, and when it is moved across the bar-code a sensor measures how much light is reflected off the individual stripes. A computer then interprets the number from the signal it has received, and looks up this number in its database.

In a shop using an electronic point-of-sale (EPOS) system, scanners are also used to record all sales. Using the article number as a reference, the computer checks its database for information about that product, such as the name of the item and the price. It passes this information back to the till. The till adds the price to the total for all the other goods the shopper is buying, and prints out an itemised receipt. It may also update the shop's stock position on the computer's database.

1 *What are the advantages to the shop of having an electronic till?*
2 *What are the advantages to the customer?*
3 *How does it change the way in which the checkout operator works?*
4 *With an EPOS system, how can prices be changed? How might this affect the customer?*
5 *The shop can keep a detailed record of the items sold each day. How could the shopkeeper use this information to decide which goods should be sold in the shop? How would this benefit the consumer?*
6 *What are the implications of the development of bar-coding for people working in the retail trade today?*
7 *What are the implications for manufacturers, wholesalers and retailers?*

Changing attitudes to leisure

Today many people have more **leisure time** than used to be the case. Employees' representatives have managed to secure reductions in the working week, and in the working day. **Standards of living** are also rising, so that people can afford to spend more time

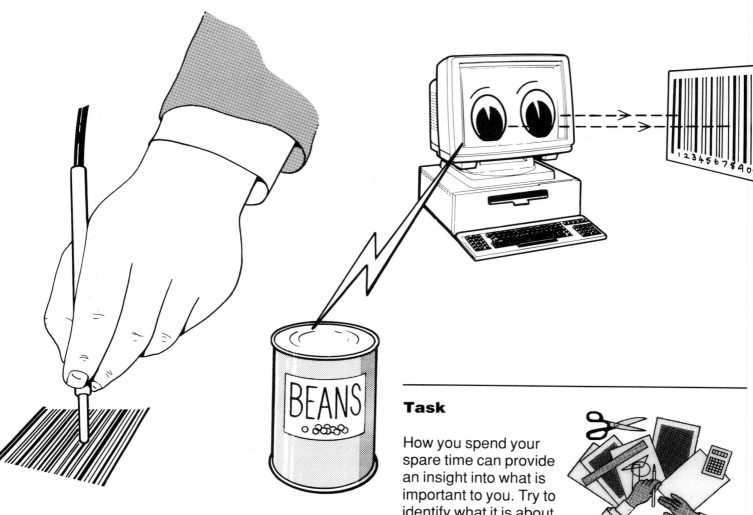

Figure 14.17 Reading a bar code

on leisure, and it is more socially acceptable to have free time. A range of new leisure pursuits has developed.

Employers are beginning to realise more the importance of leisure to a happy and fulfilled workforce. Going back to Maslow (Chapter 3), we can see that individuals can satisfy their needs through their leisure activities as well as their working activities. If it becomes possible to combine the two in a fulfilling lifestyle, then all well and good.

Task

How you spend your spare time can provide an insight into what is important to you. Try to identify what it is about the activities you do that attracts you to them. Consider keeping a record of your leisure activities, adding information about benefits (such as diplomas, music grades etc.).

Then think about objectives you can set yourself to improve your leisure time. How can you go about achieving these aims? You should refer back to the notes earlier in this chapter on managing change.

What information do you need to find out more about leisure opportunities? What skills and attitudes do you need to improve your experience and enjoyment of leisure?

Case Study – Work and leisure

Study the data in Figures 14.18 and 14.19, which show some information about work and leisure in the United Kingdom. In Figure 14.19, 'essential activities' covers essential domestic work and personal care, including shopping, child care, washing and getting up and going to bed.

1 *Which groups seem to have the most leisure?*
2 *How does your own leisure pattern fit in with those shown?*
3 *Do you think that the groups will have different attitudes to leisure?*
4 *What interesting features do the pie-charts show about how different groups divide their leisure time?*
5 *How do you think the use of leisure affects peoples' attitudes to their work?*
6 *How can organisations cater for the leisure needs of their members and employees? Should they?*

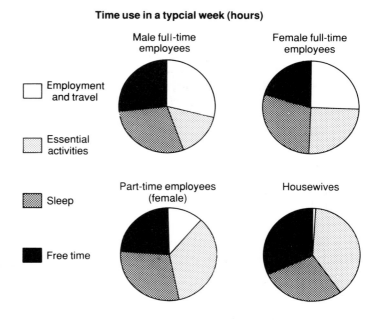

Figure 14.19 Time use in a typical week (hours)

Environmental issues

Product development can offer better, more reliable, more convenient, more accurate goods. However, it is important to look carefully at the all-round costs of new technologies. Should we accept the **pollution** it can bring, and in some cases the destruction of the natural environment? Should we accept job losses and the break-up of communities?

Clearly, pressure needs to be exerted on the movers of changing technology to make sure that ecological balance is preserved and that the environment is effectively protected. As we shall see in Chapter 15, this pressure comes from both internal and external sources. Today, the environment is a highly sensitive issue. Changes in attitudes towards the environment have had a dramatic impact on developments.

For example, in late 1991 the European Commission took issue with Britain over seven controversial and highly damaging road-building projects. These included the Channel Tunnel rail link and King's Cross terminal, and an extension

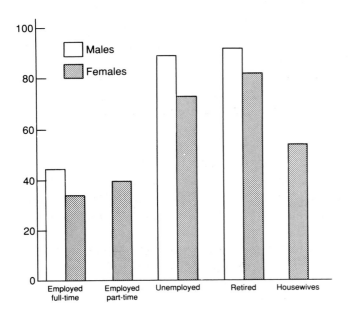

Figure 14.18 Leisure time in a typical week (hours)

to the M3 near Winchester. The Commission argued that when planning approval was sought for these projects a specified full environmental study was not included. A European court judge warned that Commission rules override any decision by the British government.

This case is interesting because it shows not only the powers of supra-national bodies, but also the importance attached today to environmental issues. Ten years ago environmental pressure groups were very much 'on the fringe', whereas the environment is now near to the centre of the political stage. Such a dramatic change has had a profound effect on all organisations.

Task

Set out a *personal action plan* showing how you can plan a change to improve your local environment.

Set out an *organisational action plan* showing how an organisation you are familiar with can plan to improve its local environment.

In each case, *start out by doing a force field analysis.*

15
Organisational Responsibilities

Organisations have responsibilities towards the people who work for them, their members, their shareholders, and many other groups and individuals. They have a wider responsibility towards their neighbours and the community. Indeed, the security and future of the planet are largely in the hands of organisations. Individuals and groups who work for organisations share in the responsibility for the way their organisations function.

Fundamental responsibilities are explored in this chapter. There are a number of key ways in which these responsibilities regulate and influence an organisation's operations. We look at the legal framework of consumer protection and competition policy, and at environmental responsibilities and auditing. Finally we consider how ethical responsibilities influence the running of modern corporations.

Pressure and responsibility

An organisation is not a machine. Rather it is a body representing the interests of a large number of people, some of whom work within the organisation, or are members (e.g. club members), or are part or total owners (e.g. shareholders).

Others are people whom the organisation comes into contact with as a result of its external relations – customers, suppliers, neighbours, government bodies and so on.

Every organisation must take very seriously both its **internal** responsibilities and its **external** responsibilities.

Examples of external pressures

Some of these responsibilities are forced upon an organisation by **outside pressures**, whilst others are **voluntary practices**. Outside pressures set the minimum levels of responsibility, and the voluntary practices build on these bare requirements.

Laws nowadays establish minimum safety standards, codes against unfair trading, restrictions

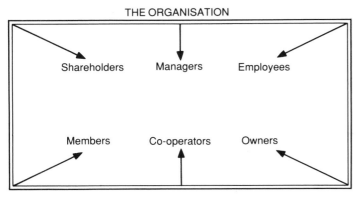

Figure 15.1 Examples of internal responsibilities

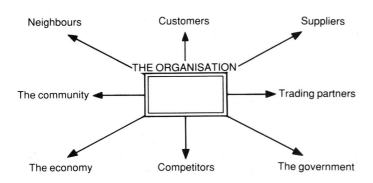

Figure 15.2 Examples of external responsibilities

on shop opening hours, environmental standards, and so on. These are outside pressures. In addition the government, after liaising with certain **regulatory bodies**, oversees the establishment of voluntary **codes of practice** – in advertising, for example.

Consumers can exert considerable pressure, because they can choose what and what not to buy. **Suppliers** can apply pressure by insisting on certain terms of any buying and selling. **Competitors** can add to the pressure by changing the strength and nature of the ways in which they compete.

Pressure groups influence organisations in many ways. They give adverse publicity to some products, they arrange consumer boycotts, and lobby the press and politicians in an effort to force an organisation to change. Unorganised groups of individuals can also exert pressure, and with support can soon become a highly vocal pressure group.

An organisation, whatever its business, must try to be highly sensitive to all of these external pressures.

Examples of internal pressures

An organisation is like an organism made up of many parts, of which the most important is probably the **people** who work for it. Other elements of the organism are the processes and procedures that take place within the organisation.

Running an effective organisation with dissatisfied employees is difficult. Most people would rather work for an organisation that they can be proud of, rather than one which embarrasses them in some way. Employees will therefore try to put pressure on an organisation to reflect their own values and ambitions. Of course, some employees have more power and influence than others – a managing director has more than a young trainee. However, a business that ignores a young trainee's views is very short-sighted.

We saw in Chapter 9 that the modern idea of **quality circles** is spreading. Small groups of employees meet together to talk about problems, possible improvements and ideas for change.

Shareholders are another important internal pressure group. As part owners of an organisation they can voice their opinions by making comments at shareholders' meetings, proposing motions for discussion and voting in the way they see fit. Unhappy shareholders can withdraw their support from a company by selling its shares.

The **Board of Directors** is intended to represent shareholders' wishes. It has the crucial responsi-bility of appointing the managing director of a company.

Trade unions and **staff associations** exert internal pressures. Groups of employees within a company or plant are formed to represent the wishes of all employees, and much of their influence comes from informal discussions with the managers. More severe pressure can be applied through strike action or other means of removing full co-operation.

If an organisation is of the type to have **members**, these also have an important influence. For example, members of the Church of England may express views about the role of women in the church's ministry. Supporters of a football club may call for the directors to sack the manager, and members of a film club may show their preferences for certain types of film.

Task

What organisations do you belong to? Set out your answer in the form of a diagram like the one shown here for Howard Sykes.

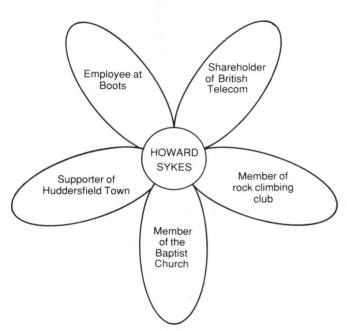

Figure 15.3 The organisations to which Howard Sykes belongs

Now consider in turn each organisation that you belong to, and set out a list of some of the internal and external pressures.

It is, of course, not just people that exert pressures – we also have to consider organisational **processes.** For example, every organisation must generate a cash flow – financial controllers need to ensure that every day there is sufficient cash available to meet the payments it is necessary to make that day (as we saw in Chapter 10). Production planners look at the demands that production flows and the operation of machinery make on the way in which a company

operates (Chapter 16). Marketing people assess the needs and wants of consumers and relate these to the capabilities of an organisation (Chapter 4), and so on.

Responsibility is two-way

One of President Kennedy's well-known sayings was: 'Do not ask what your country can do for you; instead think of what you can do for your country!'. This remark expresses the idea that responsibility is a two-way affair. Yes, any organisation that you belong to will have responsibilities towards you, but you too will have responsibilities – to that organisation.

Task

Choose one organisation of which you are a member. What responsibilities does this organisation have towards you? What responsibilities do you have? You may need to do some research to find out more about these responsibilities. Who can you ask? Are there any leaflets or other documents that set out your rights and obligations?

Case Study – Exploration and production by Shell UK

The following extract is taken from a Shell UK company report for 1991, describing the activities of the exploration and production division (Expro).

'For Shell, the year not only marked the twenty-fifth anniversary of the start of North Sea exploration but, significantly, also saw new "low-cost" oil and gas fields brought on-stream ahead of schedule at a time when a programme was being put in hand for rejuvenating many of the original platforms.

'Oil sales fell by 13 per cent to 208 thousand barrels a day, the lowest for nine years. Gas sales were similarly depressed by 10 per cent.

'Expenditure on exploration and capital investment in production was £495 million, the highest level for some years. In the harsh environment of the North Sea, safety must be given the highest priority, and the improvement of performance in this area is a prime concern of management. It was a matter of the deepest regret, therefore, that ten fatalities occurred in our operations in 1990. These included six people killed when an S61 helicopter crashed while attempting to land on the Brent Spar tanker loading facility.

'Although the sector's performance gives no cause for comfort, there were signs that the company's commitment to safety has begun to yield some general improvement. In 1990, the frequency of lost-time incidents amongst employees and contractors improved from 6.3 to 5.1 per million man-hours worked. In particular, a third year of operation without a lost-time incident was completed on Brent Alpha, demonstrating that substantial further improvement of the safety record is achievable. Strenuous efforts are being made to enhance the effectiveness of safety management.

'Lord Cullen's report on the Piper Alpha disaster, published in November, made 106 recommendations for the improvement of safety on offshore installations. Our staff were prominent in presenting technical evidence on safety management to the Cullen enquiry. Along with other operators, we welcomed the recommendations, many of which had been adopted ahead of the report. Among the physical changes recommended in the report, the most significant were the installation or relocation of emergency shut-down valves, nearing completion in early 1991.

'Our normally good relations with contractor employees offshore were disrupted by a period of unofficial industrial action which affected maintenance programmes on a number of installations.

'Recognising the need for a motivated, stable and skilled contractor workforce offshore, we introduced forward-looking approaches. These give contractors more responsibility for the work and enable them to offer improved terms and job security to their employees. Rather than purchasing services on a job-by-job basis, the five-year engineering services contract provides long-term engineering support and design; the four-year modification and maintenance services contract will enable the contractor to assemble and train a core team of workers who will become part of the platform team.

'A prime target is to minimise the impact of our activities on the environment, including the reduction of emissions during operations and plans for dealing with environmentally hazardous accidents. An inventory of all discharges and emissions was completed, providing a quantitive basis for achieving further improvement and monitoring progress. In August, staff took part in a mock oil-spill exercise, which successfully tested all aspects of our response.'

1 *Identify the groups highlighted in the extract to whom Shell Expro has responsibilities.*
2 *Explain why it is crucial that these responsibilities are met.*
3 *How can internal and external individuals and groups influence the activities of Shell Expro?*

Responsibilities to employees

New employees must be given a written contract of employment within thirteen weeks of starting a job. However, the employer and the employee are said to have formed a contract even before the written contract has been drawn up and signed. This contract is recognised in law when the employee agrees to work for the employer, and the employer agrees to pay the employee a wage or salary.

By law the contract of employment must include the following:

- the title of the job
- the date the job starts
- hours of work
- the rate and method of pay
- holiday arrangements
- the period of notice that must be given
- pension scheme arrangements
- rights concerning trade unions
- the organisation's rules concerning discipline.

New employees agree a date for work to start, and the contract becomes binding from this date.

Task

Obtain a copy of a contract of employment (your own or that of someone else) and identify its various parts.

Imagine that you have to write a contract of employment for an apprentice hairdresser. You may need to carry out some research into rates of pay, and other terms of employment for a hairdresser.

Health and safety at work

Task

Look at the pictures in Figure 15.4. Can you spot the dangers illustrated? List them, and suggest possible action to be taken in order to ensure a safer working environment in each case.

Figure 15.4 Hazards at work

Health and **safety** at work are the responsibility of the **personnel department**. Official regulations covering these topics occupy thousands of pages of text. The details are very important. We shall examine the three main laws that apply.

The Factories Act

The Factories Act covers most businesses that use machinery. It therefore applies to a wide range of premises, including garages, printing works, and engineering works, as well as building sites. Note that it does not apply just to 'factories'. Some of the important details of this Act are:

- Adequate toilet and washing facilities must be provided.
- The inside of buildings must be properly heated and ventilated.
- Floors, stairs and passageways must be free from obstructions such as boxes and furniture.
- Floors must not have slippery surfaces.
- Machinery such as presses must have fenced screens to prevent serious injury.
- Fire escapes must be provided and kept in good order. Fire doors should not be locked or obstructed.

The Offices, Shops and Railways Premises Act

This Act is particularly important in relation to office and shop conditions.

- Temperatures must not fall below 16 degrees centigrade in places where people work for any length of time.
- There must be adequate supplies of fresh or purified air.
- Toilet and washing facilities must be adequate for the number of employees and kept in a clean state. There must be running hot and cold water with soap and clean towels.
- Suitable lighting must be provided wherever people walk or work.
- The minimum amount of space for each person is 12 square metres of floor area.

The Health and Safety at Work Act

This Act establishes a responsibility for both employers and employees to provide safe conditions at work. The employer's duty is to ensure, so far as is reasonably practicable, the 'health, safety and welfare at work of all employees'. The employee's duty is to take reasonable care to ensure both his or her own safety and the safety of others who may be affected by what he or she does or does not do. Employers or employees who do not abide by these rules can be punished in a court of law.

An example of an area covered by the Act is protective guards for cutting machines such as food-slicing machines and industrial presses. Accidents occur if the guards are faulty or if they are removed. Generally the workplace must be designed in such a way as to minimise the risk of accidents.

The Act also lays down training standards for employees in potentially hazardous occupations.

This Act is backed up by a Health and Safety Executive which includes representatives of employers, employees and local authorities. Inspectors make sure that the law is being observed.

The safety officer of an organisation must be aware not only of general laws, but also of specific laws and codes relating to particular industries. For example, there are laws relating to workers in mines, the explosives industry, and textiles. On top of this, many industries establish their own safety regulations, often in conjunction with trade unions. A firm's safety officer will normally attend conferences and refresher courses on safety as a regular feature of his or her work.

Task

Investigate the health and safety features that apply either to you in your place of work, or to a parent or friend at

their place of work. Set your findings out as a written report.

If you have the facilities, work in a group to produce a video to highlight the health and safety lapses that affect the members of your college. This video could be a short 'commercial' lasting no more than 45 seconds. You should first construct a story board to clarify your ideas, before you shoot the video.

Welfare responsibilities

Many organisations nowadays provide **social facilities** for employees, with special functions at Christmas. The organisation may subsidise a canteen and provide premises for a sports and social club. There may be company 'outings'. A good personnel manager will keep an eye on the well-being of employees and their families.

Although **staff appraisal** is usually seen primarily as a means of assessing employees' skills, it is also a useful tool to find out the ambitions, concerns and interests of employees. Regular meetings can be arranged between employees and their line managers to discuss how things are going, and possible pathways for job enhancement and promotion.

A common starting point for appraisal is a **job description**, for which a suggested framework is shown in Figure 15.5. The job description will aim to:

- achieve a shared understanding of the job, working relationships and needs and requirements
- bolster co-operation and teamwork by encouraging discussion on the basis of agreement and common acceptance of areas of responsibility
- provide a means of self-assessment
- provide a useful management document for recruitment, selection, organisational review and development, appraisal of training and career developments and requirements.

Every employee should have a job description, which is negotiated between the employee and his or her manager.

Name:	
Salary grade:	
Relationships:	Responsible to: Supervises: Others:
Purpose of job:	
Responsibilities:	These should not exceed eight in number. The responsibilities will cover tasks which the postholder does not necessarily do, but must ensure are done to fulfil the job purpose.
Key tasks:	These should not exceed eight in number. They are tasks to be done by the postholder, each task crucial to the fulfilment of the purpose of the job.
Context of the post:	Facts, factors and circumstances which have a bearing on the fulfilment of the job.

Figure 15.5 Suggested framework for devising an agreed job description

---

Task

Using Figure 15.5 as a basis, draw up a possible job description for your business studies lecturer. Discuss your description with others.

Discrimination at work

Discrimination against anyone on the grounds of their sex, race, colour or national origin is illegal, whether it be in recruitment, conditions of work, promotion, training or dismissal. Job advertisements must clearly not discriminate. It is then necessary to make sure that interviews are fair, pay is equal for similar work, and that there is no sexual or racial harassment.

There must be no discrimination of any sort. Alleged cases of discrimination can be taken to an **industrial tribunal** or a body such as the **Race Relations Board**.

Task

The advertisements in Figure 15.6 appeared in a local newspaper. Do you think that they discriminate in any way?

The **Sex Discrimination Act** set out rights for both men and women. Unlawful discrimination means giving less favourable treatment to someone because of their sex or because they are married or single, and can be either **direct** or **indirect**. The Act also covers victimisation.

Direct sex discrimination means being treated less favourably than a person of the opposite sex would be treated in similar circumstances. For example, a policy to appoint only men to management positions is clearly illegal.

Direct marriage discrimination means being treated less favourably than an unmarried person of the same sex. A policy not to recruit married people for a job that involved being away from home would not be allowed.

Indirect sex discrimination is less easy to identify. It means being unable to comply with a requirement which on the face of it applies equally to both men and women, but which in practice can be met by a much smaller proportion of one sex. For example, organisations may be indirectly discriminating against women if access to certain jobs is restricted to particular grades which in practice are held only by men.

Victimisation means being treated less favourably then other people because you have in good faith

---

SALES REPRESENTATIVE

Get in the fast lane with one of the fastest growing frozen food firms.

PILGRIM FROZEN FOODS

Pilgrim Frozen Foods need a Sales Representative for the area bordered by Leicester, Loughborough, Stamford and Grantham.

You should be presentable and articulate, able to assimilate the latest marketing strategies and be able to develop new sales outlets. Experience of the food trade would be helpful.

In return we offer an attractive remuneration package and company car.

Send your CV together with a hand written letter explaining why you should fill this demanding position to:-

Philip Parker
Sales Manager
Pilgrim Frozen Foods
Blue Street
Boston
Lincs PE21 8UW

RESPONSIBLE PERSON

required to deliver the

Citizen GRANTHAM

in Denton
Tel. (0476) 71739

MERES STADIUM POWERSPORT
require
One Full Time and One Part Time

FITNESS INSTRUCTOR

Must have a sporting background, good communications and first aid certificate. Experience as a fitness advisor would be advantageous but training will be given.
Salary negotiable upon experience.
Apply in writing to Box No. 339
c/o Grantham Journal
46 High Street, Grantham,
Lincs NG31 6NE.

Figure 15.6 Job advertisements

306

made allegations about discrimination in relation to the Sex Discrimination Act or any other regulation.

A person who thinks he or she has been treated unfairly with regard to sex discrimination can lodge a complaint with the Central Office of Industrial Tribunals within three months of the alleged wrong-doing.

An industrial tribunal is a relatively informal 'court' which will usually meet locally. It consists of a legally qualified chairperson and two ordinary members of the public with experience of industry and commerce. A complainant can either present his or her own case to the tribunal or seek help from the Equal Opportunities Commission.

Figure 15.7 An industrial tribunal panel

If the tribunal finds in your favour it can do any or all of the following things:

- make an order declaring your rights
- order that you be paid compensation, which could include lost earnings, expenses, damages for injury to your feelings or damages for future loss of earnings
- recommend that the person or organisation you complain against should take a particular course of action within a specified period – for example to consider you for promotion within the next year.

The **Race Relations Act** makes it unlawful to discriminate against a person, directly or indirectly, in the field of employment on the basis of race, colour or national origin. **Direct discrimination** is

treating a person, on racial grounds, less favourably than others are or would be treated in the same or similar circumstances. Segregating a person from others on racial grounds constitutes less favourable treatment.

Indirect discrimination consists of applying a requirement or condition which, although applied equally to persons of all racial groups, is such that a considerably smaller proportion of a particular racial group can comply with it. Examples are:

- a rule about clothing or uniforms which disproportionately disadvantages a racial group and cannot be justified
- an employer who requires higher language standards than are needed for safe and effective performance of the job.

The **Commission for Racial Equality** has produced a code of practice for the elimination of racial discrimination and the promotion of equality of opportunity in employment. This code aims to give practical guidance which will help employers, trade unions, employment agencies and employees to understand not only the provisions of the Race Relations Act and their implications, but also how best they can implement policies to eliminate racial discrimination and to enhance equality of employment. This code covers a variety of areas including recruitment, training and appraisal.

Responsibilities to consumers

Any product or service that is provided to the market-place must meet certain standards. Some of these standards are established by law, some by voluntary codes of practice within an industry, and others are set by individual businesses.

Before the 1960s, consumers had very little protection under the law. They had to rely on their own common sense. The Latin expression *caveat emptor* – 'let the buyer beware' – applied.

Businesses supply goods or services for consumers in return for payment. The legal system exists to provide a framework within which transactions can take place, and to provide a means of settling disputes. Large or well-developed organisations often deal with relatively small consumers, so there is a need for the law to make sure that this inequality in bargaining power is not abused.

Task

When did you last make a complaint to a shop about something you had bought? How did you make the complaint? What rights were you aware of? What was the outcome of your complaint?

How do disputes arise?

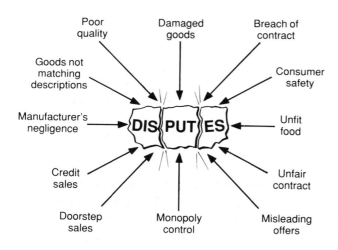

Figure 15.8 Some causes of disputes

Damaged or poor quality goods. It quite often happens that purchased goods do not function properly. They may have been damaged in transit or they may be of poor quality and not suitable for the purpose for which they are intended.

Goods not matching descriptions. Goods may not be as described on the packaging or in an advertisement.

Manufacturer's negligence. Faulty manufacturing processes or bad design might lead to the personal injury of the consumer or damage to other goods. For example, a faulty electrical component might cause fire.

Breach of contract. This could include the failure of the supplier to supply, a failure to meet the required quality, or a failure to supply by a given date. For example, a shop selling bridal gowns might fail to supply the dress by the agreed date.

Consumer safety. Goods may not be safe and could cause injury to consumers.

Unfit food. Eating unfit food can have particularly unpleasant consequences and consumers need to be protected against this.

Misleading offers. Consumers can easily be misled by offers, bargains and their rights concerning sales items.

Unfair contracts. Contracts may contain exclusion clauses or disclaimers which might make the relationship between the buyer and the seller unreasonable. It would be unacceptable for a company to disclaim responsibility for an injury caused by its own negligence.

Doorstep sales. There need to be guidelines to protect clients who might have been intimidated into buying goods from doorstep salespeople, particularly if these goods are expensive and have been bought on credit.

Credit sales. Customers 'buying now and paying later' over an extended period leave themselves open to abuse. They could well be charged excessive interest rates, pay large administration costs or be tied to an expensive maintenance agreement.

Monopoly control. Monopolies and mergers produce a situation where one or just a few companies control a market. Lack of competition can be to the disadvantage of consumers in terms of quality and prices.

Task

Interview a selection of 20 consumers to find out the sorts of disputes they have been involved in with sellers. Do most complaints fit into a small number of headings, or do their complaints go right across a wide range of areas? What actions did consumers take in each case? Is there scope for more consumer protection? If so, what form should it take?

Legal processes of consumer protection

The consumer may need help to ensure that he or she gets a fair deal when making an exchange with an organisation. Various Acts of Parliament set out to ensure that organisations keep to their responsibilities.

The **criminal justice system** deals with cases where the laws of the country have been broken. These laws attempt to protect members of society and to punish offenders whose actions have been harmful to the community. Cases might, for example, be brought to court for dishonesty and for selling unhygienic foodstuffs. Punishments could be fines, imprisonment or both.

The **civil law** is concerned with disputes between individuals and groups. Laws have been built up over the years dealing with buying and selling activities. Laws related to **contracts** set out the obligations that individuals have to each other every time they enter into an agreement, while the law of **torts** protects individuals and groups from each others' actions, particularly if an individual or group suffers injury as a result of these actions. Individuals and groups enforce their rights by suing in the civil courts.

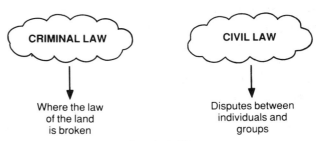

Figure 15.9 Criminal and civil law

Consumer laws

Numerous Acts of Parliament are concerned with consumer protection. Although it is not possible to know each Act in detail, it is necessary to understand the reasons for the more important Acts, and their general effects. They all create legal responsibilities for organisations.

We shall look at these Acts under three main headings (see Figure 15.10). **Competition** laws, which are concerned with creating a healthy climate of competition within the economy, are the subject of a separate section later in this chapter.

Figure 15.10 The three divisions of consumer laws

The provisions of **credit** laws cover most forms of credit transactions. Under the **Consumer Credit Act** all businesses involved in some way with credit have to be licensed by the Office of Fair Trading. Advertisements offering credit have to state the annual percentage rate of interest (APR) so that consumers can compare the true cost of one credit offer with another. It is illegal for traders to send you a credit card that you have not asked for and, if you are refused credit, you can ask for the name and address of the credit reference agency that has reported you as a bad risk. You can then put the matter to rights if the refusal has been based on false information.

We now turn to Acts covering the quality of goods or services.

The Sale of Goods Act

Sellers must provide goods that are of '**merchantable quality**' – that is, they must not be damaged or broken. Goods sold must also be **fit for the purpose** intended. If you bought a pair of shoes and they fell apart at the seams within a week, they would not have been fit for the purposes for which they were sold – serving as footwear.

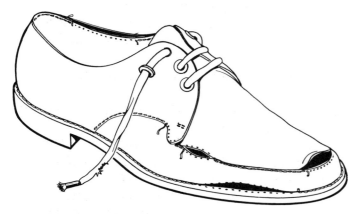

Figure 15.11 Unfit!

Under this law you can ask for replacements if goods do not meet the requirements you specified to the seller. For example, if you bought spare parts for your car from a garage on the understanding that they were for a Mini, and found that they would only fit a larger car, you would be within your rights to ask for your money back or replacements.

The Trades Description Act

The description given of the goods forms part of the contract that the buyer makes with the seller. This Act makes it a criminal offence for a trader to describe goods falsely. A type of case frequently prosecuted under this Act is the turning back of mileometers on used cars to make them appear less used.

Figure 15.12 Won't fit!

The main objective of the Trades Description Act is thus quite straightforward – descriptions of goods and services must be accurate. Terms like 'waterproof' and 'shrinkproof', if used, must be genuine.

The Weights and Measures Act

The aim of this Act is to ensure that consumers receive the actual quantity of a product that they believe they are buying. For example, pre-packed items must have a declaration of the quantity contained within the pack. It is an offence to give 'short weight'.

The Food and Drugs Act

This Act is concerned with the contents of foodstuffs and medicines. The government needs to control this area of trading so that the public is not led into buying harmful substances. Some items have to carry warnings – tins of kidney beans, for example, must have clear instructions that they need to be boiled for a fair length of time before they can be eaten.

The Act lays down minimum contents for various foodstuffs. For example, a sausage can only be called a sausage if it contains a certain amount of meat. Similar rules apply to items like Cornish pasties and beefburgers.

The contents of medicines are strictly controlled by this Act. Certain substances are not allowed at all.

Case Study – Food safety

Safety laws are passed both to protect employees at work, and to provide safety standards for the users of particular products.

Workers in a modern food processing plant are used to following strict procedures aimed at ensuring hygienic (i.e. germ-free) working conditions. For example, they must usually take off watches and rings, put on a hairnet and hat, a coat that is laundered daily and a pair of wellington boots. Any dressings on cuts or grazes must be replaced by metal-lined plasters that can be found by metal detectors should they fall off. There are several other rules that have to be followed.

Despite these precautions, between 1982 and 1989 the number of reported cases of food poisoning tripled to 52 700. Food manufacturers' sales and profits were hit by scare after scare, from salmonella to listeria, from botulism to bovine spongiform encephalopathy ('mad cow disease').

In January 1991 the government brought in a new Food Safety Act, giving environmental health officers the power to shut down offending premises iimmediately, and to seize suspect food before it

reaches shops. Regulations on refrigeration temperatures, chemical residues in food and the use of certain technologies have been tightened, and from now on all food premises will be compulsorily registered. Staff training has to improve. Ministers have the power to oversee the introduction of new technologies such as irradiation. Perishable foods must carry 'eat by' rather than 'sell by' dates.

The EC has decreed that member governments must achieve adequate standards of inspection at the point of production by 1993.

1   *Why is food safety so important?*
2   *Could it be left to manufacturers and retailers of foodstuffs to regulate their own trades and industry?*
3   *Why is it necessary to update good laws constantly?*
4   *Comment on the likely effect of the new laws on:*
   a *the production of ood*
   b *the sale of food*
   c *the quality of food*
   d *the price of food*
   e *consumers*
   f *the number of food producers in the industry*
   g *the use of new technology in food production.*

Sources of consumer help and advice

There are numerous sources of help and advice for consumers, providing opportunities for people to follow up complaints and grievances. It is therefore important to consider carefully the circumstances of each grievance before deciding on the most appropriate way forward. Through these channels, consumers and bodies representing consumer interests are able to put pressure on organisations to meet their responsibilities in full.

The **Office of Fair Trading,** a government body, was set up to look after the interests of consumers and traders. It publishes a wide variety of information, and encourages businesses to issue codes of practice to raise the standards of their service. A trader who persists in breaking the law must give an assurance that he will mend his ways. As we shall see later, the OFT also keeps an eye on anti-competitive practices, monopolies and mergers and might suggest changes in the law.

The **National Consumer Council** represents the consumer to the government, nationalised industries, public services and businesses. It also carries out research and publishes its recommendations.

Citizens' Advice Bureaux, of which there are some 900 in various parts of the country, cover many aspects of day-to-day life. A CAB will often agree to act as a 'go-between' in disputes between traders and consumers.

Local authorities have **trading standards departments** that investigate complaints about misleading offers or prices, inaccurate weights and measures, and consumer credit.

Environmental health departments enforce legislation covering the health aspects of food – or example, unfit food, or unhygienic storage, preparation or serving of food.

Nationalised industries are vast monopolies with the potential to put consumers in a weak position. **Consumer and consultative councils** represent consumers and aim to prevent the misuse of monopoly power.

Standard setters

The **British Standards Institution** is financed by voluntary subscriptions and government grants. Its primary concern is with setting up standards that are acceptable to both manufacturers and consumers. Goods of a certain standard are allowed to bear the BSI kitemark, showing consumers that the product has passed the appropriate tests.

Professional and trade associations promote the interests of their members as well as the

development of a particular product or service area. In order to protect consumers their members often agree to abide by voluntary codes of practice. These codes aim to keep up standards and will often set up funds to safeguard consumers' money. For example, the Association of British Travel Agents (ABTA) will refund money to holidaymakers should a member company fail.

Independent consumer groups and the media

The **Consumers' Association** examines goods and services offered to the public and publishes the results of its research in *Which?* This magazine was founded in 1957 and has developed a circulation of over half a million. It has become an invaluable source of information for consumers.

The National Federation of Consumer Groups is a coordinating body for voluntary local consumer groups. Local groups survey local goods and services, publish reports and campaign for changes.

There is no doubt that, when consumers' rights and obligations are abused or when dangerous goods are brought into the market-place, feelings run high. The **media** – newspapers, television and radio – increasingly become involved in campaigns for changes. High TV viewing figures, in particular, clearly demonstrate the public's interest.

Case Study – Ice-creams found to contain bacteria

The report below is adapted from an article in *The Independent* newspaper on 4 August 1989.

'Nearly half of the ice-creams tested by a consumer group contained levels of bacteria which were unsafe. Eight could have caused food poisoning.

'In the study, published by *Which?* magazine, 21

ice-creams were unsatisfactory. Seven soft ones, sold from vans, had bacteria counts way over the government safety standards.

'Inspectors bought ice-cream cones from 23 vans and 24 shops and cafes. The ice-cream included scoops, wrapped blocks and soft ice-cream. The soft ice-cream was the most contaminated. Twelve out of twenty-eight soft ice-cream cones had high bacteria levels. Nineteen of the scoops failed the bacteria count test. Wrapped ice-cream caused no problems, passing the test with flying colours.'

1 *Name the organisation that publishes* Which?
2 *What does this organisation do?*
3 *How did* Which? *magazine:*
   a *collect information about different types of ice cream?*
   b *make the public aware of the findings?*
4 *How is the* Which? *report likely to affect:*
   a *ice-cream consumers?*
   b *ice-cream retailers?*
   c *ice-cream manufacturers?*
5 *How does government try to maintain standards in the food industry?*

Competition policy

Organisations in modern society frequently have to compete. Petrol stations compete to make sales, as do fast food outlets, cafes and pubs. Colleges compete for students and hospitals compete to provide patient services.

Competition is an essential element in the efficient working of markets. It encourages enterprise, productivity and choice. In doing so, it enables consumers to buy the goods they want at the best possible price. By encouraging efficiency in industry, competition in the domestic market also contributes to our international competitiveness.

The overall aim of United Kingdom competition policy is to encourage and enhance the competitive process. When that process is adversely affected, the law provides a number of ways in which the situation can be examined and, if necessary, altered.

Task

Do you think that competition should operate freely in all markets? Can you think of exceptions to the general principle? Explain why you think these exceptions should exist.

Competition is not regarded as an end in itself. With some exceptions, there is no assumption that a particular type of action or a particular situation is necessarily wrong. The legislation provides for case-by-case examination, and only when a matter is found to be, or likely to be, against the public interest can it be prohibited.

Task

Search the national press for examples of cases where actions by companies were thought to be anti-competitive. Why were the actions regarded as against the public interest? What were the government rulings in each case?

The administrative framework

Overall responsibility for competition policy is in the hands of the **Secretary of State for Trade and Industry**. Working with the Secretary of State are two bodies specifically set up to deal with matters affecting competition. They are the **Office of Fair Trading** and the **Monopolies and Mergers Commission**. Both organisations are given specific roles and responsibilities by Act of Parliament. The **Restrictive Practices Court** also has an important role.

The Director General of the OFT acts very much as a watchdog, keeping an eye on commerce as a whole, carrying out initial enquiries, calling for in-depth investigations by the Commission and, depending on the response of the Secretary of State to the Commission's recommendations, asking companies for specific undertakings and then watching them. He or she also maintains a register of **restrictive trading agreements** and may refer these agreements to the Restrictive Practices Court.

The Commission has no power to initiate enquiries. It investigates specific markets or the actions of companies in detail and decides what is and what is not in the public interest.

The final authority to prohibit actions rests either with the Secretary of State or with the Restrictive Practices Court in the case of restrictive agreements or the imposition of minimum resale prices.

The legal framework

United Kingdom competition law is made up of four principal Acts of Parliament, dealing with separate aspects of competition policy. They are the Fair Trading Act 1973, the Restrictive Trade Practices Act 1976, the Resale Prices Act 1976 and the Competition Act 1980. Each Act gives the Director General of the OFT and the Commission, or the Restrictive Practices Court, different responsibilities. These laws can be split into two categories:

- In the case of the Restrictive Trade Practices Act and the Resale Prices Act, action is taken in the courts.

- In the case of the Fair Trading Act and the Competition Act, practices are examined by the Director General, the Commission and the Secretary of State.

Task

Keep a diary of newspaper cuttings dealing with cases involving the four laws relating to competition. What happens to companies that infringe these laws?

Monopolies

Where a company or group of companies has market power, there is the potential for the market to be harmed in a number of ways. Excessive prices, reductions in the level of service and unfair restrictions on entry into the market are typical examples of what can happen, in the absence of effective competition. This will harm consumers.

Defining a monopoly

Although we normally think of a **monopoly** as the sole supplier to a particular market, United Kingdom law uses a wider definition. Under the Fair Trading Act, a monopoly is defined first as a situation where a company supplies or buys 25 per cent or more of all goods or services of a particular

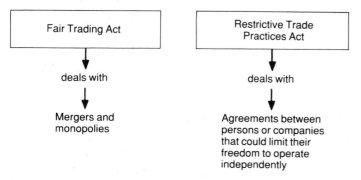

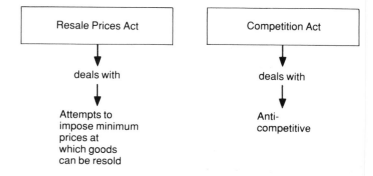

Figure 15.13 Four competition Acts

type in the whole country or in a particular area (e.g. the South East).

The Act also defines a complex monopoly as a situation where a group of companies that together have 25 per cent of the market all behave in some way that affects competition.

Task

Think of examples of national or local monopolies. In each case try to suggest why the monopoly position might help consumers, or be harmful to them. How would you go about testing this?

The public interest

There is no assumption that monopolies are wrong in themselves. The invention of a new device, for example, will inevitably make the inventor a monopolist to start with, even if the device provides a benefit to the public. The 1973 Act simply defines situations where it is *possible* that market power could be misused, and recognises that this *may* be against the public interest. It is for the Commission to say what is and what is not in **the public interest.**

Dealing with monopolies

The Director General keeps a constant eye on British industry, looking at how major companies are operating, and at allegations and complaints.

Once he or she feels that there may be evidence of monopoly malpractice in a particular industry, the case is referred to the Commission. However, at this stage no companies are named; it is simply suggested that the Commission should investigate a particular aspect of competition (e.g. prices) in that industry.

The Commission then investigates and makes a report to the Secretary of State, with suggestions for possible action. The Secretary and the Director General then decide what should be done. This might involve asking companies to make promises to change, or asking for promises backed up with measures to make sure that the promises are kept.

```
┌─────────────────────────┐
│ Director General keeps an│
│ eye on all industries    │
└─────────────────────────┘
            │
            ▼
┌─────────────────────────┐
│ Suspects malpractice in  │
│ a particular industry    │
└─────────────────────────┘
            │
            ▼
┌─────────────────────────┐
│ Asks Commission to       │
│ investigate particular   │
│ industry without naming  │
│ suspected companies      │
└─────────────────────────┘
            │
            ▼
┌─────────────────────────┐
│ Commission reports findings│
└─────────────────────────┘
            │
            ▼
┌─────────────────────────┐
│ Actions taken by Director│
│ General and Secretary    │
│ of State                 │
└─────────────────────────┘
```

Figure 15.14 How monopoly malpractices are handled

Case Study – Newspaper distribution

In October 1991, the Office of Fair Trading decided not to refer the distribution of national newspapers to the Monopolies and Mergers Commission. The decision was described as a gross injustice by the National Federation of Retail Newsagents, which represents about 30 000 small newsagents and which campaigned for the enquiry.

Newspaper and magazine distribution in the UK is dominated by three wholesalers which account for more than 80 per cent of the market between them. WH Smith speaks for a 45 per cent share, followed by John Menzies at about 25 per cent and Surridge

Dawson at around 10 per cent. The balance is accounted for by local wholesalers.

Newsagents are worried about changes in the distribution network which have led to major wholesalers obtaining exclusive distribution rights for titles in a particular area. The complaints were about a lack of alternative wholesalers for newspapers and magazines in their area, increases in carriage charges, and being forced to stock publications they did not want. Although the OFT admitted there were restraints on competition in the way newspapers were distributed, 'it could see no reason for believing that there is any loss to the public sufficient to justify a reference'.

However, the OFT was concerned that there may be restrictive agreements between wholesalers. It was considering court action against one such local agreement in the Blackpool–Preston area. The OFT found that one wholesaler had agreed not to supply certain newspapers and magazines to newsagents in the Preston area in return for another wholesaler agreeing not to supply these newspapers and magazines in the Blackpool area.

1 *Why is there considered to be a monopoly situation in newspaper and magazine distribution?*
2 *Why did retailers want this monopoly position to be investigated?*
3 *What does your local newsagent think? Perhaps you can also find out what the local wholesale manager thinks.*
4 *Does the article present any evidence of unfair monopoly practices?*
5 *Why do you think the OFT decided not to refer this case to the Commission?*
6 *Do you think the Director General was justified in failing to call for an investigation?*

Anti-competitive practices

In a competitive market, companies can be expected to adopt policies intended to give them a competitive edge. This can lead to benefits in terms of efficiency, better quality goods and services, and so on. However, sometimes firms use practices which may be harmful to competition. Practices that may be acceptable in one market where competition is strong may be unacceptable in another where there is less competitive activity.

Under the Competition Act, an **anti-competitive practice** is defined as *any practice that has, or is intended to have, or is likely to have the effect of restricting or preventing competition.*

The ability of a firm to influence the market depends on its **market power**. Market power stems from

"BUY SUPERBRAND PATENTED PRODUCTS WE HAVE 90% OF ALL SALES IN THE MARKET"

SUPER BRAND

Figure 15.15 Market power

having a large share of the market, having a leading brand name, or being able in some way to prevent new firms from entering the industry (perhaps as a result of patent rights). Companies are covered by the Act if they have more than 25 per cent of a market or a turnover of more than £5 million.

If an alleged anti-competitive practice is reported to the Director General, he or she can set up an investigative team to look into it. On the basis of the investigation the Director General must decide whether he or she thinks that it is anti-competitive. If it is felt to be so, the practice can be referred to the Commission which must decide whether it is against the public interest. A report is then produced within a period of four to eight weeks. The Secretary of State and the Director General may then insist that the businesses involved abandon the practice if it is felt to be unacceptable.

Resale price maintenance

Attempts by manufacturers or suppliers to enforce a minimum price at which their goods can be resold by dealers or retailers restricts competition and can keep prices higher than they would be otherwise. Resale price maintenance is unlawful under the Resale Prices Act except for goods granted an exemption. Goods exempted at present are books and pharmaceuticals.

Task

Why do you think that books and pharmaceuticals are exempted by the Resale Prices Act? Try to find out by interviewing somebody in the book trade. You may find that different opinions are given by the small and the large bookshops.

Under the 1976 Act it is unlawful to try to establish minimum prices. It is also unlawful to stop supplies or to offer less favourable terms to dealers whom the supplier believes to be responsible for price cutting. A supplier is, however, entitled to withhold goods from a dealer who is pricing them as 'loss leaders' (that is, as goods sold at a loss in order to attract customers towards profitable items).

The Director General has the power to seek a court injunction to force the parties involved to scrap a retail price agreement.

Mergers

Under the Fair Trading Act, a **merger** is said to take place when two or more companies 'cease to be distinct'. The aim of competition policy is not to prejudge mergers but to examine the merits of individual mergers. The advantages in each case must be weighed up against the disadvantages.

The 1973 Act lays down two tests to decide whether a particular merger can be investigated:

- *the assets test* – that the total gross assets of the company to be taken over exceed £30 million in value
- *the market-share test* – that, as a result of the merger, 25 per cent or more of the supply or purchase of goods or services of a particular description in the United Kingdom or a substantial part of it comes under the control of the merging enterprise.

The critical factor in deciding whether a merger should be allowed to take place is again the public interest. Those most likely to cause concern are **horizontal mergers**, where two companies supplying the same sort of product or service combine. However, vertical and conglomerate mergers may also be investigated.

Companies are expected to notify the Director General if they hope to merge. The Director General will conduct a preliminary investigation before deciding whether to advise the Secretary of State to refer the merger to the Commission. Companies are stopped from acquiring each other's shares while the investigation takes place. If they have already started to merge they will be ordered not to join their operations together. The Commission reports to the Secretary of State who decides, in consultation with the Director General, whether or not the merger is in the public interest.

Case Study – A merger in the public interest?

Two companies are hoping to merge. At present one company has 32 per cent of the market and the other has 26 per cent. The assets of each company are in excess of £50 million.

These companies both manufacture finished goods for retail sale. Because of the perceived high quality of their product, they will only deal with selected retail outlets, and under the new (merged) company structure these outlets will be allowed to sell the product only if they agree to a mark-up of exactly 35 per cent. In addition there will be a number of regulations as to how the product can be displayed and offered to customers. The companies are confident that the new company will shortly capture all of this exciting and rapidly developing market.

Prices are expected to remain high in this industry, and product performance and quality are likely to improve rapidly with breakthroughs in research and development. The UK is a world leader in this product, and many new jobs will be created. UK prices compare favourably with those of the foreign competition.

1 List the facts making is likely that this proposed merger would be referred to the Commission.
2 What arguments can be put in favour of this merger?
3 What do you think the likely outcome would be?

Restrictive trade practices

All commerce is based on agreements of one form or another. The buying and selling of goods and services would be impossible without them. In such agreements, businesses agree to do certain things. However, some of these commitments may restrict competition.

The Restrictive Trades Practices Act covers agreements affecting goods and services. Companies must **register** certain types of agreement that they make with other companies. These may cover all sorts or areas, including:

● restrictions on prices or charges
● conditions on which business is conducted
● geographical divisions of business
● people with whom business can take place
● the quantity of goods to be produced
● the manufacturing process to be used.

Agreements can be in any form, including the spoken word. All such agreements must be registered.

The Director General of Fair Trading refers suspect agreements to the Restrictive Practices Court, which will strike down any restrictions found to be against the public interest. Parties to an agreement therefore need to be able to prove to the Court that there are real benefits from their restrictive practices.

Task

Describe the roles of the following in the United Kingdom's competition policy:

a the Director General of Fair Trading
b the Secretary of State for Trade and Industry
c the Monopolies and Mergers Commission
d the Restrictive Practices Court.

European Community competition law

The European Community has its own competition regulations which in a number of cases go above and beyond national laws. Article 85 of the Treaty of Rome forbids agreements which may adversely affect trade between the 12 member states, and in particular which have as their object a limitation of competition within the European market. This includes price fixing, market sharing, restriction of production or technical development, and the imposition of discriminatory terms of supply. Such agreements are automatically not allowed unless given an exemption by the European Commission.

A European Merger Control Regulation allows the European Commission to control mergers which have a 'community dimension'. This is defined as those mergers where the parties have a total worldwide turnover exceeding 5 billion ECU and at least two of the parties have a Community turnover exceeding 250 million ECU unless each of the undertakings achieves more than two-thirds of its turnover in one and the same Member State. Special rules apply for banking, financial, and insurance institutions.

The role of the European Commission

The European Commission is directly responsible for the application of European legislation in the United Kingdom. The Commission may act on the basis of agreements which have been made before them, on complaints or on their own initiative. They may seek information in writing or by inspectors making visits to firms who would always be accompanied by staff from the Director General's Office. Commission inspectors have wide-ranging powers to ask questions and to obtain information. Before deciding that a law has been broken, the Commission issues a statement of objection to the parties concerned, who then have the opportunity to reply to the Commission, both in writing and orally, before representatives of Member States. The European Commission also hears the opinion of an advisory committee of competition experts from Member States, including a representative of the Director General.

Task

The section above looks in detail at UK competition policy. The student should sort out the detail and concentrate on:

a understanding the four main areas covered by legislation
b the main officials responsible for putting these laws into effect
c actions which can be taken to create a more competitive environment.

A good way of studying this area is to follow cases reported in the press. This should reinforce the idea of varying interpretations of the 'public interest'.

Case Study – Restrictive practices by Tetra Pak

In October 1991, the European Commission fined Tetra Pak, the Swedish/Swiss company that invented sterilised packaging for liquids, a record £52.5 million for abuse of its dominant market position. The Commission's investigation began as the result of a complaint in 1983 by an Italian competitor, Elopak.

Tetra Pak was accused primarily of adopting restrictive contract clauses. Sir Leon Brittan, the Commissioner responsible for competition policy, said: 'The infringements have involved almost all products manufactured by Tetra Pak and have had a damaging impact on competition in all EC member states.'

By insisting that customers use only Tetra Pak packaging machines and cartons, the company effectively stifled competition. Product guarantees were made dependent on this commitment. The company also controlled delivery and fitting of spare parts for machinery owned or rented, and in many contracts imposed a monthly maintenance charge that was adjusted in line with customer loyalty rather than the actual maintenance required. Rental agreements ran for a minimum of three years – nine in the case of Italy – and sometimes included punitive discretionary penalties for companies that allowed contracts to lapse. Carton labelling and, in some cases, monthly reports were required of clients, who risked finding themselves host to surprise inspections.

The measures ensured that the company could safely adopt predatory pricing policies. The costs of machines and cartons in different member states varied by factors of 300 per cent and 50 per cent respectively.

Tetra Pak is appealing to the European Court of Justice.

1 Why was the European Commission concerned with this case of abuse?
2 What seem to be the most telling allegations of abuse against Tetra Pak?
3 Give examples of the restrictive practices involved.
4 Which of these practices seem to be in the public interest and which against the public interest?
5 Why do you think Tetra Pak employed these restrictive practices?
6 What do you think will be the verdict of the Court of Justice?

Responsibilities for financial reporting

All public companies must produce an annual set of audited financial statements, as we saw in Chapter 11. The auditors need to be able to say that they have seen a true and fair picture of the financial state of a particular company.

However, in 1991 it became very obvious that clarification was needed as to exactly who should be held responsible for presenting that true and fair picture. A number of companies whose accounts had been recently audited found themselves in trouble when it came to light that their figures were a gross misrepresentation of the truth. It has been apparent for a number of years that it is almost impossible for an external auditor to get a true picture of company affairs. Auditors work with the set of figures that the company presents to them. As lawsuits multiply amid the collapse of unstable business empires whose accounts have been passed by some of the most distinguished accountancy firms in the land, auditing looks to be an increasingly pointless, if expensive, exercise.

In October 1991, the Auditing Practices Board proposed changes to make it clear that it was a company's board of directors, rather than its auditors, who were primarily responsible for uncovering and reporting fraudulent practices. Such practices may include devices for inflating profits and disguising the receipts from one-off transactions – such as the sale of land or other assets – as though they were part of a company's continuing income.

A piece of government legislation passed in October 1991 makes it an offence for auditors not to be registered with one of the four auditing institutes recognised as registered supervisory bodies (RSBs).

It is the task of the RSBs to monitor the quality of audit work performed by their members. An RSB may send in an inspector to any firm it sees fit. Incoming auditors must now report on their predecessors if they discover poor quality work. At the same time a Financial Reporting Council has been established. This organisation is made up of members from across the business world. It now has the responsibility of making and policing the rules under which companies report, so removing this power away from accountancy institutes.

Ecological and environmental responsibilities

Your environment is everything that surrounds you – where you live, the people you know, the living and non-living things around you:

Environment to each must be,
All that is, that isn't me.

All living things have four vital needs:

SUN	EARTH
AIR	WATER

For millions of years, plants and animals have been on this planet. For 40 000 years they have shared it with us, humankind. In the last few decades, however, we have begun to destroy this world by damaging the balance of our four vital needs.

- We damage the balance of sunlight by making holes in the ozone layer.
- We fill the air with harmful gases.
- We put acid into the rain.
- We poison the earth with chemicals.

Everything we do to our environment affects us and every other thing which shares this world with us.

The surge of **environmental awareness** reinforced by pressure groups and political and media activity has resulted in an important cultural shift – environmental concern has joined other commonly held values. *It is a shift that organisations cannot escape.*

The environmental challenges to industry are now well established. First, there is **regulation.** Regulation can be seen as a relatively quick and visible way of changing industries' behaviour. In Britain, the Environmental Protection Act – and specifically 'integrated pollution control' – has changed the basis of pollution regulation. Membership of the European Community also forces the UK to adopt community standards.

Perhaps more important is **consumer pressure.** More consumers are looking for products that are 'ecologically friendly'. There is also **investor pressure** – those who provide finance for businesses are increasingly questioning the environmental soundness of their investments.

From the inside there is **employee pressure.** People who are concerned citizens at home do not become environmental slobs when they arrive at work. Management pressure is also very important. For example, the Advisory Committee on Business and the Environment, set up to help thrash out environmental issues with the government, is made up of senior managers from major companies.

The Environmental Protection Act 1990

This Act created two new systems for regulating industrial pollution. **Integrated pollution control** (IPC) will apply to more than 5000 existing industrial processes with the largest pollution potential, and will regulate all their releases to land, water and air. It will be enforced by an Inspectorate of Pollution. The second system, to be enforced by local authorities, will cover 27 000 **complex processes**, and will control only their emissions to air. Under both systems, operators will have to employ the 'best available techniques not entailing excessive cost', to minimise releases of the most polluting substances, and to 'render harmless' all releases from their processes.

IPC extends the sorts of control previously applied only to air pollutants to all the wastes – gases, solids and liquids – generated by companies. The new Inspectorate will ensure that the least environmentally damaging solution overall – the 'best practicable environmental option' or **Bpeo** – is chosen to deal with these.

Task

Obtain some petroleum jelly, which you can get in a chemist's shop. Take six stiff white cards and

smear them with some of the jelly. Place the cards in a variety of places – some where you would expect the air to be clean (perhaps in a tree) and some where it is dirty (maybe near a busy street). Leave the cards in place for a few days and then collect them. Write down the signs of pollution you found and what they appeared to be from.

Develop a proposal for reducing some of these pollutants. Try to make your proposal one that fits in with the notion of being the best practicable environmental option – Bpeo.

Responsibility for pollution

There can be no doubt that we must all play a responsible part in preventing or reducing pollution. Individuals and organisations can work to control the pollution they cause. An essential starting point is an awareness of pollution and its causes.

Water pollution

Much **water pollution** comes from factories, which take fresh water in from a river, use it in a manufacturing process, and then discharge it back into the river. The discharge often contains chemicals and oils which kill fish and other living things in their food chain. Other causes of water pollution are agricultural waste and chemicals which seep through the soil into rivers and lakes.

Oil is a potent pollutant. In March 1989, the ship the Exxon Valdez poured more than 10 million gallons of oil into Prince William Sound in Alaska, following which millions of fish and birds died. When sea-birds dive through oily waters the oil sticks to their feathers, which then can no longer keep out the cold and wet. The birds die if the oil is not cleaned off.

Air pollution

As yet, we have not been able to harvest the forces of wind, sun or water to meet all our energy needs, and we will probably continue using coal, oil and gas for many more years. These are responsible for a lot of **air pollution**. Power stations burning coal or oil pour dangerous sulphur dioxide into the air. Car and lorry exhausts add nitrogen oxide.

To produce one unit of electricity, a power station sends into the air ten grams of sulphur, three grams of nitrogen oxide and a thousand grams of carbon dioxide. One kilogram will fill 20 balloons.

Task

Check back on your electricity reading chart at home and find out how many units of electricity your family uses in a day. Multiply your units by the amounts of pollution given in the text to discover how much your family adds to air pollution from your use of electrical power alone.

Noise pollution

Noise is experienced when the ear picks up unwanted vibrations, most of which come from machinery of some kind. At its most intense – for example a jet plane taking off – noise can cause actual physical pain.

New roads can bring the nuisance of traffic noise into people's homes, often in areas which previously enjoyed peace and quiet. New road developments to carry freight from the Channel Tunnel are a case in point.

Noise is particularly annoying at night, when it can interrupt sleep. There is nothing new in this. In the times of the Roman Empire the capital's residents complained so vigorously about the disturbance caused by cart traffic that the Emperor Augustus put a ban on all carts leaving or entering Rome at night!

Case Study – Public concern about the environment

The public's attitude towards the environment is a key influence on organisational activity. Opinion polls suggest that most people's concern for the environment is a little fickle and strongly influenced by media coverage.

When times are good and the economy is growing, people worry about the fate of the planet and that of future generations. When recession bites, these concerns tend to be pushed aside by more immediate concerns about personal security. However, polls do indicate that a substantial proportion of the population – about a fifth – have had their environmental consciousness raised permanently.

For example, once a month for a number of years MORI has been asking the public: 'What would you say is the most important issue facing Britain today?' and 'What do you see as other important issues?'. In the late 1980s the environment appeared high on the public's agenda of concerns.

MORI has also been asking people whether they have done any one of twelve 'green activities' in the last year or two. These include walking in the countryside, buying 'green' products in supermarkets, joining an environmental group and writing letters on environmental issues to MPs and newspapers. Those who answer 'yes' to five or more of these activities are counted as **environmental activists**. The percentage of these rose from 14 in 1988 to 31 in 1991.

1 *What conclusions would you draw from the bar-chart?*
2 *Do you feel that raised environmental awareness is likely to be a short-term or long-term trend?*
3 *What are the implications for organisational activities?*
4 *Design an action plan for your organisation to improve its environmental consciousness.*
5 *Carry out a market research survey along the lines set out by the MORI survey. Do your findings coincide with the MORI findings? Explain your results and compare them with the MORI survey.*

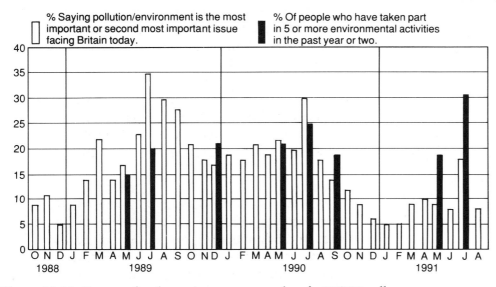

Figure 15.16 **Concern for the environment – results of a MORI poll**

Green audits

In 1986 a new environmental law was passed in the United States. It did not require organisations to fix anything, install anything or clean up anything. All it obliged them to do was submit (to the Environmental Protection Agency) an annual list of the quantities of hazardous chemicals they had released into the environment. The Agency would publish the information in a Toxics Release Inventory. The aim was to create a massive shift in power away from government and industrial regulation and towards the public.

Local communities in the USA are now able to knock on companies' doors armed with detailed information about what is being put into their air and water. Environmental groups have found the inventory a valuable campaigning resource. In industry, senior management and other employees have started asking pointed questions about why such large amounts of costly raw materials and valuable products are being thrown away. Many businesses have been able to set up new strategies for saving waste and cutting down on pollution. In Britain there is growing pressure for **environmental auditing**. The Environmental Protection Act paved the way for further registers on industrial pollution, waste disposal sites, contaminated land and so on.

Some of the 'green' investment funds have joined environmentalists in arguing for compulsory audits which provide information on companies' raw material and energy consumption as well as pollution. The Trades Union Congress (TUC) has urged its members to demand **green audits** in workplace negotiations.

Leading oil and chemical companies have been running auditing programmes since the 1970s. These are generally intended to show up weaknesses in environmental management systems and breaches in internal standards. Companies also like to take an audit of another company's environmental legacy before considering a merger. The findings of such audits are intended for management's eyes, rather than the public's.

In 1990, the European Commission produced a draft idea to enforce environmental audits on companies in a number of leading industrial sectors. However, the Commission is now expected to suggest only a voluntary scheme.

Task

Carry out a rough environmental audit of the place where you work. Are there any obvious areas for environmental improvement? Are there policies which could be changed to improve the environment?

Costs and benefits of organisational activity

When weighing up the effects of any activity it is necessary to assess:

- who are the winners and who are the losers
- the size of their gain or loss.

This is difficult because people have varying views and give different values to things. Whereas one person would not mind the property next door being converted to a fish and chip shop, another would regard this as an absolute disaster. Where one person sees a new road as being a benefit because it reduces the time taken to get to work, another sees it as a danger to children. Where one person sees fast food outlets as being an improvement to the quality of life, another sees them as representing unhealthy eating standards.

Task

List what you consider to be the benefits of fast good outlets. Who benefits? How do they benefit?

Now list the disadvantages. Who suffers? How do they suffer? Is it possible to say whether the disadvantages outweigh the advantages?

Even when it is possible to measure costs and benefits in money terms, it is easy to underestimate the 'real' effects. For example, if a new office development creates 100 jobs paying average salaries of £10 000, it is quite easy to compute the increased earnings in the area. However, it is impossible to attach a value to the excitement felt by somebody who is being taken on to work in the office and who has not worked for the previous five years. Attaching money values to costs and benefits, therefore, can at best be only a very rough measure. Costs and benefits can be **private** or **social**.

Private costs and benefits

When an individual or organisation carries out a project, costs and benefits are calculated from a private point of view. For example, when a business decides to build an extension it will weigh up the extra costs and revenues that will flow from that extension.

Social costs and benefits

Social costs and benefits go beyond the individual or group to consider all the individuals and groups who will be affected by an action or policy. If a business wants to build an extension, the local planning authority takes into consideration all the other groups and individuals who would be affected – the builder of the extension and his employees, the people who would work in the new extension, the implications for neighbours, and so on.

Task

Produce a report seeking planning permission for a proposed service station. Your particular responsibility is to explain the benefits that the new station will bring to local people. In your report, you are expected to explain the various ways in which a service station 'adds value' to the products it sells – fuels and lubricants, tyres and accessories, items for the shop – to the advantage of customers.

There are many possible ways of setting out your report, but you should aim for clarity and ease of reading. The sequence of thoughts must be simple to follow. Here is one possibility:

Title. This tells the reader what the report is about.

Contents list. This reveals in more detail what the report is about.

Terms of reference. This informs the reader what you were asked to do. You could say: 'I have been asked to study the proposed service station and report on the benefits it would provide for the community. The report will be presented to the planning committee.'

Procedure. This explains how you set about collecting the information. Did you write to people to ask for their opinions? Did you carry out face-to-face interviews? Did you visit other service stations in nearby towns?

Findings. This could well be the longest part of the report. It should give all the facts you have collected.

Summing up. This is a brief reminder of your findings.

Recommendations. These are the actions you think should be taken by the planning committee as a result of your findings.

Signature. This tells everyone that it is your work.

Ethics

Ethics are moral principles or rules of conduct which are generally accepted by most members of a society. An ethic is a guide as to what should be done or what should not be done. It involves what one believes to be right and what is considered to be wrong. From an early age, parents, religions and society in general provide us with moral guidelines to help us to learn and form our ethical beliefs. Many ethics are reinforced in our legal system and thus provide a constraint to business activities, while others are not. In areas not covered by law, pressure groups often form to put forward their cases.

The media often bring to our attention examples of both successful and questionable business activities – insider trading of shares, the use of animals for testing cosmetic and pharmaceutical products, tobacco sponsorship, trading links with nations such as Iraq, and so on. As a result, consumers have become increasingly aware of the ethical values underlying business decisions.

A new breed of environment-friendly, caring, community-conscious corporate citizen is emerging in British industry. For example, Peterborough-based Thomas Cook is funding the building of a local hospital; Butlins is offering day visits for under-privileged children; and Cadbury raised about £500 000 for young sufferers of cerebral palsy with its 'Strollerthon', which attracted 12 000 walkers. Kentucky Fried Chicken is operating with the Tidy Britain group to remove litter and educate people on how to improve their environment.

Two factors are accelerating the switch to corporate responsibility. First, according to work carried out by both the Henley Centre and MORI, there is a massive swing away from the attitudes of the 1980s. Greed is no longer good – ethics are in.

Secondly, products are becoming increasingly similar, so that one way to differentiate products is emotionally. Companies are trying to prove they have social values, which have an emotional impact on their consumer. There are four main areas in which this can be shown: the environment, the local community, the 'fitness' of a company and its employees, and investments in the community.

Task

Produce a list of what you consider to be the ten main ingredients of an 'ethical' company. How can you as an employee contribute to the creation of company ethics?

16

Producing Goods and/or Services

This chapter is concerned with the planning and management of operations that result in the product being available to satisfy consumer needs that have been identified by the marketing process.

It is often argued that the production function in an organisation is the most difficult to understand, coordinate and carry out. This function often accounts for the largest allocation of an organisation's resources, so it is essential that managers have strategies worked out to deal with problems as they arise.

In order to analyse production, we break it down into five broad areas – product, plant, programmes, processes and people.

What is production?

An organisation exists for a purpose – it produces goods or services (or sometimes both) as a central activity. Whereas marketing activities discover consumer needs and provide the direction for an organisation's activities to fulfil those needs, **production** is the process of making the finished outputs available for the market-place. During this process there is **wealth creation**.

Wealth creation provides the goods and services that we need. Almost everything we see around us has been provided through a series of wealth-creating activities, which add value at every stage to transform raw materials or **inputs** into finished goods or **outputs**. Managing this process is known as **production management** (or sometimes **operations management**). This is a key function in the organisation because without it the objectives could not be achieved.

All activities playing a part in providing goods and

Figure 16.1 Meeting objectives through the production of goods and services

services create wealth. Wealth creation therefore involves various *types* of production.

Primary production is the first essential stage in the whole production process because it is concerned with extracting the gifts of nature. Examples of primary activities are agriculture, mining, fishing and tree felling.

Secondary production may involve changing the raw materials (inputs) into finished or part-finished goods through construction or manufacture.

Companies receiving part-finished goods as their inputs, and turning these into more part-finished or finished goods, are also involved in secondary production.

Tertiary production comprises all the support services that make primary and secondary production possible. **Commercial services** such as banking and insurance do this, as well as **direct services** (e.g. teachers, police, nurses, civil servants).

Task

Set out a table like the one in Figure 16.2. Then make a short list of occupations which fall under each heading.

Primary production	Secondary production	Tertiary production	
		Commercial services	Direct services

Figure 16.2

Just as a worker on a production line adds value to an item in order to satisfy the needs of customers, a footballer also adds value, but with a service. *All* industries and *all* occupations are concerned with adding some value to a product or service so that customer satisfaction can be created. For example, managing a school involves dealing with a budget, setting a timetable, monitoring activities in and out of the classroom, creating a sense of identity, keeping parents happy and developing an overall strategy for the organisation. Such **operational** activities are not dissimilar in nature from the activities of an operations manager in a large factory.

The abilities of the production or operations team are therefore a vital element in carrying out activities designed to satisfy the needs of the customer.

Producing goods or services can be a highly complex act. Many would argue that this function is the most difficult to understand and carry out. The operations area usually demands the largest amount of capital, assets, labour and other factors, and it is important that an organisation has a definite strategy for dealing with problems as and when they arise. For example, while an operations manager must make effective use of technology and consider long-term plans, this must *not* be at the expense of day-to-day issues of the organisation – such as allowing orders to become overdue, quality to fall or morale to wane.

We can therefore say that an operations manager must be concerned with all the following issues:

- the costs of production
- the condition of the means of production (machinery etc).
- keeping production going
- health and safety
- keeping employees motivated
- keeping up-to-date with technology
- satisfying the requirements of customers
- maximising the use of plant
- minimising the use of materials.

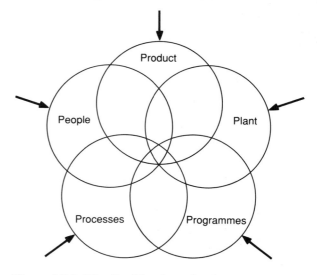

Figure 16.3 The five P's of production

328

These issues can be broken down into five broad areas, as shown in Figure 16.3. In the real world there is considerable overlap.

Case Study – Glaxo Pharmaceuticals

Glaxo is the only British company in the top ten of the world's pharmaceutical league table. The company's products are sold in virtually every country through a network of 70 subsidiaries and associate companies employing more than 30 000 staff worldwide.

Glaxo's major manufacturing unit in the UK is at Barnard Castle in County Durham, where more than 1500 people are employed. The aim is to build-up quality from the start of every process, and that each stage of a production cycle should maintain the quality, if not enhance it. For example, a large proportion of raw materials for the factory are supplied by Glaxochem Ltd, a sister company. Standards of supply for materials from both this and other suppliers are strictly controlled.

The factory has five production departments – Cephalosporins, Injections, Primary, Tablets and Topicals – each with its own high degree of specialisation and expertise. Production management is based upon product business group responsibility to achieve optimum customer service.

At short notice the factory may be called upon to meet an order from across the world for any of more than 2500 preparations, and this requires that at least 3500 types of purchased materials be held in stock. It also demands meticulous planning, to make sure that stock levels do not tie up valuable working capital.

Production schedules for the smooth and efficient operation of the factory rely on the company's sophisticated database management system which connects customer orders and forecasted requirements with production resources. The system also includes stores, accounting and quality assurance sub-systems. Glaxo's philosophy of 'get it right first time' helps to create greater certainty of success and is designed to ensure that customer requirements in a competitive environment are always met.

1 *What information from the case study reveals to you that managing operations at Glaxo's Barnard Castle factory is a highly complex task?*
2 *How does the organisation approach some of the problems of managing its operations?*

The product

An organisation's **product** is the good or service it offers to consumers. A dry cleaning service is just as much a product as is a washing machine or tumble dryer.

As we saw in Chapter 6, all organisations have to analyse what their product means to their customers. Too often in the past, organisations have ignored marketing information and developed products simply because production costs appeared to be low, or because efficient use could be made of materials; they did this instead of looking at how they could develop products to meet consumer needs. Their approach was clearly **product-led**

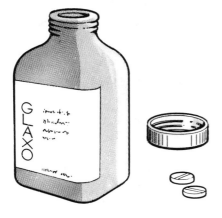

Figure 16.4 A Glaxo product

rather than **market-led.** In our modern competitive world where the wishes of the consumer are ever more demanding, it is rarely possible for organisations to survive without becoming market-led.

Case Study – Have the Cubans become market led?

After the world's largest McDonald's opened in Moscow, Cubans probably felt a little jealous. The response from Fidel Castro, Cuba's leader, was that his regime could do anything the reforming Russians could do, but without the help of the Yankee capitalists! Over recent months a chain of hamburger restaurants has sprung up on the streets of Havana.

Known locally as McCastro's, the kiosks serve burgers and one type of soft drink, but beyond that they have little in common with McDonald's. At McCastro's, surliness and incompetence are the order of the day. Despite this, the kiosks are proving popular and Cubans now munch 80 000 hamburgers daily.

Some people remain suspicious, because meat has not been widely available in Cuba for many years. One aspiring entrepreneur was recently arrested for trying to pass off cleaning rags dipped in vinegar as beefsteak. Though the ingredients remain unknown, one official newspaper in Cuba claimed the burgers are highly nutritious and contain a minimum of 60 per cent pork. It failed to identify the other 40 per cent!

1 *How have the Cubans responded to the desire of consumers to follow Western eating habits?*
2 *Have their efforts been successful? To what extent may this move have been market-led?*
3 *What might happen to the market for burgers if a McDonald's opened up in Havana? How would the Cuban kiosks have to respond?*

Research

No matter what the source of new product ideas, it would be foolhardy for an organisation to develop a new product without first conducting **research.** Research is the systematic search for facts and information to solve problems.

Market research tries to anticipate the needs of potential and existing customers by means of a thorough understanding of their behaviour patterns. **Product research** then takes this further – it uses the knowledge of consumers' needs and wants to make changes to existing products or to develop new ones.

Distinguishing between the different characteristics of consumers to develop a product to appeal to a particular group in a particular market segment is known as **differentiation.**

Where do new ideas come from?

Product developments sometimes arise out of **chance ideas.** These ideas may develop from discussions with colleagues, from suggestion schemes or from brainstorming sessions.

Market gap analysis is often used. An organisation's existing range may have a number of gaps which

Figure 16.5 McCastro's fast food

need to be investigated and filled. Gap analysis will identify under-exploited market segments so that products can be directed at them.

Organisations will look to maximise their use of **idle resources**. Machines that are not fully used are wasteful to the organisation. By developing a new product an organisation may be able to mobilise this excess capacity.

There may be a need to spread the financial risk through **product diversification**. A narrow range may present a danger, particularly in markets such as clothes where fashions change frequently.

An organisation may have a desire to gain prestige. Producing a **flagship product** may improve the image of the whole range.

Finally, an organisation may have been asked by a customer to develop and produce a product for a specific application. The product is thus produced to **special order**.

Task

Work in small groups to brainstorm ideas on the following marketing issue.

'Market research reveals that consumers are unhappy about the choice of products available for washing their cars. They feel that the products currently available have hardly changed over recent years.'

If time allows, discuss your ideas with other groups.

Design

A new product should be **designed** to meet the needs of customers. A 'new design' is a product with details that are different from earlier products intended for much the same use.

Customers should be able to identify features of the new product that are different from and better than those of competing products. Good product design is generally agreed to relate directly to commercial success.

For most major projects a **design team** is established which is led by a design manager. The team then remains with the project throughout its development.

Nowadays, computer systems help designers to develop new products and solve engineering problems. **Computer-aided design** (CAD) involves the use of a computer, a workstation and a graphics board with a magnetic pen, which enables the

The changing face of design

operator to touch symbols and select operations so that a design can be made up. This technique can be used to draw two-dimensional shapes or three-dimensional views and models. CAD has completely transformed the role of the designer.

Case Study – Design at Ford

The planning, design, engineering and development of a new car at Ford is an extremely complex process. With anything up to 15 000 parts, the modern car is the most complicated piece of equipment built in high volume.

Each new product starts with a series of detailed paper studies aimed at identifying the most competitive and innovative product in whichever part of the market is under review. Original research into systems and concepts is balanced against careful analysis of operating characteristics, features, performance and economy targets, projected cost of ownership and essential dimensional requirements.

Research into competitors' vehicles, market research to judge tastes in future years and possible changes in legislation are all factors that have to be taken into account by the product planners when determining the specifications of a new vehicle.

Such information is passed on to the design team. The skill and judgement of the trained and experienced automotive designer is vital to the creation of any design concept. To assist in the design process, Ford use some of the most advanced computer-aided design equipment. For example, computer-controlled measuring bridges that automatically scan model surfaces are linked to Ford's computer centre through a highly-sophisticated satellite communication network. The design process involves:

- designers formulating ideas as sketches and coloured drawings
- producing full-scale clay models to review the design
- development engineers testing engines in a computer-linked test cell
- wind-tunnel testing to enable designers to maximise aerodynamic efficiency
- hand-building a prototype
- using mobile laboratories to monitor test vehicles
- using prototypes for rigorous crash testing to improve safety standards
- extensive durability testing on a variety of surfaces in all conditions.

Another major responsibility of the designer is **ergonomics.** This is the consideration of human factors in the efficient layout of controls in the driver environment, and is a fundamental part of design. For example, the design of the instrument panels must take into account the driver's reach zones and field of vision. Designers also have to ensure that designs are capable of being manufactured efficiently and economically.

Five years of research, planning, design and development take place ahead of production. Today's new Ford is more than just a pleasing shape. It represents the culmination of an extensive process of development. The product's launch determines whether all of the years of work have been justified.

A very familiar design

1 *What role does research play in the design process?*
2 *Identify areas of importance for designers when developing a new motor car.*
3 *How does technology help the designer?*

Stages of product development

A number of steps can be clearly identified in the development of a new product. As ideas and products go through successive stages of research and testing, those considered less likely to succeed are eliminated (see Figure 16.6).

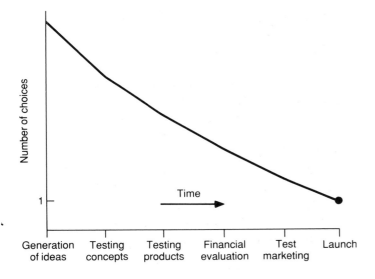

Figure 16.6 Elimination of choices

Testing concepts involves assessing whether or not product designs might succeed in the market-place. This means asking questions such as:

● What appeals to the consumer?
● What benefits would this product offer?
● Does the product meet the needs of the market?
● Could the idea be improved?

Testing products of the manufactured kind involves developing models or prototypes. At this stage the designer will be looking at areas such as quality, performance, safety, ergonomics and appearance. The economics of production must be taken into account, and it may be decided to build in **planned**

obsolescence so that the product will need to be replaced after a certain period of time.

In some cases it may be worth while for an organisation to apply for a patent, giving it the exclusive right to produce and sell a given item.

Financial evaluation of a new product's potential is essential. Will it ultimately generate profits? Techniques of investment appraisal, and cost–volume–profit predictions using marginal costing and break-even analysis, are essential at this stage. One major difficulty, however, is the reliability of data – prediction always carries an element of risk.

Test marketing involves setting up a market situation that is as near to the real thing as possible. This is a 'dry run' and brings back information to reduce some of the risks of a full launch. Test marketing often takes place in defined television areas. For example, M&M's (the sweets) were originally test-marketed in the Tyne Tees television area – a popular choice with marketing people because the viewing public is close to the national profile, and the area does not have large areas of overlap with other TV stations.

The **launch** is the time when the product is presented to the market and is exposed to the ultimate critical test. Ideally, the launch will create an awareness of the product, followed by an interest and then a desire to purchase.

Task

Think of an item of packaged food you have recently consumed (a yoghurt perhaps, or a new soft drink). Comment on how the product would probably have been tested in its development stage.

Value analysis

The objective of **value analysis** is to satisfy consumer needs as economically as possible. All elements in the product and in its **marketing mix** are examined in order to eliminate any unnecessary or wasteful expenditure.

For example, if designers were free to operate without any cost control guidelines, they might use components or materials of a higher quality than those required to complete the task. This influences the price that has to be charged, and means that the product may not be viewed as 'value for money' by the consumer.

A value analysis team will be made up of personnel from a range of areas able to contribute to cost-cutting decisions. The team might comprise:

- a designer – for knowledge of the product
- a marketeer – for knowledge of consumer needs and the marketing mix
- a production engineer – for knowledge of processes
- an accountant – for the ability to analyse costs
- a work study expert – for experience of working procedures
- a buyer – for knowledge of sources and prices of supply.

The product life-cycle

The acceptability of a product to the market-place will determine how long it will be in demand and its overall success or failure. Designers have to base their plans upon what they expect the product's life-cycle to be. This involves working closely with marketeers to ensure that the right type of product is launched into the market at just the right time. Careful timing of the launch into the product portfolio is essential. These are matters discussed in Chapter 6.

Case Study – The products of the future

Products in the process of development for launch in 1995 include robot vacuum cleaners, microwave ovens that know what is in them, irons that sense the fabric they are pressing, and food mixers that bake cakes.

Moulinex, Europe's largest manufacturer of domestic appliances with 14 per cent of the market, recently inaugurated a £3.5 million research centre at Caen in France. Here, 35 specialists in materials, motors, robotics and computer-aided design work to raise the IQs of products to match their futuristic designs.

Figure 16.7 The cake of the future?

The pace of development and change is astronomic. With product life-cycles shortening, companies are fast making obsolete even their own inventions. A vacuum cleaner used to last twenty years and an iron seven, but now people replace vacuums every seven years and irons every three.

Moulinex planned to spend about 2 per cent of their revenue, or £16 million, on research and development in 1991. Soon they will launch a home controller that uses electricity lines to communicate commands (such as 'on' and 'off') using specially built plugs with computer chips. These plugs can be used for appliances made by any manufacturer and the system will probably retail for about £300.

Meanwhile, in the kitchen of the Caen centre, home economists throw eggs, flour and milk into a food mixer which blends them and then bakes a cake at a touch of a button. A vacuum cleaner that looks more like R2D2 moves around a room on its own and knows where objects are. One cannot help thinking what might happen if such appliances one day decided to turn against their owners!

1 *How does this case study indicate a need to tie in marketing with research?*
2 *What does shortening product life-cycles imply for the work of the designer?*
3 *Briefly discuss the ethics of shorter product life-cycles. (Mention: care of the environment, quality of goods, consumer satisfaction, employment, standard of living.)*
4 *Identify areas in your home where you feel gadgetry could improve your quality of life.*

The plant

In order to produce a product or service some form of accommodation is required. The **plant** may account for a large proportion of an organisation's fixed assets and represent a considerable financial investment. The location, size, design, layout and safety of the plant are all of fundamental importance if it is to operate efficiently.

Location

The **location** of a factory or shop where an organisation intends to operate undoubtedly has a major effect on its performance. Locating an organisation is expected to be a long-term commitment and clearly decisions taken today will have lasting implications. The owner of a small organisation may not want to leave his or her neighbourhood, and the problem then may be not where to locate but rather finding a suitable site. In contrast, large organisations view the world as their market, and numerous factors taken together influence the choice of location.

Whatever the type of organisation, the aim will be to locate where the difference between benefits and costs is maximised. It is important to minimise unit costs and maximise outputs from given quantities of resources.

We now consider the most important factors influencing the choice of location.

Transport

Transport costs are particularly crucial if raw materials or finished goods are bulky. If the output of an industry is more expensive to transport than its inputs, it is a **bulk-increasing** industry, and common sense suggests that it is more likely to locate near to its market. Market orientation is also important when the product is perishable – bread is an example.

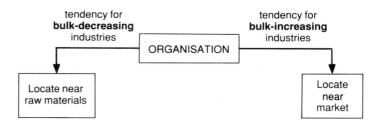

Figure 16.8 Location of plant

On the other hand, if the raw materials are bulky and costly to transport and the industry is a **bulk-decreasing** industry, it is beneficial to save on transport costs by locating close to where the raw materials are available. For example, steel plants tend to be located on or near the coast where they have access to imported iron ore.

In practice, decisions are not quite as clear-cut as the above might suggest – markets tend to be spread out and raw materials come from a number of suppliers. So, the nature of the industry, the spread of the market, the availability of raw materials and their influence upon costs of transport all have to be weighed against each other.

Case Study – Technical Operations Ltd

Technical Operations Ltd, a manufacturer of specialised computer components, is in the process of reviewing its factory location, at present at site A in Figure 16.9. The company has identified three other possible locations for a factory – at B, C or D.

The management of TOL understands the need to take many factors into consideration when deciding upon the most appropriate new location. These factors include:

- grants from the government
- labour costs
- the cost of transporting raw materials to the plant
- the cost of transporting finished goods to the market.

TOL will relocate its plant where the sum of all these costs is minimised. Production costs are constant wherever the factory is located.
It has been established that national and local government grants will reduce all costs by 25 per cent at locations B and D only. As for the other costs, *for each 10 000 components produced* they are as follows:

- labour: £7300 at A, £7500 at B, £8400 at C and £7900 at D
- transporting *raw materials:* £14 per mile by road,

£8 per mile by canal, £9 per mile by rail
- transporting *finished goods* to the market *at C:* £18 per mile by road, £10 per mile by canal, £12 per mile by rail.

You are required to compare the costs involved and then provide a recommendation to the TOL management. You can do this by calculating the total costs of providing specialised computer components at each of the alternative locations and comparing these with the total cost of staying at the existing site. The preferred location will be the one with the lowest total cost.

To help you to keep your figures organised, copy out the table below and fill it in as your calculations proceed.

	A (£)	B (£)	C (£)	D (£)
Labour				
Raw materials transport				
Finished goods transport				
Totals				
Less government grants				
Total cost per 10 000 units				

1. *Find the location with the lowest total running cost.*
2. *How would the cost of removal of existing stocks be taken into account in a real situation?*
3. *What other information might TOL require before making a relocation decision?*
4. *How much is the difference in total cost between the lowest and highest cost locations if sales reach 95 000 next year?*

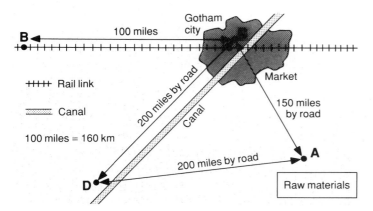

Figure 16.9 Details of the area

Integration with group companies

A large organisation will usually want to locate its plants where work can be easily **integrated** with other plants in the same group.

Labour and housing

Labour and certain skills are more readily available in some areas than in others. House prices and rents vary considerably between areas, and this may limit **labour mobility.**

Services

There are five standard **services** to be considered: gas, electricity, water, waste disposal and drainage. Some industries use considerable quantities of water (e.g. metal-plating, food preparation). Disposal of waste can be expensive, so a careful assessment has to be made of all requirements.

Land

Land costs vary considerably from area to area. Sometimes the geology of land has to be looked at to see whether it can support heavy weights

Regional characteristics

Each region has particular characteristics. For example, **climate** might be an important factor in the manufacture of foodstuffs or perishable goods. **Local regulations** may affect certain types of activity on a site. Finally, some organisations like to locate in an area with a reputation for hosting similar businesses, or where training facilities are available locally.

Safety requirements

Certain types of industry may be considered to be a **danger** or nuisance to their local environment (e.g. nuclear power stations, chemical plant or munitions works). Public concern increased during the 1980s after the Union Carbide disaster in Bhopal, and the catastrophe at Chernobyl.

Communications

The accessibility of sea ports, airports and motorways is an important factor. A good **infra-** structure encourages industries to move to a region. Towns such as Northampton, Peterborough, Telford and Milton Keynes can all credit some of their development to their infrastructure.

Government influences

Disproportionate rates of **unemployment** in various parts of the UK have been a prominent feature of the last thirty years. Government intervention in the location of industry is designed to provide more balanced economic growth which distributes wealth and employment more evenly. There are financial incentives for organisations to locate in certain areas. In particular, selective assistance is provided for projects that create or safeguard employment.

Good communications are important

Task

List the factors that would be important for locating each of the following:

a a college
b a brewery
c a bank branch

d a car manufacturing plant
e a large supermarket
f a steel plant.

Ranking of factors

There will be certain **limiting factors** to the choice of site. For example, a chemical plant needs to be near a major water supply, manufacturers need to be close to a source of labour, and a bookshop ideally needs to be in the centre of a town or city. Choosing a site means taking all of the relevant factors into consideration and attempting to assess them in relation to each other. One technique of doing this is **ranking.**

Weights are assigned to each of the factors, the most important being given the highest numbers. The choices of site are ranked according to the relative strengths of the factors at those sites – for example, the ranks would be 3, 2 and 1 if there were three choices of site. Finally, for each site the weights are multiplied by the ranks and a total score obtained. This is easier to understand when we look at an example.

In Figure 16.10, the ranks attached to the relative importance of four locational factors for each of two

locations appear on the left of each cell, and the ranks multiplied by the weights appear in bold type after the diagonals. Location B is the most desirable location using this method.

Case Study – Teesside Development Corporation

Teesside was hit heavily by the recession in the early 1980s when many thousands of workers lost their jobs with major employers such as ICI and British Steel. During the 1980s Teesside became an area of extensive industrial dereliction, with continuing high rates of unemployment.

Teesside Development Corporation came into operation on 15 May 1987 with a remit to regenerate 19 square miles of derelict industrial land on both banks of the River Tees and in the town of Hartlepool. It was set up by the government to stimulate the economy and improve the living and working environments of those living on Teesside. The initial development strategy was to achieve this with new jobs and services to enrich the quality of life. Nine initiatives formed the overall strategy for Teesside (see Figure 16.11).

Factor	Weight	Possible locations	
		A	B
Transport	5	1/5	2/**10**
Land	3	2/**6**	1/3
Amenities	3	1/3	2/**6**
Communications	3	2/**6**	1/3
Totals		**20**	**22**

Figure 16.10 **An example of the ranking technique**

☆ **Industrial development** – New sites and factories, including the Enterprise Zone at Middlesbrough

☆ **Commercial development** – New offices, leisure and shopping facilities

☆ **Land** – Strategic purchases of land to achieve regeneration

☆ **The river** – Rejuvenate its use with developments such as Hartlepool Marina and Tees Offshore Base

☆ **The environment** – Stimulate environmental change

☆ **Marketing** – Create a new and deserved image for Teeside

☆ **Training and retraining** – Meet the needs of new industries in the manufacturing and service sectors

☆ **Housing** – Improve existing housing stock and encourage new house-building

☆ **Transportation** – Improve the road infrastructure

Figure 16.11 **Initiatives for Teesside**

In the Corporation's first three years of development work, it brought in over 100 new companies and created 7500 jobs. One such company was a pipe-trailer manufacturer from Bradford-upon-Avon. Teesside Corporation helped by providing:

- abundant semi-skilled and skilled labour, wages paid for the first three months
- freehold land at £35 000 per acre
- grants to cover 15 per cent of capital costs, including land and building
- low-interest finance for 50 per cent of capital costs
- assistance towards consultancy costs
- direct consultancy from Corporation staff
- a site linked to a motorway.

Such companies have come to recognise the benefits Teesside can provide and have served to provide a wave of confidence about the future of the area.

1 Why did the government set up Teesside Development Corporation?
2 What does the Corporation aim to do?
3 Describe how the Corporation helps:
 a companies
 b the people of Teesside
 c the infrastructure
 d the environment.

Plant size

The **scale of operations** is usually measured by the number of units produced over a period of time. Large organisations are able to produce their goods and services at more competitive prices because they can spread their fixed costs over a larger output. If the amount of production increases, average unit costs over most production ranges are likely to fall because the organisation will benefit from **economies of scale** (the advantages it gains from becoming larger). All organisations aim for the scale of production which suits their line of activities best, and this is achieved when unit costs are at their

lowest for the output produced. Beyond this point an organisation starts to find that inefficiencies or **diseconomies of scale** (the disadvantages of being too large) push unit costs up (see Figure 16.12).

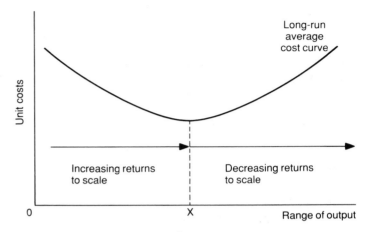

Figure 16.12 Returns to scale

If output increases at a faster rate than the inputs, average unit costs will be falling and an organisation is said to be benefiting from **increasing returns to scale**. Beyond the point at which average unit costs are at their lowest, the increase in output will be less than the increase in input, so that average unit costs are pushed up and the organisation is suffering from **decreasing returns to scale**.

Internal economies of scale enable an organisation to manage its operations more efficiently. They result from an organisation being able to use better technology, management and business practices as it gets larger. *External* economies of scale are factors outside the direct control of an organisation from which it benefits as an industry becomes larger or an area prospers.

Internal economies

Technical economies. Larger organisations have the ability to use techniques and equipment which cannot be adopted by small-scale producers of the same good or service. For example, an organisation might have three machines, each producing 2000 units per week at a unit cost of £1. As the organisation becomes larger it could replace these three machines with one machine producing 10 000 units per week at the lower cost of 75p per unit. If a small organisation tried to use such a machine, costs would be excessive in relation to its output and the machine would probably become obsolete before the end of its physical life.

Labour and managerial economies. In a very small business it is not unusual for one person to be 'jack of all trades', constantly adjusting skills and switching from one job to another. A large organisation, on the other hand, employs a number of specialised staff on its management team – accountants, marketing managers, personnel officers etc. Specialised roles tend to improve the overall quality of work and decision-making processes, and reduce overall unit costs if the output is sufficiently large.

Commercial economies. In the commercial world, larger organisations enjoy considerable benefits. For example:

- They can afford to devote more resources to market research and product research.
- Raw materials can be bought in bulk and larger discounts obtained.
- They can exercise buying power in their markets (i.e. demand extended credit periods).
- They sometimes have a financial stake in suppliers or retail outlets.
- Overheads may be spread over a larger output.
- Centralisation may make the organisation more efficient.

Financial economies. Large organisations are viewed in a different light by the financial world. As they are (usually) a more sound investment, they find it easier to raise finance, often at preferential interest rates. A further financial advantage is that they may be able to raise capital by issuing new shares on the Stock Exchange.

Risk-bearing economies. As well as having a financial stake in both suppliers and outlets, a larger organisation may have the ability to diversify across a range of products and operations to spread risks. By doing so an organisation covers itself against too much dependency on one area.

Task

Explain why a small organisation may be at a disadvantage when attempting to serve the same market as a large organisation. Can you think of any advantages that the small organisation may enjoy?

External economies

Concentration. If similar organisations develop in the same geographical area, a number of benefits arise – for example, a skilled labour pool, a reputation for the area for the quality of its work, local college courses tailored to meet the needs of that particular industry, and better social amenities.

Information. Larger industries have information services and employers' associations designed to benefit the actions of members (e.g. the Motor Industry Research Association).

Disintegration. In areas where certain industries develop, component industries or service industries develop to help with maintenance and support processes.

Case Study – ZX Hardware Ltd

ZX Hardware Ltd has responded to the general growth of interest, amongst young children and teenagers, in both computers for educational purposes and computer games. Over the last few years the organisation has developed through a massive expansion programme and rapidly increasing popularity. The following figures have been drawn from the financial statements of the business:

	1989	1990	1991	1992
Yearly outputs (units)	1350	1670	2940	5000
Number of machines	12	15	18	20
Number of employees	18	20	24	28
Number of products	2	3	5	9
Cost of manufacture per unit (£)	74.50	69.70	62.30	50.10

1 *Examine the figures carefully. What economies of scale have taken place? Describe how they might help ZX Hardware Ltd.*
2 *What other information can you extract from the table (e.g. output per machine, labour productivity)? What do these figures tell you about growth taking place in the company?*
3 *What other benefits not shown by the table will ZX Hardware Ltd obtain as it becomes larger?*

Growth

Organic growth is said to occur when an organisation obtains economies of scale through gradual development, often through re-investing profits, expanding its market share and developing new products. Such growth can take a long time. A quicker and more dynamic type of growth is possible through mergers, takeovers, deals and acquisitions which involve the integration of a number of organisations under a single umbrella organisation.

A **horizontal merger** takes place when two or more organisations with products of a similar nature at the same stage of production join together. A horizontal group will therefore consist of a number of integrated organisations at the same stage of production – for example, a group of motor manufacturers or supermarkets. By bringing organisations 'under the one roof', economies of scale can be achieved. Profitability should be increased and the integrated group will have greater market power and will have reduced competition.

A **vertical merger** takes place when two or more organisations producing products of a similar type but at different stages of production join together. **Backward vertical integration** involves the takeover of a supplier, and **forward vertical integration** involves merging with an organisation at a later stage in production. A vertical integration helps to secure sources of supply or secures outlets in the market-place. In doing so it helps an organisation to achieve closer control at every stage of production. Breweries tend to be vertically integrated throughout their stages. In Figure 16.13 it can be seen how an organisation may integrate both horizontally and vertically.

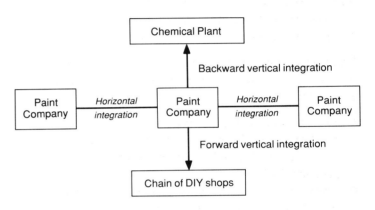

Figure 16.13 **Forms of integration**

Case Study – Horizontal mergers

All the following mergers took place in 1991:

● Aérospatiale Helicopters (France) and MBB (Germany) joined forces to become Eurocopter International to compete with the powerful American helicopter manufacturers.
● Northern Foods paid £25.9 million for Bodfari Foods of Cheshire to increase its share of the national milk market from 13 to 13.5 per cent.
● Clarke Foods bought Lyons Maid to become the second largest ice-cream manufacturer after Unilever.

1 Identify economies the above organisations might obtain.

2 How might these integrations affect the actions of their competitors?

Not all integrations are either horizontal or vertical. It is a common practice today for organisations that are only loosely connected to join together in order to maximise risk-bearing economies. This is a feature of **conglomerate integration.** A conglomerate spreads risks by choosing different types of organisations in which to invest. This allows it to balance out variations in return – swings and roundabouts. As a result each of the subsidiaries may be substantially different in nature. For example, Hanson PLC is a conglomerate with widely diversified interests, including tobacco, batteries and building products.

Task

Scan the financial pages of newspapers and professional business magazines. Make a short list of recent mergers, takeovers and acquisitions. Comment on the motivations behind them.

Diseconomies of scale

Large organisations are significantly more difficult to manage, and tend to suffer from certain inefficiencies.

Human relations. Large numbers of employees are more difficult to coordinate and manage. For example, communicating information and instructions may be difficult, especially through many layers of management. Contact between those who make the decisions and those who receive instructions is reduced, and this can lead to a low level of morale, a lack of purpose and industrial relations problems.

Decisions and coordination. The sheer scale of production may limit the ability of management to respond to the market and make good decisions. In a large organisation both the quality of information reaching the decision maker and the quality of instructions passed on can be severely affected by size. Difficulties may also arise because of excessive paperwork, regulations and meetings.

External diseconomies. Large organisations become well known in the community and efficient public relations is essential to overcome unfavourable attitudes of interest groups. For example, public displeasure with the actions of a large organisation may lead to consumer boycotts or necessitate the development of alternative products.

Design and layout of plant and equipment

The working environment should enable people and machines to function efficiently. Though designing the layout is normally an 'organisation and methods' (O&M) responsibility, it will be carried out after extensive consultation with administrative staff and specialist engineers who might be concerned with features such as power availability and maintenance requirements.

Factors influencing the layout of plant include:

- flow of work
- type of work
- cost
- legal requirements
- safety
- ergonomics.

The **flow of work** has to be analysed to establish links between people, materials, paperwork and resources. The aim is to reduce unproductive movements to a minimum. Where frequent movements take place, people and resources need to be located close to each other. In a **product layout**, products, paperwork and materials flow constantly from one stage to another. Control is simplified because the paperwork, material handling and inspection procedures are reduced (see Figure 16.14).

In a **function** or **process layout,** all operations of the same type are performed in the same area (e.g. in

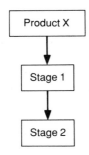

Figure 16.14 A product layout

the typing pool or print unit). Although this system is flexible, considerable planning is necessary to ensure that people and resources are not either over- or under-burdened (see Figure 16.15).

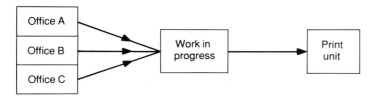

Figure 16.15 A process layout

In a **fixed-position layout,** operations are performed and then the materials or paperwork are returned to a fixed location after each process (see Figure 16.16).

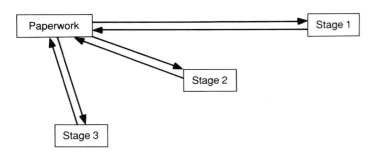

Figure 16.16 A fixed-position layout

The **type of work** will influence the layout of plant. Some functions may need to be in certain areas. For example, a typing pool has to be accessible to many users, a reception area has to be at the main entrance, and certain manufacturing processes need to be near specialist services.

Whenever redesigning a layout is considered, **cost** must be borne in mind. A budget is normally set and layout modifications have to be catered for within prescribed limits.

Legal requirements must also be met, as we saw in Chapter 15. The layout has to take into account health and safety – physical conditions such as space, ventilation, noise, cleanliness, cloakroom facilities etc.

Ergonomics is important in the design of the plant. Ergonomics considers the relationship of employees to equipment and machinery, and tries to understand how these relationships can affect performance. Workplaces should be designed from the outset around the capabilities of operators.

Hence, in planning a layout it is necessary to:

* analyse links between people, work and departments
* plan departmental locations
* take into account legal requirements, health and safety, facilities and cost
* draw a scale plan
* liaise with staff throughout the process.

Whatever techniques are used in setting up a layout, the aim must be to maximise flexibility and the ease of coordination so that process time and costs will be minimised.

Task

You have been given the responsibility for redesigning the foyer of your local college. Draw an outline plan of the floor area of the foyer, and suggest locations for the following:

* reception desk
* students' union shop
* toilet facilities
* caretaker's lobby
* display board
* student services counter
* college map.

Design a suitable layout to avoid congestion, and justify your decisions. In what way is this problem typical of the problems any designer of a plant layout would have? What should you aim for and what should you avoid?

Performance, maintenance and safety of plant

The justification for expenditure on new equipment is that it contributes towards the quality of goods and services being provided. Before equipment is bought the general effects upon the organisation have to be evaluated, and standard economic appraisal techniques have to be applied to find out whether such changes will be worthwhile.

Maintenance of plant and equipment is essential for the efficient provision of goods and services. If the size of the organisation warrants it, a typical maintenance department will have call on the services of specialists like electricians and plumbers. The maintenance department will work to a plan to ensure that all equipment is checked and serviced in turn. The effectiveness of a maintenance department can be judged on the basis of freedom from emergencies.

It is the duty of an employer to remove all potential causes of **accidents**. Accidents can cause distress, time off and delayed production. Employers need to anticipate circumstances that might lead to injury, eliminate hazards quickly, and encourage staff to adopt good (i.e. safe) practices at all times.

The process

In looking at the **process**, we have to distinguish between goods and services. Whereas goods provide a **tangible** product, services are a benefit of an **intangible** nature received by the customer. The important distinction between the two at operations level is that a service cannot be stored – production and consumption take place at the same time. Most services, however, do come with a physical element. For example, when you open a bank account you are kept informed of your balance by means of statements and other literature.

There are three main types of process: **job, batch** and **flow**. The operation of each type of production depends upon the stage of each organisation's development as well as the nature of the work, the type of product and the needs of the market. Some organisations start with job production and then, as they grow, move to batch production and then finish up with flow production. Production is **intermittent** when it involves changing operations from one product to another, and **continuous** if the product emerges as a continuous stream.

Job production

Job (or make-complete) **production** is the manufacture of single items by either one operative or teams of operatives. Ships and bridges are made this way. It is possible for a number of identical units to be produced in parallel under job production (e.g. several similar frigates for the navy). Smaller projects can also be seen as job production – for example, writing this book or knitting a sweater. What characterises job production is the fact that the project is considered to be a single operation which requires the complete attention of a range of resources.

The desirable features of job production are:

- Each output is a unique product that, from the design stage, exactly matches the requirements of a customer. It will often, therefore, be a response to a customer order.
- As the output is a single unit, inspection and supervision are relatively straightforward for all but massive projects.
- The customer may be able to specify details during the production process.
- Working on a single project in a team, from start to completion, provides workers with a greater degree of satisfaction.

There are, however, a number of potential drawbacks. Resources have to be versatile to adjust to the range of specialised tasks associated with the same job. For example, imagine building a house on your own – how many different skills would you need?

Another problem is that, as job production is unique, costing is based upon uncertain predictions of costs in the future. The larger the job, the more potential there is for error. Projects like the Channel Tunnel have huge potential in that respect.

A further drawback is that unit costs tend to be high since there are few economies of scale.

Task

Identify a product manufactured by job production. Explain why job production was used in that instance.

Batch production

Batch refers to a specific group of items that go through a production process together. As one batch finishes, the next one starts.

For example, on Monday a particular machine might contribute to the manufacture of wide-lined stationery, on Tuesday plain stationery, on Wednesday narrow-lined stationery etc. Batches are constantly processed through the machine before moving on to the next operation. This method is sometimes referred to as 'intermittent production' as different job types are held as work-in-progress between the various stages of production.

The desirable features of batch production are:

- It is particularly suitable for a wide range of similar goods.
- It economises on the range of machinery required and reduces the need for a flexible workforce.

- It is possible to respond quickly to orders by finishing off work-in-progress.
- It makes economies of scale possible.
- It makes costing easier and provides better information for management.

There are potential drawbacks. There may be difficulties scheduling batches to meet customer orders, whilst avoiding holding stocks for excessive periods. The time lag between investment in materials and the completion and sale of the final product may not be acceptable. Additionally, this method of working tends to require a lot of paperwork, and careful attention to plant utilisation. It is necessary to avoid waiting time for each batch at a particular stage before it is able to move on to another stage.

Flow production

Batch production is described as 'intermittent' production because it is characterised by irregularity. However, if each of the rest periods in batch production disappeared it would then become **flow production** (sometimes called **mass production**). Flow production is therefore a continuous process of part-finished products passing on from one stage to another until completion. Units are worked upon and passed straight on to the next stage without waiting for others to reach the same stage of completion. For the production line to work smoothly there should be no movements or **leakages** from the line. It may be a single-stage process or it may involve an assembly line.

For flow production to be successful there has to be continuity of demand. If demand varies there is persistent overstocking or shortage of finished goods.

Achieving a smooth flow of production requires considerable pre-production planning to ensure that raw materials are purchased and delivered on time, that sufficient labour is employed, and that all operations take the correct time.

Consider an example. Assume that a production level of 1000 units per hour is required, and the four stages in the process require the use of the following types of machines:

For stage 1: machine type A, which can process 500 units per hour
For stage 2: machine type B, which can process 250 units per hour
For stage 3: machine type C, which can process 1000 units per hour
For stage 4: machine type D, which can process 250 units per hour

For a balanced flow to be achieved, the job would require these machines: two of type A, four of type B, one of type C, and four of type D. This can be seen clearly in Figure 16.17. Study the diagram and follow the process through each stage to convince yourself that a smooth flow will be achieved.

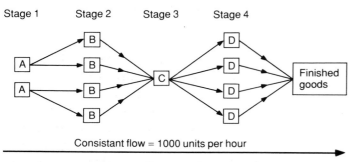

Figure 16.17 Achieving flow production

The benefits of flow production are:

- Labour costs tend to be lower.
- Inspection can easily spot deviations in the line.
- As there is no rest between operations, work-in-progress levels can be kept low.
- Minimal storage space is required.
- Physical handling of products is reduced.
- Investments are quickly converted into sales.
- Material and line requirements are easy to assess, so control is more effective.

Problems do occasionally arise, however. Flow production requires a constant demand – if the demand falters, overstocking may take place. It is sometimes difficult to balance the output of one stage with the input of another, so on-going work study is required. Parts and raw materials must arrive on time, and maintenance must be

preventative to ensure that emergencies do not cause the line to stop. Finally, staff absences may have far-reaching effects upon the flow.

Task

Identify which of the following situations, in your experience, are job production, batch production or flow production:

a visits to the dentist
b your local town traffic
c bus services
d visiting the bank
e ordering a drink in a busy pub.

CADCAM and CIM

Over recent years considerable developments have taken place in production industries. As well as computer-aided design (CAD), developments have taken place in machine tools. Many are now controlled numerically by a computer (computer numerical control – CNC). Other developments have taken place in robotics. With CADCAM (computer-aided design/computer-aided manufacturing), data from the CAD system is used to drive machines, making the CAD system part of the manufacturing process.

A more recent development is called **computer integrated manufacturing** (CIM). Not only is the product designed on a CAD system, the software also orders materials, drives CNC machine tools and has its own control system which provides data for purchasing, sales etc.

The programme

All organisations have to plan their operations within a framework of policies. Developing a programme involves looking at:

- what needs to be done
- when it needs to be implemented
- the resources necessary to fulfil the task.

The role of the planning process depends upon the type of production. With flow production, considerable thought has to be given to designing and setting up the operation. With job production, the timing of the availability of skilled workers and resources is vital. In all these situations the programmer will aim to get the most from materials, labour and plant, timetable them for use at the most appropriate times, and aim to achieve the objectives of the organisation.

Production planning and control also need to be carefully coordinated with marketing information. One aspect of this is the **product life-cycle**. The operations management needs to be aware of the changing circumstances during a product's life. For example, the initial volume requirements may be low and production may be by the batch process. As growth is achieved flow production may be more appropriate, and smaller volume may be required in a product's maturity, as demand drops away.

Scheduling (or timetabling) is concerned with determining what should be done and when. Scheduling therefore develops detailed programmes out of initial broad plans.

Critical path analysis

A further technique in the programming process is that of **critical path analysis** (CPA). CPA is used to schedule related tasks in a way that minimises time and costs. A series of lines is drawn in the form of a **network** to find the 'critical path' of a project. Activities are thus linked diagramatically. For example, when building a house, walls have to be built before putting the roof on (see Figure 16.18).

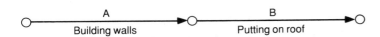

Figure 16.18 A simple network

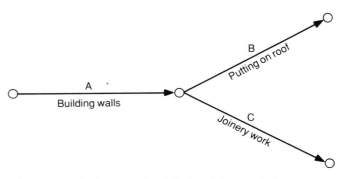

Figure 16.19 A network with simultaneous jobs

Other activities are, of course, carried out simultaneously, so that at the time the roof is put on joinery work may be completed (Figure 16.19). Network analysis can be used to programme these events in such a way as to create the most effective plan.

A further ingredient in constructing a network is the element of **time**. If time is incorporated into the diagrams it becomes possible to calculate the minimum amount of time to carry out a particular project. Those activities which take the longest time to complete in moving from one stage to the next are described as **critical activities**. The 'critical path' of a project is therefore the line along which these activities flow. If these activities are delayed the whole project will be delayed.

Today, CPA is applied with the aid of computer software. Packages are available to determine the best way of scheduling a complex series of tasks.

Task

Draw a network of activities for baking a cake. Indicate the time likely to be taken for each part of the process. Identify the critical path.

Purchasing

Procuring materials is a key management function for any organisation. The importance of its role can be appreciated when one realises that an average manufacturer spends about one-half of its income on supplies of raw materials and services.

The purchasing department will aim to provide the organisation with a steady flow of materials and services, with continuity of supplies. It will also aim to obtain the best value for money – to provide the best for a low cost. The use of value analysis often makes it possible for considerable savings to be made, though a danger is that quality can be sacrificed to cost considerations. A successful purchasing department will keep costs down, produce a fast stock turnover, reduce obsolescence, ensure continuity of supplies and reduce lead times (the interval between the realisation of a need and its ultimate fulfilment upon delivery).

Just-in-time is a system that relates purchasing decisions and stock levels to current production requirements. It involves working with the lowest possible stock levels, but at the same time making sure that materials *are* available when required, that they are of good quality and that they are fit for the purpose intended.

Case Study – Using expert systems in purchasing

The development of expert systems has improved the quality of decision-making in purchasing and supply. Expert systems are computer programs concerned with capturing the knowledge of experts and presenting it in such a way that it can be interrogated by non-experts. They are designed to hold the specialist knowledge and experience of an expert and then allow this to be accessed so that someone with less knowledge can make comparable decisions.

An expert system is of most value where reasoning rather than calculating is required, so that decisions can be made with the benefit of knowledge which an expert has acquired through experience.

Expert systems in purchasing can be used to:

- analyse a problem (e.g. economic ordering levels)
- explain a process (e.g. documentation in the purchasing office)
- make a choice (e.g. selection from a group of suppliers).

Expert systems make expertise more readily available at all times, whereas an expert would have to be paid for a consultation. By helping with key decisions they help an organisation to become more competitive.

1 What is an expert system?
2 How might such a system benefit a purchasing department?
3 Can you think of any drawbacks to using an expert system, rather than employing an expert or providing suitable staff training?

Stock control

In an ideal world where organisations knew demand well in advance and where suppliers always met delivery dates, there would be little need for stocks. In practice, however, demand varies and suppliers are sometimes late with deliveries, so stocks act as a protection against unpredictable events. Stocks are normally held of:

- raw materials
- work-in-progress
- finished goods.
- consumables
- plant and machinery spares

The aim of any **stock control system** is to provide enough stocks to cater for current demand and uncertainties, while keeping minimum levels so working capital is not wasted. Keeping stocks at just the right level is therefore important. Very low stocks or excessively high stocks can have harmful effects on a business – if stocks are very low an organisation might not be able to take on and meet orders, but if they are too high they represent money lying idle when it could be put to better use.

Problems of low stocks	Problems of high stocks
1 Shortages can lead to loss of business.	1 The risk of stock loss is increased.
2 It may be difficult to satisfy customer demands.	2 There is an increased risk of a stock item becoming obsolete.
3 The situation can lose goodwill.	3 Costs of storage are high.
4 Ordering needs to be frequent, and so handling costs are higher.	4 Stocks can tie up an organisation's working capital.

Figure 16.20 Implications of stock levels

Buffer stocks can be built up as a preventative measure against running out as a result of unexpected variations in demand. A minimum level will be set, below which it will be hoped that stocks will not fall, though this may depend upon the lead time between placing an order and its receipt.

In an ideal situation stocks should never fall below the set minimum stock level or go above the set

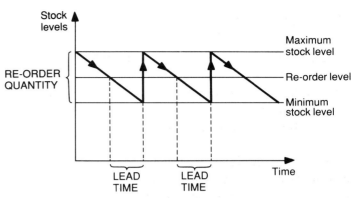

Figure 16.21 Managing stock levels

maximum level (see Figure 16.21). Stocks should therefore be replenished just at the point at which the minimum stock level is about to be breached. In the real world, delivery times, re-order quantities and rates of usage will all vary, to complicate the ideal picture.

Quality control

Quality relates to the individual characteristics of each product or service which enable it to satisfy customers. The objective of any control system is to provide a product with reliability and value for money. In doing so quality control looks at:

- *Design quality* – the degree to which features within a design satisfy customers
- *Product manufacture quality* – the success of a manufacturing process in matching design specifications
- *Product quality* – the degree to which the finished good or service satisfies the wishes of the customer.

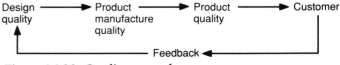

Figure 16.22 Quality control

There are five essential parts to the quality control approach:

- setting the quality level required by the customer:
- planning to achieve the required quality (e.g. by

selecting the right materials, aiming for prevention by means of regular maintenance and shop-floor vigilance, carefully training operators)
- monitoring the manufacturing process
- correcting any problems
- providing long-term planning.

An essential requirement of any system is **feedback,** so that deviations from planned performance can be picked up and faults corrected (and avoided in future).

Task

Think about the quality of service provided by your local fish and chip shop. Identify problems of quality such a shop may encounter. How is it possible for the owner to both monitor and correct these problems? How could the owner avoid such problems in the future?

Modern approaches to quality

Over recent years many organisations have adopted a much broader approach to quality under the guise of **quality assurance**. With this approach, deliveries are expected to be of an appropriate quality and the operations of the organisation providing the good or service are designed in such a way as to **assure** that quality is achieved. The idea is that this approach makes sure an organisation gets the quality right first time and thus avoids the problems arising from failure.

British Standard 5750 was developed by the British Standards Institution to provide a framework within which organisations can be certified as having comprehensive quality management. This is the subject of a case study at the end of the chapter.

Quality circles, formed of groups of workers at the workplace to identify problems, try to present

solutions. These have been discussed in Chapter 9. Another modern idea is the **zero-defects** approach, which aims to get workers to develop a commitment to flawless working.

All such approaches are designed to eliminate problems and thereby ensure that quality is achieved.

Some organisations interpret quality more widely and talk about **total quality management** or the **total product.** Quality is considered not only in the product but also in all other areas of the organisation – so that quality becomes everybody's business, from the most junior member of staff to the most senior member of the management team. In this way an organisation develops a framework enabling quality to be achieved at all levels, to create a genuine competitive advantage over rivals.

Task

Find an organisation which makes a claim about quality. Why do you feel it makes such a claim?

The people

The successful operation of an organisation's activities depends ultimately on its people. The abilities of the labour force are the result of training, background and experience. Managers who wish to obtain the most from their labour force treat them as a valuable resource and keep them motivated. As many of an organisation's labour force tend to work in operational activities providing goods or services, operations managers need to be involved with policy decisions affecting employees within their area of responsibility.

Organisation and methods (O&M) (quite commonly called **work study**) has developed as a managerial science to help managers to use their labour force more effectively. Its primary concern is to analyse efficiency in order to maximise the use of resources. By looking at the ways in which activities are carried out by human and material resources, O&M tries to ensure that the techniques used create the maximum possible benefits for the organisation. Its objectives are:

- to reduce costs by establishing the most cost-effective methods of doing a job
- to standardise such methods
- to establish a time pattern of working
- to install the findings as standard working practices.

Work study consists, therefore, not only of a study of *methods*, but also *measurement* in order to achieve higher productivity.

Method study involves examining both existing and proposed methods of undertaking a job, in order to find a way to do the job more easily and therefore increase output. The steps are shown in Figure 16.23.

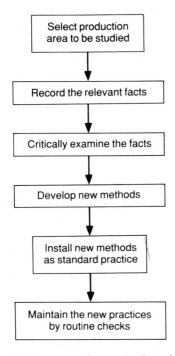

Figure 16.23 **Stages of a method study**

Work measurement is the establishment of techniques to time activities so that they can be carried out with a defined level of performance – for the purpose of improving worker motivation, creating incentives and improving future performance. The steps are shown in Figure 16.24.

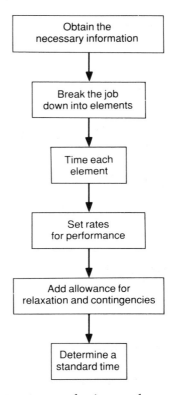

Figure 16.24 **Stages of a time study**

Task

In this activity you should look at how you manage your studies. First conduct a method study of your techniques to discover whether you could work more efficiently. Then conduct a form of work measurement to analyse what you should be expected to undertake over certain periods of time.

After a method study and work measurement process have been carried out, management must decide what changes, if any, need to be made. The information available will cover the placement of machinery, ergonomics, the main communication channels and how they interact, the way in which people work, their incentives, facilities, problems and motivation.

Work study can make its practitioners unpopular because of its association with sensitive areas such as payments, incentives and working methods and speeds. Success in handling the exercise depends upon the extent of the trust between managers and those involved in producing the goods or services. Some organisations run **appreciation courses**.

Case Study – The evolution of mass production

In the early days Ford built cars the way everybody else built them. The chassis was the foundation. It was left standing in one spot until the car was finished. Helpers and stock runners brought parts to the mechanics who assembled it.

Henry Ford intended from the very first to produce the simplest car he could make and produce it in the largest possible numbers at the lowest cost. His aim was mass consumption, and in order to achieve that he had to invent mass production.

A new era in industrial history took place in 1913 when Henry Ford opened up a moving final assembly line in his automobile factory in Michigan. To break away from hand production, Ford and his engineers devised machines for making parts in quantity, as fast as they were needed, and methods of assembling parts as fast as they were made. Using principles of manufacturing pioneers, Ford made massive use of interchangeable parts, which unskilled workers could assemble into finished goods, and this eliminated his dependence upon skilled labour. He experimented with gravity sides, conveyors and the placement of men and tools for maximum efficiency. Breaking each manufacturing operation into its constituent parts, he multiplied the production of flywheel magnetos to complete engines, often by a factor of four. All of these developments led to the birth of mass production with the Model T Ford.

1 *Henry Ford wanted to produce in large numbers at low cost. To what extent is this the philosophy of all mass producing industries?*
2 *What is the difference between a mass production technique and the production of individual products?*
3 *How do mass production techniques alter the nature of the skills required?*
4 *Find out more about:*
  a *the division of labour*
  b *the history of Ford*

Case Study – British Standard 5750

BS 5750 is in fact a series of national standards for use by UK suppliers and purchasers. They tell suppliers and manufacturers what is required of a quality orientated system. They are practical standards for quality systems, whether you employ 10 or 10 000 people. They identify the basic disciplines and specify the procedures and criteria to ensure that products or services meet customer requirements.

Since BS 5750 was established in 1979, more than 9000 firms have become assessed and registered under BS 5750 or equivalent standards; and as a result of links with other countries, national standards have developed in other parts of the world.

The benefits of BS 5750 are easy to realise. Building-in quality at every stage reduces waste and time-consuming reworking of designs and procedures. This saves an organisation money because it helps to establish more soundly-based quality-related procedures which ensure satisfied customers.

1 *What are the reasons for BS 5750?*
2 *Explain how BS 5750 might influence:*
   a operations
   b the training of staff
   c customers.

Case Study – The opportunity of Europe and 1992

The removal of trade barriers throughout Europe gives industry in the United Kingdom access to a potential market of 320 million people. This market is larger than the USA or Japan and will increase the potential for growth and success of regional industry. The development of the Channel Tunnel is forecast to transform the economics of rail freight.

A custom-built Rail Freight Centre to serve the North East of England presents a unique opportunity for organisations to avoid the congestion taking place on the M25 and the south-east road network generally and allow industry to deliver its goods more efficiently to improve performance in the European market.

The freight centre is proposed for development at the Faverdale Industrial Estate on the north-west edge of the town of Darlington. A key factor in the development of the Faverdale site is all of the supporting communication links. For example, the Darlington Cross Town Route is due for completion by 1995. The A1(M) lies one mile to the west of Darlington. Teesside Airport lies close to Darlington. The Faverdale estate already contains many companies which have indicated a wish to use the Rail Freight Centre. They will benefit from direct access to the centre and the links it provides.

It is intended that the freight centre will be a road/rail transfer development. Custom-built facilities will be designed to enhance services to customers and add value to their operations. A firm of independent consultants has indicated that a modern custom-built centre will capture a large share of the transportation market by providing better opportunities for north-eastern companies to transport their goods overseas.

1 *What factors influence the location of organisations?*
2 *How important are good transport links?*
3 *What are the benefits of sending goods by rail?*
4 *Explain why rail links should become more important after the opening of the Channel Tunnel.*
5 *What other methods could be used to encourage organisations to move to Darlington?*

17
Making the Most of People

In this chapter we look at the personnel function at work and the roles of trade unions and employers' associations.

We begin by describing the 'employment procession', which is the path taken by a person from the time when he or she joins an organisation. The path consists of a number of steps, the personnel department being concerned with managing each of these steps. We look at important stages which affect every employee.

We examine the important part played by trade unions in supporting the rights of employees. Some people argue that trade unions no longer serve a useful purpose, whilst others point to their changing yet still vital functions. Industrial relations in the workplace are discussed.

Finally we look at the roles of government and the European Community in influencing working conditions.

An organisation's most valuable resource is its **workforce** – the people who work for it. Managers therefore need to give careful thought to the needs of employees. An organisation can have all the latest technology, and the best physical resources, but unless it looks after its people it will never thrive and achieve optimum results.

The 'employment procession'

The **personnel** department of an organisation has the prime responsibility for recruiting and looking after employees – the human resource. A key part of this function is administering what is known as the **employment procession.**

Employees have needs from the time of their selection for employment until they cease working for the organisation. The employment procession starts with the **recruitment** process – finding

potential new recruits and choosing whom to take on. New staff then need to be helped to 'fit in', so they go through a period of **induction.** During their employment they will need to be **trained** to upgrade their skills and knowledge. Then, when the need arises, they can be **transferred** to other jobs or areas. When they finish working for the organisation they need to have their jobs **terminated** in a satisfactory way – this includes making sure that pension and other matters are dealt with according to the law.

Among the personnel department's other functions, it is responsible for:

- health and safety
- equal opportunities
- bargaining
- appraisals
- discipline
- payment systems.

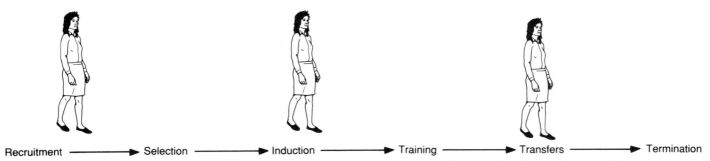

Recruitment ——————▶ Selection ——————▶ Induction ——————▶ Training ——————▶ Transfers ——————▶ Termination

Figure 17.1 The employment procession

Recruitment

From the personnel department's point of view, the purpose of recruitment is to buy in and retain the best available human resources to meet the **organisation's needs**. Hence the first requirement is to define and set out what is involved in particular jobs.

This can be done by carrying out a job analysis, which leads on to an outline **job description**. For example, the job of a trainee manager in a supermarket could be described under the following key headings:

- title of post
- prime objectives of the position
- supervisory/managerial responsibilities
- source(s) of supervision and guidance
- range of decision-making
- responsibility for assets, materials etc.

Task

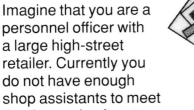

Imagine that you are a personnel officer with a large high-street retailer. Currently you do not have enough shop assistants to meet the demands of customers, particularly at weekends. There are long queues at the tills, and it has become impossible to stack shelves neatly or to price all items accurately. Set out a *job analysis* for a shop assistant, by answering the following questions:

a What tasks need to be performed?
b What skills and qualities are required?
c How can these skills be acquired?

Once the appropriate managers in the organisation are happy with the outline job description, the personnel department can use this outline to produce a fuller job description to be applied in advertising the job vacancy.

A **job specification** goes beyond a simple description of the job, by highlighting the mental and physical **attributes** required of the job holder. For example, a recent Prison Service advertisement specified the following: 'At every level your task will call for a lot more than simple efficiency. It takes humanity, flexibility, enthusiasm, total commitment and, of course, a sense of humour.'

The personnel department may therefore set out, for its own use, a 'person specification' using a layout similar to the one shown in Figure 17.2.

Summary of job			
Attributes	**Essential**	**Desirable**	**How identified**
Physical			
Qualifications			
Experience			
Training			
Special knowledge			
Personal circumstances			
Attitudes			
Practical and intellectual skills			

Figure 17.2 Layout for a person specification   ✿

The job specification can be used to:

- make sure that a job advertisement conveys the qualities that prospective candidates should have
- check that candidates for the job have the right qualities.

Case Study – A job at Mothercare

Figure 17.3 shows the essential information contained in a recent advertisement for a job vacancy at Mothercare.

AREA MANAGER

Southern England

£24–28k + car + benefits

The concept of Mothercare is unique in the world of retailing. With over 250 stores nationwide and a clear market leadership in its chosen field, it is an essential part of life for nearly all of Britain's parents-to-be and new parents.

We are seeking an Area Manager to operate in the South with responsibility for around 20 stores. Your role will be to maximise sales, working closely with your Store Managers and appreciating the individual needs within your area . . .

Imagination, flair, an entrepreneurial attitude and problem-solving skills are just some of the qualities you will need, as well as the ability to lead and motivate your team. Our culture is changing and our Area Managers are at the forefront of this. Substantial retail experience is obviously essential . . .

Figure 17.3

1 What do you think the job analysis for the Mothercare vacancy indicated to the personnel department?
2 What are the key ingredients of the job description?

3 How appealing do you find the job description?
4 What other details might a prospective recruit be interested to know?

Other uses for the job specification

The job specification can, in addition to serving as a recruitment instrument, be used in **staff appraisal.** As we have seen in earlier chapters, this is a means of monitoring staff performance and is a feature of promotion assessment in modern organisations. In some organisations – such as hospitals, schools, and profit-making businesses – employees and their immediate line managers discuss personal goals and targets for the coming period (e.g. the next year); the appraisal then involves a review of performance during the previous year, and the setting of new targets. Job details thus help to focus discussions. Job descriptions can be used to arbitrate on who should be doing what in an organisation, and job analysis can serve as a way of setting standards.

Internal recruitment

Organisations can recruit internally or externally. A decision has to be made as to whether to select an existing employee to fill a job vacancy or to find a suitable outsider (see Figure 17.4).

Advantages	Disadvantages
1 You know what you are getting	1 No new ideas are brought to the organisation
2 It saves on recruitment costs	2 There is no buzz of efficiency that follows an external appointment
3 It saves on induction costs	3 The person moved to a new position will need to be replaced
4 Promotion is seen as an incentive for all members of the organisation to work harder	4 Promotion of one person may upset someone else who is 'overlooked'

Figure 17.4 **Advantages and disadvantages of internal recruitment**

An insider knows the culture of the organisation, and his or her qualities are already familiar to the managers. On the other hand, an outsider may introduce a lot of new ideas which he or she has picked up elsewhere, but the person is very much an unknown quantity. Job references can be very deceptive.

External recruitment

The way in which **external recruitment** takes place depends on the type of job involved. Generally speaking, the more junior the position the less elaborate will be the means of recruitment. For example, the post of a junior mechanic may be advertised in a local newspaper, whereas a senior management position may be advertised in national media, including specialist magazines and newspapers.

Task

Why are some jobs advertised only locally and some nationally? (*Hint*: Your answer should mention skills and costs.)

Recruiting through newspaper and magazine advertisements

Job **advertisements** form an important part of the recruitment process. An organisation is able to communicate job vacancies to a selected audience by this means. Most job advertisements are written (or at least checked) by the personnel department, involving the same skills as marketing a product. Advertisements must reach those people who have the qualities to fill the vacancy.

Job advertisements therefore take many forms, according to the current requirements. Good advertisements contain at least the following information (check the list against Figure 17.5):

- *Job title* – This should form the main heading, possibly in bold print.

New Globe Theatre Company
DIRECTOR
London

Basic £20k + car + bonuses

The New Globe Theatre Company is a new group which will be staging productions in major London theatres. The Director will receive an initial salary of £20 000 but can expect to progress steadily to higher rates as the size of the company increases and the scale of operations expands.

We are looking for someone with extensive experience of theatre production and management who will probably have worked in a similar capacity for at least five years in regional theatre productions.

If you wish to take the opportunity of pioneering this new and exciting venture, please forward a letter of application to:

Director of Personnel,
The New Globe Theatre Company,
1001 The Strand,
London WC2 0NG
Telephone 071 900 1234

Figure 17.5 Advertising a job nationally

- *Job description* – This should highlight the major requirements of the job in a concise format.
- *Organisational activities and market-place* – There should be a brief description of the environment in which the organisation operates.
- *Location* – Applicants need to know the location of the organisation and the location of the job (which may be different).
- *Salary expectation* – Figures are not always necessary, but an indication of the salary level (or a recognised grade) should always be given.
- *Address and contact* – This should appear, with a telephone number if appropriate.
- *Qualifications* – Certain jobs require a minimum entrance qualification, which should be clearly stated.

- *Experience* – This should be quantified as it will have a bearing on the expected salary level for the job.
- *Fringe benefits* – The advertiser may wish to mention a company car, a health scheme, and so on.
- *Organisation identity* – This may be in the form of a logo (or simply the name of the organisation).

A good job advertisement, while providing prospective candidates with helpful information, also helps to deter people who do not have the required qualifications for the job.

Presentation of the advertisement is very important as it gives prospective employees a first impression of the organisation.

Task

Cut out three newspaper job advertisements and highlight what you consider to be the strengths and weaknesses of each.

Task

Think about the features of what you would consider to be an ideal job for you. Try to make out a realistic job advertisement to describe this job. You may need to carry out some research to find out such features as a realistic wage and the experience required.

Commercial employment agencies

A number of commercial agencies recruit employees for organisations in return for a fee. These agencies often specialise in particular areas of employment (e.g. office, manual, technical, managerial).

Agencies are widely used in the field of recruiting temporary secretarial help. A secretary signs to work for an agency. The agency then finds a temporary appointment for that person with a company. The company pays the wages direct to the agency, which takes a commission from the pay packet before handing it on to the worker.

Government-run employment agencies

Government-run **employment agencies** play a major part in finding jobs for people who are unable to do so by other means. The job-finding agency established to help school-leavers is the **Careers Service**. Every school has a careers officer who interviews all potential school-leavers. The careers officer works from a local careers office where a list of local job vacancies is displayed. The careers officer puts school-leavers in touch with the personnel departments of organisations in which they are interested.

The **Employment Service** has brought together the Jobcentre network and the network of unemployment benefit offices. The Employment Service aims to:

- give encouragement and help to unemployed people, particularly those who have been unemployed for a lengthy period
- make accurate and prompt benefit payments to claimants, at the same time ensuring that payments are made only to those who are entitled to them.

Jobcentres are to be found in prominent places in many towns. Cards advertising jobs are on open display, and members of the public can ask Jobcentre staff to make appointments for interviews with appropriate personnel departments.

Selection and induction

Recruitment and **selection** are closely tied together. Selection is the process of *choosing* people to work in an organisation. The selection system should attempt:

- to get the best people within existing budgets – that is, those with the most appropriate skills, experience and attitudes
- to select people who will stay with the organisation for a reasonable time
- to minimise the cost of recruitment and selection relative to returns.

Selection **interviews** should be well organised. They should be arranged at convenient times and at convenient locations, and should present to candidates a realistic picture of what the job entails and what working for the organisation will be like.

Before selecting candidates for interview, the organisation should have a clear picture of the 'ideal' candidate. Preparatory work should be done through careful job analysis, description and specification. It is then a matter of sifting through all the applications to find candidates who best meet the organisation's requirements, and drawing up a 'shortlist'.

As part of their interviews, candidates may be given **tasks** to complete to test their aptitude. Also, to check whether applicants are likely to stay with the organisation, it is important to ask them about their future intentions, and to show them the working environment. While the organisation needs to select suitable employees, it is also important that employees select the organisation.

Case Study – Recruitment and selection of older employees

At the B&Q do-it-yourself store in Macclesfield, the average age of the sales staff is 57. The store works very efficiently and consistently achieves profits that are 30 per cent ahead of the targets.

B&Q now has a policy of aiming job advertisements at older people. A national advertisement prompted 7000 replies, and more than 600 over-50s applied for 57 job vacancies at Macclesfield.

The scheme was started because of B&Q's difficulties with the youngsters it employed – in some areas the staff was turning over faster than the stock, so senior management decided to see whether older people would stay longer. Research has indicated that they do, and they take fewer days off for sickness. Employee turnover at Macclesfield is nearly one-sixth than at similar stores, and absenteeism is 40 per cent less. Shoplifting is also low.

As a result of this experiment, B&Q's target is to have 10 per cent of its national workforce aged over 50. The company feels that older staff are prepared to work harder. In addition, many have had a lot of experience of using the materials that the company sells, so that they can give useful advice to customers.

1 *What qualities do you think B&Q looks for in its sales staff?*
2 *Set out these qualities in the form of a job specification for a sales person.*
3 *Would older people fill this job specification better than younger workers?*
4 *What disadvantages will there be to B&Q from employing older sales staff?*

Interview assessment

An interview assessment form like the one in Figure 17.6 is a useful tool for summarising all the quantities of candidates interviewed.

Factors	INTERVIEW ASSESSMENT					
	Rating					Remarks
	A	B	C	D	E	
Appearance Personality Manner Health						
Intelligence Understanding of questions						
Skills Special skills Work experience						
Interests Hobbies Sports						
Academic						
Motivation						
Circumstances Mobility Hours Limitations						
OVERALL						

A = Exceptional   B = Above average   C = Satisfactory
D = Below average   E = Unsuitable

Figure 17.6 An interview assessment form

Task

Work in groups. Choose a job advertisement from your local newspaper, and draw up the appropriate job specification. Decide on the questions that an interviewer would be most likely to ask. You can use the interview assessment form in Figure 17.6 to hold mock interviews for this post.

Handling job interviews

Interviews can be nerve-racking. In a short space of time the candidate must convince the interviewer

that he or she is the person the organisation needs. Both the interviewer and the candidate need to be prepared. The candidate can prepare by practising answers to the questions likely to be asked, possibly with the help of a friend who takes the role of the interviewer.

It must be remembered that interviews are a two-way activity. The candidate has a chance to ask questions and find out if the organisation and the job are suitable. Questions can, for example, be asked about training, promotion prospects and social facilities.

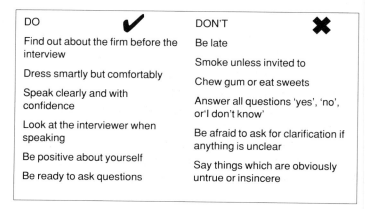

DO ✔	DON'T ✘
Find out about the firm before the interview	Be late
Dress smartly but comfortably	Smoke unless invited to
Speak clearly and with confidence	Chew gum or eat sweets
Look at the interviewer when speaking	Answer all questions 'yes', 'no', or 'I don't know'
Be positive about yourself	Be afraid to ask for clarification if anything is unclear
Be ready to ask questions	Say things which are obviously untrue or insincere

Figure 17.7 A candidate's interview checklist

Induction

New members of an organisation need to have **an induction** period – a time during which they are 'shown the ropes'. This might involve a short familiarisation course, following an experienced employee around, part-time working, or some other means of gentle induction. However, in some organisations it may be considered more appropriate for new recruits to be thrown in 'at the deep-end' – to swim or to sink in the organisation according to their ability.

Training

Many organisations develop schemes to enable **training** to be carried out 'in-house'. At the same time staff may be encouraged to attend college courses to learn new skills. Thus training can be divided into two sorts:

- **on-the-job training** – learning new skills through experience at work
- **off-the-job training** – learning through attending outside courses.

There are various government-sponsored training schemes. For example, the government currently subsidises organisations to employ and train school-leavers. Promotion within an organisation often depends on gaining qualifications to do higher grade jobs.

Skilled workers will be more in demand in the 1990s because of falling numbers of young people entering the job market. Some older people with suitable skills will be tempted back from retirement. Changes in work and child-care patterns will enable more women to combine motherhood with having a career – women will confidently tackle jobs which have been dominated by men in the past, and men will share responsibilities in the home.

Flexibility at work will be vital. Boundaries between traditional trades are breaking down as 'multi-skilling' – the ability to do different jobs – becomes more and more desirable. Workers with transferable skills will be the ones able to train or re-train as new markets develop and expand.

Opportunities are expected to abound for people trained and skilled in technology, in electronics, in science, in management and in the service industries.

Training and Enterprise Councils (TECs)

In the 1990s, **TECs** are expected to play an important role in encouraging training in particular skills. Training and Enterprise Councils are employer-led independent local bodies whose aims are to foster economic growth and regeneration. TECs arrange training and enterprise programmes in local areas to meet the needs of the local business community. The TECs receive start-up funds from central government, but are expected to become increasingly financed by the local businesses they serve. While this idea might be effective in some densely populated areas where there are concentrations of industries, it may not be so effective in sparsely populated areas with a diversity of small businesses.

Task

Find out about your local TEC. How is it financed and run? What is it doing about training in your area? Is it getting a favourable or an unfavourable press?

National Vocational Qualifications (NVQs)

An **NVQ** is the expression of a person's ability to do a job satisfactorily, and is awarded by a combination of exams and an assessment of competence at the workplace.

It is important for everyone starting work or training to check that they are being given the opportunity to obtain a relevant NVQ.

These are well established in service industries, and in construction, engineering, clerical jobs, clothing manufacture, retail sales, agriculture and horticulture and many more sectors.

It is now possible for older people with experience but no qualifications to have their experience assessed. If they are judged to be competent, they will be awarded an appropriate qualification.

Reforms of training and education

The government has introduced a series of reforms aimed at providing TECs with the opportunity to work in partnership with local education authorities and the Careers Service, and to equip young people with stronger basic skills and more higher level skills. The key changes are as follows:

- More NVQs have been introduced.
- New diplomas have been developed to record achievements in academic and vocational areas.
- Schools are to be allowed to admit part-time and adult students to their sixth forms.
- Employer influence in the education system has been extended through TECs.
- By 1996, Training Credits will be offered to every 16- and 17-year-old leaving full-time education. These credits may be used to buy training.
- Careers and vocational work in schools has been strengthened.
- More places have been made available in higher education.
- All pupils aged 16 have to stay in school to the end of the summer term.
- Further-education and sixth-form colleges have been given the freedom to expand and respond to their markets.

Transfer or retirement

From time to time, a member of an organisation may need to be **transferred** from one section to another. This may be for the purpose of promotion or to widen experience, or for disciplinary or other reasons.

Retirement

When people reach retirement age they still need to be looked after. Some large organisations, such as Shell UK, prepare employees for retirement by running special courses. Members are given advice and support in preparing for retirement. Their rights and entitlements can be ensured. Once they have retired they can still be looked after by the organisation. It is also possible to look after the dependants of personnel.

Involuntary termination

Redundancy occurs when all or part of an organisation closes down, or when particular types of employees are no longer required. It should be noted that it is jobs that are made redundant, not people.

Dismissal

Over the years an elaborate system for the **dismissal** of staff has developed as a result of the large number of cases that have been before industrial tribunals or other courts. The heart of the matter lies in the difference between what is termed **fair** dismissal and what is regarded to be **unfair** dismissal.

The **period of notice** that an employee must be given when being dismissed is stated in the contract of employment, which is a legal document.

Task

Study your own contract of employment or that of a friend. How long a period of notice must be given before employment can be terminated? What does it depend on?

Fair dismissal

If a dismissal is disputed, it may be up to an **industrial tribunal** to decide on the fairness of the action (see Chapter 15). An organisation member can be fairly dismissed under certain circumstances, including the following:

- wilful destruction of the organisation's property
- sexual or racial harassment
- continuous bad timekeeping
- a negligent attitude at work

- inability to do the job which the employee was appointed to do
- sleeping on the job.

Some circumstances may lead to instant dismissal where there has been gross misconduct (e.g. theft from a factory). It is usual for an employee to receive a written warning before being dismissed.

Unfair dismissal

Dismissal for the following reasons would be judged to be unfair.

- *Pregnancy* – A pregnant woman can be sacked only if she if unable to do her job properly (e.g. as a shelf stacker).
- *Race* – A worker cannot be sacked on the grounds of his or her race.
- *Homosexuality* – If an organisation member is a homosexual, that is no reason why he or she should be sacked unless it can be proved that it affects his or her standard of work, or leads to sexual harassment.
- *Union membership* – An employer cannot sack a worker for belonging to a trade union.
- *Criminal record* – If an employer does not find out about an employee's criminal record until some time after employing him or her, the employer cannot sack the worker on these grounds unless it was a very relevant crime (e.g. a cashier who has a record of stealing the petty cash).
- *Religion* – An employee cannot be sacked on grounds of religion.

Task

During your time at work you will go through a number of important phases of self-development. At first you will have few skills and little experience. As time passes you will build up more skills, confidence and experience. It is helpful to review

your own progress in a particular job: by looking at where you are now you can get a better picture of where you want to go. Here is a useful review sheet to help you to do this:

The purpose of my job is . . . . .
I moved into this job because . . . . . .
I believe I am effective in my present job because . . . . .
One aspect of my job that I do well is . . . . . .
The part of my job that I get most satisfaction from is the same/different from what I do well, because . . . . . .
The area of my job that I do least well is . . . . . .
And I believe I could improve on this by . . . . . .
An area of training and development that I would really like to pursue is . . . . . .
The teams I work in/lead are . . . . . .
As a team member I am . . . . . .
I feel I make my best contribution when . . . . . .
The times I contribute least are . . . . . .
The particular skills that I bring to work are . . . . . .
One area I need to be more skilful in is . . . . . .
Some evidence of my success (or lack of success) includes . . . . . .
Some ways in which I have personally developed over the last two years are . . . . . .

Other personnel functions

In this chapter we have so far focused on 'employment procession'. In addition, the personnel department plays an important role in managing health and safety laws, equal opportunities policy, and appraisal and disciplinary procedures. The personnel department is responsible also for representing the management side of organisations in industrial relations matters.

Employers and employees need to have a system for communicating their views and requirements to each other. The aims of a business organisation may be to win more orders and to make sales and profits; employees working for that business, on the other hand, may be more concerned with having a longer holiday break, job security and improving their wages and conditions of service. A forum of some

Figure 17.8 Viewpoints require a forum

description needs to be set up to make these different viewpoints known. Employers and employees need to come together to discuss their needs and problems. Arrangements for such **industrial bargaining** vary a lot.

Trade unions

The media's reporting of **trade union activities** can easily give the wrong impression of the full role of unions in modern industries. Unions are, in fact, involved in all aspects of industrial relations.

A trade union is an organisation of employees, which aims to protect and promote the interests of its members. A trade union is therefore a **promotional pressure group** and a **protective pressure group**. It exerts pressure by means of **collective bargaining** with employers.

Trade unions are organisations formed, financed

and run by their members in their own interests, and several have existed for over 100 years. Trade unions today consist of many groups, from bank managers to bank clerks, from school caretakers to school teachers, and from lorry drivers to civil servants.

In British law, a union must be 'independent' – that is, it must not rely on an employer for funds, facilities or organisation. It must show that it can provide adequate services to its members and is able (if necessary) to sustain itself during disputes.

In the United Kingdom there are over 200 certified independent trade unions, although the vast majority of members belong to the largest few unions. They can be divided into three main categories:

- manual worker unions
- white collar unions
- managerial/professional unions.

Task

Using newspapers, library sources and your memory of news programmes, write out the full names of the unions listed in Figure 17.9.

	Initials	Full name of union
Manual	ASLEF	
	NUM	
	TGWU	
	NUPE	
	EETPU	
White collar	NUT	
	APEX	
	NALGO	
	NASUWT	
Managerial and professional	NATFHE	
	BALPA	

Figure 17.9 Some familiar unions

Decline of the unions

During the 1980s and 90s there has been a decline in union membership. However, the fall in numbers has not been fastest in the UK under a Conservative government – it fell faster in France with a Socialist government. Indeed, union membership as a proportion of the workforce fell in *every* major industrial country. In the UK the proportion in 1988 was 41 per cent and in France 12 per cent. By 1991 it was down to 37 per cent in the UK.

The central causes of union decline are the changes in industrial structure and the nature of the workforce that have been taking place across the industrial world. These changes include the decline of numbers employed in 'heavy' industries such as coal and steel, the shift of manufacturing employment from production to design and marketing, the increase of women in the workforce, the shift to part-time work, and the growth of small companies and self-employment. Lower inflation in the eighties may also

have contributed because people did not have to fight so hard to keep up with price rises.

Internationally, the main area where unions have kept their memberships – though not necessarily their influence – has been the public sector. Where unionisation is lowest, as in France or the United States, the public/private sector balance of union membership is even more heavily skewed towards the public sector.

It is unlikely that union memberships will continue to decline as the factors which created the unions become less significant. It is possible that trade unions will, by the beginning of the twenty-first century, be seen as having had a natural life of a little more than 100 years, for the conditions that led to their growth will no longer apply. The appaling abuse of workers by industrial management that made the unions necessary rarely occurs today in the developed world, and the ineffective management that operated in the public sector will no longer be tolerated. As industry in the developed world increasingly shifts production (though not design, finance and marketing) to less developed countries, where labour costs are lower, union memberships will be further eroded. This shift is already widespread in the USA and Japan.

Task

A new freight company has been set up, and the management is approached by a trade union official expressing a desire to represent the employees. In your opinion, which union is most likely to approach the company? Think of reasons for and against recognising the uniform from the points of view of employees and the management.

Some major union aims

A trade union tries to protect its members' interests in a number of ways, including:

- protecting their levels of wages and other payments
- negotiating their hours of work and other working conditions
- keeping an eye on health and safety at work
- protecting promotion opportunities and seeing that employees get fair treatment
- providing benefits for members who are ill, unemployed, retired or injured
- representing members in disputes at work.

However, trade unions do not concern themselves simply with matters related to employment. They also debate issues such as education, political freedom and the international economy, as well as running their own educational courses and giving cash donations to various causes.

Recognition

Prior to 1971, if a trade union wanted to be **recognised** in an organisation, it had no legal backing. Disputes about recognition were resolved by negotiation or a trial of strength between the parties.

However, the Industrial Relations Act 1971, and subsequently the Employment Protection Act 1975, gave a trade union the option to apply to the Advisory, Conciliation and Arbitration Service (**ACAS**) if it was being denied recognition, and therefore bargaining rights.

ACAS has a legal duty to encourage collective bargaining, and will put pressure on an organisation to recognise a union. It cannot force the organisation to agree, it can only encourage recognition. It may take a ballot of employees' wishes, and will usually accept a vote of 30 per cent in favour as grounds for recognising the union.

The objectives of a **recognition policy** are:

- to negotiate bargaining procedures that will be effective and viable in the long term
- to minimise the need for intervention by a third party in disputes

- to ensure that bargaining procedures are consistent with the decision-making structure of the organisation
- to negotiate arrangements conducive to the orderly and peaceful settlement of disputes.

Task

This activity continues with the freight company example of the previous task. After studying the recognition objectives outlined in the text, decide what issues should be included in a recognition policy, and prepare a presentation from either the management or union point of view.

a At what level of support should the union be recognised?
b Should there be only one union?
c How much involvement should the union have in decisions on pay and conditions?
d Should the union have to promise not to call for a stoppage of work?

Your presentation should form the basis for a discussion document. You may wish to adopt a hard stance on some issues at first in order to compromise during negotiations. In a classroom situation you could role-play the negotiations.

Trade union representatives

In medium-sized and large organisations it is not really possible for each employee to negotiate individually with management on every issue or grievance that arises. Instead, trade unionists elect or appoint **representatives** who negotiate on behalf of all the members. These representatives can be divided into two groups.

Shop stewards are elected by union members at their workplace, their task being to represent the views of trade unionists on day-to-day issues. They are not paid a wage by the union since they work at their own job when not involved with union business. However, they are trained by the union to carry out their union duties.

Full-time officials of a union are either elected by the members or appointed by the union's executive team. They are paid out of the union's funds.

To do their jobs well, trade union representatives need skill in talking to members and in gaining a clear view of their problems. They must be able to organise and speak at meetings and present arguments to management, and have an understanding of accounts, production levels, the market and basic economics. They must also have a good knowledge of present laws concerning health and safety, dismissal, redundancy and employment in general. The job of a trade union representative is therefore an extremely demanding one.

Task

The National Union of Students represents the interests of students. Write out a job specification for a union representative at the college you attend.

Case Study – Out of tune

The Royal Opera House in London has experienced some industrial problems. The management offered the musicians a 5.5 per cent increase in payments, but the musicians wanted 20 per cent spread over two years. The Musicians' Union wanted to avoid strike action by using other methods to force the management to negotiate.

For example, the orchestra played some performances in casual dress instead of full

evening dress, and the musicians planned to add extra intervals, to make the performances up to 45 minutes longer.

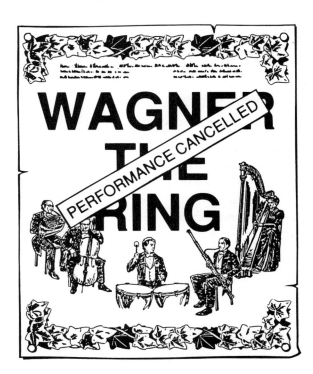

Figure 17.10 **The show must (not) go on**

The director of the ROH told the musicians to stay away from work unless they were prepared to work normally. The musicians failed to attend a final dress rehearsal, and the ROH had to cancel all performances until further notice. The Musicians' Union said that this was a 'management lockout' – that is, not their responsibility.

The union said: 'Our members have been staging a limited action because they didn't want to jeopardise productions.'

The management said: 'The musicians' action was in breach of their contracts and threatened the security of their jobs and those of other employees.'

1 If you were the director of the ROH, what action would you take to avoid the disruptive actions of the musicians?

367

2 What other actions could the musicians take in support of their claim?

3 Do you think that this dispute should go to arbitration, or can the management and the union come to an agreement?

Running a trade union

Full-time union officers in most unions are in three or four grades (see Figure 17.11).

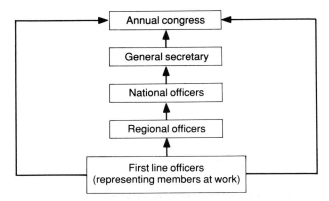

Figure 17.11 A typical union structure

At the top is the general secretary who is an elected official. Next come the national officers, who are usually recruited internally and operate from their union's headquarters. A third band of officers run the union in regions or districts, and they are responsible for the first-line officers who not only organise the union at local level, but also are closely involved with the union membership at the place of work and the local branch. The first-line officers make up the vast majority of all full-time officers.

The annual conference

National officers are responsible for arranging the annual general meeting (often called the **annual congress**) of the union. At this meeting delegates from the regions meet to discuss issues and pass resolutions setting out the future policy of the union. This annual meeting is very important because, if the union is to truly represent its members, it must listen to and then carry out their wishes.

Unofficial action

Disputes often boil up very quickly at the workplace, and the official union structure may be too slow in moving to deal with such problems. Employees are therefore represented at the workplace by a shop steward who deals with these local matters. Sometimes a shop steward will ask the employees if they want to take industrial action without first getting the union's permission. This is known as **unofficial action**, for which the union will not offer financial or other support unless the action is subsequently made official.

In large factories and other workplaces, there will be a committee of shop stewards supervised by a leading shop steward called a **convenor**.

Task

In a factory making cast-iron pipes all the workforce are in the 'GMB Union'. There are four divisions in the factory – the melting shop, the pipe spinning shop, the pipe coating shop and the despatch department. Draw a diagram showing how the GMB could be organised in this factory.

Case Study – Changes in the labour force

Over the next few years there will be dramatic changes in the structure of the labour force. These will stem from shifts in the population structure, advances in technology, and changing attitudes at work, as well as other factors.

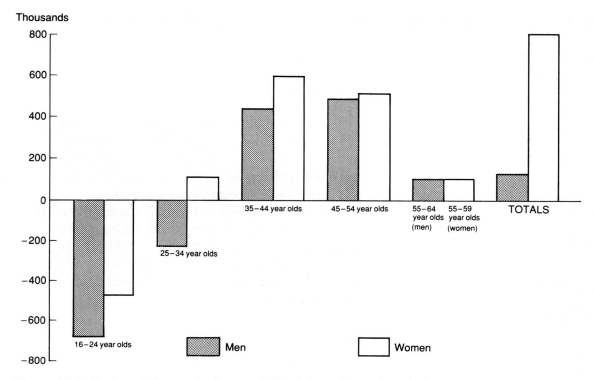

Figure 17.12 Projected changes in the UK civilian labour force of working age, 1989–2001

Figure 17.12 shows the projected changes up to the year 2001.

1 *What impact are these changes likely to have on the size, structure and influence of trade unions in the UK?*
2 *How should trade unions adjust their recruitment policies to accommodate for these changes?*

Trade unions and disputes

The mass media often give the impression that trade unions set out to create industrial disputes. In the UK the number of disputes is low when compared with other countries. Many trade unionists have never been involved in industrial action.

Trade union representatives help to ensure the smooth running of industry. Wherever people work or meet together, disputes and grievances will occur, and in industry the problems of new technology, complicated payment systems and work that lacks

stimulation are bound to create occasional dissatisfaction. Many of these everyday problems are easily dealt with by meetings, discussion and bargaining.

It is the trade union representative who expresses the views of employees. Shop stewards often complain that, while most of their activity is concerned with preventing disputes or strikes, such information is not reported in the newspapers.

Disputes usually occur when all the available channels of discussion and negotiation have been tried. Reasons for disputes are usually very complicated, and one needs to be cautious about saying that one party is 'wrong' or 'right'. If the causes of disputes were that simple, then they would rarely occur.

Negotiation

The way in which **negotiation** takes place varies from plant to plant. **Collective bargaining** means that representatives of employers and employees get together to discuss and bargain. At one extreme, negotiation may involve just two people. This is a very common arrangement – the personnel manager and a representative of each trade union will have short meetings every week. Most collective bargaining over major issues, however, involves inter-party negotiations. These can range from fairly small groups on each side of the bargaining table to over 20 representatives from management and a similar number from different trade unions. It is important to remember that discussion is the major tool of industrial relations, not industrial action.

Types of industrial action

Non-cooperation. This can take the form of working without enthusiasm, a go-slow or a work-to-rule. Working-to-rule means sticking firmly to the rule book, elements of which might normally be set aside to speed up procedures.

Overtime ban. This is a weapon that needs to be used carefully because employees lose earnings while employers pay out less in wage and production costs. It can be most effective when management has important orders to meet.

Strike. A strike is the ultimate weapon of a trade union and occurs when employees withdraw their labour. A strike will normally involve some form of **picketing** action. A picket is a union representative who stands outside the place of work to explain to people why the strike is taking place and why they should not go into the workplace.

Sit-in/work-in. In response to their jobs being made redundant, employees may continue working and 'lock out' the management until negotiations take place.

Types of employer action

Employers and management can themselves take industrial action to put pressure on employees. Actions can include the withdrawal of overtime, mass suspensions, changes in working standards and payment rates, locking employees out, the closing

A P&O picket line

down of enterprises and the removal of plant and machinery at the workplace. The withdrawing of overtime or mass suspensions, for example, are sometimes used by the management to put over the point to union negotiators that it proposes to stand firm on a particular point.

The Trades Union Congress

The trade unions as a group have their own organisation known as the Trades Union Congress (**TUC**). Every year delegates from the separate unions meet together at a conference to discuss and vote on general union policy. The TUC itself has a permanent body of national officials under the leadership of a president. The TUC puts forward the unions' collective point of view to the government and others. It has a major interest in employment laws, training and conditions at work.

Trade unions in a changing environment

Earlier in the chapter we saw that the number of people in trade unions has declined. There are many challenges and changes which trade unions must face in their environment today, not least of which is the increased affluence of the general labour force.

There has been the decline of manufacturing industry – the traditional base for large unions – and its replacement by the supremacy of the service sector of the economy. Large factories and plants have increasingly been replaced by smaller units of employees, but where large concentrations of employees still work together they tend these days to be part-time or unskilled workers with limited bargaining powers.

The separating-off of non-core service functions by large businesses means that individual employees have closer contact with their immediate managers.

There has been a move towards increased co-operation between managements and employees. A new style of management increasingly stresses the importance of including employees in decision-making processes, and in return employees are expected to take on wider responsibility for their own actions. For example, **multi-skilling** involves employees being prepared to do many different jobs rather than concentrating on a single job skill. At the same time many employers have introduced **single-union deals** – rather than bargaining with many individual trade unions they recognise and bargain with a single union.

Case Study – A single-union deal

In November 1991, engineering union leaders and Toyota signed a single-union agreement that was heralded at the time as likely to give the company the lowest labour costs in the motor industry. Five unions competed for the prize of recognition for up to 3300 workers to be employed at Toyota's new plants at Burnaston in Derbyshire and on Deeside. The deal offered workers 'stable employment' in exchange for total flexibility between skills and a commitment to maintain production goals.

Wage levels offered were at a high level for the time. Employees were expected under the agreement to work a 39-hour week despite the Amalgamated Engineering Union's successful campaign for the introduction of a 37-hour week throughout the engineering industry.

The Japanese owners wanted to establish productivity levels comparable to those of Japanese plants. The agreement also sorted out arrangements for industrial action. If the two sides could not be brought together in their thinking by an independent third party, then a ballot of members would need to be called before any industrial action could take place. The expected output from the plant is 200 000 cars a year from a tiny labour force compared with that of domestic competitors. Workers will have representatives on the company board and they have also been given the strongest commitment to job security in the car industry.

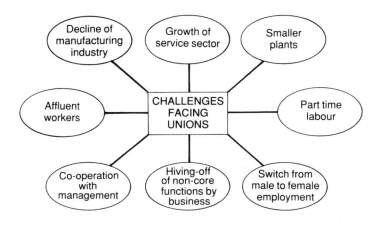

Figure 17.13 Challenges

1 *What have the management at Toyota contributed to make this deal a success?*
2 *What contribution has the Amalgamated Engineering Union made?*
3 *How will each side benefit from the deal? Who else might benefit?*
4 *What weaknesses can you see in this deal?*
5 *What ingredients of this arrangement do you see as 'forward looking'?*

Case Study – Union structure in Germany

The German union structure has been shaped by the country's history. In the 1920s the German economy was racked by huge inflation and strikes. In reaction, a new concept known as *Mitbestimmung* (co-determination) grew up. This was based on the radical idea that workers and managers should have equal power in a company. Under Hitler, unions were suppressed but the movement came back after the Second World War. Ironically it was the British who were largely responsible for the shape of the post-war unions in Germany. As the occupying power they saw the need for a stable industrial relations set-up, and brought in experts to create the structure that still survives.

A small number of unions were created (there are now sixteen, headed by the engineers' IG Metall, the biggest union in the world) and a one-plant-one-union rule was established. With everyone from cook to toolmaker in the same union, there was never any possibility of **demarcation** (who does what job) disputes.

Mitbestimmung took on a definite legal form. It was introduced first in the steel industries and later spread to all large companies. Its basis was a two-level board system, with the workforce and employers equally represented on the supervisory board. If it came to the crunch, employers could always get their way, but the set-up did have a calming effect. Management was able to find out the wishes of labour early on in negotiations.

In addition a **works council** – a non-union body that represents the workers' interests (except on pay) – has been in place since 1972. Conflict is illegal. The principle of co-determination sets the scene for the whole industrial relations atmosphere, which is remarkably free from confrontation. But the other leg of the system – the legal framework – ensures that even if the unions do want to push wages up, their actions are strictly limited.

Wage talks are carried out between unions and employers' organisations. Some are countrywide, while IG Metall negotiates state by state. One state will be chosen by the union; the battle will be fought there, and other states will fall into line.

The idea is to thrash out collective deals which set basic pay levels for different grades of employee. These are binding and, as individual companies are not involved in the negotiations, there is no scope for one company to offer bigger wage increases than another.

The basic wage level is, however, rarely paid, because virtually every company adds a top-up that can boost basic pay by perhaps 25 per cent. These top-ups reflect local skill shortages, and tend to be more generous in large companies. So the idea of the centralised coordinated pay settlement in Germany is really a myth.

1 What are the main differences between the union structures in Germany and in the UK?
2 How and why did the differences develop?
3 Which do you think is the better system?
4 Why do companies in Germany pay more than the negotiated basic wage levels?

Employers' associations

Just as employees have formed and joined trade unions in order to protect their common interests, so employers have formed and joined their own groups. Examples are the Confederation of British Industry (**CBI**) and the National Farmers Union. These associations have two main functions:

- to represent employers in dealings with trade unions
- to give help and advice to employers on a wide range of issues, such as training, calculating tax, etc.

In some industries an employers' association will bargain with trade unions to establish a minimum wage for a given period of time. Individual employers then negotiate additional payments at a company, plant or workplace level with shop stewards.

Most employers' associations today operate principally at a regional rather than a national level.

The Confederation of British Industry

This body was set up to provide a national organisation giving the views of employers. The CBI acts as a mouthpiece for the employers to present their opinions and feelings to trade unions, government, the media and other interested parties.

The CBI collects and makes known information on a wide range of matters. Its *Industrial Trends* survey, published quarterly, gives up-to-date information on the state of business. It also produces a magazine,

CBI News, giving employers up-to-the minute information on a wide range of business issues.

The CBI has a permanent staff involved in collecting statistics, processing information, publishing articles, and dealing with queries from industrialists. It is led by a Director General.

Professional associations

A **professional association** offers exclusive membership for suitably qualified people in order to enhance the status of their work. There are many types, reflecting the wide range of **professions**, and many were established under the Companies Acts or by the granting of a Royal Charter. Their functions include:

- acting as examiners of standards and providing study facilities and guides (for example, prospective bankers take exams organised by the Chartered Institute of Bankers)
- controlling entry into the professions
- preserving high standards of professional conduct in order to protect the public
- providing members with technical information and keeping them in step with new knowledge.

With more specialisation in the professions, and more people working in the service sector, professional associations have increased in number in recent years.

The government and industrial relations

ACAS

The Advisory, Conciliation and Arbitration Service (**ACAS**) was set up in the 1970s to act as a 'third party' in industrial disputes. It can do this in a number of ways.

Conciliation is a process through which an independent outsider, such as an ACAS official, tries to act as a channel of communication between an employer and a union. The conciliator will usually meet the parties separately before trying to bring them together.

Mediation is a stronger process whereby an independent outsider proposes the basis for a settlement. However, the parties involved do not have to accept it.

Arbitration involves both parties agreeing to accept

Figure 17.14 The functions of ACAS

the recommendations of an independent body like ACAS.

Task

The national and local press frequently refer to industrial relations issues in which ACAS has been involved. Try to keep a diary of such events over a three-month period. What actions did ACAS take? How was it involved in different disputes?

New initiatives

Smooth industrial relations are an important ingredient in a prosperous economy. The government meets frequently with representatives of employers and employees to discuss issues of national importance. The government will actively seek the co-operation of trade unions and employers in launching **initiatives** such as training schemes and new health and safety laws.

The government establishes the general framework

in which industrial relations is set.

Throughout the 1980s the government established a comprehensive set of new laws limiting the actions of trade unions. Important pieces of legislation have been the banning of secondary picketing (i.e. the picketing of premises not directly involved in a dispute), establishment of the right of individuals and groups to sue unions for damages (including lost business) caused by illegal industrial action, and provisions for balloting members on strike action.

The general feeling is that during the eighties the powers of the unions were increasingly restricted, and that unions became more fully accountable under the law. In 1991 the government published a fresh **Green Paper** (a discussion document) setting out some ideas for the future. The title was *Industrial Relations in the 1990s*. The main proposals are shown in Figure 17.15.

☆ Members of the public to have a new right to seek injunction to halt unlawful industrial action disrupting public services

☆ Seven days' notice of any industrial action

☆ The right for an individual to join the union of his or her choice

☆ The right for workers not to have union deductions made from their pay without their individual consent

☆ Rights to information about their union's affairs, including the salaries of principal officers

☆ New rights to combat fraud and vote-rigging in union elections, including the right to inspect voting registers

☆ The right to an independently scrutinised postal ballot before strikes

☆ Postal ballots on union mergers

☆ Collective agreements to be legally binding unless they include provision making them unenforcable

☆ New powers for the government-financed Certification Officer to investigate mismanagement of union finances

☆ Higher penalties for union leaders failing to keep proper accounts

Figure 17.15 Main proposals of *Industrial Relations in the 1990s*

Case Study – European social policy

The major changes introduced in 1987 by the Single European Act included giving the community wider powers in the social field to create a European social policy. The social dimension is a vital part of the single market project. It stresses the need to make full use of resources and to distribute benefits more fairly.

After all, the single market would be pointless if it weakened people's living standards and levels of protection. People are now free to move and work within Europe. The European Commission is also working to raise training standards, with the focus on encouraging schemes for further training and the rapid integration of young people into working life. Improving health and safety at work is another major problem being tackled by the Commission, the emphasis here being above all on rules for the protection of workers exposed to hazardous substances.

The main focus for social policy is dealing with **unemployment**, and in particular fighting long-term unemployment and helping young people to find work. Projects assisted by the Social Fund range from training in new information technology, to aid for migrant workers and vocational training for the disabled.

Article 119 of the Treaty of Rome requires men and women to be given equal pay for equal work. Women can insist on these rights through their national courts. In the mid-1970s women's rights were strengthened by three Directives which extended the legal guarantees of equal treatment at work beyond the field of equal pay to include access to employment, vocational training, working conditions and promotion, and social security.

The European Commission aims to underpin the foundations of community social policy by means of

a **Social Charter** of basic rights which will reflect the European model of society, social dialogue, and the rights of each and every individual in the community.

The Social Charter is still being developed. It is a package of new measures planned to harmonise working conditions and protect employees throughout the EC. One of the key proposals being debated is to restrict the working week to a maximum of 48 hours. Other suggestions are: a minimum period of four weeks' paid holiday guaranteed to all employees; a rest period of at least eleven continuous hours every day; a maximum eight-hour shift of 96 hours per fortnight for night staff; and, in principle, every Sunday off. Under the charter, part-time workers would have to be given a proportion of full-time workers' benefits (such as paid holidays, pensions and sick pay).

1 Explain what you think might be the consequences of the proposals for:
   a part-time workers
   b full-time workers
   c small businesses
   d large businesses
   e the British economy.
2 You will be able to discover the most up-to-date information about the Social Charter from newspapers and TV and radio news broadcasts. Have the proposals outlined above come into being? Have they been modified?

18
Reviewing Performance

All organisations have to live with and accept changes. This chapter attempts to improve your awareness of this, and the need to monitor and review performance constantly. It starts with hints on how to plan and review personal performance, and goes on to consider organisation performance.

In our changing world, all business functional areas such as marketing, human resources, production and operations, information and finance are important. In many situations they will be integrated so that an organisation can develop a better overall picture of where its competitive advantages lie. From such information it can spot opportunities and then develop a strategy to act quickly to exploit them.

In this book we have provided you the reader with challenges. You have been asked to communicate effectively, to work in co-operation with others, to make decisions, to investigate new areas of skill and knowledge, to interpret data, to reflect on work experience, to manage tasks and to do many other things. You have also been asked to reflect on these experiences and to set yourself realistic new targets.

In doing all this, you should have developed a better self-awareness and an increasing ability to review your own performance as well as the performances of others.

Review of performance is very important. It is important for **individuals** (e.g. how well can you do a particular task, and what improvements can you make?). It is important for particular **processes** (e.g. how well is a manufacturing process being carried out, and are there areas that can be improved?). Finally, it is important for **organisations** (e.g. how effectively is an organisation meeting its objectives and how can this performance be improved?).

Planning and reviewing personal performance

We can break down a new experience or task that we need to perform into three stages, using a simple PIE model:

P = Planning
I = Implementation
E = Evaluation

The stage of **evaluation** involves reviewing the planning and implementation in order to make improvements.

Aims and objectives

Planning an activity must start with you deciding on your aim and objectives. What are you trying to achieve?

In military terms, your **aim** is your main focus for concern – for example, to win a war. Your **objectives** are the main means you establish to pursue your aim: to fight a number of battles, to ensure that you have available the best possible weaponry, to strike when you have the maximum advantage, etc.

Task

a What is your main aim in following the college course you are currently doing? What objectives have you set to pursue this main aim?

b What is your main aim in carrying out a particular piece of work experience? What objectives have you set to pursue this aim?

It should be apparent that if you are not clear about an aim and objectives then you will not be able to define the direction in which you wish to go. If you have not yet set an aim and objectives, then try to do so now. It often helps to talk through your goals with someone else.

The next stage is to look at the 'nitty-gritty' – the means of following up your aim. What exactly do you need to do?

On a college course you may need to:

● learn new skills
● learn and be able to use new knowledge
● develop new attitudes.

The same applies to work experience.

Competency statements

Today, many of the things that you need to be able to do are expressed as **competency statements**. These show a number of CAN DO's. For example, it could be said that teaching well involves these CAN DO's:

● *can* start a lesson with interest
● *can* organise an interesting discussion
● *can* use an overhead projector with clarity
● *can* provide a range of interesting experiences for the class.

Task

Draw up lists of about ten competency statements for two of the following:

a a teacher
b a nurse

c a hairdresser
d a shop worker.

One way in which you can review your own performance in a particular activity is to make a list of competency statements for yourself. Better still, you can draw up the list after discussing the matter with colleagues. Then refer to any existing literature giving details of competency statements for a particular trade. Of course, there will be different *levels* of competency, not just 'CAN DO' or 'CAN'T DO' – you should try to find out what these particular competencies are.

One word of caution at this stage. In some areas it is quite easy to draw up competency statements (e.g. mending a bicycle tyre). However, there are other areas in which it is not so clear – for example, it is not clear-cut what makes a good teacher, or a good comedian.

Task

Think of about five activities or occupations for which it is difficult to draw up lists of competency statements.

Short-term and long-term plans

Having established your aim and objectives, you can set about developing plans to implement the objectives. Some targets that you set will be short-term while others will cover much longer periods.

- A **strategic plan** sets out long-term aims.
- A **medium-term plan** outlines the main objectives to be achieved over a period of time.
- A **short-term action plan** identifies immediate targets.

Personal action planning

You may want to set out your own **action plan** to cover some aspect of personal development during your BTEC course. For example, you may want to improve your study skills, or to develop competencies at work, or to score high grades on your assignments.

Example – Action plan to develop a work-related competency

You can develop an action plan using the following headings:

- *Area for development*. Set out here the skill that you want to develop. You will then have a clearer idea of what you want to change.
- *Name of person responsible for implementing the change*. This should be you, because you are responsible for managing your own learning in this new area.
- *Task group*. Who will support you in bringing about the change? By identifying this group you will know who can help. Indeed, the task group may help you to develop the action plan. The more you communicate your needs to them, the better chance there is for them to help you.
- *Statement*. This should explain what the task group is set up to achieve. You can then communicate this mission statement to an outside group.
- *Roles*. Who should do what in the task group? What is your responsibility? What is the

responsibility of your tutor or work supervisor?
- *Analysis of needs*. Carry out an analysis to identify the **strengths, weaknesses, opportunities** and **threats** in relation to the identified change. This is a SWOT analysis which we met in Chapter 5. The template in Figure 18.1 can be used.

STRENGTHS	WEAKNESSES
OPPORTUNITIES	THREATS

Figure 18.1 Template for a SWOT analysis

- *Action steps*. List the main steps you will need to carry out your planned change. List them both in order of importance and in the order in which they will need to be carried out. The action steps will help to make it clear what you will have to do, and any resources needed to help you make the change.
- *Evaluation*. Try to identify the criteria that will be used to assess the success of your action steps. It is very important that you set these out from the start. You will need to know how to measure your success. Clearly the task group will be of great use in helping you to measure changes and improvements.

If you carry out an action plan successfully it should help you to have a greater awareness of your own ability to learn, and of your own strengths and weaknesses. It should also help you to plan new learning experiences.

Evaluation

It is important that you try to develop ways of measuring how effective you have been. You should then compare your own assessments with those of other people.

For example, imagine that as part of this BTEC course you have to plan an effective presentation (this was one of the suggested activities in Chapter 1). Your action plan could include the evaluation sheet in Figure 18.2. You could ask other people to fill in the evaluation sheet to see how their assessments compare with your own. Who could you ask to fill in the presentation evaluation sheet? How could you discuss the sheet with them? What might you do if their evaluations of your performance were different from your own?

PRESENTATION EVALUATION SHEET

Name of presenter: Sheet filled in by

	Weak			Strong	
	1	2	3	4	5

CONTENT
Planning of presentation
Language at right level
Objectives clearly stated
Communication of ideas
Use of visual materials
CONTROL OF PRESENTATION
Used time well
Handled questions well
Signposted different stages
Used questions
Paced session
CONTACT WITH AUDIENCE
Involved the audience
Listened to points raised
Acted naturally and confidently
Looked for feedback
Asked for questions
Tested that audience understood

OVERALL ASSESSMENT

Figure 18.2 Presentation evaluation sheet

Continuing personal awareness

The PIE model of planning, implementation and evaluation provides opportunities to develop greater self-awareness, awareness of others and awareness of important planning procedures. This book set out to encourage you to develop suitable skills. You have found out how organisations operate, but just as importantly you will have found how you can fit into an organisation.

You should remember the practical experiences that you have gained from the course and be aware of your own relationships with organisations through a process of critical review.

Case Study – Your work experience

Your own work experience is the subject of this case study. Specifically, think of the work experience that has been the most important in terms of your personal and career development.

1 Give a brief job description of what was involved.
2 Who were you responsible to? What were you responsible for?
3 Comment on how you gained from this work experience in terms of:
   a increased knowledge about the work involved
   b increased skills or aptitudes
   c changed attitudes to work
   d changed plans for future career development
   e increased insights about the operation of organisations.
4 Set out a short action plan giving details of steps you may want to take to:
   a find out more about career choice, or
   b find a new appropriate work experience opportunity.

Reviewing processes and products

Most modern processes involve a range of specialist skills. People work together amidst a lot of detailed planning.

Even a simple process such as preparing a meal at home involves careful planning, skilled implementation, and critical review. The inputs need to be collected and blended with skill. The processes need to be carefully balanced and timed, if the output is to be of the highest quality.

Think how much more complex this process needs to be in a modern food-processing plant producing on a 24-hour basis. Food technologists, chefs, production planners, financial managers, information planners, marketing departments, distribution coordinators, skilled operatives and many more employees are involved in producing foods in bulk for the public.

Control

Control is an essential requirement if processes are to be effectively managed to convert inputs into outputs. **Performance standards** must be established. **Measurement** is required to make sure that actual results can be **compared** against the planned performance. If the results are not to the required level of quality or quantity, then information needs to be fed back so that **corrective action** can be taken. This is called **feedback**.

For example, in a modern food-processing plant there is a central testing area. At regular intervals a tasting panel made up of food technologists, marketeers, production staff and others meets regularly to taste the products to check that they conform to the required standards. If the results are below what is required, then the source of the problem must be quickly identified and corrective action taken.

New product development

Another key change process is **product development.** Product development in the food industry involves a number of stages. Figures 18.4, 18.5 and 18.6 show the stages adopted by one very large supermarket business.

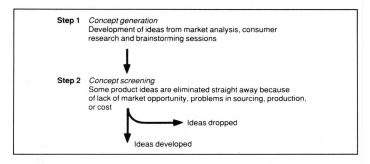

Figure 18.4 The concept stage of product development

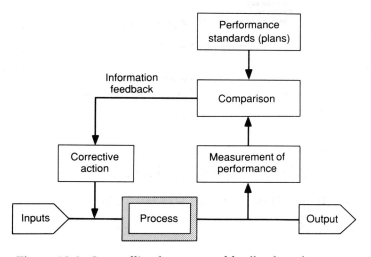

Figure 18.3 Controlling by means of feedback and corrective action

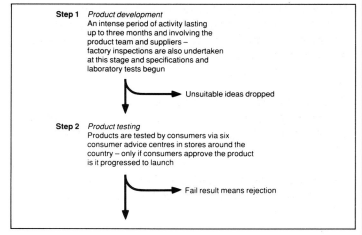

Figure 18.5 Product selection

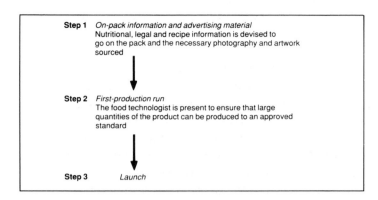

Figure 18.6 **Progression to the launch**

Task

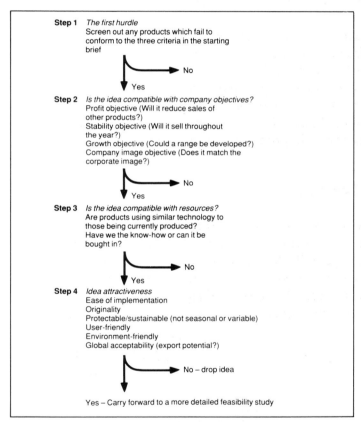

Working in a small group of three or four, **brainstorm** as many ideas as possible in 15 minutes for *Project Instant Start*. The brief for this product range is given below:

> The breakfast cereal market is well developed. Although new own-label products are launched at a rate of approximately one every three months, there is little market innovation. Changes in the late 1980s reflected the increasing health consciousness of consumers, with sales of wheat and oat bran cereals and muesli-based products increasing.
>
> Moves away from the 'cooked British breakfast' are evidenced by decreasing sales of bacon, eggs and sausages. Product innovations such as the microwave sausage and the breakfast pizza have been unprecedented flops!
>
> Weekday breakfast is no longer a leisurely occasion for the majority of the population. Breakfast 'on the hoof' is becoming increasingly common, but product choice is limited.
>
> Recent customer surveys have identified a need for products designed to be eaten in the car on the way to work or school.
>
> YOUR TASK is to devise a list of products suitable for

inclusion in the Instant Start Breakfast Kit range. Products must be:

- EASY TO EAT, WITH A GOOD TEXTURE
- REASONABLY HEALTHY
- NOT LIKELY TO GO OFF!

Once you have brainstormed as long a list as possible in the time available, you should be able to start **screening out** unsuitable products. To carry out the screening process you should carry out a step-by-step review of all the products suggested, as shown in Figure 18.7.

Figure 18.7 **Your screening guide**

Reviewing organisational performance and managing change

An organisation should constantly review its past and current performances in order to compare the direction in which it is going with alternative directions.

At the heart of effective evaluation is the availability of existing standards, or **benchmarks**, against which to check performance. The most important benchmark is the organisation's **core purpose**. The core purpose is the combined answer to the questions:

- Why does the organisation exist?
- What contribution does the organisation make to a wider system?

The core purpose of the organisation should be written in the form of a very simple **mission statement**. The mission statement should be in language that a child can understand – it should tell everyone inside the organisation and outside the organisation what the organisation 'stands for'.

Task

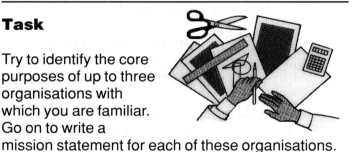

Try to identify the core purposes of up to three organisations with which you are familiar.
Go on to write a
mission statement for each of these organisations.

The core purpose of an organisation is often taken for granted, but it is vitally important that there be agreement amongst the key members of the organisation as to what it is. Without it you will hear comments such as 'I don't know what we are supposed to be doing!' and 'What is the point in this?'.

Having a core purpose makes it possible to establish:

- goals
- priorities
- structures
- the allocation of resources.

The core purpose will also reflect the **values** of the organisation. For example, it might exist to serve the community, to provide maximum employment, or to maximise profits.

Business decisions

With a clear purpose it is possible to make plans and implement business decisions. As we have seen, there are three main types of business decisions – strategic, structural and operational.

Strategic decisions focus on long-term goals – for example, whether the organisation should diversify into new lines. **Structural** decisions deal with organising the human resource in such a way that the organisation is likely to realise its potential and meet its strategic objectives. Decisions about the organisation's day-to-day activities in such fields as marketing, finance and purchasing are classed as **operational** decisions.

There is a clear connection between these three types of decision. An organisation should first establish its strategic objectives and then design an appropriate organisational structure in order to meet those objectives and control its detailed operations. Strategic objectives should be achieved through operational plans. Without this interrelationship between the three types of decision, an organisation is likely to run into difficulties.

The strategic audit

Strategic management involves the setting out of objectives for the total enterprise. An important part of this is the carrying out of a **strategic audit,** to find out what has been achieved in the past and what can be achieved in the future. Managers should set out to create a balance between resources and opportunities. All the key functional areas should be involved in this process in an **integrated** way.

The **marketing** function keeps the organisation in tune with the wishes of consumers. The **production** system needs to be geared towards using resources in the most effective ways to meet market needs. The

financial system must provide long-term and short-term cash flows to service the needs of the organisation. The **administrative** and **information** functions should service the other functions with appropriate systems for processing useful data and making sure that everything is running smoothly.

Task

Identify the main sub-systems that exist in a business with which you are familiar. Why do all of these functions need to contribute to an overall strategic audit?

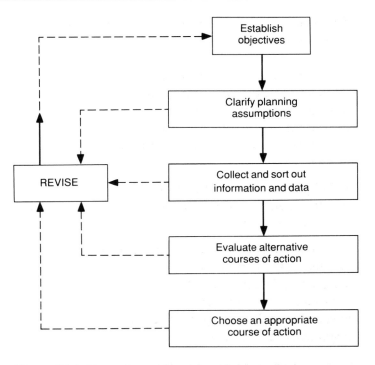

Figure 18.8 Preparing and revising plans

Organisational planning

Organisational planning helps to bring the objectives out into the open. There is a well-known saying that 'if you do not know where you are going then any road will take you there'. The point is that without clear planning you may achieve *something*, but it is unlikely to amount to much. If company objectives are clarified then individual departments have clear guidelines and it is possible for all departments to work in a coordinated way.

Planning also makes it possible for managers to evaluate performance. Without evaluation there cannot be adequate control. Of course, plans are unlikely to be met in every detail, but they do establish guidelines against which performance can be checked and if necessary modified.

Planning should be a continuous process. A useful model (although not the only one) is to establish objectives, clarify the planning assumptions that are being made, collect and sort out useful data, evaluate alternative courses of action, select an appropriate course of action, then re-evaluate the chosen course, and modify planning in the light of results. This is summarised in Figure 18.8.

A planning system establishes standards of control. When these standards are not met then corrective action should be taken, as we saw in Figure 18.3.

Planning should establish a whole organisation plan, as well as sub-system plans for each of the parts of the organisation.

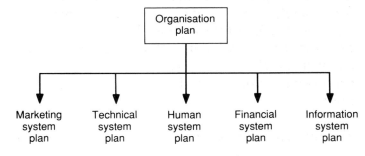

Figure 18.9 The whole organisation plan

An alternative planning approach

Another way of approaching planning involves the following:

- *Diagnosis* – Where are we and why? (This usually involves some form of audit of company performance, which is then analysed.)
- *Prognosis* – Where are we going? (This involves looking at possible future scenarios in the light of present performance and trends.)
- *Objectives* – Where do we want to go?
- *Strategy* – What is the best way of achieving our objectives?
- *Tactics* – What specific actions will enable us to meet day-to-day targets?
- *Control* – How far have we progressed? (A company will need to establish performance indicators against which it can measure its success.)

Case Study – Changing corporate priorities

In this book we have referred often to the changing business environment. When the environment in which an organisation operates changes dramatically, then it becomes necessary for that organisation to change its strategy and tactics.

In 1991, the well-known writer and broadcaster David Bellamy suggested that companies should move further to consider their impact on the natural environment. Professor Bellamy said progress was being made by a growing number of industrial companies, but he urged action on a wide number of fronts. Specifically, he proposed ten 'Bellamy guidelines' for the greening of business:

- Carry out cradle-to-grave, independent environmental audits of all company activities.
- Develop comprehensive environmental policies based on the audits.
- Produce action plans with specific environmental targets.
- Integrate the action plans into strategic business planning.
- Ensure action and control by setting up environmental management systems, with environmental affairs managers in charge.

- Ensure that staff know about the policies and be organised to meet the challenges; training might be needed.
- Ensure that top management is committed to the 'green' initiative.
- Link the environmental plans with quality programmes.
- Seek to enforce the new British Standard on the environment, once it is implemented.
- Adopt an environmentally sensitive approach to development of new products and processes.

Professor Bellamy argued that industry was proving again and again that new technologies made recycling and reuse of waste profitable. He said: 'The challenge before industry, from shopfloor to boardroom, is to speed the process on its way before legislation of a more negative kind sends many businesses to the wall of bankruptcy.'

He suggested some broad-brush criteria for success, such as 'fishability' and 'swimmability' of rivers, lakes and inshore waters. He said industrial water users should be willing to put their water intake points downstream of their own outfalls. 'Working on the principle of maximum profitability, no raw materials should be wasted. They are paid for, including the costs of their transport to the factory. Companies would be foolish to face the costs of dumping anything with downstream consequences. Anything that enters a production system for any purpose should end as part of a saleable product or as a saleable or reusable byproduct.'

1 *How practical are Professor Bellamy's suggestions?*
2 *How might businesses adopt such suggestions in their planning?*
3 *Would this necessitate a change of core purpose, and mission statements in some cases?*
4 *Comment on the type of changes needed in:*
  a strategic planning
  b operational planning
  c control mechanisms.
5 *Which business sub-systems would be most likely to be affected?*

6 *How would you go about convincing people within an organisation that the changes are necessary?*

7 *Who would you need to convince outside of the organisation, and how could they be convinced?*

Managing changes

Making changes in the way that an organisation operates is not easy. Clearly, people affected by the changes need to be convinced that they are necessary, so these members of the organisation must be identified as a first priority.

Task

Imagine that it has been decided to run college course for four extra weeks a year so that syllabuses can be covered more effectively.

a *Make a list of all the groups and individuals who will be involved in and affected by this change.*

b *What do you think each group would have to say about the change?*

c *What could you say to each group to persuade them that the change is necessary?*

d *How could you involve each group in the process of change?*

Managing the process of change can be broken down into four discrete elements (see Figure 18.10).

Building the vision involves making people clear about what a particular change involves and how they are involved in it. Once again, a number of questions can be asked:

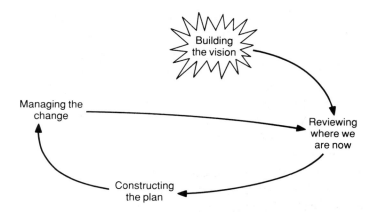

Figure 18.10 **Managing the process of change**

- What is involved – that is, what is the proposed change?
- Why should we do it?
- What will the major effects be?
- How can we manage the change?

Reviewing where we are now involves assessments of the following:

- current provisions
- resources
- roles and responsibilities
- development needs
- the climate for change in the organisation.

Constructing the plan involves:

- the planning process
- a policy statement
- action plans for implementing the change
- getting all parties committed to the change.

Once it is decided who is involved, what is involved and how the change is to be made, the next step is to put the plans into action and manage the change. It is necessary to:

- manage the people involved
- check on and record progress
- overcome problems during implementation
- make sure that the change is permanent
- evaluate the change
- improve on any weak areas.

Task

Imagine that you have been asked to make members of your organisation more 'environmentally aware'. How would you go about this? How would you seek to build the vision? How would you review where your are now? How would you construct plans? How would you manage the change?

Conclusion

During your life you will be a member of many organisations. In some of these you will have a key 'organising role' – for example in running a local football team, arranging meetings, planning presentations, organising a set of accounts, fixing a venue for a dance and so on. At other times you will simply respond to a set of routine procedures established by an organisation for carrying out particular tasks.

Whatever the situation you are involved in, you should remember that an organisation is essentially a human system that has been set up for a particular purpose. As an organisation member you are part of key processes. The way in which you perform your roles always has a bearing on the image and success of that organisation.

From time to time you will find that an organisation has lost a sense of its purpose. This can lead to frustrations. However, as a result of following this BTEC course you should be more fully aware of how organisations operate, and their strengths and weaknesses. The new knowledge, skills and attitudes that you have developed will make you a more critical – yet more effective – member of any organisation of which you are a part.